CARL SCHURZ

REFORMER

AMERICAN POLITICAL LEADERS

EDITED BY ALLAN NEVINS

RUTHERFORD B. HAYES
By H. J. Eckenrode

THOMAS B. REED
By William A. Robinson

JAMES A. GARFIELD
By Robert Granville Caldwell

JOHN G. CARLISLE
By James A. Barnes

CARL SCHURZ
By Claude M. Fuess

In preparation

GROVER CLEVELAND
By Allan Nevins

ANDREW JOHNSON
By St. George L. Sioussat

JOSEPH G. CANNON
By William Allen White

CHESTER A. ARTHUR
By George F. Howe

THEODORE ROOSEVELT
By Charles R. Lingley

JAMES G. BLAINE
By David S. Muzzey

ROBERT M. LaFOLLETTE
By Frederic C. Howe

SAMUEL J. TILDEN
By Alexander C. Flick

JOHN HAY
By Tyler Dennett

WILLIAM McKINLEY
By Geoffrey Parsons

GEORGE FRISBIE HOAR
By Frederick H. Gillett

WILLIAM JENNINGS BRYAN
By Henry Steele Commager

ULYSSES S. GRANT
By William B. Hesseltine

JOHN SHERMAN
By Roy F. Nichols and
Jeanette Paddock Nichols

CARL SCHURZ IN 1906

CARL SCHURZ

Reformer

(1829-1906)

By

CLAUDE MOORE FUESS

Illustrated

DODD, MEAD & COMPANY

New York 1932

109629
92
Sch 88

COPYRIGHT, 1932
BY DODD, MEAD AND COMPANY, INC.

ALL RIGHTS RESERVED
NO PART OF THIS BOOK MAY BE REPRODUCED IN ANY FORM
WITHOUT PERMISSION IN WRITING FROM THE PUBLISHER

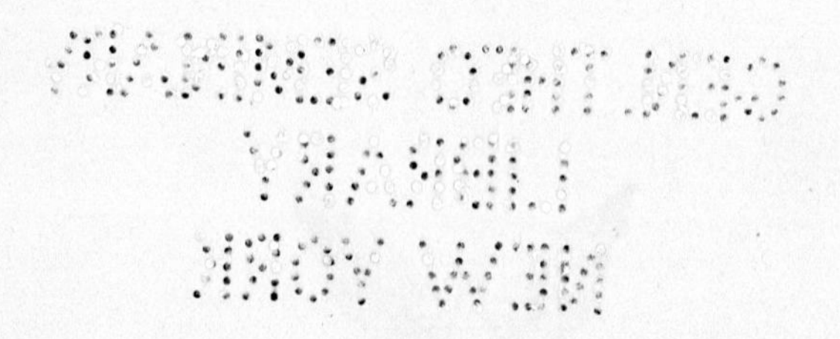

PRINTED IN THE UNITED STATES OF AMERICA
BY THE VAIL-BALLOU PRESS, INC., BINGHAMTON, N. Y.

Dedicated to the Memory
of my Grandfather
JACOB FUESS
of Annweiler, Germany
and His Fellow Revolutionists of 1848

FOREWORD

No one can write on Carl Schurz without being under deep obligation to three men, all of them fortunately still living: Dr. Frederic Bancroft, of Washington, who, with Professor William A. Dunning, completed with rare tact and skill the unfinished *Reminiscences* which Schurz left behind him at the time of his death, and who selected and edited for the Carl Schurz Memorial Committee the six-volume edition of Schurz's *Speeches, Correspondence, and Political Papers;* Dr. Joseph Schafer, of Madison, Wisconsin, editor of the *Intimate Letters of Carl Schurz,* author of *Carl Schurz, Militant Liberal,* and an authority upon most phases of Schurz's career; and Mr. Chester Verne Easum, author of *The Americanization of Carl Schurz,* a book which added much to the available information and settled some perplexing questions.

Mr. George McAneny, former friend and associate of Schurz, has assisted me in collecting material; and Mrs. McAneny, daughter of Schurz's intimate comrade, Dr. Jacobi, has contributed her recollections of both Schurz and her father. I have been aided also by Mr. Oswald G. Villard, Honorable Franklin MacVeagh, Mr. Nelson S. Spencer, Mr. Richard Henry Dana, Mr. John T. Morse, Jr., Mrs. Joseph Lindon Smith, Dr. Warren King Moorehead, Mr. Dirk H. van der Stucken, Dr. Carl F. Pfatteicher, Mrs. Winfield M. Sides, Mr. Robert Lincoln O'Brien, Professor David S. Muzzey, Mr. Mark A. de W. Howe, Mr. and Mrs. Alan R. Blackmer, Reverend Frederick W. Fuess, the officers of the Carl Schurz Memorial Foundation, and Professor Allan Nevins.

In preparing this volume, I have read with some care files of newspapers in New York, Boston, Washington, Cincinnati, Milwaukee, and St. Louis, and have consulted all accessible diaries, journals, and autobiographies for the period. Although certain unpublished letters of Schurz have been beyond my reach, it is improbable that they would have modified my estimate of him as man and statesman. My indebtedness to the authorities of the Oliver Wendell Holmes Library at Phillips Academy, of the Massachusetts Historical Society, and of the Boston Athenæum—where most of my researches have been carried on—is difficult to express. My wife has aided me greatly by her frank criticism and unfailing encouragement.

My own household as a boy was rich in memories of the "Forty-Eighters," and my mind was early filled with stories of their courage and idealism. Possibly something of the spirit which I learned at my grandfather's knee may have been transferred to these pages. I hope so; for Schurz and his comrades were, like the Pilgrims, lovers of liberty, and their sons and grandsons should not forget their tradition.

C. M. F.

December 1, 1931
Hidden Field
Andover, Massachusetts

CONTENTS

CONTENTS

ILLUSTRATIONS

CHAPTER I PRELUDE

DURING the stormy period between the outbreak of the Civil War and the close of the nineteenth century, most Americans grew familiar with the tall, erect, and vigorous figure of Carl Schurz, known to the newspapers as "that Dutchman." Thomas Nast's drawings of Schurz in *Harper's Weekly* showed a grotesque, lanky form, apparently all spindle legs and bristling beard, with heavy spectacles veiling piercing eyes. Something about his irregular features lent itself readily to caricature, and his whiskers became as well known as Roosevelt's square teeth or Mark Twain's shaggy moustache. In Nast's sketches, Schurz seemed like a modernized Ichabod Crane or, better still, a Teutonic Don Quixote tilting indiscriminately at both windmills and giants. In his later years, he was easily recognized as he strolled with rapid nervous gait down Fifth Avenue or stepped blithely on the platform in Carnegie Hall. He was never insignificant. If he did not always inspire affection, he could arouse fear.

The apprehension which Schurz excited was not, however, in the hearts of the guiltless. For forty years or more he was the self-constituted, but exceedingly useful, incarnation of our national conscience. In an age dominated by such unidealistic leaders as Roscoe Conkling and James Gillespie Blaine, Thomas Collier Platt and David Bennett Hill, Schurz was almost an anomaly. Nevertheless, during a period notorious for the frailty of its legislators and the stolid indifference of the ordinary taxpayer, Schurz dared to take a stand against political corruption. Few men have done more than he to cleanse our American governmental system. Zealous in his insistence on justice, he buzzed persistently about, lecturing all our Presidents, from Lincoln to Roosevelt, and reminding officials of their moral obligations. Naturally he did not make himself popular, but he did, without being at all sanctimonious, become a mighty spiritual force.

Schurz spent his life, on both sides of the Atlantic, as an agent of reform. Beginning as a fiery youth in Germany, where he rebelled against autocracy, he continued his career in the United States by fighting for the abolition of Negro slavery, for the rehabilitation of the Indians, for the conservation of our national resources, for sound money, for free trade, for a merit system in the civil service, for international peace, for fair treatment of the Filipinos, and for honesty in public affairs, to say nothing of countless lesser causes by which he was from time to time attracted. Thus he had a part to play in most of the important events of his generation. A politician like Blaine, as Mr. Charles Edward Russell has recently pointed out, leaves nothing behind him but the memory of an engaging personality; [1] but Schurz will long be associated with far-reaching policies and reforms.

In pursuing his aims, Schurz, early an adherent of the Republican Party, developed later into the perfect type of the Independent, or Mugwump, attaching himself for the moment to that party from which reforms might be expected. Averse to blind partisanship, he was always ready to change sides when the sides seemed to him to have exchanged principles. Although he held national office for only brief periods—six years as senator and four years as member of the Cabinet—he gained influence through his public utterances and was in many quarters listened to as a prophet. Historians have been forced to admit that he was right on most issues; and, even when he was wrong, he was sincere.

Schurz's methods of operation, after he had gained experience, did not vary greatly from campaign to campaign. He called conferences of kindred spirits, moved the adoption of minatory or commendatory resolutions, and wrote letters of ad-

[1] Russell, *Blaine of Maine,* 432–33. Mr. Russell, Blaine's latest and best biographer, says of the Maine statesman, "No other man in our annals has filled so large a space and left it so empty."

vice and warning. He spoke frequently and eloquently before large audiences; he reasoned with those German-Americans of whom he was the flawless idol; and he brought legitimate pressure to bear on wavering legislators. He was aggressive, tireless, irrepressible. He and his kind were often prodigiously annoying to executives like Cleveland, who complained of "the querulous impracticability of many self-constituted guardians of civil service reform," or like Roosevelt, who spoke scathingly of "those political and literary hermaphrodites, the mugwumps." But Cleveland and Roosevelt could not help respecting the rare combination of patience and audacity with which Schurz impressed his ideas upon the more intelligent voters.

Schurz's enemies, of whom there were many, searched his record indefatigably, hoping to reveal something to his discredit. If there had been any indiscretion or secret vice, they would have discovered it. Intermittently, as if in desperation, they accused him of cowardice on the battlefield, of disloyalty to his friends, and of inordinate personal ambition; but very few took these charges seriously. His private life was spotless. He had never been involved in any intrigue. When his opponents had paid for their detective work, they had learned that he was of alien birth, that he was fond of his family, that he could not be bribed or seduced, that he was tenacious of his opinions, and that, while not unstirred by a desire for fame, he wanted little for himself. The inquisitors were baffled when they found a man devoted to "plain living and high thinking."

Carl Schurz was a very useful person. Under a monarchy, he would have been an unwearied rebel, instigating revolution after revolution until either he or the king perished. In a democracy, he employed less violent methods. He was, however, able to compel both Republicans and Democrats to move more carefully and keep in mind the effect which a course of action would have on the Independents. His opinion on disputed questions became a matter of some concern to those who wrote party platforms. Since his death in 1906, there has been no one precisely like him in American affairs. He himself was not unaware of both his gift for leadership and his soundness of judgment. "In my public life," he announced, without undue humility, "I have not seldom seemed to stand alone, and deserted, but never long."

Stiff and aloof though he sometimes seemed to be, Schurz was really a very human person, and those admitted to intimacy with him found him most companionable. He was always happiest in his home, and rejoiced when, after a prolonged period of lecturing, he could rejoin his wife and children. He loved music, both as listener and performer, and expressed his moods by playing Bach and Beethoven. His genial humor and expansive sympathy endeared him to his friends. Especially fond of outdoor life, he was a striking figure at his summer home on Lake George, where he dashed impetuously along the woodland paths with his dachshunds yelping at his heels. He was different in his tastes from the usual American political leader. To those who had heard the stories of his youthful adventures, he seemed to carry about him an atmosphere of melodrama. In more than one sense, his entire career was glamorous. "Schurz is a wonderful man," wrote John Hay in his *Diary*, "an orator, a philosopher, an exiled patriot, a skilled musician! He has every quality of romance and of romantic picturesqueness."

"I WAS born," said Carl Schurz in one of his early speeches, "not far from that beautiful spot where the Rhine rolls his green waters out of the wonderful gate of the Seven Mountains, and then meanders with majestic tranquillity through one of the most glorious valleys of the world." [1] It was a district rich in history and legends; and Carl himself was born in a castle, with a stone-paved courtyard, a medieval moat, a drawbridge, and the coat-of-arms of the owner, Count Wolf Metternich, carved on a shield above the massive pillared portal. But Carl was not of noble ancestry. Nobody of his name had ever attained distinction in war or peace. His father, Christian Schurz, was a respectable schoolmaster, of peasant stock, in the tiny village of Liblar, about ten miles west of the Rhine and some fourteen miles southwest of Cologne. Of Carl's paternal grandparents nothing is recorded except that they died at a very early age. Their lineage has never been traced.

Of his mother's family, however, the boy heard much. Her maiden name had been Marianna Jüssen, and her father, Heribert Jüssen, known throughout the countryside as *Der Burghalfen,* was a tenant and overseer on Count Metternich's estate, locally called "The Gracht." The Burghalfen was an arresting personality, a magnificent animal of huge size and herculean strength, who ate and drank prodigiously, who could fell a mad bull with a sledge hammer, carry a ponderous anvil in his arms for rods, and lift unaided a loaded wagon from the ruts of a muddy highway. Carl inherited much of his grandsire's abundant vitality, although not his superb physique. Without school training, the Burghalfen dominated others through his shrewdness and magnetism. Around him myths in-

[1] *Speeches, Correspondence, and Poltical Papers of Carl Schurz,* I, 49. These volumes will be hereafter referred to as *Writings.*

evitably clustered, for he inspired admiration, whether he outstripped his subordinates at labor in the fields or appeared, gorgeously arrayed, at festivals, with his formidable rifle, *Der Ferkelstecher*, "The Pig Sticker," on his shoulder. Through Carl's transmuting imagination, he seems as dazzling as Porthos, but he was actually merely a supervisor on the Metternich farm, dividing the profits with the owner. With him, Carl's mother and father made their home for some years after their marriage; and it was in the tenants' portion of the castle [1] that their oldest son, Carl, was born, on March 2, 1829.

Carl's earliest recollections were of the ancient Burg, with its ivy-covered walls, its neatly kept parks, its granaries and stables. Even in his old age, he could remember the horn of Hermann, the Count's huntsman, as he balanced himself on the railing of the drawbridge and played his merry tunes with the gusto of a feudal retainer. Carl's first vivid memory was of himself, as a small child in petticoats with a white bonnet on his head, looking down at the wild boars with their gleaming tusks in the pit where they were kept. His mother, who presided over the servants' quarters and the dairy, sometimes took the lad with her into the immense cow-barn, built like a church, with a nave and aisles. By contrast with her burly husband, she was a slight, graceful woman, with a thin face and light-colored, curly hair, delicate, sensitive, and nervous by temperament. She superintended the meals in the vaulted hall, with its stone columns, and watched over the spinning of the flax. It was a primitive community, in which all the activities depended on the will of the master, and in which the bondmen who ate their porridge with clumsy wooden spoons out of wooden bowls had changed very little for three centuries. But the French Revolution and the Napoleonic Wars were be-

[1] The exact room, on the ground floor facing on the court, is now marked by a bronze tablet on the outside brick wall, placed there in 1929 by a group of German admirers. When my friend, Dr. Carl F. Pfatteicher, visited the castle in 1931, the heavy ivy had almost obscured the tablet and had to be cut away before the inscription could be read.

ginning to have their effect, and Carl Schurz was to grow up in a world in which even the common people were to demand —and to secure—their rights.

When Carl was about four years old, his father left the Metternich castle to take a house of his own in Liblar, an insignificant hamlet of not more than eight hundred inhabitants, whose chief boast was that its one street was paved with cobblestones.[1] Finding it difficult to bring up his family of four children on his teacher's salary of less than a hundred dollars a year, Christian Schurz resigned and opened a hardware shop, hoping thus to increase his income. A man of some learning, he had secret ambitions for his sons, Carl and Heribert. But he had little practical ability, and his dreamy nature was a disadvantage to him in business. On the walls of his living room were hung the portraits of his heroes, Schiller, Goethe, Wieland, Körner, Tasso, and Shakespeare, and he encouraged Carl to patronize a circulating library. The boy read good literature, including such classics as *Robinson Crusoe* and Schiller's *The Robbers*. The father, who had a passion for music, could play the flute, and Carl, as a lad of six, began to practice on a battered piano, thus laying the foundation for perhaps the most enduring solace of his life. Later he went twice a week to Brühl, a village four miles away, to take lessons from an organist. Eventually he became a first-class performer, skillful enough to impress John Hay. But Christian Schurz, although a kind father, lacked steadiness of purpose, and his career was one of melancholy futility.

Frau Schurz, Carl's mother, had been one of Christian Schurz's pupils in his singing school. Although she had received only a rudimentary education, she had a good mental endowment and stimulated her children to industry; but it was

[1] Liblar, entirely rural in the early nineteenth century, now boasts of several briquette factories and has been considerably industrialized. The one picturesque object of interest in the vicinity is still what is locally called *Das Schloss*. Liblar erected to her "Great Son," in 1929, an appropriate *Denkmal*, or memorial, consisting of a granite pedestal, surmounted by a bronze bust of Schurz and approached by a flight of stone steps.

her moral force which distinguished her above her neighbors. "I know no virtue that my mother did not possess," wrote Carl long afterwards. "Her disinterestedness in every trial proved itself capable of truly heroic self-sacrifice. . . . Her very being exercised a constantly elevating and stimulating influence, although she could aid her children but little in the acquisition of what is commonly called knowledge." [1] Her correspondence with Carl, although not beyond criticism in grammar, was rich in common sense, and her earliest letter to him, written in 1841, when he was in his thirteenth year, urged him to be industrious and not to neglect his religious instruction. Both parents lived to follow their son to the United States and see him become famous. Christian died in 1876, in his eightieth year, and Marianna died a year later, at seventy-nine.

The factors which determine a child's thoughts and aspirations are usually complicated and obscure, but the military bent which Carl at one time displayed may be traced to boyhood experiences. His father had seen the great Napoleon and, at the age of eighteen, had joined an infantry regiment and marched to Belgium, arriving just too late for the battle of Waterloo. Later he was promoted to be a corporal, but, to his lasting regret, was never under fire. Frau Schurz's four stalwart brothers, Peter, Ferdinand, Jacob, and George, all over six feet tall and each one of exceptional ability, had dramatic stories to relate, not only of battles but also of the busy world outside of Liblar. Meanwhile the Burghalfen, with his shaggy eyebrows and piercing eyes, who seemed as rugged as the Drachenfels, had a stroke of paralysis, which, leaving the upper part of his body still sound, did not permit him to walk, or even to stand. The disabled old autocrat, condemned to lie helpless with his legs swathed in flannel bandages and occupy tedious hours in killing flies, thrilled his grandson with stories of cannon bombardments and bayonet charges. The lad who listened so eagerly was to be a general before he was thirty-five.

The unhappy Burghalfen was not yet at the end of his mis-

[1] *Reminiscences*, I, 24.

THE CASTLE WHERE CARL SCHURZ WAS BORN, NEAR LIBLAR, GERMANY

ENTRANCE TO THE CASTLE WHERE SCHURZ WAS BORN

THE ROOM WHERE CARL SCHURZ WAS BORN, SHOWING THE TABLET PLACED THERE IN 1929

fortunes. Old Count Metternich died, and his son, although amiable, did not get along well with his crippled overseer. As a consequence of a quarrel, the Burghalfen left his comfortable quarters in the castle and took a house in Liblar. Most of his belongings had to be sold at auction, and the battered hero could not survive the disgrace. His wife died first, and he followed her to the grave twelve days later. With them, a whole generation, antiquated and outworn, seemed to pass away. The eighteenth century was fading, and a new era was about to dawn.

In his ninth year, Carl was withdrawn from the village school at Liblar and enrolled in a more pretentious institution at Brühl, walking the eight miles there and back every weekday during the summer. In the winter, however, he was allowed to remain at Brühl, boarding himself in the house of a butcher's widow. On his long walks through the woods, the small boy held a book in his hands and actually, complying with a suggestion from his father, perused the entire twenty cantos of Klopstock's *Messiah*—a feat which only those who have glanced at the ponderous hexameters can really appreciate. On these journeys, also, he memorized Tiedge's *Urania*, as well as shorter poems by Gellert, Herder, Bürger, Langbein, Körner, and other writers hardly suited, it would seem, to an immature mind. But Carl was a precocious student, who had already picked up a little Latin; and he made rapid progress in this language and in the other subjects taught in the cheerless Franciscan monastery in which the classes were held.

Carl's early life was not free from misfortunes and restrictions. The sudden death of his brother, Heribert, only fifteen months younger than he, was a blow for which he could find no consolation. His father's financial difficulties obliged the boy to practice such systematic economy that he had no opportunity for self-indulgence. This, however, he always regarded as an advantage, for it left him undebilitated by luxurious living. In his autobiography, he said:

Education can render young people no better service than to teach them how to make their pleasures independent of money. This is far easier than we commonly suppose. It requires only that we learn to appreciate the various good things which cost nothing and some of which are offered by almost every environment.[1]

In reflecting on his childhood, Schurz felt that he was fortunate in having been surrounded by "simple and modest circumstances, which knew neither want nor excessive affluence, and which did not permit any form of luxury to become a necessity." Throughout his life he had sufficient to live upon, but little more.

Carl was an impressionable lad, sensitive to his environment and quick to respond to the influence of older minds. Like many Germans, he was inclined to sentimentality and vague reverie, but a certain robust practicality kept him at his work. "You have talent," his mother wrote him when he was only sixteen; and, even at an earlier age, he stood out above his comrades because of his quickness in grasping ideas. He was a serious youth, self-conscious, rather egotistical, and without much sense of fun, but he had no difficulty in making and retaining friends. His father, who liked to show off his son's musical proficiency, might easily have spoiled the boy. Carl, however, showed no disposition to sow wild oats, and remembered some trivial experiences which early warned him against gambling and drinking. Having been warned that much was expected of him, he did not intend to disappoint those who trusted in him.

Nature and outdoor life stirred in him powerful emotions. He thought later that he was blessed in being able to spend his early days in the country, "where one feels himself not only nearer nature, but nearer to his kind than in the confinements and jostling crowds of the city." There were plants and song birds in every room of the little one-storied plaster

[1] *Reminiscences,* I, 76.

house in which they lived; and, on his walks to and from school, he quickly became an amateur botanist and ornithologist. "This love for the woods has never left me," he wrote, "and often in later life, at the aspect of a beautiful spreading landscape or of the open sea, I have asked myself whether what I had seen and felt in the forest did not surpass all else." [1]

Carl learned to enjoy and understand architecture and painting, and, in an unsophisticated way, took an interest in the theater—first of all, in the puppet shows in the tiny dance hall in Liblar, where he was fascinated by "Die Schöne Genovefa" and other melodramas. Later, when he saw "Hedwig, the Bandit Bride," performed by real actors, he was irresistibly impelled to plot a drama of his own. With Schurz, the impulse to put thoughts on paper developed early. Under favoring conditions, he might have been diverted into a literary career, in which he would have been successful.

There was not a Protestant in Liblar, and, like virtually everybody in the neighborhood, Carl was brought up in the Roman Catholic faith. But some liberalizing influences of his boyhood prevented him from a blind credulity. The errand man, called "Master George," taught him to be skeptical of miracles and dared to criticize the sermons of the parish priest. His uncle Ferdinand, a disciple of Voltaire, indulged in scoffing jests on religious subjects. When the boy heard the priest declare that all except Catholics were doomed to everlasting hell fire, he wondered about his wise friend, Aaron, the Jew, and moved toward tolerance. His mother would have been glad to have him study divinity, but, although he reached the conclusion that it was impossible not to believe in God, he could not choose the church as a career.

It was a childhood rich in romance. During warm August days were held in the various parishes a succession of kirmesses, or festivals, to which the entire family went for eating and drinking and making merry. While the older ones sat from four to six hours at dinner, the children watched the juggler

[1] *Reminiscences,* I, 44.

or ran to the booths on the village green. Most exciting of all was the "Schützenfest," on Whitmonday, at which the local sharpshooters contended to see who could hit the last jagged fragment of the wooden bird and thus become the *Schützenkönig*, or King of the Day, privileged to wear a crown of gold tinsel and artificial flowers and to carry around his neck the ancient silver chain. Once Carl himself, home on a vacation, became a member of the Sanct Sebastianus Society, enrolled as a competitor, and carried off the prize as the substitute for an old washerwoman, who, like him, was adorned with ribbons and flowers. It should have been an hour of triumph! But, as he looked at the "Queen," both he and she seemed grotesque, and his success was tinged with bitterness. The incident offered him an opportunity to moralize "that the fulfillment of a wish usually looks very different from the anticipation."

To Carl Schurz, brought up in monarchical Prussia, the United States seemed the hope of the world—a land, as he later described it, "covered partly with majestic trees, partly with flowery prairies, immeasurable to the eye, and intersected with large rivers and broad lakes—a land where everybody could do what he thought best, and where nobody need be poor, because everybody was free." Once one of the neighboring families started out with household utensils and boxes and trunks for the nearest port to sail for America, and Carl watched them wistfully as, in the gray dawn, the wagons climbed over the hill and disappeared in the shadow of the forest, on their way to a country "without kings, without counts, without military service, and, as was believed in Liblar, without taxes." Carl's father, showing the lad a picture of George Washington, described him as the noblest of men—a patriot who, after commanding armies, had returned to the plow as a simple farmer. To the Schurz family, the United States was a favorite theme of conversation, and ultimately most of them emigrated there in quest of liberty.

These German expatriates carried with them to their adopted

fatherland something of the simplicity and charm of their life in the Rhine valley. Even in Ohio and Missouri and Wisconsin they kept up for some years their quaint festivals, their fondness for athletic sports and Turnvereins, their musical gatherings, and their observance of holidays like Easter and Christmas. In venturesome moods they even wore the picturesque costumes which had not seemed out of place in Prussia. But the "melting pot" usually did its work with the children, and the second generation were molded into Americans, standardized, each one like the other.

When he was ten years old, Carl, now the sole hope of his father's heart, was entered in a gymnasium, or school, in the large city of Cologne—"good old, respectable, stupid Cologne," he called it. There he boarded very modestly at the house of a locksmith, sleeping in the same bed with the locksmith's son —a mechanic. Fortunately he was thrown into contact with a young Westphalian, Heinrich Bone, a teacher of unusual magnetism, who urged his pupils to write with directness and clarity and trained them in independent thinking. It was Bone who made Schurz a scholar. The course of study comprised mainly Latin and Greek, and the boy read widely in classical literature and history. Later he sometimes asked himself whether schools ought not to substitute for Greek and Latin the study of modern languages. But, even while recognizing the validity of many of the arguments for change, he admitted that, if given the choice once more between the ancient classics on the one hand and the so-called "useful studies" on the other, he would undoubtedly stand by the curriculum to which he had been subjected. "I personally owe to the old classical courses," he said, "very much that was good and beautiful, and that I would not forego." [1]

In Cologne, Carl spent six restless years. "I am truly frittering my life away," he wrote in the earliest of his letters to be preserved, written, September 28, 1845, when he was sixteen. But he was highly ambitious, especially in literature.

[1] *Reminiscences*, I, 89.

He scribbled verses, fraught with Byronic melancholy; he planned to write "something in the nature of a novel"; he resolved, after seeing *Hamlet*, to become a dramatist. But he was unable to settle down to any steady course of action. "All sorts of crazy ideas come to me now and then," he wrote his friend, Theodore Petrasch. But he made an impression on his instructors, and once, when his father was visiting him, the great Professor Putz had put his hand affectionately on Carl's shoulder and said to Christian Schurz, "A hopeful boy."

While Carl was learning to enjoy the *Iliad*, Christian Schurz was passing through dark days. In anticipation of Carl's entering the university, Christian had sold his property in Liblar and moved to Bonn, a town about twenty miles to the southeast of Liblar, on the west bank of the Rhine, where, in 1818, the Frederick William University had been founded. There Christian Schurz, with his usual financial ineptitude, was thrown into a debtors' prison, and Carl, still only seventeen and about to enter the highest class in the gymnasium, had to withdraw from school at Cologne and make arrangements with the family creditors. It looked as if his desire to enter the university would be thwarted.

A youth with his aspirations, however, was not easily frustrated. Settling down with his parents in Bonn, he pursued a course of lectures at the university, aiming, by his own private studies, to prepare himself for the graduation examination from the Cologne gymnasium. Although he could not yet matriculate at Bonn, he was thrown into the company of a brilliant group of undergraduates, notably Theodore Petrasch and Ludwig von Weise, and, although then ineligible for membership, was welcomed as a guest at the meetings of the Burschenschaft Franconia, the best of the student clubs. Schurz's admiring friends had introduced him to Johannes Overbeck, president of Franconia, as a youth of great promise; but Carl, at his first appearance, was so much embarrassed that he could only blush and stammer. "I had much rather be thought awkward than insignificant," he wrote in excusing his conduct. Later he redeemed himself by writing a parody of the Auerbach Cellar Scene in Goethe's *Faust,* in which he whimsically satirized some of his associates. Made self-confident by this success, he lost his shyness and soon developed into a leader. During this period he wrote also some *Poetical Letters* and a novel, *Richard Wanderer,*[1] which he repeatedly revised but never tried to publish. It was evident that he possessed intellectual power and literary ability, but what direction they would take was not yet clear.

By sheer dogged persistence Schurz covered the preparation for the final gymnasium examination and, in September, 1847, returned to Cologne for the ordeal. The examiner in Greek assigned him for translation a portion of the sixth canto of the *Iliad* which he knew by heart; and his proficiency in history and languages led his judges to overlook certain weaknesses in mathematics and the sciences. In a few weeks he was a regularly matriculated undergraduate at Bonn, where he threw himself enthusiastically into the student life. Now a full-fledged member of Franconia, he wore its tricolored ribbon across his breast, took long walking trips into the tributary valleys of the Rhine, and reveled in freedom of thought and action. Although dueling was banned among the Franconians, Carl learned to wield "a deft and powerful blade," and he joined the others in the beer drinking so common in German universities. His friends remembered him as a youth who was exuberant but not frivolous, and who threw himself ardently into both study and play.

It was in philology and history that Schurz was most absorbed, and his chief ambition was to become a professor. Stimulated by some brilliant scholars, especially Professor Gottfried Kinkel, who was then lecturing on the history of art, Carl's mind opened like a flower in the sun. Kinkel, fourteen years older than Schurz, was a handsome stalwart man, with

[1] This novel, recently reprinted and edited by Professor Julius Goebel, turns out to be a very sentimental and melodramatic tale—as Schurz himself described it, "an impossible story about impossible characters."

a heavy black beard and piercing eyes, who made himself picturesque by his broad flowing necktie, his old gray hat, and his green coat with its velvet collar. Under Kinkel's guidance, Schurz studied the art of speech and trained himself in the theory of rhetoric and oratory. When the need arrived, Carl carried these principles into practice and could address an audience with native eloquence controlled by artistic skill. The talented youth also won the heart of Frau Johanna Kinkel, who was a gifted musician, and found in the Kinkel home a circle of congenial people, most of them liberals in their political philosophy.

At eighteen, Carl Schurz was rather short of six feet in height, slight of figure, with long hair and a sensitive mouth and a face which, while not handsome, was thoughtful, even though marred by heavy spectacles. He affected an artist's cravat and a Byronic collar, and his favorite pose was like that of Daniel Webster, with his left hand thrust across his body into his coat. Young though he was, he was self-assured and serious-minded. Already his individualism had shown itself in a fondness for debating any difference of opinion and in a willingness to bestow unsolicited advice upon his friends. He was a hard worker, but he was not a recluse. It was fortunate for him that his membership in Franconia brought him into contact with his equals and superiors. He might easily have become introspective and conceited to a degree which would have destroyed his usefulness.

At the close of 1847, Carl Schurz, busy with a tragedy based on the story of Ulrich von Hutten, was thinking only of a scholastic career. A friend named Friedrich Althaus, of similar tastes, had encouraged Carl in this project, and the two formed an intimacy which was of long duration. Apparently another professor was in the making. It was at precisely this moment that new desires and motives swept into his life like a whirlwind, carrying him from the sheltered university cloisters into the tumultuous arena of politics and transforming him from a thinker into a doer.

CHAPTER III REVOLUTION

On a warm summer evening in 1849, Carl Schurz looked for the last time from his study window at his father's house in Bonn out over the Rhine to the lovely Seven Mountains. Scattered around him on desks and tables were the books and manuscripts in which he had recently been absorbed. Often, gazing upon those hills and that river, he had dreamed of a scholar's placid life. But now all that must be relinquished. A conflict was imminent, and duty was driving him into the battle for liberty. His mother, taking down the old broadsword from the wall, had handed it to her son with one admonition—that it should be used with honor. As Carl Schurz took a final glance at the beautiful scene, he had a premonition that he should never return to the seclusion of the university. He was right.

So marked an individualist as Schurz had already shown himself to be was not likely to be in sympathy with autocratic government. Under normal conditions, however, he might have been content with a closet liberalism as the expression of his individualistic philosophy. But Europe, as he grew to manhood, was entering on a period when liberal ideas were being transmuted into revolutionary acts. The stupidly reactionary attitude of Metternich, the Austrian prime minister, was producing its natural harvest in popular uprisings all over the continent. In several countries simultaneously a national self-consciousness was developing which was to be dangerous to autocracy.

What we call today the German Republic, was, in 1847, a group of separate and independent states of various sizes, ranging from the diminutive principality of Schwarzburg-Rudolstadt to the powerful Kingdom of Prussia, and including former grand duchies, bishoprics, margraviates, and electorates. The Treaty of Vienna, in 1815, in order to indemnify Prussia for her losses during the Napoleonic Wars, had transferred to her the Rhine Provinces, including Cologne and Coblenz. Carl Schurz was thus born a native of Prussia. Austria, a motley conglomeration of Germans, Magyars, Slavs, and Italians, was a vigorous rival of Prussia for leadership of the German peoples.

The dream of a united Germany had haunted the minds of progressives since 1813, when, in desperate revolt against the tyranny of Napoleon, King Frederick William III had summoned his subjects to arms, promising them a constitutional government. Patriotism ran high, and, after the great battle of Leipzig, October, 1813, the Czar, embracing General Blücher, hailed him as "the liberator of Germany." After Waterloo, however, the Prussian monarch, controlled in his ideas by Metternich, sank back into the comfort of his palace and conveniently forgot his pledges. The Congress of Vienna, in repatching the map of Europe, formed the so-called German Confederation, comprising thirty-nine states, with Prussia and Austria struggling for preponderance among them. Its population was heterogeneous, with conflicting racial, political, and religious traditions. There was, nevertheless, some national sentiment in Prussia, especially in the universities, where the Burschenschaften, adopting the watchwords "Honor, Liberty, Fatherland," had gained a firm footing. But King Frederick William, alarmed by some patriotic manifestations at the Wartburg Festival in 1817, dissolved the Burschenschaften and relapsed into a policy of repression, under which nationalism was discouraged. The establishment in 1833 of a Zollverein, or Customs Union, under the supervision of Prussia, was actually a step toward unity, although its full significance was not realized at the moment, and, according to Alison Phillips, made "the unity of Germany under Prussian leadership inevitable."

When Frederick William III died in 1840, and was succeeded by his son, Frederick William IV, the hope of reform revived, and the new sovereign's first announcements seemed to promise important concessions. But he was a man who, although versatile and idealistic, had, according to Schurz, "sudden conceits, but no convictions," and he had no intention of curtailing the authority or perquisites of the crown. He talked in glittering generalities and made graceful gestures, but did little to relieve the discontent. Meanwhile the dissatisfaction among the people, especially among the university students, spread and deepened; and the Burschenschaften, tolerated by the new king, fostered a spirit of nationalism. Such was the situation in Prussia when Schurz was growing to maturity. Temperamentally a liberal, he had learned at the house of Gottfried Kinkel to become the advocate of a united Germany, resting upon a foundation of a popular and constitutional government. The members of Franconia wore constantly under their coats the black, red, and gold ribbon of their fraternity, now the symbol of revolution.

As 1848 opened, there was trouble in the air. The convocation of the "United Diet," by Frederick William IV, in April, 1847, had culminated in his refusal to grant a written constitution, and optimism had turned to gloom. Then, on a February morning in 1848, while Schurz was bending over his desk in Bonn at work on his tragedy of "Ulrich von Hutten," a friend rushed in crying, "The French have driven away Louis Philippe and proclaimed the republic!" It was the spark which ignited the ready tinder. Abandoning his manuscript forever, Schurz rushed out into the snow. Soon the market square was seething with excited young students. Lectures seemed profitless; the routine of the curriculum was dull and futile; the undergraduates, ardent and untrammeled, wanted to sacrifice themselves for the Fatherland. Their aspirations were vague, and the movement for German liberty lacked coherence and definiteness, but they were in earnest. The ferment was manifesting itself in public meetings all over Prussia. On March 18, headed by Professor Kinkel, a procession of students, faculty, and townspeople marched through the streets of Bonn to the City Hall, where their leader, waving a black, red, and gold banner, addressed them in burning words. On that same day, in Berlin, two shots fired accidentally precipitated a clash between a mob and the royal infantry, in which several citizens were slain. This shedding of blood was the signal for a revolutionary outburst.

Up to this point Schurz, although recognized as one of the most prominent undergraduates, had been satisfied to follow his teachers, Arndt, Dahlmann, and Kinkel. But, young though he was, he was not content to be a mere private in the ranks. At a crowded meeting in the Aula, the university auditorium, the impulse to express his ideas became irresistible. As if impelled by some uncontrollable force, he climbed to the platform and found himself addressing the assembly. Thoughts came to him in an uninterrupted flow, and he spoke with vehement rapidity. His fervor and sincerity were convincing, and the applause indicated that his first public speech had been a success. He was indeed a natural orator, of whom his contemporary, Spielhagen, wrote, "*Schurz ist das grösste rednerische Genie, das mir in meinem Leben begegnet ist.*" [1]

That spring of 1848 was a time of wild, if somewhat aimless, enthusiasm. Schurz wrote to Petrasch that he was in the midst of "a lively and reforming activity," trying to organize "a universal union of associated students." He confessed in June that his participation in the movement had made him a "public character" and had pushed him "far into the foreground." Elected president of a student meeting to protest against the acts of an unpopular royal official, he was soon engaged in the formation of a democratic club of citizens and students, the members of which addressed one another as "Citizen," in imitation of the societies during the French Revolution. In the early autumn he attended with Kinkel a congress of similar associations at Cologne, where he listened to Karl Marx, the socialist philosopher, who impressed him as being intolerably dogmatic and condescending. From him, Schurz learned the valuable lesson—which, however, he occasionally forgot—that "he who would be a leader and teacher of men must treat the opinions of his hearers with respect." [2]

[1] Dannehl, 122.

[2] *Reminiscences,* I, 140.

During this summer of "work and worry," Schurz neglected his studies, devoting himself largely to writing editorials for the *Neue Bonner Zeitung*, a newspaper which Kinkel had started in August. In late September, he went as a delegate to the Studentenkongress in Eisenach, where he made many friends and threw himself, heart and soul, into the cause. After the regular sessions were over, Schurz, with some of the more ardent spirits, held a festival at the historic Wartburg, where trouble had developed more than thirty years before, and prepared a solemn *Address to the German Nation*, voicing the most radical sentiments. On the return boat journey from Frankfort down the Rhine, the nineteen year old agitator sat alone and shivering on the deck, sobered by the cold and wondering when he would be arrested. Quite resigned to martyrdom, he was a little disappointed that the government paid no attention to his seditious utterances. Later Schurz wrote an interesting pamphlet describing this patriotic gathering.

Meanwhile, on May 18, the German Parliament, comprising "several hundred German professors and lawyers, utterly unversed in politics," had assembled at Frankfort-on-the-Main. Although composed of intelligent men and probably representative of the German people, it wasted time in debate when action was more needed than words. While it was getting down to business, King Frederick William IV, intimidated by his monarchical neighbors and unwilling to defy Austria, had sunk back into a reactionary mood, in which he was resolved to block all liberal measures. Hence the National Parliament, sitting day after day in St. Paul's Church, was sure to find itself at odds with the reigning monarch of the strongest purely German state. Furthermore the parliament itself was not proceeding altogether for the good of liberalism. In September, after some vain protests, the delegates declared that the carrying out of the infamous Truce of Malmö could not be prevented; and an angry mob proceeded to murder two of the deputies and start a riot. Schurz, on his way to the Studentenkongress in Eisenach, stopped for a day or two in Frankfort just after this affair had occurred and was much troubled by the spirit of which it was a symptom. Only through Prussian troops could this uprising be suppressed; thus, as Schurz expressed it, "the backbone of the revolution begun in March, 1848, was substantially broken." The National Parliament was wasting time in mere talk. Instead of striking while the iron was hot, it was allowing the revolutionary ardor to cool, and every hour of delay operated in favor of the reigning dynasties.

There was, indeed, as Schurz later confessed, a fumbling amateurishness about this nationalist movement. It was a period of confusion, when steadiness of purpose was lacking. Not until after sitting for five months did the Parliament begin the discussion of a constitution. In late October, a motion was passed providing that the proposed constitution should apply only to strictly German states, thus virtually splitting the Austrian Empire into two parts. After prolonged debate regarding the model which the new Germany should follow, the majority of the delegates voted for an hereditary Kaiser, with only a suspensive veto over legislation, and, on March 28, 1849, formally elected Frederick William IV to that position. Within a few days twenty-three German states had accepted the Constitution, and there was hope that Germany might at last be really united.

Meanwhile the wily Prince Schwarzenberg, the Austrian Chancellor, had brought pressure to bear on the Prussian monarch, and the Austrian delegation, numbering ninety-five, had withdrawn from Frankfort. When a committee went to Berlin to notify King Frederick William IV of the news, he hesitated and then perversely refused the leadership of a united Germany. He announced that the National Parliament was without the power to make him, or anyone else, Emperor, and it was obvious that he did not wish to affront his powerful neighbor, Austria. His combination of obstinacy and timidity dampened the enthusiasm of the revolutionaries, and Schurz and his friends in Bonn were naturally dismayed.

On May 4, 1849, the National Parliament, in a final appeal, urged the German people "to stand up for the recognition and the introduction of the national constitution." In several states, especially along the Rhine, popular uprisings ensued, and Prussian troops were employed to crush rebellions in Saxony, Baden, and the Bavarian Palatinate (Rheinpfalz). It was to Prussia that the terrified sovereigns of these smaller states turned for the preservation of their tottering thrones, and King Frederick William IV was not reluctant to employ his dragoons in sustaining the regal, or ducal, prerogative.

Carl Schurz, hitherto only a revolutionary orator, was now to become an actor in the drama. The Prussian Government had issued an order mobilizing the *Landwehr*, or military reserve, for possible use against the rebels in the Rheinpfalz and Baden, but the members of the militia, many of them young men with families, had no desire to take up arms against fellow Germans who were in favor of national unity. In Bonn, Professor Kinkel, now the recognized democratic leader, conceived the plan of seizing the arsenal at Siegburg, on the east side of the Rhine, where the *Landwehr* had been directed to concentrate, and where quantities of ammunition were stored. The operations which followed gave Schurz his first opportunity to see what war was like. It was then that his mother handed him the sword, bidding him not to disgrace it.

The expedition, stirred up by Kinkel but actually directed by a former artillery lieutenant, Fritz Anneke, was a complete failure. It was badly planned, and the one hundred and twenty volunteers who appeared were inadequately equipped. Schurz himself, who had been placed in charge of the ferry, made the inexcusable blunder of allowing the boats to return to Bonn, and it was easy for the Prussian cavalry, when informed of what was happening, to cross the river in pursuit. As Anneke was marching along on the road to Siegburg, the report came that the Prussian horsemen were coming. Anneke ordered his men to disperse into the cornfields along the highway, and the thirty dragoons rode unmolested into Siegburg, while four times their number retreated stealthily to their homes. Schurz himself, disdaining to hide, stood still with about twenty others by the side of the road while the dragoons trotted by. But he was overcome by a "feeling of profound shame." The enterprise started with such noble hopes had ended as a fiasco.

Schurz, realizing that he might now be proscribed, and unwilling to endure the ridicule of his friends in Bonn, did not wish to return to his home. Only a few weeks before, he had written rather haughtily to Kinkel, "The whole agitation is rather completely under my control." Now he was humiliated, and, to regain his own self-respect as well as the good opinion of others, he felt that he must "expiate a sin." Having become implicated in revolution, he was driven by his pride to vindicate his conduct in the affair at Siegburg. Like many another patriot, he became a rebel without realizing what had happened.

Going up the Rhine by steamboat with his friends, Meyer and Wessel, Schurz entered the Rhine Palatinate, where, in the city of Kaiserslautern, he rejoined Kinkel and Anneke. Here, among the beautiful hills of the Rheinpfalz, was a widespread spirit of revolution. The King of Bavaria lived at some distance,[1] and, when he refused to recognize the new constitution framed by the National Parliament, the people of the Palatinate obeyed the counsel of Parliament and abjured their sovereign. The Prussian Government, after completing diplomatic arrangements with the Grand Duke of Baden, then dispatched two army corps to quell the popular uprising in the Rheinpfalz. It was much the same as if the National Guard of New York should be sent into Massachusetts to suppress a revolt in the vicinity of Boston.

The provisional government in the Palatinate had thousands of volunteers for military service, but very few competent officers to drill them. The generals were, for the most part, renegade Prussians or Polish refugees, who did not command the confidence of their men. It was obvious that the only hope

1 The Congress of Vienna had returned the Rhine Palatinate (Rheinpfalz) to the Kingdom of Bavaria, the capital of which was Munich.

of the nationalist movement was to gain the sympathy and support of liberals in other sections of Germany. But when sagacious leaders, like Franz Sigel, urged an offensive march into adjacent states, they were overruled, and the Palatinate leaders did little except to await an attack from the invaders.

Serious though it seemed at the moment to Schurz, the affair had many of the aspects of a comic opera war in Zenda or Ruritania. No muskets being available, recruits were usually supplied with spears, and, as each soldier dressed according to his fancy, the effect was frequently ludicrous. On one occasion, Schurz, who had received an appointment as lieutenant on Anneke's staff, was sent with a little body of fifty men, armed with a dozen flintlocks and some spears and scythes, to arrest a priest who was reported to be keeping his parishioners from enlisting. When the ecclesiastic, in defense, had the tocsin rung and summoned the peasants to protect him, Schurz drew his unloaded pistol and, pointing it at him, ordered the reverend father to direct them to disperse. Afraid of being summarily shot, the priest obeyed orders and went with his captors, and, when he later discovered the trick which had been played on him, was merry over the deception.

When Prussian regiments crossed the Palatinate frontier, the provisional government officials retreated into Baden and occupied Karlsruhe. At Bruchsal, a few miles north, Lieutenant Schurz, on June 23, 1849, was in a skirmish, with bullets, grape, and shrapnel whizzing about him, and received his first wound—a grazing shot on the shinbone, which bled a little but did not prevent his remaining on horseback all day. Writing to his parents and sisters, he said, somewhat grandiloquently, "I swear to you that never in my life did I feel so happy and never so purified as during this baptism of fire." During the battles along the Murg River, in the last days of June, he was, he told his family, "often in the bloodiest fighting, in the most murderous fire." He rejoiced that he thus helped to save his honor from the "mockeries and revilings" of his adversaries.[1]

[1] *Intimate Letters*, 60–61.

The culminating absurdity of the campaign for Schurz came on June 30, when Colonel Anneke sent him into the fortress of Rastatt, with a message to the commander, Governor Tiedemann. After discharging his duties, Schurz went to the rendezvous designated by Anneke and there fell asleep from sheer fatigue. When he awoke at twilight, the citadel had been surrounded by Prussians, and every avenue of escape was cut off. By a trick of fate, he had been separated from his own army and immured in the fortress.

Obliged to make the best of his situation, he told his predicament to Governor Tiedemann, an able and vigorous commander who attached him to his staff. During the siege of twenty-three days, Schurz kept a careful record of events, and his account was later published in the *Neue Bonner Zeitung* during August and September.[1] When the Prussians opened a bombardment and it was learned that the army of the Palatinate had retreated, it was evident that the garrison could not long hold out. Aware that the enemy would be especially severe on Prussians who had joined the revolutionists, Schurz expected the death penalty. On July 21, he penned a farewell letter to his family. Two days later, when Colonel Tiedemann decided to surrender, Schurz, after preparing a message for his friends, calmly awaited the hour of four, when the beleaguered soldiers were to march out through the gates between two lines of Prussian grenadiers and lay down their arms.

From the tone of Schurz's farewells, there can be no doubt that he thought himself about to be executed. At the moment, he was filled with a Byronic egotism. Face to face with death, he could not refrain from sentimentalizing over his fate. He

[1] In November, 1928, Dr. Joseph Schafer, to whose thorough and persistent investigations we owe much of our knowledge of Schurz as a young man, visited Bonn and went through the files of the *Neue Bonner Zeitung,* where he found Schurz's account of the siege printed in eight installments. Dr. Schafer later translated the document, and it was published in the *Wisconsin Magazine of History,* XII, 239–70, March, 1929. The surrender, as finally arranged, was unconditional, and Colonel Tiedemann, with twelve of the higher officers, was condemned by a Prussian court-martial and shot.

pictured his acquaintances saying of him, with a shrug of the shoulders: "Too bad about him; he had a fine talent, but he was over-eager and excitable. He might have become an able young man." In what he undoubtedly imagined to be his last words, he wrote: "Remember occasionally a friend who pledged his life for the realization of an idea before he knew the means of achievement; whose greatest sin it was, contrary to his own theory, to be too regardless of egoism. Again, farewell." [1]

But he was to be saved for better things. As he was preparing to go to headquarters to march out with the garrison, he recollected a subterranean sewer which he had noticed leading from within the city of Rastatt under the fortifications to the country outside the walls. The entrance to it in Rastatt was from a trench near a garden hedge. Schurz mentioned the matter to his orderly, Adam, and to an artillery officer named Neustädter; and the three men, equipped with provisions, slipped out of the rear ranks of the column, turned into a side lane, and entered the mouth of the sewer, which was nearly six feet high and lined with brick. This was between one and two o'clock on the afternoon of July 23, 1849.

After struggling through the drain tube and being almost drowned by an unexpected rush of water after a rain, the fugitives found the outlet guarded by a patrol of Prussian guards and were compelled to retreat to the town. Here they took refuge first in a barn and then in the loft of a shed, where they lay hidden for three days and two nights almost without food. Luckily they found a laborer who brought them something to eat and drink, and later notified them that the sentinels at the other end of the sewer had been withdrawn. With this workman's aid, the three refugees emerged from their retreat at midnight, ate a supper in their friend's kitchen, and, making their way through the sewer, arrived in a cornfield. Their guide—whose name was Augustin Loeffler—accompanied them to the banks of the Rhine, where he had engaged a skiff. In a few moments they were on Alsatian territory, where, on

[1] *Intimate Letters*, 67.

French soil, they gave shouts of relief at their escape. When he reached the inn at Selz, Schurz slept without a break for twenty-four hours. He would have been altogether happy if he had not been notified that Kinkel had been wounded and captured, and was soon to be tried by court-martial.

Schurz was free, but his lot was not an enviable one. He was still among strangers, and he at once set out for Switzerland, where Anneke and other patriots had sought an asylum. Still in military uniforms covered with alpaca dusters, they boarded the train from Strassburg to Basel. Adam was left behind, assurance having been given that he would be pardoned, and Schurz never saw him again; indeed he never knew his orderly's last name. Schurz and Neustädter, crossing the border, finally reached the village of Dornachbruck, where Schurz, utterly enervated by his privations, lay for ten days in bed in a melancholy lethargy, from which he revived sufficiently on July 31 to send a letter to his anxious parents, assuring them that he was "rescued and free," but without funds. He wrote that, although he was in "a state of deathly exhaustion," he was laboring incessantly on his diary, which he wished to have published. He begged his father to send him some money and to procure for him a passport under an assumed name. "Just a little more help and I am wholly saved," he added as he closed.

Schurz's father, who had given the youth up for dead, immediately sent Carl's friend, Strodtmann, to Switzerland with letters and money. Schurz's gloom was dissipated, and he set out with Strodtmann for Zurich, where, after the latter had returned, he was attacked by a fever, the aftermath of his exertions, which confined him to his couch for two weeks more. When he had finished his convalescence, he found himself without any occupation, in the midst of a group of refugees in the same condition. As he regained his strength, the need for something to occupy his teeming mind became imperative. His fellow exiles were content to spend their time in taverns, reminiscing about the past and plotting for the future. But Schurz decided to continue his studies. "A restless craving for systematic mental activity has seized upon me," he wrote. He registered for courses in the University of Zurich. He discussed problems of military tactics with some Prussian officers and carried on some historical researches in the local library. Soon he was writing articles for Dr. Hermann Becker, editor of a Cologne newspaper. He even considered becoming a professor in what the Swiss expected would be a great university, conducted by the federal government in Zurich. And then, just as he was worrying because the local police were becoming bothersome, he was drawn into the most romantic adventure of his career.

Although Carl Schurz was not yet of legal age, he had won for himself a fame which extended throughout the Rhine provinces. He was disposed later to look back with some dissatisfaction on the revolutionary movement of which he had been a part; but at the time he regarded himself as a person of some importance. "My popularity and standing among the people have risen considerably," he wrote in the autumn of 1849, with that lack of humility which was always one of his distinguishing characteristics. Wishing to appear as a man "whose honor and principles are dearer than his happiness," he refused to apply for an amnesty. The spring of 1850 found him in excellent health, hoping for a possible new uprising in Germany and living on money supplied him by loyal friends in Bonn. He wanted action but did not know where to find it.

CHAPTER IV RESCUE

In a poem written in 1906 to commemorate Carl Schurz's career, Richard Watson Gilder wrote:

> In youth he braved a monarch's ire,
> To set the people's poet free.

It was chiefly Schurz's rescue of Gottfried Kinkel from the penitentiary at Spandau which made him a hero to his fellow countrymen, giving him the reputation of Bayard or of Galahad. When he later arrived in the United States, he found himself known because of this exploit, and it was easy for him to claim and hold a place of leadership.

After being taken prisoner, Professor Kinkel had been incarcerated in Karlsruhe, where he expected to be condemned and executed like many of his comrades in arms. When he appeared before the court-martial on August 4, however, his eloquence was so moving that he was sentenced only to life imprisonment in a fortress. The Prussian Government, viewing this as too lenient, altered the punishment to life imprisonment in a "house of penal servitude." Confined for a few weeks in the Bruchsal, in Baden, he was then transferred to Naugard, in Pomerania, where he was treated like a common malefactor. There he remained from October 8, 1849, until April, 1850. Popular sentiment was strongly with Kinkel, but, when Strodtmann wrote his "Spinner's Song," referring to the prisoner's fate, the poet was promptly expelled from the University of Bonn.

Meanwhile Frau Johanna Kinkel was trying desperately to induce some one to rescue her husband, and, in February, 1850, sent an entreaty to Carl Schurz, who, actuated by both affection and duty, resolved to make the attempt. During the following summer, he devoted himself entirely to plans for freeing his friend and former teacher. The first step was to secure a passport in the name of Heribert Jüssen, his cousin, a young man of his own age and physique. With this identification in his pocket, he could travel without embarrassment in districts where he was not personally known to the authorities. Posing as an emissary of the liberal club in Zurich, he entered Germany and visited several cities. He later described vividly how, reaching Bonn at three o'clock in the morning, he stole into the house of his parents and sat in their bedroom until dawn woke them and they recognized their beloved son. Here Frau Kinkel called, and Schurz arranged to correspond with her by means of a "magic ink," invisible until touched with a chemical solution. Enough money was collected from Kinkel's friends to make it feasible to continue with the project, and Schurz was determined to carry it through.

Thinking it best to absent himself from Germany for a while, Schurz went to Paris for a few weeks. While he was there, Kinkel was brought to Cologne to be tried for his share in the luckless attempt on the Siegburg arsenal. Schurz himself was one of those named in the indictment, but he and five others had not been apprehended. Kinkel, on May 2, made an eloquent defense of his conduct, and the jury, amid thunderous cheers, returned a verdict of "Not Guilty"; but, having still his sentence to serve on other charges, he was now transferred to the penitentiary at Spandau, about eight miles west of Berlin.

As soon as this excitement had subsided, Schurz returned to Germany, conferred again with Frau Kinkel, and then proceeded to Berlin, where he found lodgings with some of his brothers in Franconia. Although he thought it necessary to preserve the utmost secrecy, he could not resist seeing the famous actress, Rachel, in Racine's *Phèdre.* He was so stirred by her genius that he went again and again to the theater until he came one evening face to face in the lobby with a former member of the Democratic Club at Bonn, a man who had been suspected of being a spy for the Prussian police. This ended his pleasure, but Schurz saw Rachel again later, both in Paris and in the United States, and thought her greater than Ristori, Wolter, or Sarah Bernhardt.

The conspiracy for releasing Kinkel had been progressing with all the romantic surreptitiousness that attends the action of a romance by Anthony Hope. Not even his parents knew where he was, and his only letter of that period to be preserved was written while he was convalescing from a severe contusion of the hip which he received as a result of a fall in a public bath—an injury which confined him to his lodgings for almost a month. When he recovered, he drove to Spandau in a cab and there took into his confidence a Dr. Ferdinand Falkenthal and later an innkeeper named Krüger, who offered his tavern as headquarters. Here Schurz began his operations.

The story of the release of Kinkel was later decorated with all sorts of fantastic embroidery, until it seemed as elaborate as the escape of Edmond Dantès from the Château d'If. The account which Schurz gave in his *Reminiscences* is, however, so straightforward and detailed that there is no reason to go further for the truth. Ascertaining after a cursory inspection that it would be impossible to extricate Kinkel by force, Schurz next tried to bribe a turnkey. He approached three of the guards in succession, only to find that no one of them had the courage to help with the plot. Temporarily thwarted, Schurz became alarmed and withdrew for a few weeks to Hamburg. When he returned to Dr. Falkenthal's residence, he posed as a physician, and, to further the deception, carried with him always a set of surgical instruments.

After one or two other failures, Schurz at last interviewed a jailer named Brune, who had the daring and the inclination to join in the conspiracy. From the fund collected by Kinkel's friends, he was able to promise Brune a considerable sum of money, which, in case of his detection, would be turned over to his wife and children. In late October, 1850, Schurz arranged a series of relays from Spandau to Mecklenburg, at the port of Rostock, from which Kinkel could embark for England.

CARL SCHURZ AND HIS WIFE

It was planned that the prisoner could go in less than thirty hours from his cell to the sea.

On the night of November 5, everything was in readiness. Schurz had even handed Brune the reward agreed upon. All the details had been carefully checked. Brune, having secured the keys to Kinkel's cell, was to bring him down the stairs to the gateway, and, after the night watchman had passed on his rounds, was to hurry the fugitive to Krüger's hotel, from which he was to be spirited away in a carriage driven by a man named Hensel. At the appointed hour, Schurz waited in the shadow of a doorway for Brune. Minute after minute passed, and no one came. At last, after half an hour, a spectral figure stepped out, his finger upon his lips. It was Brune—but without Kinkel! "I am unfortunate," he whispered. "I have tried everything. I have failed. The keys were not in the locker. Come to me tomorrow and get your money back."

There was nothing for Schurz to do but to go back to Krüger's inn and from there set out to notify the waiting relays that the plan had failed. It was a melancholy journey through the darkness, and Schurz was sick at heart. When he returned to Spandau, he had an interview with Brune, who explained that the inspector, instead of placing the keys as usual in the locker, had carelessly thrust them into his pocket and taken them to his home. It was an accident which could not have been foreseen—just bad luck.

Brune, no less disappointed than Schurz, had rejected the money given to him in the expectation of success. He suggested, however, another plan which, he thought, could be accomplished that very night. The guard on the second floor had been taken ill and Brune had volunteered to be his substitute. It was his idea that he might let Kinkel out of his cell and lower him from a dormer window to the street below. If Schurz could arrange to keep the street free from passers-by, the project was feasible. His optimism renewed, Schurz procured a rope, which Brune wound around his body; and Hensel agreed to be waiting again with his carriage and horses.

Shortly after midnight, on a still and slightly overcast evening, Schurz, with his companions, stood hidden in the recess of the door of a house opposite the penitentiary. Suddenly Brune gave the signal from the window, and Schurz, looking to see that the street was clear, struck sparks from his flint and steel to indicate that all was ready. Then Schurz could see a dark form moving slowly down the wall, accompanied by tiles and brick, which, loosened by the descent, began to strike the pavement. As soon as Kinkel touched the ground, Schurz was there to greet him. "This is a bold deed," were the prisoner's first words. In a minute or two, Kinkel had been disentangled from the cord and Hensel's vehicle had driven up. The two entered Krüger's hotel through a rear door, and there Kinkel was attired in a black cloth suit, a huge bearskin overcoat, and a Prussian officer's cap. While this exchange was being effected, Krüger entered, bringing some glasses of punch which had been mixed in an adjoining room by some convivial penitentiary guards.

Schurz drove off with Kinkel through the Potsdam gate, later, however, turning in another direction in order to elude any possible pursuit. On and on dashed the carriage, to the north through Oranienburg, Teschendorf, and Löwenberg, to Gransee, thirty-five miles away. As dawn brightened, Schurz could see how Kinkel had been altered by his imprisonment; how his face had become furrowed with anxiety and his black hair streaked with gray. The sun was well up when they crossed the Mecklenburg line into comparative safety. But they did not linger, and continued their journey, still at top speed, with fresh horses, until they passed through Rostock and arrived at Warnemünde, a coast resort, where Schurz for the first time saw the sea. They were exhausted, for they had been two nights on the road. Here Kinkel had at last a chance to dress his hands, which had been badly lacerated by the rope; and the two refugees, now regarded as heroes, were royally entertained by a democrat named Brockelman, who also provided them with one of his own vessels, the *Little Anna,* a forty-ton schooner. This was ready to sail on Sunday, the seventeenth of November.

As the tiny vessel weighed anchor on a frosty morning, Kinkel and Schurz stood on deck, gazing back rather forlornly at the shore of their fatherland as it slowly faded from view. The fact that they were exiles weighed heavily upon them both. When Schurz returned to Germany eleven years later, he was Minister of the United States of America to Spain. The fugitive had become an ambassador.

The voyage across the North Sea was so tempestuous that Schurz, to avoid being washed overboard, had himself lashed to the mainmast. After an ordeal of eleven days, they docked at Leith, the port of Edinburgh, where they were welcomed by friends and acquired presentable clothing. Schurz once told Bliss Perry that, when he stepped off the ship at Edinburgh, he knew only two words of English—"sherry" and "beefsteak"—to which he soon added "oxtail soup." From there they proceeded south to London, and then, after a week of sight-seeing, to Paris, where Kinkel rejoined his wife. At the French capital, Schurz found himself famous. Newspapers printed garbled, but picturesque, stories of his share in Kinkel's liberation, and countless legends were spread about the gallant young German who had risked his life for a friend. During the remainder of his career, the splendor of this exploit clung to him, and he was regarded as a national hero. As late as 1903, he received a picture postcard, signed by several German statesmen, showing a photograph of the White Cross Inn, near Rostock, where he and Kinkel had stopped in their flight from Berlin and where the room in which they had breakfasted was still being pointed out to guests. That was fifty-three years after the event. It was Kinkel's *Befreiung* which made Carl Schurz a distinguished man.

Schurz now settled down for six months in Paris, picking up a few francs by writing for the newspapers. His financial resources seem always to have been sufficient, even at periods when he had no visible means of earning an income; and it is probable that he was supported in part by contributions from his parents. Although he lived frugally, as always, he had money enough to buy an occasional book or a ticket to the theater. Under the instruction of an excellent teacher, the Princesse de Beaufort, he was soon able to write short letters to French journals, which, to his delight, were published without correction. He read French history, met a large number of public men, and attended meetings of the National Assembly at that interesting period when President Louis Napoleon was contemplating the seizure of the imperial title. Schurz, always a student of human nature, made keen observations on what was going on around him. He did not, however, find the atmosphere of Paris altogether congenial, and he was glad to spend a short time with Kinkel at the latter's new home in London.

On March 7, 1851, Schurz wrote to his parents, "My position continues to be very precarious, my earnings uncertain." While he was meditating literary projects and trying desperately to earn a few francs to send to his father, his peaceful routine was rudely interrupted. In late May, as he was walking with Frau Folger, the wife of one of his friends, near the Palais Royal, he was called aside by a police agent, notified that he was under arrest, and, after a preliminary examination, was taken to the Prefecture of Police and thrust into a cell, without any explanation. Schurz spent the night with a thief as his companion, but at once demanded pen and paper and wrote to the authorities, asking the reason for his detention. Not until four days had passed, however, was he brought before the chief, who treated him courteously but announced that the French Government wished Schurz to withdraw outside its borders. Later he learned that his release was due mainly to the efforts of the Petit family, with whom he had been living. His indignant protests were futile. Not until he had agreed to move immediately to London was he set free. Apparently Louis Napoleon, already preparing to make himself Emperor, was taking measures to drive from the country such avowed revolutionaries as Schurz, who was regarded as a clever and audacious conspirator.

In June, Schurz moved to London, where he took lodgings in the midst of a little German colony on St. John's Wood Terrace, not far from his friends, the Kinkels, who introduced him into their own social circle. His youngest sister, Antonie—known to her intimates as Tony—soon came from Bonn to live in the Kinkel household. Meanwhile Carl himself studied piano playing under the expert guidance of Frau Kinkel and earned some money by giving lessons in German and music.

Among the exiles who had sought a haven in London from various European monarchies, Schurz, young though he was, soon claimed a conspicuous place. Kossuth, the Hungarian, and Mazzini, the Italian, were there, and Schurz met them both. He seems, however, to have been rather vaguely restless, and the chimerical schemes of the "patriots" among whom he was thrown made him impatient. In the autumn, he ventured to the continent, stopping for a few hours in Paris and visiting Switzerland, where he secured the coöperation of certain German refugees in raising a "German National Loan," incidentally spending two weeks on a walking tour through the high Alps. Meanwhile Kinkel had sailed for the United States, hoping there to obtain funds for the same purpose. He was warmly received in the larger cities, but the financial assistance which he had expected did not materialize, and he returned disappointed. Kossuth's mission during that same autumn was equally barren of definite results. The truth was that the hour was not propitious for revolutionary enterprises. In Kinkel's absence, Schurz had acted as his vicegerent in London, carrying on his vast correspondence and keeping two printing presses active. Momentarily stimulated, he wrote that he had "great hopes for the development of things in the year 1852." But Louis Napoleon's *coup d'état* in December, 1851, was the death-knell to the aspirations of continental refugees.

The story of Schurz's decision to seek a refuge in the United States introduces another of those romantic incidents with which his life was filled. On a chilly winter morning, he wandered restlessly through the London streets, at last reaching Hyde Park, where he sat down on a bench to meditate. The conviction struck him that the Revolution of 1848 had lost its impetus and that a period of reaction was opening in Europe. The kind of plotting and intrigue in which he had been occupied would no longer be productive. With his Fatherland barred to him, America was the land where hopes were highest. Then and there, shivering in a London fog, he resolved to set out for "a new world, a free world, a world of great ideas and aims," as he optimistically described it in his *Reminiscences*.

Absorbed in his thoughts, Schurz had ignored a little man who had been sitting dejectedly on the other end of the park bench. Suddenly, however, he looked up and recognized Louis Blanc, the French Socialist, whom he knew slightly. As Schurz rose to steal away, Blanc lifted his head, stared at him with eyes which had not been closed for many hours, and said, "*Ah, c'est vous, mon jeune ami! C'est fini, n'est ce pas? C'est fini!*" This was the verdict at which two revolutionists, one French and one German, had arrived in that mid-century despondency. The two men pressed one another's hands silently and parted.

The motives which led Schurz to select the United States as an asylum are difficult to disentangle. His parents, paying the penalty for their son's radicalism, were in straitened financial circumstances and eager to join some relatives, the Jüssens, who had already emigrated to Wisconsin and were prospering. Schurz himself had received golden reports from Kinkel and hoped to be able to make a living in America by lecturing. There was the additional argument that nothing could be accomplished in London. Teaching had somewhat broken down his health, and he did not like the English climate. Finally, he confessed to his family, he felt "the most pressing necessity for activity on a large scale." But he had not yet decided to burn his bridges behind him. To his friend, Friedrich Althaus, he wrote, "I am saying farewell to Europe with the certainty of being back again at the right time."

In the autumn of 1851, Schurz, calling at the house of Johannes Ronge, in Hampstead, on business, was introduced to Margarethe Meyer, daughter of a well-to-do Jewish manufacturer of Hamburg. She was only eighteen years old, described by Carl as having something childlike in "her beautiful features and large, dark, truthful eyes." Recently graduated from school, she had come to England principally to help her sister, Mrs. Ronge, whose husband, an ex-priest and ardent revolutionary, had fallen on evil days. Apparently Margarethe and Carl fell in love almost at first sight. They were betrothed in February, 1852, and Carl, replying to some questions from Margarethe's brother, Adolf Meyer, wrote a very illuminating autobiographical letter, in which he explained his financial condition, pointing out that he was earning by teaching "what would suffice in a pinch to cover the common needs of two," but adding that he proposed to seek in America "a broader and more fertile field." "My nature," he continued, "cannot content itself with the life aims which are contained within my four walls." Adolf Meyer did not altogether approve of his sister's going to the United States, and some difficulties had to be overcome. Fortunately for Carl, however, Margarethe, although she had always been sheltered and protected from annoyance, did not lack courage, and she was sufficiently in love to be willing to disregard the wishes of her family.

Margarethe Meyer and Carl Schurz were married on July 6, 1852, in the Parish Church of Marylebone, in London, and went for their honeymoon to "a charming little cottage in rural Hampstead." They had planned to sail almost immediately for America, but both Schurz and his wife were attacked by illness,[1] and they were compelled to delay their embarkation. While he was convalescing, Carl was very impatient and did

[1] Schurz, writing on July 26, described his illness as scarlet fever, but it was too brief in duration to be like the disease which we know by that name today. He wrote, "My sickness, as is usual with me, was swift and severe in its onset, prostrating my whole organism for a short time; then just as quickly broken, and a prompt convalescence."

not enjoy his "floundering state of suspense." The bride and groom finally engaged passage in mid-August, on the *City of London,* a sailing vessel which took twenty-eight days for the trip. They landed in New York on September 17, on a bright autumn morning. "With the buoyant hopefulness of young hearts," wrote Schurz, "we saluted the new world." He was then in his twenty-third year.

CHAPTER V READJUSTMENT

THE EMOTIONS which filled Carl Schurz's breast as he sailed up New York harbor, past islands radiant with sunlit splendor, must have been very like those which had stirred those earlier immigrants on the *Mayflower* and the *Lady Arbella* in the seventeenth century. "We felt," he wrote, "as if we were entering, through this gorgeous portal, a world of peace and happiness." He has recorded vividly his impressions as they ate their first dinner at the Union Square Hotel, at five o'clock in the afternoon, with Negro waiters who made an elaborate ceremony of the occasion, or as they walked about the city observing the people. Naturally still a German in habits, spirit, and loyalty, he was uncertain whether or not to choose a new allegiance. As late as April 12, 1853, he wrote, "I am no less attached to Germany in America than I was in Europe." To him the United States seemed not so much an adopted fatherland as a place of new hopes and unlimited opportunities. His Americanization, as Chester Verne Easum has pointed out, was a gradual, even an unconscious, process, but it was eventually to be thorough.

Schurz's first outburst of elation was followed by a mood of gloom. For a fortnight, his wife, never very strong physically, was ill, and the young husband, sitting at evening in the park at Union Square, had some of the most melancholy hours of his life.[1] He missed the friendly consolation of his fellow exiles

[1] Speaking many years later, Schurz said: "I well remember my first wanderings through the streets of New York, some of which were at the time decorated with the trappings of a presidential campaign. . . . I remember my lonely musings on a bench in Union Square, the whirl of the noise and commotion near me only deepening the desolation of my feeling of forlornness; the future before me like a mysterious fog bank; my mind in a state of dismal vacuity, against which my naturally sanguine temperament could hardly bear up." *Writings*, VI, 41.

in St. John's Wood, and he found that his ignorance of English was a handicap to him in making acquaintances. As soon as Mrs. Schurz was convalescent, they went to Philadelphia, where there was a considerable German colony, among them Schurz's old ally, Adolph Strodtmann, who was running a bookshop and editing a newspaper. What Carl needed most was work—some outlet for his restless energy. He perceived, however, that he could not enter into the activities around him until he could talk the language in which they were conducted. Why he had not learned English in London has never been satisfactorily explained. The speed with which he mastered French would seem to indicate that he had some linguistic facility. But he apparently lived for several months in England without speaking any tongue but German, and he was now compelled to take up a task which should have been accomplished before he set out for America.

His methods were unorthodox but productive. Ignoring a grammar, he began with the aid of a dictionary to read—first the *Philadelphia Ledger*, then the classic English novelists, and finally Macaulay, Blackstone, and Shakespeare. He read, he declared, with the utmost conscientiousness, never letting an unusual word slip by without looking up its meaning. He used the *Letters of Junius* for practice exercises, translating passages into German and then back again into English, and then comparing the result carefully with the original version. Within six months, as a reward for almost unceasing devotion to his system, he could carry on a conversation in English with ease and could write a letter in the American idiom. To the end of his life, he remained bilingual, speaking as readily in one language as in the other. When he was composing the reminiscences of his childhood, he fell naturally into the phrases which he had then employed; but he always preferred English for public speaking and for the discussion of political subjects and business affairs.

During these months of adaptation to his new environment, Schurz had obviously no means of earning his living, and his biographers have been justifiably puzzled to explain how he managed to support himself and his wife, to say nothing of the baby, Agathe, born in the summer of 1853. He traveled somewhat in Connecticut and Pennsylvania, and later took a trip to Washington. Within the next few years he made two journeys to Europe. Yet he never in his letters mentions any lack of ready cash. It has been suggested that Schurz, for some time after his arrival in the United States, may have been the paid agent of the German revolutionary group in London, commissioned to maintain and stimulate the sympathy of German-Americans; but there is no evidence to prove this supposition. Much more plausible is the theory that Margarethe Schurz used up a considerable portion of her own small fortune—which amounted approximately to fifteen thousand dollars—in giving her husband time to prepare himself for the competition of American life. The problem is really wrapped in mystery, and Schurz himself says nothing in his correspondence to offer a solution. We do know that, in the spring of 1853, Carl's father, mother, and two sisters joined him in Philadelphia, and that the entire family took a house there, the daughters finding employment in a millinery shop.

Having acquired some facility in the language of his adopted country, Carl Schurz next undertook to learn something about its politics and people. It was a kind of interregnum in Washington affairs, during which the chief issue was Negro slavery. Calhoun, Clay, and Webster, the great leaders of the nation for almost four decades, had all died at the middle of the century. Schurz had arrived in America only a few weeks before the death of Daniel Webster and the election of Franklin Pierce as President, and he had found it difficult at first to differentiate between Whigs and Democrats. New leaders were coming to the front—Seward, Sumner, Jefferson Davis, Chase, and Douglas—many of whom were not satisfied with the Compromise of 1850, prepared so carefully by the older generation. Schurz soon ascertained that most German-Americans had joined the Democratic Party, attracted, perhaps, by the party name and by its generous policies toward citizens of foreign birth, especially the Irish and the Germans. He wisely, however, did not commit himself until he had taken the opportunity to learn what the issues really were.

During the winter after his arrival in America, Schurz lived very quietly, saying little and inquiring much. He wrote a book in German on the French Revolution and its results, and planned a volume dealing with the United States; but the first, although used later as a basis for lectures, was never published, and the second was never written. During the autumn of 1853, he was still meditating whether or not he should settle permanently in America, and, to help his decision, he made a visit during the following winter to Washington. His motives in going to the capital were not altogether clear, even to himself; but he did have in his mind an idea that he might be able to influence the foreign policy of the Pierce administration,[1] and he was doubtless seeking an agreeable opening in political life.

Schurz's early glimpses of the operation of American democracy had filled him with "dumb amazement," as he saw "the principle of individual freedom carried to its ultimate consequences." In Washington he was at once thrown, as an unprejudiced and disinterested spectator, into the very midst of the seething turmoil of American politics during the debate over the Kansas-Nebraska Bill. He soon discovered that, although the country was at the moment badly governed, democracy had not altogether failed. He wrote to his wife that President Pierce was a man placed at the helm of a great republic "without possessing the necessary strength of character or the equally necessary clearness of mind." Through Francis Grund, then a newspaper correspondent, Schurz received his initiation

[1] In a letter to his wife, dated March 23, 1854, Schurz said, rather mysteriously and vaguely, "It was my intention to urge upon the people I came in contact with—especially if I should be able to reach any member of the Cabinet—a certain course in their foreign policy"; and he reported that, with members of Congress, he had had some success that was "quite pleasing." *Writings,* I, 12.

into the corruption of our public affairs and the operation of the "spoils system." An idealist in his philosophy, he was shocked at the abuse of patronage and at the discovery that office-holders were interested not so much in their salaries as in the "pickings" which their positions permitted. Schurz was, of course, in Washington at a period when the Democratic Party, rejoicing in the fruits of its recent victory, was making sure that lucrative places were held by loyal partisans. But he was peculiarly and permanently impressed by the toleration with which men apparently high-minded regarded the conditions around them. Carl Schurz, the civil service reformer, received his inspiration from what he saw in Washington in 1853.

To a man who had observed parliamentary bodies in Germany, France, and England, the American Congress did not seem imposing, and the majority of its members struck him as being "easy-going and careless of appearances," as well as excessively fluent. The most conspicuous figure in the Senate was Stephen Arnold Douglas, then only in his fortieth year, but at the apex of his influence. Schurz has left in his *Reminiscences* a graphic picture of the "Little Giant," with his diminutive but sturdy body and massive head, "the very incarnation of forceful combativeness," and his sentences, driving "straight to the mark like bullets, and sometimes like cannon-balls, tearing and crashing"—a splendid "parliamentary pugilist." For him Schurz promptly conceived an intense aversion, thinking him to be "the very embodiment of that unscrupulous, reckless demagogy which . . . is so dangerous to republics." [1]

Schurz's dislike of Douglas was doubtless actuated in some degree by his own strong opposition to Negro servitude. He could not understand how a party calling itself Democratic could be "the mainstay of the institution of slavery." His first interview in Washington, ironically enough, was with the Secretary of War, Jefferson Davis, who impressed him by his dignity and courtesy. But he also conversed with Seward and Chase and Sumner, whose point of view was nearer his own,

[1] *Reminiscences,* II, 33.

and found himself sympathizing with "a small band of anti-slavery men faithfully fighting the battle of freedom and civilization." As he listened to Southerners like Butler, Toombs, and Mason on the floor of the Senate, he pondered on the arguments which could be advanced to overcome their logic. When Schurz reached Washington, Douglas's Kansas-Nebraska Act, declaring the Missouri Compromise inoperative and void, had unnecessarily reopened the question of slavery extension, which Clay and Webster had thought to settle forever through the Compromise of 1850. Mainly through Douglas's personal efforts and aggressive eloquence, the bill passed the Senate on March 2, and later became a law through the President's signature on May 30. Whatever were Douglas's motives—and they have been more and more generously interpreted—his action led directly to the Civil War. On Schurz himself the passage of the measure was to have some effect. A group of anti-slavery men, meeting in Jackson, Michigan, on July 6, formed the Republican Party, with which he was shortly to be identified, and the German-Americans of the Northwest abandoned in large numbers the party which Douglas headed. Early in 1855, Schurz wrote to Kinkel, "I am decidedly opposed to any extension of the domain of slavery"; and he declared that the United States would never interfere practically for the freedom of the peoples of the world until the slaveholders had ceased to be a political power.

There must have been something about this brown-haired, brown-eyed young foreigner which attracted attention, for he found little difficulty in making acquaintances, even with the political leaders. Always self-confident, he wrote, after looking about him, "Nature has endowed me with a goodly capacity that only awaits an opportunity to make itself useful, and I do not think I am over-estimating my value when I say that I would be second to very few here, not now, but in a few years."[1] He was encouraged by certain assurances made to him in the capital to hope that, if he established citizenship in

[1] Letter to Mrs. Schurz, March 23, 1854. *Writings,* I, 11.

one of the western states, he might expect within a very short time to be chosen a Congressman, with a brilliant career ahead of him. "When I come in touch with this atmosphere of political activity," he confessed to his wife, "I feel the old fire of 1848 coursing in my veins as fresh and young as ever." After his return to Philadelphia in 1854, he had definitely decided to become an American citizen.

He now could speak the language and had seen the rulers of the nation. The next step was to investigate the country, especially the Northwest—that "real America," where so many of his friends and relatives had already settled and in which he was planning to seek an opportunity for development. As an agent for a Philadelphia company interested in installing a gas-lighting system in Indianapolis and other cities, Schurz set out in the early autumn of 1854, traveling alone and endeavoring to absorb impressions of the places which he visited and the people whom he met. What he saw and felt has fortunately been preserved in a series of letters to his wife, who, less robust and audacious than he, was fearful about moving toward the west. One of Carl's difficulties was to convince Mrs. Schurz of the advantages to be derived from another change of residence. Passing through the Alleghenies at night, he saw nothing of Pittsburgh except the "yellow, burned-out fires" which had been started in the streets as a precaution against cholera. In Ohio, he could watch from his car window the pioneers, many of them still in log cabins, enclosed in dense forests and reached only by narrow trails. Near Cincinnati, the woods were thinner, and the magnificent valley of the Ohio opened up, showing the city which even then was known as the "Queen of the West" and in which Schurz was later to play the role of political leader. He was much impressed by the large amount of new construction, but was obliged to proceed directly to Indianapolis, then a city of eighteen thousand people, where he found two thousand Germans, living together in their own section of the municipality. The Indiana capital bore a "rural character," and men and women rode in from the environs on horseback, sometimes followed by young colts. Then and always, Schurz was a shrewd observer, accustomed to record what he saw and experienced, and his letters can be relied upon for their accuracy and credibility.

After having ridden by train from Indianapolis to Chicago, across the "grand prairie" and "the unbroken, inexorable, dead plains," Schurz confessed that, although he already loved the West, he would not care to dwell on those endless meadows. He arrived in Chicago at two o'clock in the morning and, unable to find a room or a bed in a hotel, roamed through the lonely streets, where, as he said humorously to his wife, he met millions of rats, "of all sizes and colors, old and young, white and gray," who "played charmingly" about his feet. He finally found a refuge in a windowless closet, the walls of which bore evidence of "bloody bedbug battles." This was his first experience in Chicago, a city which he was later to enter almost as a conquering hero.

Throughout the Middle West, Schurz met relatives and acquaintances, who entertained him lavishly. In St. Louis, for example, he was welcomed by "a multitude of old and new friends," who overwhelmed him with invitations. It is significant, however, that he noticed how the existence of slavery cast a shadow over the industrial and commercial developments of that city. A strong German element existed there, chiefly liberal-minded men who had been driven out of the Fatherland during the political upheavals of 1830 and 1848. Among them was the patriot, Friedrich Hecker, leader of the revolutionary movement in South Germany, who lived on a farm at Belleville, Illinois, and who, although only a little over forty, was pitiably ill. As the two discussed politics, they agreed in denouncing Douglas's "iniquitous attempt . . . to permit slavery unlimited expansion over the Territories" and pledged themselves to meet on the field in a common endeavor if the anti-slavery cause ever needed their aid.[1] Everything he saw made Schurz more opposed to slavery as an institution.

[1] *Reminiscences,* II, 40–41.

Courtesy of the Estate of Carl Schurz

THE CITY OF WASHINGTON IN 1852

Returning to Chicago, Schurz took the night steamer along the coast of Lake Michigan to Milwaukee, a city which, in his opinion, suffered from the presence of too many Germans. He was better pleased with Watertown, Wisconsin, about fifty miles to the west, where he was strongly urged by his uncle, Jacob Jüssen, to settle. While it was a community deficient in cultural advantages and social refinement, it was young and full of opportunities, and an immigrant could become a voter after only one year of residence. By the middle of October, Schurz was back in Philadelphia with his wife, evidently impressed by the beauty of the West, the cheerfulness and breeziness of the people, unhampered as they were by any traditions of the past, and the grandeur which was "the characteristic of all western life." Equipped with more accurate information about Wisconsin, he was able to talk more persuasively to his wife, who responded to his infectious enthusiasm.

Some family conferences resulted in a decision to move to Wisconsin. Before the winter ended, Schurz accompanied his parents and his sisters to Watertown, which they reached on March 3, 1855, after a cold and unpleasant journey. There Schurz bought some real estate and saw that the family were comfortably established. In April, he took passage, with his wife and child, for Europe, his chief purpose being to benefit the health of Mrs. Schurz, who was far from well. During his short visit to London, he renewed his acquaintance with Louis Kossuth, finding him old and depressed. The Kinkels were leading an unperturbed existence, the professor as a lecturer on art and Frau Kinkel as a music teacher. Carl went with Frau Kinkel to a concert at which Jenny Lind sang and Richard Wagner conducted the overture to his own *Tannhäuser*, and became a captive to the great composer's new form of musical art. Schurz confessed that the revolutionary ardor of the exiles in London had cooled, and, recognizing this, was more than ever convinced that he had chosen rightly in deciding to become a citizen of the United States.

Leaving Mrs. Schurz with her family in Europe, Carl came

back alone to America, arriving in July and proceeding at once to Watertown, from which place he wrote her, saying, "There are many persons who seek my acquaintance, and from the manner in which I am received I may conclude that I could easily attain prominence." Lack of confidence in himself was never one of Schurz's weaknesses. His self-assurance, tactfully concealed from others, revealed itself constantly in his letters to his wife. Watertown itself was then growing rapidly and had a population of 8500; indeed, since Schurz's previous visit, whole rows of wooden three-story buildings had sprung up like mushrooms. There was every reason to believe that a "boom" was on, through which a far-sighted investor in real estate might profit.

Impressed by such possibilities, Schurz purchased a piece of land on the outskirts of the community. Before signing the deeds, he again visited Milwaukee to investigate prospects for investment there, but eventually determined to choose Watertown, where he was being urged to participate in local politics. The sale was closed on September 23, 1855, and Carl Schurz became a resident of a place which, although still small, was the second town in Wisconsin, apparently about to become a great railway center. Writing to his wife, Carl described it as "created from nothing by sheer industry, initiative, and persistence," and drew a picture of the streets crowded with wagons and the sidewalks packed with people—"a picturesque, lively scene, full of cheerfulness." New arrivals were coming every day, and everybody was optimistic.

The farm which Schurz had bought, subject to a heavy mortgage, contained eighty-nine acres. There, on a site overlooking the river and the town, Schurz built a house, typical, architecturally, of that ghastly period in American civilization, with hideous rococo decorations and no symmetry. He undoubtedly felt that he had made a shrewd investment. As a matter of fact, the panic of 1857 was already imminent. The railroad boom was soon dissipated, and Watertown became, not a center, but just another town along the route; real estate, instead of appreciating, dropped in value; and the population increased only a few hundred beyond the point which it reached in 1856. The truth is that Schurz had bought at the very height of the inflation. Within a year money became very scarce, and well-to-do people resorted to barter. It is needless to say that his ventures in real estate were unprofitable.

Confident in his future prosperity, Schurz sailed again for Europe in the autumn of 1855, meeting his wife on December 17, in London, and accompanying her in early February, 1856, to Montreux, in Switzerland, where they spent several months together. Carl thought that Margarethe's health was much improved, but he was warned that it would take longer than a year to restore her completely. They sailed back to the United States on June 21, 1856, and, after a few days in New York and Philadelphia, set out for Watertown, where they were disappointed to see that their new house was not quite ready for occupancy. By autumn, however, they were established, and Schurz wrote, "Anything pleasanter than Margarethe's and my suite cannot be conceived." Mrs. Schurz herself felt invigorated in the crisp climate and soon took an active share in the management of the home. In the midst of a snowstorm, Schurz wrote to Kinkel, describing himself as living "in a handsome country house, upon a gentle acclivity, a gunshot distant from the town" and picturing in the bay window of one room "a lovely young woman at work and a red-cheeked, angel-faced child at play," while he sat in another, at a writing table, surrounded with books, including Blackstone, Kent, and other legal tomes.[1] Even in that frontier community, there were evening parties, charades, and dances of a simple kind; and once they had a masked ball, which lasted until dawn. The German immigrants had brought with them their singing societies and their festivals and their spirit of *Gemütlichkeit*. The activity and inspiration around him compensated Schurz for the en-

[1] Letter to Kinkel, December 1, 1856, *Intimate Letters*, 175. The house itself was burned down some years ago, but the owner of the new residence on the same site calls his place "Carl's Hügel"—Carl's Hill.

joyments of civilized life which he had been obliged to abandon.

Nothing could keep Schurz from being busy. Soon he secured an appointment as notary public, and, with his partner, C. T. Palme, undertook to carry on business as a land agent. Having become a citizen, he was elected alderman for the Fifth Ward, as a Republican, as well as supervisor for the Fifth and Sixth Wards; and he seems to have been for a brief period Commissioner of Public Improvements. In his spare moments, he studied law and was actually admitted to the bar; but, although he entered into a partnership with Halbert E. Paine, of Milwaukee, he never practiced in the courts. He was even president of an Insurance Company. Countless projects entered his restless mind, and he had his hands in nearly every local enterprise.

Above all, however, it was politics which seized and held his interest. Although most of his German associates were Democrats, he was attracted by the platform of the newly formed Republican Party adopted at Philadelphia in June, 1856, and became a staunch supporter of its nominee, John C. Frémont, the "Pathfinder." Believing that slavery for the moment transcended all other issues, he felt that, in the presidential campaign of 1856, "the old cause of human freedom was to be fought for on the soil of the new world." Sitting on a cracker box in front of a store on Watertown's Main Street, Schurz talked to his neighbors about the horror of slavery, and made some converts.

Soon he was to have a wide audience. The party managers perceived his ability and potential influence. L. P. Harvey, a Wisconsin State Senator, urged Schurz to make a little speech in German at a Republican mass meeting in the country town of Jefferson; and, when he pleaded lack of preparation as an excuse for declining, Harvey invited him to attend as a guest. Schurz found himself on the stage, among the local dignitaries, and later, at a certain point in the program, heard himself being introduced by the chairman as "Mr. Carl Schurz, of

Watertown, who has fought for human liberty in his native country and who has come to us to do the same in his adopted home." Before he realized it, he was on his feet, stammering at first but then regaining his confidence and appealing to his hearers to remember their duty, as American citizens, to check the spread of slavery. This was Schurz's first political speech on American soil.

A recruit like Schurz was a godsend to the Republicans in Wisconsin. Invitations poured in, and he was soon busy addressing German gatherings in his native tongue—for he did not yet dare to make a public address in English. His speeches were not widely reported, even in the German newspapers, but he became well known, and stories of his adventures at the siege of Rastatt and of his liberation of Kinkel were spreading throughout the State.[1] For the vote in Wisconsin, which gave Frémont a substantial majority over Buchanan, Schurz was unquestionably largely responsible. His experience in this kind of rough-and-tumble electioneering was useful to him, for he had occasionally to meet and overcome an opposition which manifested itself in "heckling" and even in the throwing of missiles.

The Democratic victory in the national campaign, although not unexpected, was a disappointment to Carl Schurz. On December 1, 1856, he wrote to Kinkel, "At last the slavery issue has become the watchword of the day; the time for compromise has passed, and the last chance for a peaceful solution has come." In this same letter he expressed the opinion that a civil war over slavery was altogether probable. Two months later he wrote Althaus, explaining certain factors in the situation which the latter had not understood, and prophesying eventual victory for the Republicans. "Never has a beaten army gained so many advantages after a lost battle," he boasted. Nevertheless he confessed that the Republican defeat was a "stunning

[1] With characteristic self-assurance, Schurz wrote, November 20, 1856, to his brother-in-law, Henry Meyer, "As for myself, my brief activity brought me such widespread influence that I shall probably not keep out of official life very long." *Intimate Letters,* 174.

blow," from the bewilderment of which it took him some weeks to recover.

In March, 1857, on a business trip to New York, he attended a concert by Thalberg, where he "heard for the first time what real piano playing is." When the landlord at the Prescott House learned that his guest was the rescuer of Kinkel, he produced a bottle of champagne at breakfast and insisted on drinking to his health. "My fame is now almost seven years old," Carl wrote to his wife, "and in the seventh year it still brings me a bottle of champagne!"

In the following August, after a brief career as editor of the Watertown *Anzeiger*, Schurz started a newspaper of his own—the Watertown *Deutsch Volks-Zeitung*—which, although declaring itself to be "independent but not neutral," came out in uncompromising opposition to slavery and could not, therefore, be considered as anything but Republican. As a matter of fact, it was subsidized from its inception by Republican funds, and it maintained a precarious existence in a community which was consistently Democratic. The newspaper, however, did increase Schurz's prestige in the Republican Party, the leaders of which recognized that his influence was not to be ignored. It was these considerations mainly, together with an appreciation of his oratorical gifts, which led the Republican leaders of the state to turn to him as a candidate for office.

Sent as a delegate to the Republican State Convention, on September 3, at Madison, he was offered a place on the ticket as state treasurer, but declined to accept any position lower than that of lieutenant governor,—amazing audacity from a young German who had hitherto held no office higher than that of alderman. He had his will, however, and was nominated for lieutenant governor on the first formal ballot, securing 145 votes against 22 for D. D. Cameron. When the proceedings opened, Schurz was merely a name to most of the delegates. But, after stepping to the platform to accept the nomination, he delivered a speech which convinced the audience that "the ablest man in the hall was Carl Schurz." The

Courtesy of the Estate of Carl Schurz

NEW YORK CITY IN 1854

Milwaukee *Sentinel* reported that, as Schurz concluded his "eloquent remarks," the convention stood up spontaneously and gave him "three thundering cheers." There was a definite feeling that a captain had appeared.

The ensuing campaign, although no worse in Wisconsin than in other closely contested sections, was very bitter. The Republicans circulated romantic versions of Schurz's exploits as a revolutionist in Germany; and the Democrats, in retaliation, accused him of being a rebel and a traitor, and of having misappropriated funds entrusted to his charge. His enemies spelled his name "Shirts" and ridiculed his physical peculiarities. Meanwhile he spoke frequently, on an average of five times a week, often in German but sometimes in English. His most notable address was delivered on Friday, October 16, in the Court House at Madison. This he had carefully prepared, and it was printed in two installments in the *State Journal* of October 19 and 20. Schurz wrote Kinkel,[1] "Upon this speech is based the greater part of my reputation in this country. So with becoming modesty I herewith lay it at the feet of my master and instructor in the art." Horace Rublee, editor of the *State Journal*, described Schurz as "an easy, fluent speaker, without any of the rant and bluster of the stump orator." The speech itself was clear and direct in style, without a trace of foreign idiom, and went straight to the mark. Dealing almost exclusively with the question of slavery, it was especially bitter toward Stephen A. Douglas and his doctrine of "squatter sovereignty." He ended with a spirited glorification of Liberty, in a passage which he deprecated as "a somewhat florid piece of oratory," but of which he was really very proud. The obvious sincerity of his words, coming as they did from a man who had spent his boyhood under a despotic government, was very moving.

But Schurz, then, as later, had something positive about him which either attracted or repelled very strongly, and made him enemies as well as friends. The remainder of the Republican

[1] Schurz to Kinkel, February 23, 1858, *Intimate Letters*, 185.

ticket, including Alexander W. Randall, the gubernatorial candidate, was successful by a small margin, but Schurz was defeated by forty-eight votes. He wrote his brother-in-law, Heinrich Meyer, that he was the victim of an obvious "election fraud," but this explanation is not convincing. The truth is that his enemies in his own party had scratched their ballots in favor of his opponent. The Republicans voiced their regret at this misfortune, and even the editor of the Watertown *Democrat* confessed, when the campaign was over, that Schurz had been its "ablest and most eloquent speaker, either in German or in English." He wisely declined the clerkship of the State Senate and returned home to repair his finances and meditate. Although he was much chagrined and called 1857 "an abominable year," he had actually profited much by his experience. The significant fact was that, although he had not attained his ambition, he had become known throughout his own state. His Americanization had proceeded very rapidly. He now began to spell his name "Carl" instead of "Karl," and he had definitely become a citizen of Wisconsin. Soon, immersed in political controversy, he was to lose all his desire to return to his Fatherland and was to throw in his lot with the United States of America.

CHAPTER VI ORATORY

LIKE Daniel Webster, whom in other respects he did not at all resemble, Carl Schurz was essentially an orator, a master of the spoken word, and the influence which he exerted was due largely to what he said and the way he said it. Like all good public speakers, he was something of an actor, but he never relied on mere trickery, and he paid his listeners the compliment of assuming that they were, like himself, interested in getting at the truth. A man who heard him often has said that the secret of Schurz's eloquence was its "terrible sincerity." Not until late in life did he become a good extemporaneous speaker. In his earlier years, he took the utmost pains with each address, even writing out his lectures and memorizing them word for word. Much of this carefulness was due to the fear that he might otherwise make blunders in grammar or in idiom; but he was also exceedingly conscientious, and wished to be quoted accurately or not at all. He was a delight to reporters, for, when they asked for copy, he always had his manuscript ready for the printer. He mastered spoken English very thoroughly, and, by 1860, traces of his German accent were barely perceptible.

It was through his oratory that Carl Schurz became nationally known. During the months following the Wisconsin campaign of 1857 his reputation spread rapidly, until, on April 18, 1859, he, a recent German immigrant, was to speak in Faneuil Hall, in historic Boston, on "True Americanism." He was then only a little over thirty. No man of alien birth has ever risen more quickly to prominence in the United States. That he did so was due, of course, to an unusual combination of circumstances, but even more to his genius, which needed only a fertile soil and a sympathetic atmosphere to flourish and expand.

After his successful campaign speeches in the autumn of

1857, Schurz, confronted with a "dreadful scarcity of money," prepared a lecture on "Democracy and Despotism in France," based on the manuscript over which he had labored during his first months in the United States. What was to be a long and conspicuous career on the lyceum platform opened in January, 1858, with a lecture before his neighbors in Watertown, followed by others at Janesville, Madison, Racine, and Milwaukee. Soon, making use of his knowledge of European history, he composed other talks on such topics as "Germany," "Germany and France," and "American Civilization."

Those were the golden days of the lyceum, when even the most famous of American orators, including Edward Everett and Wendell Phillips and Charles Sumner, were for weeks "on the road," subjecting themselves to the hardships of "one-night stands" and promiscuous hospitality and hot rides on dirty trains, but gaining in reputation and bank account. The forms of diversion then available in small towns were less enticing and diversified than they are today. With no radio or motion pictures to keep them in touch with the outside world, people were glad, after a hard day's work, to drive several miles in order to receive instruction from the lips of some famous lecturer. Carl Schurz, scholarly, lucid, and dignified, made an excellent impression on an audience. Although he did not always try to thrill them, he did leave them with the feeling that they had received their money's worth in education.

When, after an introduction by some effusive local chairman, Schurz stepped forward and began, "Ladies and Gentlemen," the audience saw an awkward looking figure, somewhat over six feet tall, excessively thin of body and rather loose-jointed, wearing clothes which fitted him badly and bore obvious signs of wear. Bespectacled and serious of countenance, he looked like an unworldly college professor whose cherished aim was the improvement of his fellow men and women. He was entirely happy when, during the summer of 1858, he was fulfilling a series of engagements at middle western colleges, talking on historical subjects, at a fee of never more than fifty dollars and frequently less. In July he spoke before the Archæan Society, at Beloit College, on "True Americanism," a theme which he also chose for an address two weeks later before the Literary Society of the University of Wisconsin. Both lectures were commented upon favorably, although one critic complained that Schurz's delivery was "not sufficiently forceful"—a strange comment in view of the impassioned fervor of his stump speeches. In August, Schurz was appointed by Governor Randall as a member of the Board of Regents of the University of Wisconsin, in which position—which was greatly to his liking—he was active on committees and exerted no small influence. With characteristic devotion to his friends, he at once offered Althaus an appointment as Professor of Modern Languages and even discussed a similar proposal with Kinkel. When these two declined, he secured the place for Dr. J. P. Fuchs.

Always in Schurz's heart there was a struggle between two ambitions—scholarship and statecraft, literature and politics. In one sense, his life was a compromise between them; but, when a choice had to be made, he always turned to practical affairs. In the autumn of 1858, the senatorial campaign between Abraham Lincoln, Republican, and Stephen Arnold Douglas, Democrat, was reaching a climax in Illinois, and attracting the notice of a public far beyond the borders of that State. Schurz, who had for Douglas a dislike which was emotional rather than reasonable, gladly accepted an invitation to become a Lincoln crusader among the Germans of Illinois. "I found myself," he wrote later, "for the first time on a conspicuous field of political action." On September 28, in Mechanics' Hall, Chicago, he addressed a huge mass meeting in a speech of which later a million copies were printed and distributed. He entitled it "The Irrepressible Conflict," thus putting into circulation, apparently for the first time, a phrase which William H. Seward used with such decisive effect at Rochester, New York, about a month later. The Chicago gathering had been called primarily for the purpose of ratifying the

Republican nominations. Schurz, however, with broader vision, devoted himself, with the utmost eloquence of which he was capable, to arguing the broad proposition that Negro slavery should be treated as a purely sectional or local institution, under the protection of State laws, and concluded with the expression of the hope that slavery might gradually be eliminated in the South by Southerners themselves. This speech, vigorous, pungent, aggressive, made a sensation which extended as far east as New York, where the *Tribune* said of Schurz, "He speaks with an eloquence, force, and intelligence which prove him an invaluable acquisition to his adopted country." The Republican party was indeed glad to welcome a leader who could do so much to win the German vote. After his Chicago speech, Schurz was no longer a provincial politician. He had emerged into national prominence.

For several days Schurz remained in Illinois, addressing audiences in both English and German at several places in the interior of the state. The most significant occasion was at Quincy, on October 13, where he was scheduled to speak on the evening of the day when the next to the last of the Lincoln-Douglas debates was to be held. Schurz, accompanied by a member of the Republican State Committee, was on a train bound for Quincy when, at a way station, a tall man, wearing a battered "stove-pipe hat" and carrying on his left arm a gray woolen shawl, looking uncouth and even grotesque with his faded cotton umbrella and black satchel, entered the car and was hailed effusively by the crowd. It was "Abe" Lincoln, whom Schurz now saw for the first time. After the necessary introductions were effected, Lincoln greeted Schurz with an "off-hand cordiality," well aware of what this scholarly German had been doing for his cause. Lincoln talked "in so simple and familiar a strain" that Schurz felt as if he had known him all his life. The two sat down side by side, Schurz observing Lincoln very carefully, a trifle perplexed by the latter's personality. It was the beginning of a relationship which was to mean much in Schurz's education and progress.

On the following afternoon Schurz was, of course, present at the Quincy debate, with a seat on the pine-board platform, and left, in his *Reminiscences,* quite the most vivid account of the proceedings.[1] He wrote of Douglas: "As I looked at him, I detested him deeply; but my detestation was not free from an anxious dread as to what was to come." He noted, however, that when Lincoln made a reply full of rapid thrusts and humorous retorts, "the scowl on Douglas's face grew darker and darker." After the debate, Schurz said good-by to Lincoln, and they were not to meet again until the latter's nomination for the presidency at Chicago, in May, 1860. The Illinois elections, held on November 2, 1858, gave the State officials to the Republicans but left the Democrats with a majority in both branches of the Legislature, the result being that Douglas was elected senator on January 6, 1859, by a vote of 54 to 41. Certain features of this Illinois experience made a profound impression upon Schurz: the evils of a narrow party loyalty; the effectiveness of Lincoln's unornamented but shrewd method of reasoning; and, above all, the democratic nature of the appeal made by the two great protagonists to the intelligence and patriotism of the people. The German immigrant could find inspiration and encouragement in the example of Abraham Lincoln.

Schurz now returned to Wisconsin and its tumultuous politics. At the State Republican Convention, on October 5, he had served again on the Committee on Resolutions, as chairman; and he furthered the candidacy of "Bowie-Knife" Potter for Congress in the First Wisconsin District. After Potter's election, Schurz delivered, on November 18, a notable address at Milwaukee called "Political Morals," in which he laid down certain principles of political independence which he was to follow all his life. It was a highly idealistic statement, assailing political corruption and insisting that a party could claim the

[1] Beveridge has said that Schurz's description "of the picturesque features of an American campaign meeting at that day" is "the best account of its kind." *Lincoln,* II, 686–87. It should be read in Schurz's *Reminiscences,* II, 89, ff.

support of the people only when its conduct was blameless. In his *Reminiscences*, Schurz declared "that the despotism of party organization constitutes one of the greatest and most insidious dangers threatening the vitality of free institutions of government." In this Milwaukee speech he announced himself to be an Independent, and he remained an Independent until his death.

Some influential Chicago business men, impressed by the brilliance of his address in that city, now urged him to open an office there and were prepared to guarantee him an adequate income. He preferred, however, to remain in Wisconsin. His application for admission to the bar was granted by the Circuit Court of Jefferson County, without any formalities except a nod from the judge, the signing of a document, and a drink at a tavern near by. Schurz at once arranged a partnership with Halbert E. Paine, beginning January 1, 1859, in Milwaukee; but he had hardly bought a desk chair before he was called away to other more congenial pursuits. By 1861, both Schurz and Paine had other affairs to settle, and the firm was never reconstituted.

During the winter of 1859–60, Attorney Schurz was busy, not with clients, but with advocating the election to the Supreme Court of Wisconsin of his friend, the fascinating Byron Paine, who had won fame by volunteering his services as counsel for the abolitionist, Sherman Booth, when the latter was arrested for assisting the fugitive slave, Joshua Glover, to escape in 1854. The critics of the Fugitive Slave Law desired Paine's election, and the campaign, fought out mainly on that issue, was actually a test of the relative strength of the slavery and anti-slavery causes. Schurz's chief contribution was his speech, March 23, 1859, under the title "State Rights and Byron Paine," in which he justified those who had defied the federal courts and had nullified the federal edicts. Paine was elected by a majority of more than ten thousand and took his seat on the bench. Within two years, however, both he and Schurz were obliged to alter their opinions. General Carl

Schurz, engaged in maintaining the authority of the federal government, could not have been proud of his speech on "State Rights and Byron Paine."

It was 1859 which saw Schurz's first appearance in conservative Boston. The large influx of Irish immigrants during the fifties had aroused in Massachusetts a strong "Native American" sentiment, resulting in the temporary triumph of the Know-nothing Party, which was pledged to exclude men of alien birth from any share in our government. For three years, from 1854 to 1857, the Governor was Henry J. Gardner, a staunch Know-nothing, but he was beaten for a fourth term, and it seemed as if the movement had spent its force. In 1859, however, the General Court of Massachusetts adopted for submission to the people an amendment to the State constitution providing that foreign born men should not be allowed to vote until two years after they had become citizens of the United States. This bigoted measure, directed principally against Irish Catholics, was opposed by the Democrats, led by Caleb Cushing, and also by a small group of liberal Republicans, including Henry Wilson. Many of the Massachusetts abolitionists, however, favored the amendment. It was Wilson and E. L. Pierce, afterward Charles Sumner's diffuse biographer, who conceived the shrewd plan of bringing Schurz to Boston as the spokesman of the anti-slavery Germans of the Northwest. Schurz, after learning that his expenses would be paid and that his presence would "do a great deal of good," seized what was really an important opportunity.

Schurz was first introduced to a Boston audience at what was called a "Republican Celebration of the Birthday of Jefferson" held on Wednesday, April 13, at the Parker House, with Governor George S. Boutwell as toastmaster. The guests, including Anson Burlingame, John P. Hale, Henry Wilson, and John A. Andrew, found the Parker House food and beverages excellent and sat eating and drinking from three o'clock until five-thirty. Schurz, the fifth on the list of fifteen speakers, was greeted by "Three cheers for our German Republican friends of the Northwest." His remarks were devoted largely to praise of the Jeffersonian principles of freedom, equality, and self-government. It was a cautious speech which did him no harm.

On April 18, in Faneuil Hall, was held what the Boston *Courier* called "a Republican Demonstration against Know-nothingism." Before an audience of more than two thousand men and women, not quite filling the auditorium, Schurz delivered a revised version of his previous lecture on "True Americanism." The local newspapers differed in their opinions as to his success. The *Transcript* declared that he "was received with enthusiasm and made an eloquent address." The *Post* said, "The hall was not full and the speaking was not of a high order." The *Courier*, even more critical, announced: "There was something of a stampede after Mr. Schurz began, those whom curiosity attracted thither not being sufficiently magnetized by the eloquence of the speaker to remain after his opening sentences had been uttered. He read his speech from manuscript, and during the merely speculative portions of his remarks excited little enthusiasm; toward the close, however, he spoke with more warmth upon the tangible politics of the country and excited from the reduced but attentive audience frequent and cordial applause." Garrison, in his *Liberator*, asserted that Schurz's speech was "with one or two exceptions, the most eloquent address that has ever been made in Faneuil Hall for fifty years."

Schurz himself was complacently satisfied. "I spoke like a god," he wrote his wife in an expansive mood, "and today I cannot get away from the praises of my speech." On April 20, he talked in Worcester, where he warned the Republican Party that any proscriptive legislation against foreigners would alienate the Germans of the Northwest. As he was leaving, he sent a note to his wife, saying; "My success in Massachusetts was decidedly brilliant." This sounds grossly conceited, and, indeed, Schurz never had a low estimate of himself or his abilities. But he had made an impression in New England. When he arrived in Boston, the newspapers discussed how his name should be spelled and pronounced. The Worcester *Spy* declared dogmatically that it should be pronounced "Shurts"; the Boston *Daily Advertiser* came out for "Schoorts." The *Courier* settled the problem by stating, "The proper way to pronounce the name of this ardent young Republican is Schurz." While this dispute was going on, the man himself was becoming better known.

Although he regarded himself, after this last experience, as "the best abused man in America," he realized that the trip had well rewarded him. He had met most of the distinguished writers and statesmen of New England, including Longfellow, Holmes, Sumner, and others. He had dined with the Gardner Brewers, at what he described as "one of the patrician houses of the town." He found Boston and Bostonians "exceedingly congenial" and was delighted to be thrown into a society which was not only intelligent but cultured. Of a few of his new friends, especially Longfellow, John A. Andrew, and Frank W. Bird, he left charming characterizations in his *Reminiscences.* He had established with the East connections which were to be of much assistance to him in later years; and to the Republicans of the Atlantic States he was from that moment on the spokesman of the Germans of the Northwest.

Despite conventional protestations to the contrary, Schurz wished to receive the Republican nomination for governor in the summer of 1859. Although he did not openly appeal for support, it is easy to read between the lines of his letters and discern his hopes. What he really wanted was to have the Republican Party rise up as a single man to draft him as a candidate; but this, it seems, that party did not care to do. Governor Randall coveted a renomination; and, at the convention held in late August, his desire was gratified. This result was inevitable, for Schurz, through his blunt expression of his views, had made powerful enemies, and even his friends had been only lukewarm in his behalf, fearing that, if he were sidetracked into State affairs, his career might be ruined. Unanimously nominated for lieutenant governor, Schurz rather petulantly declined. When he returned to Milwaukee, his admirers greeted him with a tumultuous ovation, at which he complained because some people had supposed him to belong to "that class of politicians who will take *anything* in order to have something."

During the autumn Schurz showed his loyalty by being very active in the Wisconsin campaign, even participating in two debates with Hobart, the Democratic candidate for governor. He was also persuaded to carry through a speaking itinerary in Minnesota in behalf of his friend, Alexander Ramsey, the Republican gubernatorial nominee. There he traveled six hundred miles, often under the most primitive conditions, and delivered thirty-one speeches, undergoing some extraordinary adventures which he later described vividly in his *Reminiscences*, basing the narrative on some letters sent at the time to Mrs. Schurz. The Republicans won in both Minnesota and Wisconsin, and Schurz was assigned much of the credit for the victories. He now had a few weeks in which to recoup his finances by lecturing.

Of all the vicious attacks made upon him, none irritated Schurz more than the charge that he was paid for his political speeches. In his *Reminiscences*, he presented the facts. He was obliged, he admitted, to accept compensation for his traveling expenses, but he invariably returned from such expeditions considerably out of pocket as well as so much exhausted physically that he was badly in need of a rest. He did, however, receive payment for his lyceum lectures, but for which and the income derived from them he would have been obliged to withdraw from public affairs. His real estate ventures had left him burdened with debt; his wife's property was very much reduced in amount; he had no gainful occupation except lecturing. It is not strange that he was often troubled by lack of cash.

New England had been so much pleased with Schurz's platform appearances that he returned in January, 1860, to Boston, and, making his headquarters there, gave a series of lectures at such provincial centers as Concord, Springfield, Nashua, Hartford, New Haven, and Albany. His tour opened, however, with a political address in Springfield, under the auspices of Samuel Bowles, of the Springfield *Republican*, on the subject of "Douglas and Popular Sovereignty"—a great success, reprinted not only by the Eastern newspapers but also in pamphlet form by the anti-Douglas Democrats. It was in substance a scathing denunciation of the "Little Giant" as a demagogue and an unscrupulous politician, who had endeavored "to reduce the people to that disgusting state of moral indifference which he himself is not ashamed to boast of." It was this address which Lincoln declared made him jealous.

The presidential campaign of 1860 was now under way, and Schurz, although a citizen for less than five years, was to have a noteworthy, even a decisive share in it. When the Wisconsin Republican Convention met on February 29, in Madison, Schurz was promptly elected delegate-at-large to the National Convention and was made chairman of the Wisconsin delegation—a position of much influence. On March 2, when he returned to Milwaukee, he wrote to his wife: "This is my birthday. Thirty-one years old! I have grown rapidly without growing old. I am still young in strength, ambition, and affection. The serious side of life has, indeed, taken a firmer hold of me, but I am as hale as I was ten years ago."

For the next few weeks, Schurz was occupied with little except politics. He still fulfilled lecture engagements whenever he could secure them, but, wherever he went, he kept his finger on the pulse of the voters. Although his mind was not altogether fixed, he preferred Seward. In mid-March, while on a visit to Columbus, Ohio, he spent a morning with Governor Chase, who said to him in the course of the conversation; "What do you think of my candidacy for the presidency?" Schurz, who referred to the incident delightfully in his *Reminiscences*, replied frankly; "If the Republican Convention at Chicago have courage enough to nominate an advanced anti-slavery man, they will nominate Seward; if not, they will not nominate you." If Schurz had any suspicion then that Lincoln might ultimately be the choice, he concealed it from his associates. So far as his friends were aware, he was for Seward, without any reservation.

CHAPTER VII PRESIDENT MAKING

ALTHOUGH Abraham Lincoln had declared, as late as April, 1859, "I do not think myself fit for the presidency," he was at heart an ambitious politician, who shrewdly encouraged all movements in his favor. The Democratic Convention at Charleston had adjourned in despair on May 3, 1860, without naming standard bearers, and it was evident that the deadlock between the Douglas and anti-Douglas wings could not be broken. Thus, as the day drew near for the Republican Convention, sagacious party leaders saw that the chances for victory were excellent. It was obviously William H. Seward, of New York, against the field; and Schurz, after some vacillation, had announced himself as favoring that candidate. He did, however, write to Mrs. Schurz on March 9, 1860, that he should be very well satisfied with either Seward or Lincoln.

Lincoln's adherents, with everything to gain and nothing to lose, were bending their efforts to consolidating the opposition to the New York statesman, in the hope that Lincoln would loom up as the best available compromise candidate. In the late winter, Lincoln went east, where, on February 27, he made his famous speech in Cooper Union, later appearing before large and approving audiences in several New England cities. A week before the Chicago convention opened, the Illinois delegation had decided to support Lincoln, and Indiana was won over a few days later, together with scattering votes from various sections. Thus Lincoln was sure of a powerful nucleus on the floor, and his friends, as was shown later, were clever bargainers. They were aware, furthermore, of the advantages to be gained from the fact that the convention was to be held in Lincoln's own State, where noisy enthusiasm could be easily manufactured. Superficially it looked as if Seward would win without much difficulty, but there were undercurrents flowing strongly in another direction. The New York *Herald* spoke wisely when it said, on May 14, that the contest had narrowed down to Seward, Lincoln, and Wade.

The Republican Convention opened on Wednesday, May 16, in an extraordinarily ugly structure called the Wigwam, hastily flung together from rough pine boards by the Chicago Republican Club. Standing on the corner of Market and Lake Streets, in a central location, it had deep galleries across one side and the two ends and could hold more than ten thousand persons. The delegates, representing not only the older strategists but also "young blood," were full of animation, and the spectators did their share to maintain the excitement. Organized applause and cheering were planned for both Seward and Lincoln, and the streets were colorful with parades.

In the midst of this bedlam, young Carl Schurz, attending his first national convention, moved with the dignity befitting the leader of the delegation from an important state. He had come pledged to Seward, and joined with Evarts, of New York, and Blair, of Michigan, in managing his campaign on the floor. Just before the gathering was called to order, a special meeting of the "German" delegates was held; and, although Schurz had consistently opposed the formation of any German "bloc," he attended and exercised a salutary influence on the proceedings. The chief business was the adoption of resolutions repudiating the Massachusetts amendment depriving foreign-born citizens of the suffrage for two years.

In the hall itself, Schurz, regarded as the spokesman of a large body of German-American voters whose support was essential to the success of the Republican Party, was one of the most prominent figures. When George Ashmun, of Massachusetts, was elected permanent president, Schurz was designated, with Senator Preston King, to escort him to the platform; and Schurz and King, one very tall and thin, the other short and rotund, looked as if Don Quixote and Sancho Panza had met to carry out an agreeable duty. Schurz was appointed a member of the Committee on Resolutions, and actually drafted the fourteenth section of the platform, declaring against any action which might abridge or impair the rights of citizenship previously accorded to immigrants. This resolution he defended in an eloquent speech, protesting against its modification or deletion. Schurz also shared in the writing of the anti-slavery declaration, and, in one of the most dramatic moments of the convention, shouted, amid a storm of cheers, "We defy the whole slave power and the whole vassalage of hell."

Schurz's early enthusiasm for Seward was, as he confesses, chilled even before the convention met by the intrigues of New York politicians, who, directed by the astute and unscrupulous Thurlow Weed, were resorting to every device in order to manipulate affairs in the interests of their candidate. Schurz did not like the inexhaustible supply of champagne and cigars with which the Seward men regaled other delegations, nor did he care for Tom Hyer, the Bowery prize fighter, who headed a band of professional applauders, all of whom shouted whenever Seward's name was mentioned. Nevertheless Schurz seconded Evarts's nomination of Seward, and did his best in the latter's behalf. The Wisconsin delegation stood by Seward to the end, even when it was obvious that he was defeated.

The first ballot revealed astonishing strength for Lincoln, who had 102 votes against Seward's 173½. The New Yorker was, it is true, in the lead, but Schurz knew that his nomination was now improbable, if not impossible. The opposition to Seward from powerful quarters now began to find a voice, and the Lincoln followers were everywhere, insisting that their man was the most "available." On the second ballot, Pennsylvania cast her fifty-two votes for Lincoln, and the New York delegation were stupefied. The galleries, packed with Lincoln supporters, became more vociferous in their cheers. Amid a tension almost unendurable, the third ballot opened, showing a steady gain for Lincoln. Finally, at the critical moment, the Ohio chairman changed four votes from Chase to Lincoln—and the latter was nominated. When Evarts moved that the choice be made unanimous, Schurz was quickly on his feet to second the motion, which was carried in the midst of "a strange and tremendous demonstration," lasting without a pause for more than ten minutes. A cannon from the roof of the Wigwam roared out the news that the Middle West had triumphed, and that Abraham Lincoln, of Illinois, was the candidate of the Republican Party. When Stephen A. Douglas heard the news, he said to a group of Washington Republicans, "Gentlemen, you have nominated a very able and a very honest man."

Lincoln himself, restless and depressed, had remained at Springfield, occasionally joining the throng around the telegraph office. The committee appointed to give him formal notification of the action of the convention included several distinguished Americans—Ashmun, Bowles, and Boutwell, all of Massachusetts; Evarts, of New York; Kelley, of Pennsylvania; Carter, of Ohio; Blair, of Missouri; Welles, of Connecticut; Tuck, of New Hampshire; and Carl Schurz, of Wisconsin. When these men, many of whom had been disappointed in Lincoln's nomination, reached the latter's unattractive white two-story house on the outskirts of the city, they filed into the bare and gloomy parlor, with its marble-topped center table, on which lay the family Bible and a silver-plated pitcher for water—a room which was completely without charm or good taste. There Lincoln stood, a tall, ungainly figure, with drooping shoulders, with sunken cheeks and somber downcast eyes, looking at them with a melancholy expression. But, in response to Ashmun's notification, Lincoln stood up straighter, his eyes brightened, and he made a well-phrased reply. When the ceremony was over, Lincoln talked informally in a jovial manner, and the gathering became less funereal. One of the committee turned to Schurz and said, "Sir, we might have done a more daring thing, but we certainly could not have done a better thing." Schurz himself had reason to feel much gratified at Lincoln's nomination.

Almost at once, Schurz was selected as a member of the Republican National Executive Committee, his associates being

Morgan, Fogg, Goodrich, Welles, Duer, and Judd. The responsibility devolved upon him of "rounding up" the foreign elements in the party, including Dutch and Scandinavians as well as Germans. On May 22, he wrote Lincoln a long letter, reiterating his loyalty and outlining his plans. "If I am able," he wrote, "I shall do the work of a hundred men for Abraham Lincoln's election." So far as his speaking was acceptable, he was ready to "go to all the principal points and do the heavy work." Lincoln's reply, delayed until June 18, expressed his confidence in Schurz and his approval of the latter's program. "To the extent of our limited acquaintance," he wrote, "no man stands nearer my heart than yourself."

Schurz's part in the election of Lincoln was most important if not actually decisive. For the next few months, until November 6, he labored indefatigably and almost exclusively to enlist under the Republican standard the more than one million and a half German-Americans who in so many states held the balance of power at the polls. It was clear that if any considerable proportion of those who had begun as Democrats could be converted to Republicanism, Lincoln's success was assured. Feeling himself that there had never been a political movement "in which the purely moral motive was so strong," he was animated by the fervor of a crusader.[1] To him, the Republican campaign was "simply the revolt of the popular conscience against what was felt to be a great wrong"—as he expressed it in his *Reminiscences*—and his cause was that of "liberty, right, and justice."

On May 26, at a meeting called in Milwaukee for the ratification of the Republican nominee, Schurz made a formal report to his constituents, explaining the course of events which led to Seward's defeat, praising Lincoln highly as a man and a leader, and endorsing heartily the Republican platform. After

[1] Andrew D. White, then a young man of twenty-eight, was especially aroused by Schurz's speeches. "His arguments," wrote White, "seemed to me by far the best of that whole campaign—the broadest, the deepest, and the most convincing." White, *Autobiography,* I, 86.

paying a tribute to Seward, he answered those critics who had regarded Lincoln as a third-rate Illinois lawyer, nominated for the sake of expediency. "Let his detractors ask their own secret misgivings," he said, "and in their own fears they will read the cause of the joy and assurance of his friends." Rather more rhetorically than was his wont, he ended, "Let it be known that New York and Wisconsin, who stood together to the last for Seward in the convention, will be the first and foremost in the battle for Lincoln and Liberty!" This ratification speech, printed up as a pamphlet and extensively circulated, came at the right psychological moment, and had a most salutary effect on the Republican mood. "The people here are still quite enraptured over it," wrote Schurz, with characteristic complacency, on July 1, from New York.

Although Schurz conceived it to be his duty to arouse the popular conscience, he was not without his own personal ambitions. After attending a meeting of the National Executive Committee in early July in New York City, he wrote to his wife: "The question came up in committee as to what would follow upon the election of Lincoln. That I was to go upon a European mission was treated as if it were a matter of course." Three weeks later, while Schurz was lying on his bed in a hotel in Springfield, Lincoln himself, not unmindful of his aides, walked in, wearing "a linen sack-coat and a hat of doubtful age," and chatted for nearly two hours, while Schurz, at Lincoln's urgent request, continued to recline. Lincoln, as Schurz remembered the conversation, talked about the election "with as much placid, cheerful frankness as if he were discussing the potato crop." And then he touched on a significant topic. "Men like you," he said, "who have real merit and do the work, are always too proud to ask for anything. . . . You may depend upon it that I shall know how to distinguish deserving men from drones." "All right, old Abe, thought I," wrote Schurz to his wife. Later, when composing his *Reminiscences*, Schurz somewhat naïvely declared that it never occurred to him that his efforts as a speaker "should, or might, be rewarded by appointment to a federal office." He was no selfish spoilsman, but it may be taken for granted that he was aware of his value to the party and that he expected some recognition of his sacrifice.

Nobody in American politics up to that time had ever attempted to fill a speaking schedule as irksome and exhausting as that which Carl Schurz carried through in 1860. Webster, in 1840, had taken the stump for Harrison and had astonished his friends by his vitality and endurance; but his speeches were fewer, and he had several intervals for relaxation. Schurz was almost continuously on the move, with no opportunity for quiet. In early July, after the meeting in New York, he was in Hartford, and later in Philadelphia, where he stayed with his old friend, Dr. Tiedemann. On his return west, he spoke at Cleveland, and then entered upon a whirlwind tour of Illinois, where, in such centers as Quincy, Peoria, Pekin, Havana, Beardstown, Meredosia, Springfield, and Alton, he was received with the most demonstrative enthusiasm. He stood the incessant entertaining very well, although the constant blare of trumpeters and brass bands and the inevitable serenades which dragged him out of bed just when he was slipping off to sleep were sometimes unendurable. He was still young, of course, and he tried to live hygienically, even declining to make addresses not on his prearranged program. But an occasional remark in a letter to his wife indicated that he was often very tired. "I am terribly overrun with callers," he wrote from Beardstown. "Oh, my! I am working like a horse," he boasted at St. Louis.

Carl Schurz always throve on applause and praise. Success was to him a heady form of stimulant, which made him forget fatigue. At Springfield, on July 24, he took supper with Lincoln himself, finding Mrs. Lincoln "very nicely dressed up" and "quite skillful in handling her fan." Later "Old Abe," although he had not come out on any public occasion since his nomination, took off his coat, donned the familiar linen duster, and, making what Schurz thought to be a "grotesque appearance," walked arm and arm with him at the head of a procession of "Wide-awakes" to the square where the meeting was to be held. "The cheering was tremendous. My German speech was about the best I ever made," wrote Schurz. Then he turned to English, trying to do "specially well" for Lincoln, who sat in the front row of the audience. In a letter composed on the following day, Schurz said that Lincoln "applauded with tremendous enthusiasm," but in his *Reminiscences* he wrote, "He did not join in the applause which from time to time rewarded me, but occasionally he gave me a nod and a smile." The reader may take his choice. When the affair was over, Lincoln came up to the bilingual orator to say: "You are an awful fellow! I understand your power now." Incidents like these Schurz recounted to his wife with a pride and complacency almost startling. It must be remembered, however, that he did not expect that the letter would ever be published and that Mrs. Schurz, kept at home, was eager for news.

On July 31, Schurz made an address in German, in St. Louis, and on the following evening delivered, in Verandah Hall, the speech which he later entitled "The Doom of Slavery." In preparing for it, he wrote to Mrs. Schurz, "It is to be the greatest speech of my life"; and, in his *Reminiscences*, he styled it "the best of my anti-slavery speeches." Missouri was, of course, a slave State, the first one in which Schurz had ever spoken, and there were many pro-slavery men in his audience. With tactful moderation but without fear, he attacked slavery as wrong economically, maintaining that it was incompatible with our whole theory of government. Passing over the moral issue involved, he spent his time on practical problems. "Your system," he said audaciously to the slave-owners in front of him, "is founded upon forced labor, ours upon free labor." He left them to make the obvious deduction. He pointed out that the dissolution of the Union would defeat the object at which it aimed, and that the South, even in case of separation, would still, because of the evil influence of slavery, be dependent upon the North. If the Republicans of Missouri wished to play sound politics and rehabilitate industry, they must turn to emancipation. That was the remedy for many social and business evils.

While Schurz, during most of August, was traveling about Indiana, speaking almost every day, he was preparing a speech which would, he hoped, annihilate Stephen A. Douglas. Douglas was to talk in New York on September 12, at "a barbecue at Jones's Wood"; and the Republican managers arranged to have Schurz appear as an antidote in Cooper Union on September 13. On hot summer mornings, Schurz would seek some secluded spot and assemble the ammunition with which he proposed to exterminate the most dangerous of the Democratic candidates. As early as August 16, he wrote from Terre Haute: "My Douglas speech is coming along; if I had two free days it would be finished. It is going to be a fine specimen, in which people are going to take pride."

On the morning of September 13, Schurz, usually calm, was very nervous. Restlessly he dictated his speech to a *Tribune* stenographer, and, during the afternoon, walked up and down his room repeating passages from it. After dining at the Astor House with Governor Morgan and other notables, he rode to Cooper Union. As they drove along, Morgan asked, "How long are you going to speak?" "About two hours and a half," was the reply. "Good Heavens!" cried the Governor in dismay, "No New York audience will stand a speech as long as that!" Schurz then explained that his argument was one which must be presented in its entirety or not at all, and begged that, under the circumstances, he might be excused from appearing. The Governor finally submitted with reluctance, and Schurz proceeded with what he himself thought to be the "greatest success" of his career. The spacious hall was packed to its capacity, and the audience greeted Schurz with "endless cheering." Although he did not stop for three hours, he held everybody's attention, and, as he wrote, was "so frequently interrupted by applause that the hand-clapping consumed nearly as much time as the speaking."

Schurz's speech, first printed under the title "Douglasism Exposed and Republicanism Vindicated," but later called, less clumsily, "The Bill of Indictment," filled ten full columns of the *Tribune*, and was, in substance, a devastating attack on Douglas and his political career. While professing reluctance to assailing any particular person, Schurz soon launched into an analysis of Douglas as an alleged champion of freedom, as a great American statesman, and as a presidential candidate. He indulged freely, perhaps objectionably, in sarcasm and invective, drawing tremendous applause as he arraigned Douglas for his inconsistencies and mistakes. His logic, said the *Tribune*, stripped Douglas of his plumage "with merciless coolness." The occasion was a great opportunity for Schurz, and he made the most of it. "An immense number of pamphlet copies of this speech were circulated," he wrote in his *Reminiscences*, "and I was told that it cost Douglas many votes."

By this point in the campaign, it was becoming apparent that a Republican victory was almost certain, but Schurz did not relax his efforts. He followed his New York triumph with a series of speeches in Pennsylvania and then several through Indiana, which was regarded as a crucial State. His self-assurance had now developed into conceit, and some of his letters had a tone of braggadocio. Writing from Philadelphia, on September 24, he announced: "I have scored triumph after triumph and achieved almost superhuman results. . . . I am standing in the very thick of the fight. The blows I delivered in several places were glorious. It seems as if victory could not fail us and, by Jove, I have done my share towards it." This was doubtless true, but a mood of humility would have been more becoming—and humility and meekness were virtues which Carl Schurz never acquired.

As the contest drew to a close, even Schurz's superb vitality succumbed to weariness, but a few hours of sleep usually brought him out again "as bright as a lark." We find him planning his schedule for ten days in Wisconsin, from October 24 to November 1, and asking the modest sum of fifteen dollars a day for his expenses. On November 3, he wrote: "Two more working days and the contest will be over. . . . The trumpet sounds; again to the field of battle." Finally, on November 7, he could say to his wife: "The election is over, the battle is fought, the victory is won. . . . The victory belongs to you also, and I have not been able to separate my enjoyment of it from the thought of you." He had staked all his hopes on the campaign, and success meant to him "love, peace, family, fortune."

It is futile to speculate as to how far Schurz was responsible for the defeat of the Democrats in 1860. Writing to Petrasch in 1863, he said, "I am told that I made Lincoln President. That is, of course, not true; but that people say so indicates that I contributed something toward raising the breeze that carried Lincoln into the presidential chair, and thereby shook slavery in its foundations." Lincoln himself was reported as having said that Schurz was the foremost among the Republican orators of the nation, and it cannot be denied that he had become the most influential German-American in the United States. This he had done by the sheer force of his ideas, his voice, and his personality. To gain a hearing, he had endured the discomforts of irregular hours, heat, crowds, poor food, and all the annoyances of almost continuous travel; he had accepted nearly every demand upon his time and strength; and he cannot be blamed for claiming some of the glory. If any palms were to be distributed, no one had a better right to them than he.

At a great celebration in Milwaukee on November 18, Schurz, with his customary sanity, pointed out that Lincoln's victory did not mean that there would be an attack upon the South, but merely that Negro servitude, as a social institution, would not be allowed to spread. Whether or not Schurz was then in Lincoln's confidence is difficult to say, but the Wisconsin orator did, in this speech, anticipate rather remarkably the doctrines enunciated by Lincoln in his First Inaugural.

With a young man's resiliency, Schurz rested a few days

and then, rejuvenated, started out on a lecture tour in order to earn some money. During the campaign, while neglecting his private business, he had traveled over 21,000 miles, receiving only a trifle over $1800 for his expenses. His railroad fare alone had amounted to $800; and the sum paid over to him was barely sufficient to keep his family alive during those five feverish months. He did not complain, but, when he was accused of serving the Republican Party for financial gain, even his patience was sorely tried.

Schurz prepared several new lectures which he thought might prove appealing to a public with whom Bayard Taylor and Wendell Phillips and Edward Everett had been popular. On December 4, he was in Moravia, New York, in the midst of a blinding snowstorm. On the following evening, at Auburn, to which he had journeyed in a sled, he delivered for the first time a lecture, completed that very afternoon, on "American Civilization." When he learned that a radical meeting had been broken up in Boston by "a band of Democrats and Bell-Everetts," he wrote another lecture, called it "Freedom of Speech," and had it ready just five minutes before he entered Tremont Temple on December 12. Of this address, the *Transcript* said it had seldom been surpassed "for logical power and keen analysis," and that it would sustain "the author's intellectual reputation." Although he had to compete on that evening with the rival attraction of *Romeo and Juliet,* with Charlotte Cushman as Romeo, the hall was filled with more than three thousand people. On the preceding evening, Caleb Cushing, speaking in Newburyport, had said, "Gentlemen, revolution is upon us, and we are on the high road to anarchy and civil war." Within a few days, while Schurz was still in Boston, South Carolina had passed an ordinance dissolving the bond between her and the other States of the Union.

Schurz, engrossed with lecture engagements, could not even spend Christmas with his wife and children. "I work continuously, pausing only to sleep and eat," he wrote. Between December 15 and January 15, he spoke over twenty times in the vicinity of Boston, receiving on the average twenty-five dollars a night; and he followed this with two weeks in New York, a week or two in Ohio, a week in Michigan, and a few days in Illinois. His heart was not really in this routine lecturing, but he met his appointments faithfully. His body moved from town to town, but his imagination was in Washington, where events were happening. "Action, action is the great secret of success," he wrote, "and if ever a time called for it, it is now." He was disappointed when, in February, after he had been assured that he was to be sent as a delegate to the peace conference called by the state of Virginia, in Washington, Governor Randall, who did not like him, quietly blocked his plans.

Schurz was a young man of restless temperament and overmastering ambition, who did not intend to remain in obscurity. To his friend, Congressman John F. Potter, he said, "I shall, of course, not ask or petition for anything," adding, "I will not embarrass Mr. Lincoln by any demands, nor by declining any offer, unacceptable to myself, which he perhaps might feel inclined to make." [1] But he also let Potter know that he did not propose to take "an inferior place." He particularly desired a foreign mission, and, after frankly discussing the various possibilities, eliminating those which for one reason or another seemed undesirable, he settled on Italy (Sardinia), and confessed, "I should, therefore, be very much gratified if the administration, supposing they intend to offer me anything, would offer me the mission to Turin." The matter was talked about freely in Washington circles, and it was rumored in many quarters that the position was to be his. Schurz, however, refused to make a request himself. "To ask for an office is, in my opinion," he declared, "to pay too high a price for it. . . . I must confess that my independence in political life is worth more to me than all the favors which a government can shower upon me."

There were, of course, other hungry mouths to satisfy, and, as is usual in such complicated situations, a balance had to be

[1] Letter to Potter, November 30, 1860, *Writings,* I, 165, ff.

made of claims and recommendations. On February 10, in Springfield, Schurz had a long and intimate talk with Lincoln, in the course of which the President-elect locked the door and read him the draft of his inaugural address. When Schurz warned Lincoln that he would probably ask a few offices for his friends, the latter replied, "You write to me and you may be sure that I shall attend to everything you may ask for; and as for your own case, which you have not spoken of to me, I shall never forget you."

Having completed a very exhausting lecture tour, full of what he described as "a continual succession of small accidents and disappointments," Schurz arrived on March 1 in Washington, where he found a great many friends and some grievously troubled minds. He was at once in the thick of political bickering. "People crowded around me so that I was scarcely able to move," he wrote. On inauguration day he had a front seat and was able later to write a remarkable description of the scene in which Senator Douglas held the tall silk hat of his great rival. Meanwhile he was seeing Lincoln almost daily. He was cheered by hearing from Senator James W. Grimes, of Iowa, that "Old Abe" had called Schurz "the greatest man in America" and was about to appoint him as Minister to Sardinia. On March 13, he confided to his wife, "Lincoln desires that I shall go to Sardinia, and has definitely promised me a mission of the first class." Not until later did Schurz learn that Seward had been working against him, believing that it would be a mistake to send a former revolutionist as an accredited ambassador to a monarchical court. Schurz confessed that Seward was probably right; but Lincoln, backed by Chase, Secretary of the Treasury, and Blair, the Postmaster-General, insisted that Schurz could be trusted to use discretion and that it was important for the administration not to ignore the German-Americans. Seward reluctantly yielded; and, on March 28, when Schurz called at the White House, he was admitted at once to the President, who held out a paper reading, "I nominate Carl Schurz of Wisconsin to be Minister Plenipotentiary

Courtesy of the Estate of Carl Schurz

WILLIAM HENRY SEWARD AND HIS DAUGHTER FANNY
From a photograph made about 1861

and Envoy Extraordinary to Spain." Very much elated, Schurz wrote home, "This outcome is better than the Turin mission would have been." His enemies were naturally disgusted, and the Milwaukee *News* complained, "Impudence has triumphed over all obstacles." It did not seem thus, however, to the nation at large. The appointment was confirmed without delay by the Senate, and comments from the press, both Democratic and Republican, were largely favorable. Whenever malignity or abuse appeared, Schurz could afford to ignore it.

On September 17, 1860, in his thirty-first year, Carl Schurz wrote to his wife, "I am now in the fullness of my power which, undiminished, unwasted, blossoms and brings forth fruit." He had indeed accomplished miracles. Coming to the United States hampered by ignorance of its language and unfamiliarity with its political system, he had, in eight years, grown to be a national figure, even a President-maker, so powerful through his influence with German-Americans that those who did not love him feared him. Unable in 1852 to speak a single English sentence, he was, in 1860, mentioned by serious critics as comparable with Everett and Wendell Phillips. Bliss Perry said of him, "Mr. Schurz spoke with a slight accent that seemed to add crispness and point to his sentences; he had a faultless precision of phrase, a merciless logic, and an instinctive command of idiomatic Saxon terms." And now, in 1861, he, an exile from his native land, was about to return to it as an ambassador from the United States of America to a great European monarchy. If he had become a trifle spoiled by adulation and success, we can hardly censure him. His achievement was enough to turn even a strong man's head.

ELATED over his appointment, Carl Schurz, after some business conferences in New York, returned to Wisconsin to plan for the future. Seward was anxious that there should be no delay. But while the Schurz family were packing their belongings, the news arrived of the bombardment of Fort Sumter, on April 12, followed by the President's call for 75,000 volunteers. Carl's ambitions changed over night. With his military prestige, why could he not recruit from the German immigrants who had served in cavalry regiments in the Fatherland a body of troopers who would be early effective in the field? With Schurz always a thought was quickly transmuted into an act. Putting into a handbag the pistols which he had carried while he was releasing Kinkel, he went back to the capital, where he poured his heart out to Lincoln. The President listened sympathetically, advised him not to give up the Spanish mission, but suggested that he need not hurry about going to Madrid. Seward then offered no objections, and Schurz returned to the White House with a definite plan for raising a regiment. Lincoln now sent him to Cameron, the Secretary of War, who, in turn, asked him to see General Winfield S. Scott. The latter, who had justly earned his nickname of "Old Fuss and Feathers," treated the proposal with pompous intolerance, and Schurz saw that his errand was to be futile.

During these exciting days, Schurz was often at the White House. In his *Diary* for April 26, John Hay, Lincoln's secretary, wrote: "Carl Schurz was here today. He spoke with wild enthusiasm of his desire to mingle in the war. He has great confidence in his capability of arousing the enthusiasm of the young. He contemplates the career of a great guerrilla chief with ardent longing." Three days later, Hay recorded: "He [Schurz] has obtained three months' leave of absence from his diplomatic duties and permission to raise a cavalry regiment. I doubt the propriety of the movement. He will make a wonderful land pirate—bold, quick, brilliant, and restless. He will be hard to control and difficult to direct. Still, we shall see. He is a wonderful man."[1] Armed with the necessary authority, Schurz now set out for New York to organize five squadrons of cavalry. He was doing well, and Lincoln contemplated commissioning him as brigadier general; but difficulties arose in the War Department. There was jealousy among other officers who did not wish a "political general" to outrank them, and Lincoln wrote on May 19, "I cannot make it move smoothly just yet." At that moment, Seward notified him that circumstances made it imperative to have a minister of full rank in Madrid. Behind the scenes, schemes were being formed affecting Carl Schurz and his destiny.

Once more in Washington, Schurz had a conversation with Seward, and then one with Lincoln, but did not learn then of the strained relations between the two. Schurz and his young brother-in-law, Henry Meyer, were invited to lunch at the White House, where the three men, Mrs. Lincoln being absent, sat together at the table, the President astonishing Meyer by his simplicity and friendliness. While the Marine Band played that evening on the south lawn, Schurz sat with Lincoln on the balcony. John Hay recorded in his *Diary:* "After the President had kissed some thousands of children, Carl went into the library and developed a new accomplishment. He played with great skill and feeling, sitting in the dusk twilight at the piano until the President came by and took him down to tea."

Before departing, Schurz was admonished by the President

[1] On this morning (April 29, 1861) Hay found Schurz and James W. Lane sitting together in Nicolay's room. "Jim was at the window, filling his soul with gall by steady telescopic contemplation of a Secession flag impudently flaunting over a roof in Alexandria. 'Let me tell you,' he said to the elegant Teuton, 'we have got to whip these scoundrels like hell, C. Schurz.' They did a good thing stoning our men at Baltimore and shooting away the flag at Sumter. It has set the North a-howling for blood, and they'll have it." Thayer, *John Hay,* I, 101.

to watch carefully public sentiment in Europe and to send statements, if necessary, direct to the White House. And so, his military activities having come to a sudden end, Schurz sailed in early June with his family on the *Persia* for Liverpool. He had an interview in London with Charles Francis Adams, our Minister at the Court of St. James's, who seemed very stiff and cold; and he met in Paris our Minister to France, William L. Dayton. Fearing the effect of the sultry Spanish climate on his wife and children, he sent them to Mrs. Schurz's relatives in Hamburg, while he himself hastened to Madrid, arriving there on July 12, 1861. On the following evening at ten o'clock, Carl Schurz was formally presented to the Queen, Donna Isabella—a portly lady, with "an unhandsome but good-natured looking face," whose amorous adventures were the gossip of European courts. Schurz had ordered in Paris a conventional court costume, consisting of a richly embroidered dress coat and trousers, a cocked hat, and a sword, but it had been delayed, and, to the horror of ceremonious Spain, he appeared in a black frock coat. The Prince Consort, Don Francisco de Assisi, was a harmless person, who addressed Schurz "in a cracked soprano voice, somewhat like the scream of a young hen." In fact, the whole affair impressed Schurz like "an act in an opera bouffe"—"a comical prelude to serious business"—and he could not regard it as important. It was a long step from the simple Watertown house to the palace of the Bourbons, from democracy to royalty, but it did not disturb Carl Schurz's complacency.

Fortunately, Schurz was guided through the tangle of diplomatic civilities by the Secretary of the Legation, Horatio I. Perry, one of those indispensable and talented officials who, in the nineteenth century, so often gave continuity to our consular and ambassadorial service abroad. Schurz was welcomed gracefully by his associates in the diplomatic corps, all of whom were older than he in years and in experience. Of these, the most interesting was Count Galen, the Prussian Minister, with whom Schurz spent many reminiscent hours. He confessed that the social functions entailed by his position were "agreeable, but not extraordinarily interesting." He found himself surrounded by "small diplomats," with an eye and ear for scandal, each trying to magnify his routine business into a matter of international significance. There were occasional farcical situations, such as, for example, the few days of penance which the obese but enamored queen, turning from one lover to another, passed at the huge Escorial, the enormous gray and gloomy palace near Madrid, ostensibly visiting the tombs of her ancestors but really plotting to discard her ruling favorite.

Schurz was fortunate in securing a suite of rooms in La Quinta, the Perry country house on the outskirts of Madrid, where, in a typical Spanish residence, standing in a garden of fourteen acres, he found himself fairly comfortable. Out of his salary of $12,000, he had to pay only one thousand dollars for rent; but he soon discovered that prices in Spain were about three times what they were in New York. He was hardly in a mood to be happy anywhere in Europe, for he had a bad attack of nostalgia. "I cannot deny," he wrote his parents on August 19, "that I wish myself back home again."

Schurz found in Spain a desert land and an uncultivated people at least a hundred years behind the rest of the Western Hemisphere in civilization. Superstition, in its grossest forms, existed even in the higher circles; and the lower classes were steeped in the "crassest, blackest ignorance." The political corruption was such as Schurz had never imagined, and even the higher officials were habituated to stealing. Madrid, with all its supposed splendor, did not to him exceed in magnificence a German princely capital of the second or third rank. "Splendid titles are here as abundant as blackberries," he wrote, "but usually there is little to them." Carl Schurz was not happy, nor did the news from the United States make him less dejected.

The disaster of Bull Run (July 21, 1861) was described in the European press as not only a catastrophe but even as a disgrace to the Northern arms. Schurz had emphasized in his conversation with the Spanish Foreign Office the immense superiority of the North in resources and men; and then came the report that the Yankees had run away in their first major engagement. The Spanish newspapers began to make jokes about the sprinting ability of the Northern troops. "You must fight better in America," wrote Schurz to his parents, "so that we in Europe need not be ashamed." Chafing under the "elegant ease" of his life at the Spanish capital, he could only with difficulty endure his exile. His old friend, Paine, now in the army, wrote him predicting that Schurz would soon be a major general if he would return home. To prepare himself, Schurz spent long hours in the study of military strategy—the campaigns of Frederick the Great and Napoleon and the textbooks of Jomini and Clausewitz. He even translated a French treatise on tactics into English. The most restless man in Europe in the summer and autumn of 1861 was Carl Schurz, of Wisconsin.

Meanwhile, obeying Lincoln's injunction, Schurz had been observing carefully the currents of European opinion, reaching the conclusion that popular sentiment was turning against the North. The effect of Bull Run had been to accustom people to the idea of a strong Southern Confederacy and the not unremote possibility of its separation from the Union. The only hope of regaining the ground lost by that fiasco was "to proclaim the freedom of all slaves," thus winning "the sympathies of the liberal masses." Convinced that he was right, Schurz wrote, on September 14, from San Ildefonso, a courageous and forceful communication to Secretary of State Seward, prophesying that "as soon as the war becomes distinctly one for and against slavery, public opinion will be so strongly, so overwhelmingly in our favor, that, in spite of commercial interests or secret spites, no European government will dare to place itself, by declaration or act, upon the side of a universally condemned institution." He added that "every step done by the government toward the abolition of slavery is, as to our standing in Europe, equal to a victory in the field." Remote from the intrigues of Washington politics, Schurz could not have known that Seward was afraid lest foreign nations, de-

Courtesy of the Estate of Carl Schurz

QUEEN ISABELLA OF SPAIN AND THE PRINCE CONSORT

pendent upon cotton, would do their utmost to block the abolition of slavery. Schurz was in a position not unlike that held by Walter Hines Page, at the Court of St. James's, during the World War; and he was as impatient with Lincoln as Page was with Wilson. Perhaps neither Schurz nor Page fully realized the difficulties which the President of the United States has to face at home. Lincoln's shrewd and far-sighted opportunism was never better displayed than at this period.

Seward's reply, dated October 10, was intentionally evasive, and accurately described by Schurz as an exhibition of "vague and sonorous language." Schurz rightly suspected that Seward had not shown his dispatch to Lincoln. But, even if the President had seen it, it is probable that he would have approved of Seward's answer. After all, the moment had not arrived for emancipation of the Negro, and Lincoln wished to avoid any rash step. Schurz, however, was nettled by Seward's indifference, and wrote at once to the President requesting permission to return to the United States on leave of absence, adding that, if this were refused, he should immediately resign and come home. In his letter he did not conceal his apprehension that the struggle was becoming more and more critical, and he declared that he did not desire to spend his time "in comparative idleness or easy pursuits." The necessary sanction came in due course from the Department of State.

Schurz might have been less restless if he had had more to occupy his business hours, which were devoted mainly to routine and commonplace matters. He did, however, have to deal, during the autumn of 1861, with the proposed joint expedition of military and naval forces by England and France against Mexico, the object being ostensibly to adjust the financial affairs of that country and arrange for the settlement of foreign claims against it. Spain was drawn into the agreement, and it looked as if the move might be a serious menace to the North. The United States, embarrassed by war, could do nothing but temporize; and Seward, with considerable tact and discretion, authorized Schurz to say that, while the United States did not question the right of the three allied countries to levy war on Mexico for the redress of injuries, it did deem it important that "no European or other foreign power should subjugate that country and hold it as a conquest."

The newspaper discussion regarding the contemplated invasion of Mexico brought into prominence the notorious General Don Juan Prim, probably the most picturesque figure in Spain—a handsome adventurer, completely untrustworthy, extravagant in his expenditures, dissipated in his habits, but nevertheless the idol of the multitude. In a long and interesting letter, Schurz gave Seward an account of his investigation of Prim and his ambitions; and the Secretary of State expressed his satisfaction with the prudence and diligence which Schurz had displayed. This was Schurz's only opportunity during his brief tenure of office to show his skill in diplomacy.

Meanwhile N. B. Judd, the American Minister to Berlin, had given Schurz the assurance that he would not be annoyed or molested if he entered Prussian territory. Accordingly in late December he crossed the Prussian frontier on his way to Hamburg to rejoin his family. When the train stopped in Cologne, he was wide awake, and, as he reached the bridge over the Rhine, he could hear faintly the rushing of the waters. He was then only a few miles from his birthplace and the district where he had begun his career as a revolutionist. In a few days, he embarked on the steamship *Bavaria*. On the voyage, the Schurzes passed through a hurricane lasting six days and nights, during which the bulwarks were crushed in and several sailors hurled overboard. They did not reach New York until February 2, 1862.

On his arrival in Washington, Schurz reported at once to the Department of State; but, when his conversation with Seward was interrupted by the entrance of a foreign diplomat, he hurried by the quickest route to the White House, where he was immediately admitted to the President and repeated to him vehemently some of the ideas contained in his earlier communication to Seward. As he was talking, the door opened, and

Seward's lean, astute face peered in. "Excuse me, Seward," said Lincoln. "Excuse me for a moment. I have something to talk over with this gentleman." And the Secretary of State had to withdraw. It was probably wise for Lincoln to see Schurz alone, for Schurz and Seward differed sharply on the relationship of slavery to our foreign policy.

Lincoln listened attentively to Schurz's views, thus confirming the latter's suspicion that the President had never seen his letter from Spain to Seward, and then said, after musing a moment: "You may be right. Probably you are. I have been thinking so myself." But he then continued, saying that he was doubtful whether public opinion in the United States was sufficiently prepared for emancipation. He was afraid of the result on the border states. Lincoln then asked Schurz to remain in the capital, talk with various people, and come back to tell what impressions he had received. Schurz formed at this time a very high opinion of Lincoln's reasonableness and patience under criticism.

It was at this period that Schurz became intimate with Charles Sumner, the uncompromising Massachusetts abolitionist whose influence upon him was later to become important. Sumner, then, as always, self-confident, fanatical, and humorless, could not understand the President's delay in freeing the slaves. Fortunately Schurz, although his sympathies were with Sumner, could comprehend the wisdom of Lincoln's policy in making sure of his ground before he advanced. Schurz, after studying conditions in Washington and talking with Congressmen, went to New York to get a broader view of the situation. There he helped to form an "Emancipation Society" and arranged for a public meeting in Cooper Union. When he reported to Lincoln what had been done, the latter said, "Are you going to make a speech?" "Yes," replied Schurz. "Well, now go home and sketch that speech. Do it as quickly as you can. Then come and show me your arguments and we will talk it over." In a few days, Schurz read the completed address to Lincoln, who praised it warmly and added: "Now, you go and deliver that speech at your meeting on the 6th of March. And maybe you will hear something from me on the same day."

Schurz's Cooper Union Address, later given the title of "Reconciliation by Emancipation," was one of his noblest oratorical efforts. Its essential thesis was that no restoration of the Union, even after the rebellion had been suppressed, could be permanent without the abolition of slavery. "I am an anti-slavery man," he declared. "All the moral impulses of my heart have made me so, and all the working of my brain has confirmed me in my faith." But he was not an extremist like Sumner, and, as practical proposals, he suggested that slavery be at once eradicated in the District of Columbia; that the slaves of avowed rebels be immediately confiscated and later set free; and that some fair compensation be offered to loyal slave States and loyal masters who would agree upon some system of emancipation. Schurz was especially critical of timid Northerners who were afraid to touch the question of slavery and of politicians who did not dare to face a moral issue. When Schurz had finished, a dramatic touch was added by Horace Greeley, who read a telegram from the President announcing that he was sending to Congress a special message asking for a joint resolution offering gradual emancipation, with complete compensation to slave owners. In submitting this proposal, Lincoln, in the spirit of Daniel Webster, said, "In my judgment, gradual, not sudden emancipation, is better for all." The Cooper Union meeting was noisily enthusiastic, and Carl Schurz was wildly cheered. But nothing came of it. Congress adopted the resolution suggested by the President, but not one of the slave-owning States responded. The quarrel had gone too far to be assuaged by a gesture.

On March 9, Schurz reported to Lincoln what had happened at the Cooper Union meeting. It was the day after the eventful duel between the *Merrimac* and the *Monitor* in Hampton Roads, and the President, obviously elated, told the whole story of the unexpected appearance of the little "raft with a large iron cheese-box" upon it, and its invulnerability. The two men talked over the situation, and Schurz selected a fitting moment for telling of his own desire to resign from the diplomatic service and enter the army. Lincoln urged him to confer with the Secretary of State; and Mr. and Mrs. Schurz, accordingly, dined with the Sewards. Seward unquestionably desired Schurz to resume his residence in Madrid, but the latter had other aspirations. He was aware that, when the war was over, it would be those who had fought with the colors who would have a decisive influence in reconstruction; and he was convinced—to quote his own words—that "the true place for a young and able-bodied man was in the field, and not in an easy chair." In a second interview, Lincoln reminded him that he was abandoning a large salary and a distinguished place in order to leap into "work and discomfort and danger." But Carl Schurz could not be dissuaded. Finally the President said, "I expected you to come to this decision, and I shall send your name to the Senate with the next batch of brigadiers, and I trust we can find you a suitable command." There was the usual delay. Schurz, worn out by his labors and worries, had an attack of nervous exhaustion in Philadelphia, and was ill for two weeks. As he was convalescing, he received the good news that he had been commissioned as a brigadier general in the army of the United States.

CHAPTER IX WAR

At last he was "General C. Schurz," to be addressed at the "Headquarters of General Frémont's Army." Still incurably romantic, the erstwhile politician, lecturer, and diplomat was metamorphosed into the warrior and threw himself as ardently into his new role as if a civilian dullness were forever behind him. Although too sophisticated to regard war as merely a glorious and colorful adventure, he did assume all its gaudy suits and trappings. A contemporary photograph reveals him in enormous leather boots like those affected by Cyrano de Bergerac, a resplendent blue uniform with conspicuous buttons and epaulettes, gauntlet gloves in his left hand and a riding stock in his right, looking, with his thin bony features, his dark moustache, his tangle of waving reddish hair, and his piercing eyes, incredibly ferocious. He sits with his left leg crossed over his right and his left elbow resting near his military cap on a table, as if every detail of posture had been carefully studied; but even in this artificial pose, he is every inch an officer. Another even more impressive picture shows him standing erect, garbed like a Cossack in a fur cap, a cape, and boots and spurs, wearing a heavy beard and spectacles and carrying the inevitable half-burned cigar between his fingers. Tall and cadaverous, he was sure to attract attention wherever he went. His orderly, Schiele, was a sluggish Suabian, good-natured and corpulent, who increased his resemblance to Sancho Panza by riding on a donkey; while Schurz himself, without realizing it, now more than ever had a physical affinity with Don Quixote.

Schurz was under the initial disadvantage of being a "political general"; that is, he owed his commission, not to his rather limited earlier experience during the German Revolution, but to his indispensable services to the Republican Party during the campaign of 1860. Naturally he was not popular with the professional soldiers over whom he was sometimes placed. But Schurz had led a company into action and, like nearly every young man of abounding energy, was confident that he was potentially a Murat or a Ney. When he entered the army, he felt optimistically that two major battles would end the operations in the field and allow the North to dictate terms of peace. As a matter of fact, the war was to last almost three years more, and he, after enduring some of the fiercest fighting recorded in military annals, was to emerge without even a flesh wound.

It cannot be claimed that Schurz's course as a soldier was altogether successful. From the beginning, he was the subject of controversy, and bad luck seemed to pursue him. Clearly he was not an incompetent commander. The evidence indicates that he was a strict disciplinarian, sound in his judgments, and far-sighted in the disposition of his troops. But, while no one ever accused him of hiding when bullets were flying, his division was peculiarly unfortunate at Chancellorsville and Gettysburg, with the result that he and his "Dutchmen" acquired undeservedly a reputation for cowardice which was never quite forgotten and from which they had few opportunities to redeem themselves.

Schurz was unquestionably oblivious at times to the duty which he, as a subordinate, owed to his superiors in rank. When Lincoln and he said good-by, the President asked him to write him freely regarding anything which seemed significant; and the latter, in his *Reminiscences*, commented, "This I soon had occasion to do." It was obviously subversive of discipline to have a general officer communicating informally and directly with the President concerning the mistakes of those higher up, but this phase of the matter did not trouble Lincoln, and it was a privilege which Schurz keenly enjoyed. Colonel Theodore Roosevelt, an amateur soldier in the Spanish-American War, did, on his own responsibility, almost precisely the same thing. Schurz's innate tendency to criticize and disparage soon showed itself, and his passion for interfering caused even the President some uncomfortable hours. While he was at the front, furthermore, he carried on a constant correspondence with his political friends and watched the trend of public opinion. Idealist though he was, Schurz kept always an eye open for his own future.

On June 2, 1862, Brigadier General Carl Schurz, accompanied by his staff—all of whom were German-Americans—set out from Washington for the front. Delayed on his journey by swollen streams and rainy weather, he finally reported eight days later, at Harrisonburg, Virginia, to Major General John C. Frémont, the picturesque "Pathfinder" whom he had favored for the presidency in 1856 and whose partly superficial, partly real brilliance dazzled so many of his contemporaries. It was not a moment when Northern chances looked auspicious. General George B. McClellan, still procrastinating and demanding reinforcements, was encamped in the swamps of the Chickahominy, at the head of an army which was rapidly dropping in morale. On June 1, General Robert E. Lee had succeeded General Johnston in command of the Confederates; and soon, following the Seven Days' Battles, June 25–July 1, McClellan, much to Lincoln's disgust, was to retreat and lose Richmond. By early July, it was apparent that the Peninsular Campaign was a failure. The chief source of optimism was to be found in the West, where, after capturing Fort Donelson on February 16, General Grant had held his own at the decisive battle of Shiloh and was pressing the Confederates hard, and where the Union forces had gained almost complete control of the Mississippi River.

Frémont himself had only recently been removed from command of the Department of the West, where he had shown lack of judgment though much energy, and, for political reasons mainly, had been assigned to the newly created Mountain Department, operating in West Virginia. The forces there had been improperly divided by Lincoln. In early May, "Stonewall" Jackson, the great Confederate leader, had opened a whirlwind campaign in the Shenandoah Valley and, after a succession of brilliant movements, had actually threatened

Washington. Ordered to intercept and capture him, Frémont, Banks, Shields, and other commanders had been outgeneraled. Schurz reached Frémont's headquarters just as the "Pathfinder" had fought an indecisive engagement with Jackson at Cross Keys and was withdrawing from the field.

Securing an interview with his commanding general, the newcomer listened while Frémont defended his recent maneuvers. Schurz then inspected his own division, consisting of two regiments from New York, two from Pennsylvania, one from Ohio, and one from West Virginia, besides two batteries of artillery and a company of cavalry, and sent off to Lincoln a letter presenting his conclusions. He described with characteristic vigor the poor equipment of the men and their mood of discontent, emphasizing particularly the need of "unity of command." [1] Whether or not Schurz's disclosures influenced the President or the War Department is impossible to decide; but, on June 26, the forces of the Mountain Department were joined with those of Banks and McDowell into the Army of Virginia, of which Major General John Pope, who had won distinction in the West by his capture of Island No. 10, was appointed commander. Frémont, who had a grievance against Pope and justly distrusted him, resigned, to the relief of the President; and General Franz Sigel, who had fought with the revolutionists in Germany in 1849, was placed at the head of the First Army Corps.[2] Schurz, assigned to the leadership of the Third Division, under Sigel, now put into practice the lessons which he had learned from books, drilling his brigades hard and frequently and gaining the admiration of his men,

[1] Cf. Allan Nevins, *Frémont,* II, 637–640. Schurz confessed his sympathy with Frémont's irritated frame of mind, and hinted strongly to Lincoln that Frémont's army had been unduly neglected.

[2] According to Schurz's statement to his wife, Sigel's assignment was due to Schurz, who, when he heard that General Rufus King was to be made commander of the First Army Corps, telegraphed a protest to Lincoln recommending Sigel. *Intimate Letters,* 276. Sigel, one of the foremost to organize and direct Union sentiment in Missouri, had fought gallantly in the west and came east with a fine military reputation. It was soon shown, however, that he had been overrated.

most of whom were Germans by birth or descent. He had under him officers who had had far more experience than he—indeed one of them, Colonel Alexander von Schimmelfennig, of the Seventy-fourth Pennsylvania Volunteers, had actually given Schurz instruction in military strategy at Zurich—and it required tact to assuage their jealousy. But Schurz did his best, and was rewarded by the approval of General Sigel as well as by the respect of his subordinates.

During July, a consolidation of the Union forces in the Shenandoah Valley was effected, but there was no encounter of any importance with the enemy. Mrs. Schurz wrote on the 15th describing entertainingly a visit which she had made to her husband at Sigel's headquarters near Middletown, Virginia. "Oh," she burst out rhapsodically, "he has an innocent child's countenance when he truly rejoices." She spent "six beautiful days" with Carl, who was contented and in excellent health. She was pleased at eating her Fourth of July dinner with General Sigel and thought that the encampment in the forest was "extremely poetical."

But this idyllic existence could not last all summer. On August 8, Schurz received marching orders; and, on August 22, at a skirmish called Freeman's Ford, he was for the first time within range of the Confederate rifles. Colonel Schimmelfennig, with the Seventy-fourth Pennsylvania Regiment, had waded the Rappahannock on a reconnoitering expedition and, meeting some enemy pickets, had sent back for reinforcements. After the Sixty-first Ohio and the Eighth Virginia—constituting the remainder of Schurz's first brigade—had crossed the stream, Trimble's brigade of "Stonewall" Jackson's rearguard unexpectedly turned about and charged the Eighth Virginia, which promptly ran. It was thus Schurz's first duty on the battlefield to attempt to rally broken and disordered troops—an unfortunate omen. Later he was able to advance two new regiments and drive the Confederates back. Under this cover, the discomfited Virginians extricated themselves; while Schurz, to encourage his men, moved with his staff leisurely along the river, indifferent to flying bullets, until all the regiments were back in safety. General Sigel, in his recollections, commended Schurz for his conduct, declaring that he had "acquitted himself very bravely." This unimportant skirmish was followed by a series of marches and countermarches, which left the soldiers hungry and fatigued. Schurz himself was once in the saddle continuously for more than thirty hours, and discovered the secret of sleeping on horseback. These meaningless movements culminated at the end of the month in the disaster of Second Bull Run, fought on the field of the battle of Bull Run, or Manassas, the outcome of which had so much disturbed Carl Schurz in Spain the year before.

Schurz was an intelligent and observant man, with the gift of writing, and his impressions of a battlefield are of great psychological importance. Fortunately he left a very careful analysis of what happened to him on Friday, August 29, when the battle of Groveton was fought. Jackson and Longstreet, Lee's two corps commanders, had separated, and Pope had pushed rapidly toward Jackson, hoping to overwhelm him before Longstreet could arrive. Schurz's Third Division was on the right of Sigel's First Corps; indeed it was his destiny to be on the Union right wing in virtually every engagement in which he took part. He had received the order, "Advance at sunrise and attack." At dawn, then, he galloped along the front, under a cloudless summer sky, to say a last cheering word to his subordinates. The men began to move forward. As they entered the forest, all was quiet. Suddenly two rifle shots rang out, followed by a rattle of musketry, and the soldiers divided into irregular squads, still advancing and firing as they went. Schurz himself could see nothing through the thick white powder smoke and was left in almost complete uncertainty as to the movements of other sections of his army. For five hours this desultory fighting continued.

The picture which Schurz gave is comparable with that of the half imaginary battle (supposedly Chancellorsville) in

Stephen Crane's *The Red Badge of Courage*—of well-intentioned but uninformed men, in a state of helpless bewilderment, now retreating under heavy fire, now rallying under intrepid leaders and recapturing positions which they had abandoned a few moments before—of the conflicting orders, the misunderstandings, and the delusions which exist even among generals, who are supposed to know, if anyone does, what has been and is to be accomplished. In the end, Schimmelfennig's brigade gained possession of the railroad embankment—an important strategical point—and held it against repeated onslaughts of the enemy. But there was little coördination in the Union army. Later, Schurz wrote of the affair as "the old story of the war—to be repeated again and again—time and strength and blood uselessly frittered away by separate and disconnected efforts of this and that body of troops." At two o'clock, when his men were at the point of exhaustion, they were relieved by the fresh regiments of Generals Kearney and Hooker, and moved slowly back behind the line of battle. While they were bivouacking, Schurz walked about among the wounded, amid all the horrors which accompany war. That night, he and his staff slept among the bodies of men and horses and "the tattered fragments of vehicles and clothes and accouterments." Pope felt that a great victory had been won and that it would be easy on the next morning completely to demoralize the enemy.

Longstreet, however, had now rejoined Jackson, and the Confederate army, reunited, had no intention of withdrawing. When the over-sanguine Pope ordered his forces to attack on Saturday morning, he was doing exactly what General Lee most desired. When General Fitz John Porter moved forward, the Confederates repulsed him with great loss, and soon they were taking the offensive themselves. Schurz's division, held in reserve during the earlier part of the day, found itself actively engaged in the late afternoon, and, fighting against overwhelming odds, was obliged to retreat. As night fell, it was obvious that the Northern army had been defeated, but the wearied Confederates were unable to press their advantage. At eight o'clock, Schurz was directed to join the First Corps and cover the withdrawal of the main portion of Pope's army by way of the Stone Bridge to Centerville. His own command was finally brought within the entrenchments around Washington "in a state of perfect organization, order, and efficiency." Nothing, however, could alter the fact that the Second Battle of Manassas had been a victory for General Lee, and that Pope, who had opened his campaign with a boastful general order, no longer had the confidence of the War Department.

The calamity caused Schurz much distress of mind. He had participated in it; yet he could not tell how or why it had happened. Personally he had emerged with credit. Secretary Stanton said to him, "I have heard of your conduct in the recent battle, and I thank you for what you have done." Lincoln, pausing in the midst of conferences with politicians, shook his hand warmly and said: "I hear you fought first rate. Good luck to you." General Pope's official report mentioned him among those division commanders of whom he wished to speak "in high terms." On the whole, he had made a name for himself as a soldier. But he could not forget that the army to which he belonged had been defeated.

For the remainder of the summer and autumn, Schurz, with Sigel's corps, was encamped near Washington. It was a pleasing, restful interlude after the vicious fighting at Groveton and Manassas. We have a charming picture of life at Sigel's headquarters from James A. Garfield, who, in early October, escorted Miss Kate Chase, daughter of Secretary Salmon P. Chase, on an excursion to Schurz's encampment. After supper, Sigel and Schurz, smoking cigars violently, played beautifully on the piano, and several members of their staffs joined in singing songs of the Fatherland. Schurz told Garfield that, out of his two thousand men, he could pick a choir of at least 150, all of whom would be more than ordinary musicians. Garfield added: "It is wholly impossible for me to describe the tremendous enthusiasm of these noble fellows. Full of genius, full of the fire of their own revolution and inspired anew by the spirit of American liberty and just now by the proclamation which gives Liberty a real meaning—they are really miracles of power. I am reminded of Körner and his Wilde Jäger in 1813."[1]

Meanwhile important developments had occurred in various quarters of the country. On September 5, the unlucky General Pope, on whose poor judgment the reverse at Manassas was being blamed, was relieved at his own request, and Sigel's corps became the Eleventh Corps in the Army of the Potomac, under General McClellan. The Eleventh Corps was still held within the fortifications of Washington, but the remainder of McClellan's forces had to march out to meet Lee on his invasion of Maryland. At Antietam, on September 17, at a period when Confederate prospects seemed very bright, McClellan, if he had acted with sufficient vigor, might have won a decisive victory. As it was, he compelled Lee to retreat across the Potomac into Virginia and gave Lincoln a long-desired opportunity for issuing his Emancipation Proclamation, which was dated September 22. This edict was, of course, warmly approved by all abolitionists, including Carl Schurz. The immediate consequence, however, was not what Lincoln had hoped, but rather a storm of criticism emanating from various quarters and all aimed at the patient, undaunted man in the White House.

During the autumn, Schurz himself, animated by motives probably sincere and well meant, contributed to the censure of the President and brought upon himself a just retaliation. As we have seen, he had been encouraged to express his opinions to Lincoln and had responded by pointing out what seemed to him to be certain weaknesses in the administration policy. On November 8, 1862, after it was apparent that the Democrats had made astonishing gains in the autumn elections—gains which were chiefly attributable to the failures of our armies to win victories—Schurz, sitting down at his field desk at New Baltimore, Virginia, wrote a letter charging Lincoln

[1] Smith, *Life and Letters of James Abram Garfield,* I, 243.

with having bestowed many important places upon avowed enemies of the administration, and asking that the soldiers be commanded only by leaders whose hearts were in the Northern cause. Although it seems unbelievable, Mrs. Schurz actually carried this communication to the White House and read it aloud to Lincoln. On the same day, the President drafted his reply, pointing out that the administration, if it were to retain support, must conciliate its former critics, and declaring that, in the interests of efficiency, it was essential to select the ablest leaders, regardless of party affiliations. This rather temperate but convincing justification of Lincoln's policies did not reach Schurz until November 17. Three days later, Schurz, with characteristic persistence, prepared another and longer statement, amplifying the views previously expressed, asserting that Lincoln had been dilatory and procrastinating, and urging the President to "reconquer the confidence of the people at any price." In this letter, Schurz specifically denounced McClellan, Buell, and Halleck as incompetent.

Schurz later defended himself by saying that he was simply giving voice to the widespread anxiety as he understood and felt it; but there was about his letter a certain cocksureness which annoyed the much-perplexed Lincoln. He replied on November 24 in a note which is a masterpiece of straightforwardness, candor, and reproof. "Be assured, my dear sir," he wrote, "there are men who have 'heart in it' that think you are performing your part as poorly as you think I am performing mine." He went on to say that he needed success even more than he needed sympathy, and that he seemed to get success no more from his friends than from his critics. The letter had an undertone of irritation, indicating that Lincoln was really nettled. Two or three days later, when his words had sunk in, Lincoln sent a special messenger asking Schurz to call early at the Executive Mansion. The latter was there at seven the next morning and was ushered at once into the little cabinet meeting room upstairs, where Lincoln was sitting in an arm chair before an open fire, "his feet in his gigantic morocco slippers."

The interview which followed was entirely amicable, evidently planned by the President as an explanation and a reconciliation. After unfolding some of his many difficulties and making some "quaint remarks about men and things," he slapped Schurz on the knee and exclaimed laughingly: "Didn't I give it to you hard in my letter? Didn't I? But it didn't hurt, did it? I did not mean to, and therefore I wanted you to come quickly." After an hour's conversation, Schurz departed. As he went out, he asked, "Do you still wish me to write to you?" "Why, certainly," the President answered; "write me whenever the spirit moves you." And so they parted, as Schurz said, "better friends than ever." Schurz did write again. On January 24, 1863, only a few weeks after the incident just described, he sent a letter to the President asserting that "the spirit of the men is systematically demoralized and the confidence in their chief systematically broken by several of the commanding-generals." But he did not again indulge in condemnation of administration policies. Lincoln, by tact and shrewd management, had effectually disarmed him.

CHAPTER X CHANCELLORSVILLE AND GETTYSBURG

Exasperated by McClellan's over-cautiousness, Lincoln relieved him in early November, 1862, and made Burnside the commanding general of the Army of the Potomac. Schurz, with the Eleventh Corps, was, fortunately for him, still stationed within the defenses of Washington when, on December 13, Burnside made his attempt to capture Marye's Heights at Fredericksburg—the worst-planned, most blundering episode of the war—a frontal attack on an almost impregnable position, resulting in a needless butchery of thousands of men. Frankly confessing his errors, Burnside suffered the natural penalty, and was replaced by General Joseph Hooker—"Fighting Joe"—who restored the morale of the army so that, by the spring of 1863, it was filled with a buoyant spirit.

Throughout the winter, Schurz had remained in camp, drilling his troops and composing innumerable letters. On March 14, 1863, he was promoted to be a major general, and, after a sharp but brief illness from jaundice—during which he spent a week in Washington and ten days in Philadelphia with his family—was back with his command on March 26, near Stafford Court House. On that date, Schurz wrote: "The political situation seems to me to have improved greatly. In general there is more confidence, and determination to bring the war to an end." With the reorganization of the Army of the Potomac, General Sigel, who had never been able to get along with Pope and Halleck, was relieved of the command of the Eleventh Corps, and Schurz was left temporarily in charge. Sigel had strongly recommended Schurz as his successor, but Hooker, who for some reason did not like him, selected Major General Howard, a West Point graduate, who did not impress Schurz as being "intellectually strong." Schurz retained the leadership of the Third Division, which was strengthened by the addition of some fresh regiments—the Eighty-second Illinois, the Twenty-sixth Wisconsin, and the One-hundred-and-nineteenth New York. At a review of the Army of the Potomac in April, Schurz's division was thought by the presidential party to be "the best drilled and most soldierly of the troops that passed before them." [1]

In late April, with the warmer weather, Hooker ordered the advance which was to culminate in the memorable battle of Chancellorsville. His three corps—the Fifth, the Eleventh, and the Twelfth—all in superb condition and singing as they marched, began the execution of a series of rather intricate maneuvers, ending in the crossing of the Rappahannock, where they were joined by the Fourth Corps, under General Couch, at Chancellorsville. At that point, approximately 130,000 Unionists were opposed by only 60,000 Confederates; but the latter were led by Jackson, Longstreet, and Lee.

It is the verdict of the most authoritative strategists that Hooker, in the ensuing operations, was completely outgeneraled. The story of the battle of Chancellorsville has been told many times and need not be repeated here; but it happened that Schurz had a large part in it and that the catastrophe was in some degree blamed on him. On May 1, Hooker ordered an advance, which, however, was so vigorously resisted by the enemy that he made the serious blunder of falling back to a less advantageous position. In this new line of defense, the Eleventh Corps was on the Union right, facing south, in the midst of a tangled thicket of low trees and bushes, with General Devens's First Division the farthest to the west. Lee, whose perceptions were uncanny in their accuracy, saw that nothing but a flank movement around the Union right would accom-

[1] *Reminiscences,* II, 407. General Darius N. Couch, after saluting at the head of his corps, rode back to the side of the President, who was on horseback. "Mr. Lincoln, that is General *Shurs,*" he said, pointing to Schurz and using a pronunciation of his name frequently employed. Lincoln turned quickly and replied, "Not *Shurs,* General Couch, but *Shoortz.*" *Battles and Leaders,* III, 120.

plish what he wanted. Accordingly he audaciously divided his small army, sending "Stonewall" Jackson, with thirty thousand men, early on the morning of May 2 to encircle the Northern pickets and come upon the Eleventh Corps from the rear. It was what any daring tactician, like Lee, might be expected to do; and Hooker sent a joint order, in good season, cautioning Howard and Slocum (commanding a portion of the Twelfth Corps) to be on their guard against a flank attack.

Long before noon on May 2 Schurz could see long columns of the enemy marching from east to west bent on what looked like an attempt at envelopment. He immediately reported this information to Howard and tried to induce him to make a change of front in preparation for a possible assault from the west. But Howard, certain that Lee was retreating, refused to listen to his impetuous subordinate; and, to make a bad situation worse, Hooker early in the afternoon withdrew Barlow's brigade in order to reinforce General Sickles. Thus the Eleventh Corps was weakened until it comprised only about nine thousand men and was in such a position that, in case of a strong flank attack, it might easily be overwhelmed. On his own responsibility, Schurz shifted the Twenty-sixth Wisconsin and the Fifty-eighth New York, but, without instructions from Howard, could do little more to avert destruction.

In the late afternoon, shortly after five o'clock, while the men of the Eleventh Corps were eating or resting or playing games, deer and rabbits began to rush out of the covert toward the unsuspecting Northerners. Soon there was the roar of cannon, followed by the rebel yell, and Jackson's troops, the flower of the Southern army, charged in close formation. Thus suddenly assailed, Schurz's men resisted for a moment and then fled, leaving many wounded and dead behind them. For an hour and a half the Eleventh Corps retreated, stopping occasionally to rally, but unable long to withstand the much larger Confederate force. Not until eleven o'clock, when the disorganized corps reached support, could it be divided into its original units. On the following morning, in spite of Schurz's personal protest to Hooker, the Eleventh Corps was transferred to a position on the extreme Union left, where it was inactive during the remainder of the battle. The fighting between the two armies continued during Sunday and Monday, and, on Tuesday, May 6, Hooker recrossed the Rappahannock, having been soundly trounced by less than half his number of men. "Stonewall" Jackson, the great flanker, had been seriously wounded by a shot fired by mistake from his own troops, and was to die within a few days.

The catastrophe at Chancellorsville was so unexpected and complete that it had to be explained. Long after the war was over, various Union commanders were trying to vindicate themselves. The Eleventh Corps, composed partly of German-Americans, was made the "scapegoat," and the spirit of Native Americanism found vent in denunciation of the "cowardly Dutchmen" who had thrown down their muskets and fled like sheep. Schurz's official report, finished and sent in on May 12, gave a full, dispassionate account of what had happened, but closed with a glowing defense of his men against the charge of cowardice. He said:

> I am far from saying that on May 2 everybody did his duty to the best of his power. . . . But one thing I will say, because I know it; these men are no cowards. . . . I have seen with my own eyes troops who now affect to look down upon the Eleventh Corps with sovereign contempt behave much worse under circumstances far less trying.

Some prominent German-Americans in New York City, indignant at this flagrant injustice, called a mass meeting to protest. It was easy to prove that the first division to take to flight was that of General Charles Devens, a native American if there ever was one; and further, that only a little more than a third of the Eleventh Corps was made up of German-Americans. But still the slander would not die. Schurz, ignored by Howard and Hooker, asked, as a last resort, for a congressional investigation, but it was refused. Howard declined to accept the responsibility which rightfully belonged to him, and left the impression that not he, but Schurz, had blundered. Schurz never quite lived down the popular feeling that he had brought about the Union defeat. On the other hand, later research by students of military affairs has given him and the Eleventh Corps complete vindication.

The Eleventh Corps, however, was not through with fighting. In early June, General Lee began a movement to the north through Maryland to Pennsylvania, reaching Chambersburg toward the close of the month. On June 27, General Hooker, who had been growing more and more irritable under pressure, resigned, and was at once superseded by General George G. Meade, who, according to Schurz, enjoyed the reputation of being "a brave, able, and reliable officer," whom everybody respected. Within a few days after his appointment, he was to lead his troops at Gettysburg, probably the critical battle of the Civil War. It was to be fought, strangely enough, on ground which neither Lee nor Meade had chosen, and it was brought on by a chance encounter during a reconnaissance. All students of American history are familiar with the topography of Gettysburg: the North on a five-mile front, shaped like a fishhook, extending from Round Top on the south to Cemetery Hill and Culp's Hill on the north; the Confederates to the west, beyond the Emmittsburg Road, along Seminary Ridge. Here was enacted the climax of that five-act drama which opened at Fort Sumter and closed at Appomattox.

Most of Schurz's fighting was done on July 1, the first day of the battle. After having been quartered during the previous night in a nunnery at Emmittsburg, Maryland, Schurz started with his division at dawn, under marching orders to go to Gettysburg. A little later in the morning the Confederate General Heth, hoping to find some boots for his men, entered Gettysburg, where he came into contact with the cavalry of General Buford. Soon the little market town was the scene of a hand-to-hand combat, and, as new Union and Confederate units arrived, the battle widened in scope. The First Army

Corps, under General Reynolds, was the earliest large body of Meade's troops to reach the neighborhood of Gettysburg; but the head of the column of the Eleventh Corps came along about noon, and Howard directed Schurz to lead the First and Third Divisions through the town and place them on the right of the First Corps. The fighting was soon heavy. At first the Northerners were able to push forward, but enemy reinforcements appeared, and the situation, as Schurz saw it, became very dangerous. Fearing that he might be cut off from Gettysburg and the strong position of Cemetery Hill to the south of it, he withdrew a short distance to the east. At four o'clock, General Ewell, of the Confederate army, made a vigorous attack, resulting in terrible slaughter; and Schurz, to his relief, received an order from Howard instructing him to retreat to a position on and near Cemetery Hill. The First and Eleventh Corps then withdrew in none too orderly fashion through the streets of Gettysburg, being reformed by their officers as soon as they emerged on the south side. It was not unlike the situation at Chancellorsville, when the Eleventh Corps, on the right of the Union line, had been caught in a trap. The butchery at Gettysburg was frightful, several of Schurz's regiments losing nearly half their number in killed and wounded. He himself, in the thick of the fighting, was unhurt, although a bullet passed through his horse's neck, just under the mane. Reynolds, one of the ablest of the Northern commanders, had been killed early in the action, and Winfield S. Hancock, probably the most imposing of the Union generals, was sent by Meade to rally the fugitives near Cemetery Hill and take charge of the operations there.

Under Hancock's stimulating presence, a defensive line was formed facing west and north, with Schurz's Third Division resting in the cemetery. The Northerners expected an attack from the triumphant Confederates, and, if it had been made that evening, while the First and Eleventh Corps were disorganized, it is possible that Lee might have won a great victory. Schurz himself, however, always maintained that the demoralization of the two corps was much exaggerated and that the Confederates, whose losses had also been severe, would have found it difficult to carry Cemetery Hill. When darkness fell, Schurz sat with seven or eight other generals in the lower room of the gate house of the Gettysburg cemetery around a barrel, on the top of which was a burning tallow candle stuck in the neck of a bottle; and there they talked over what had happened and agreed in hoping that Meade would decide to hold the position which they then occupied. This, after listening to Howard, Hancock, and others, he resolved to do.

On the morning of July 2, each army was busy consolidating its units and studying the terrain. In the afternoon, however, Longstreet's corps made a determined assault on the Union left, through the peach orchard and the wheat field, but were unable to gain a foothold on Round Top. A more perilous moment for the North came at evening, when the enemy attacked the batteries on Culp's Hill, at the extreme right of the Northern line, and actually scaled the breastworks and took possession of some of the guns. Schurz hastily got in touch with two of his regiments, ordered them to fix bayonets, and rushed to the rescue. In a desperate struggle, the Germans, eager to redeem themselves from the taunts which they had been receiving, tumbled the invaders down the embankment. "During this perilous hour," wrote Schurz in his official report, "my officers and men behaved splendidly." On the whole, the second day left the two armies with Lee having gained some slight advantages. Meade was on the defensive and proposed for the present to remain so, his position being satisfactory.

Before sunrise on Friday morning, Slocum, on the Union right, began an effort, eventually successful, to dislodge a large body of Confederates who had seized possession of a portion of Culp's Hill—high ground of the utmost importance strategically. After more than seven hours of fighting, the Confederates were obliged to retire, and the danger at that point was over. Then stillness settled over the battlefield, and, for at least an hour, on that warm and languid July day, there was an ominous silence, while the officers assembled in little groups, wondering what the mysterious respite could mean. Suddenly all the Confederate cannon seemed to break loose at once, and, for an hour and a half, the two armies from their opposing ridges engaged in a spectacular artillery duel. Most of the shells passed over the heads of the Union soldiers, but they were nerve racking, and Schurz, to encourage his own men, walked up and down in front of them calmly smoking a cigar. The cannonade ceased almost as unexpectedly as it had begun. Then followed the most dramatic moment of the Civil War. Lee had ordered a direct attack on the Union center. Schurz, from his vantage point on Cemetery Hill, could watch the jaunty General Pickett riding at the head of three gray lines of infantry, their battle flags flying and their bayonets gleaming in the sunlight, as they started on that mile of open field between them and their objective. Stopping halfway on their course for a moment's shelter in a ravine, they swept on once more, mowed down by a storm of canister, decimated by rifle bullets, but still pressing on until they reached the slope itself—and, after planting a few Confederate battle flags among their captured cannon, made their way back sullenly among the heaps of their dead. It was the noblest charge recorded in our history. As it became evident that this audacious thrust had failed, tremendous cheers broke out along the Union lines, and the men here and there sang "John Brown's Body." The battle was over.

It was always Schurz's conviction that Meade erred in not ordering an offensive movement on the evening of July 3. Such a general advance would have been undertaken with elation by the triumphant survivors and especially by the Fifth Corps, which was fresh and unscathed. But Meade decided otherwise. The Confederates, after concentrating in a powerful defensive position on Seminary Ridge, remained defiant until the evening of July 4, when, in a rainstorm, Lee commenced his retreat. Halted by the swollen Potomac, he was obliged to await Meade's approach, but the latter was cautious, and, while he was deliberating, the Confederates made good their escape to the south. The North had won a notable, even a decisive, victory, and it may well have been that a prompt advance by Meade would have crushed the Confederacy then and there.

So far as his own military reputation was concerned, Schurz should have lost nothing at Gettysburg. His Third Division, although opposed on the first day by superior numbers, had fought sternly, and had been so depleted that its normal strength of approximately ten thousand had been reduced to barely fifteen hundred. But the Eleventh Corps was ill-fated. Whatever it did was wrong. The fact that it had been repulsed was enough to condemn it, and the "Foreign Legion," as it was styled by its critics, was again outrageously slandered. In his *Reminiscences*, Schurz quoted with especial bitterness the description of Gettysburg written by the novelist, Captain Charles King, who said that the Eleventh Corps retreated, "its foreign-born, foreign-bred brigadiers . . . giving way before the natives sweeping down upon them in those long gray lines." The situation reached a point which led reinforcements to protest against being assigned to the Eleventh Corps, and it seemed wise to dissolve it so that its identity might be lost. Schurz, after discussing the matter with Meade and Howard, went to Washington to present his views to General Halleck; but it was finally thought best not to break up the corps. Eventually it was somewhat reorganized and, on September 25, 1863, was detached from the Army of the Potomac and sent, with the Twelfth Corps, to the Union army under Rosecrans, who had just suffered a disastrous defeat at Chickamauga.

CHAPTER XI VICTORY

THROUGHOUT the summer of 1863, Schurz remained with the Army of the Potomac, during a long series of unimportant maneuvers and skirmishes leading to no significant engagement. After Chancellorsville and Gettysburg, both sides were in need of recuperation. Schurz, who was prostrated for a time by camp fever, finally secured a furlough of two weeks in early September, spending it with his wife and children in Bethlehem, Pennsylvania. Returning to his command at Catlett Station, Virginia, on September 17, he was almost immediately ordered with his troops on a railroad journey of twelve hundred miles to Bridgeport, Alabama, on the Tennessee River, which they reached on October 1.[1] Three weeks later, they marched to Chattanooga, over a wretched road encumbered with the carcasses of horses and mules, to Lookout Valley, under the shadow of Lookout Mountain. Meanwhile General Grant, who had been placed in charge of all the military operations in the West, had replaced the irresolute Rosecrans by General George H. Thomas, as head of the Army of the Cumberland; and Grant himself arrived in Chattanooga early in October.

At Lookout Valley occurred another of those unfortunate incidents which, taken together, lead inevitably to the conclusion that Schurz had no gift for getting along with his superiors. The story is related in detail in his *Reminiscences*. With two divisions of the Eleventh Corps, Schurz went into bivouac not far from Chattanooga, leaving behind him about three miles

[1] The decision to send the Eleventh and Twelfth Corps was reached at a midnight conference in Washington on September 23, with Lincoln present. General Hooker was given charge of the sixteen thousand men involved, who were sent from Washington, via Wheeling, Columbus, Indianapolis, Louisville, and Nashville, to Stevenson and Bridgeport, Alabama. The business of transport took only eight days. Rhodes, IV, 399.

distant part of General Geary's division of the Twelfth Corps, with a wagon train, at a hamlet called Wauhatchie. In the early morning, some lively firing indicated that Geary was being attacked; and General Hooker, riding up in an excited manner, ordered Schurz to hurry his division to Geary's relief. Schurz at once marched off at the head of Tyndale's brigade, sending his chief of staff to instruct the other two brigades to follow at top speed. There was some confusion because of the roads, and, in the midst of the bewilderment, Schurz was informed that the two brigades had been held back, one by Hooker's personal order, the other by direction of one of his staff officers. To complicate matters still further, Schurz, as he was pushing through to Geary's aid, was met by one of Hooker's aides, who directed him to take and occupy a hill on his left. This he did, after a lively skirmish, and, having placed his troops in a position to sustain a possible attack, reported to General Hooker.

To Schurz's embarrassment, he was greeted by his superior in a harsh manner, and asked why he had not executed the order for the relief of Geary. Schurz explained the facts. Silence followed. Then Hooker merely said: "I gave you the order to march to Geary two hours ago. Carry it out now." Hooker's attitude was inexplicable to Schurz, who had faithfully obeyed instructions; and the sequel of the affair made him really angry. In the ensuing January his eye fell on a reprint in a New York newspaper of General Hooker's report on the engagement at Wauhatchie, in which the latter specifically excepted from commendation Schurz's brigade, saying:

> The brigade dispatched to the relief of Geary, by orders delivered in person to the division commander, never reached him until long after the fight had ended. It was alleged that it had lost its way, when it had a terrific infantry fire to guide it all the way; and that it became involved in a swamp, where there was no swamp or other obstacle between it and Geary to delay it a moment in marching to the relief of its imperiled companions.

The issue of veracity between the two generals was clearly drawn. Schurz felt that Hooker, a "very equivocal gentleman," deliberately intended to make his position "as unpleasant as possible." Highly indignant at Hooker's allegations, he at once assumed responsibility for the supposed shortcomings of his subordinates and demanded of General Thomas a court of inquiry. This was duly ordered, but was constituted of officers belonging to Hooker's command and all of lower rank than Schurz. The latter called many witnesses to testify that Hooker had held back the two brigades and sent Schurz an order to take and hold the hill. In the course of the investigation, Schurz read a statement to the court, reviewing the evidence and vigorously condemning Hooker. The verdict was substantially a vindication of Schurz, the conclusion being that he had "fully explained his delay in going to the relief of Geary, and his apparent disobedience of orders in this regard . . . and exonerated himself from the strictures contained in General Hooker's report."

On November 22, the Eleventh Corps marched to Chattanooga to join the Army of the Cumberland, and he and his men were present on the field throughout the three days of fighting which followed. On November 24, he watched from a distance Hooker's troops as, in the mists and rains, they won the "battle above the clouds" on Lookout Mountain and placed the stars and stripes on its peak. On the 25th, the Eleventh Corps easily drove the Confederates out of the front-line rifle pits, and were instructed to be in readiness to attack the enemy's right flank in force; but the discovery of a deep ravine between the two armies compelled General Sherman to hold back his orders, and the Eleventh Corps remained inactive during the battle of Missionary Ridge. The Union center, however, without orders, stormed up the ridge and won a stupendous victory.

Schurz was now sent, under General Sherman, on an expedition of one hundred and twenty miles to Knoxville, Tennessee, where General Burnside was being besieged by Longstreet. The latter, however, withdrew at the news of

Sherman's approach, and the Third Division made the long journey back again to Lookout Valley, reaching their old encampment on December 17. For the next few weeks Schurz remained there. He wrote to Petrasch that "life in this uninhabited region, despairingly desolate, is monotonous and boresome." [1] Later, on January 24, 1864, he confided to his parents: "I have been perfectly well all the time, and the more madly things go the better I feel. The thing that suits me least, physically, is the quiet camp life." In late February, he secured a furlough and went to New York to join his wife, who had been ill. He was able to spend most of the month of March with his family and did not return south until early April.

It had become clear by this time, both to Schurz and to the higher authorities, that he ought not to continue to serve under Hooker, with the relations between the two generals strained as they were; but the administration had difficulty in discovering an assignment suitable to an officer of Schurz's rank. During the spring, he remained quietly guarding the one-track railroad which conveyed supplies to the main army at Chattanooga. Then came the news that the Eleventh and Twelfth Corps were to be consolidated as the Twentieth Corps, under General Hooker, and that Schurz was placed in command of a corps of instruction outside of Nashville—a recruiting station, called Edgefield, which might have been managed by a major as well as by a major general. The War Department had evidently made up its mind to shelve Schurz, and he knew it. He wrote on July 5, from Nashville, to his parents: "As you see, I am still here. I would have been glad to spend the time of waiting elsewhere, but through General Sherman's orders, I am detained here." While he was marking time, he called upon Andrew Johnson, then Governor of Tennessee, and became

[1] Not many anecdotes of this period have been preserved. Once, when Charles A. Dana and Schurz were riding from Knoxville to Chattanooga, they were overheard by James H. Wilson conversing in both German and English. In one of the pauses, Dana remarked, "General Schurz, you speak English with greater purity and precision than any man I have ever known." Schurz replied with a similar compliment to Dana's German. Wilson, *Charles A. Dana,* 36.

well acquainted with him. He also carried on an active correspondence with political friends and made up his mind that, unless he could soon get a more active command, he would prefer to enter actively into the presidential campaign then just beginning.

The Republican Convention, meeting at Baltimore in early June, renominated Lincoln, who received the votes of all the delegates except those from Missouri, but selected as its candidate for Vice President, Schurz's new friend, "Andy" Johnson, of Tennessee, a so-called War Democrat. In spite of this apparent unanimity, there were strong elements in the Republican Party hostile to Lincoln. The notorious Wade-Davis Manifesto, published on August 5, impugned the President's motives, criticized him for his lenient reconstruction program, and indicated that he was unpopular with the radical leaders of his party.

Chafing under his inaction, Schurz made one last effort to secure active military duty and enlisted Johnson's influence in his behalf. The latter telegraphed Lincoln, July 10, that Schurz was "anxious to be placed in a position where he can render more service to the country, and distinction and credit to himself." Two weeks later, the perplexed President replied, saying, "You can never know, until you have a trial, how difficult it is to find a place for an officer of so high a rank when there is no place seeking him." Situations of a similar embarrassing kind frequently arose during the World War. Convinced now that his army ambitions were to be blocked indefinitely, Schurz listened attentively to the many requests that he go "on the stump" again. He asked, through military channels, to be relieved of his Nashville assignment, and, when this was granted, he went at once to Bethlehem, Pennsylvania. He then formally requested permission to visit Washington for a conference with the President, and, in late July, before the Democratic Convention had met, spent the evening with Lincoln in the cottage on the grounds of the Soldiers' Home, where the President occasionally found peace—or comparative peace—during the stifling summer days.

Not without characteristic dramatic touches, Schurz later recounted the substance of their conversation. Expressing his sorrow at the bitter and unjust attacks being made upon his administration, and upon himself, Lincoln declared that he could not withdraw at that moment, lest such action bring on "confusion worse confounded." Schurz wrote, "Meanwhile the dusk of evening had set in, and when the room was lighted I thought I saw his sad eyes moist and his rugged features working strangely, as if under a very strong and painful emotion." As the interview drew to a close, Lincoln became calmer and finally, after a few humorous remarks, said, as they shook hands: "Well, things might look better, and they might look worse. Go in, and let us all do the best we can."

Schurz, although himself an abolitionist and then in sympathy with the radicalism of Thaddeus Stevens, was, nevertheless, a staunch supporter of Lincoln, and was to become one of his best interpreters. Writing on October 12, to Petrasch, he made a shrewd analysis of Lincoln's personality, saying: "He is an overgrown nature-child and does not understand artifices of speech and attitude. But he is a man of profound feeling, just and firm principles, and incorruptible integrity. One can always rely upon his motives, and the characteristic gift of this people, a sound common sense, is developed in him to a marvelous degree. . . . He is the people personified; that is the secret of his popularity." He concluded with a prophecy which, at the moment, seemed ridiculous: "In fifty years, perhaps much sooner, Lincoln's name will stand written upon the honor roll of the American Republic next to that of Washington, and there it will remain for all time."

Perhaps through Lincoln's intervention, Schurz was now offered a command of considerable importance,[1] but refused it, feeling that he would be more useful in politics. The Democratic Convention, held in late August, in Chicago, nominated

[1] Schurz himself mentions this offer, but I have been unable to verify the fact by checking details.

General McClellan, and, in its platform, virtually declared that the Civil War had been a failure. McClellan himself, in his letter of acceptance, repudiated the doctrines of his platform, declaring manfully that he could not look his former comrades in the face and tell them that "their labors and the sacrifice of so many of our slain and wounded brethren had been in vain."

Almost at once, Schurz, with the President's approbation, started on a speaking tour, in the course of which he covered New York, Pennsylvania, and the Middle West, even as far as Wisconsin. The keynote of his utterances was set in Philadelphia, on September 16, when he declared that the only logical course was to fight the war through to a finish, and that a policy of conciliation and compromise would be futile. One of the ablest of his addresses, delivered on October 7, at the Academy of Music, in Brooklyn, later widely circulated under the title, "The Treason of Slavery," assailed the theory that the Union should be restored "as it was," and contended that slavery must be abolished forever within the limits of the United States. By his eloquence, Schurz counteracted the speeches of Robert C. Winthrop and Horatio Seymour and the editorials of the New York *World*, and kept the German-Americans as a body in the ranks of the Republican Party.

An even stronger factor working for Lincoln, however, was the tidings of the capture of Atlanta by General Sherman on September 2 and of his spectacular and devastating march, beginning October 17, into "the garden spot of the Confederacy," from Atlanta to the Sea, followed by the news of Sheridan's ravaging of the Shenandoah Valley in the autumn. It seemed as if Fate had planned to rebuke the Democrats for their impudent defeatism. On the night of the election, November 8, Schurz, tired but happy, was in Bethlehem with his family, absolutely confident of victory. The result justified his expectations. McClellan carried only three States—New Jersey, Delaware, and Kentucky. All the rest were for Abraham Lincoln and a vigorous prosecution of the war.

MAJOR-GENERAL CARL SCHURZ
From a war-time photograph

After the election, Schurz remained in Bethlehem, where his wife gave birth, on December 30, to a daughter.[1] He occupied his time in revising some of his speeches and preparing them for publication in a single volume; [2] but he was really "perishing with impatience and weariness." To a man of his abounding energy, nothing was more enervating than idleness. The War Department was obviously still searching for an assignment worthy of Major General Schurz. On January 31, he had a long conversation in Washington with Lincoln and Stanton, both of whom seemed cordial; but the best they could do was to tell him that Grant would soon be in the capital and decide the matter. He was in the House of Representatives when the amendment was passed abolishing slavery, and listened to the cannon announcing "this great step on freedom's path." By late February, he had extracted from Grant the promise of a command; meanwhile he was ordered by the War Department on a trip through the Middle West, with the purpose of enlisting the coöperation of governors and mayors in a project for organizing a "Veteran Corps," to be composed of men who had left the army, but were still fit for service. Schurz accomplished little in his task as a recruiting officer—which had been clearly created to provide him with an occupation—and was back in the capital at the end of March, hoping to be returned to his former command under General Sherman. As a matter of fact, the conflict was almost over. Writing on March 25, to Henry Meyer, Schurz said: "We see the end before us. It is possible that there may be still a couple of battles. It is also possible that the business will come to an end in great measure without further fighting."

[1] This child, named Emma Savannah, died in 1867. Schurz wrote of her, March 25, 1865, "Little Emmy is the most heavenly creature ever born. She is a genuine ray of sunshine."

[2] This book, published by J. B. Lippincott and Company, of Philadelphia, and dedicated to the Union League of that city, appeared in the spring of 1865. It comprised an even dozen speeches, beginning with "The Irrepressible Conflict," in Chicago, September 28, 1858, and closing with "An Appeal to Common Sense," October 28, 1864. Schurz wrote a brief explanatory introduction.

On March 29, Schurz called on General Hancock, at Winchester, and was received graciously; but no opportunity opened itself there. He then proceeded direct to City Point, on the James River, carrying with him a confidential communication from Stanton to Lincoln. Grant, with whom Schurz had expected to confer, had returned to the front, but he did spend some time with the President, who invited him to ride back to Washington on the steamboat with Mrs. Lincoln. "I learned more state secrets in a few hours than I could otherwise in a year," he confided to his wife. "I wish that I could tell them to you. She is an astounding person." He had hardly set foot in Washington again before the news of the fall of Richmond flashed over the wires. That afternoon, he was ordered to report for duty to General Sherman, at Goldsborough, North Carolina, and hurried off, hoping to be in "at the last scene of the last act." He made the journey on a government tug, through a gloomy corner of the Great Dismal Swamp. Although he was welcomed by his former comrades, he found that, as a new corps commander had been appointed three days before, he himself would have to be satisfied with a division. As he rode through the camp of his old regiments, he was greeted "with loud cheers and much handclapping."

Soon Schurz, whose position was really anomalous, was named as General Slocum's chief of staff, and advanced with him toward Raleigh. On April 11, at the village of Smithfield, he heard rebel bullets whistle for the last time, and the next day a horseman brought the tidings of Lee's surrender to Grant. On April 17, just as Sherman was about to arrange with Johnston regarding terms of capitulation, he learned by telegraph of Lincoln's assassination, and the entire army was stricken with wrathful grief. Schurz wrote sadly to his wife: "The murderer who did this deed has killed the best friend of the South. . . . Our triumph is no longer jubilant." He was not able to be in Washington for the President's funeral, but Mrs. Schurz wrote him about it: "Now you know all, and I see you sitting still and alone, thinking, thinking, thinking. What you have always said is true; that, after Washington, he is our greatest President and the greatest emancipator. How happy I am that you served him so loyally!"

As time passed on and the period arrived for making a just estimate of Lincoln's genius, no one wrote of him more intelligently or sympathetically than Carl Schurz. Shortly after the President's death, he commented to Althaus, "Lincoln indeed was not the enlightened mind who could instantly grasp the whole tendency of a period; but through clear observation and slow decision he always at last came to the right view." Thrown with him intimately, Schurz regarded Lincoln not as an idol but as a personality, emphasizing repeatedly his essential humanity, his gradual growth in greatness, his evolution from politician to statesman. Although Schurz's own impetuosity sometimes rebelled against Lincoln's patience and made him annoyed at his temporizing policy, he admired the War President more and more, and his short interpretative biography of him is a literary classic.

As Carl Schurz in after years ruminated on his military experience, he came to certain conclusions, important because there was probably in neither army a more penetrating mind than his. He was impressed by the steadiness and reliability of volunteer soldiers and later told Prince Bismarck, to the latter's unconcealed amusement, that the Northern civilian army could have outmarched any professional European troops and would have proved superior to them in every respect in the long run. He noted the unique relationship between officers and men—a relationship which led them often to fraternize in a way which a German general would have thought subversive of discipline. He made some interesting observations on physical courage, which he found to exist among men otherwise unprincipled; and he became distrustful of the moral merit of that kind of bravery which is "merely, or mainly, temperamental." So far as he himself was concerned, he declared that he was, during a battle, "entirely unconscious of any personal danger." Of all the commanders with whom he was associated, the greatest genius to him was William Tecumseh Sherman. Finally, Schurz developed "a profound abhorrence of war as such" and a conviction that, as a people, we need physical courage less than we need moral heroism, the quality which leads one isolated man to stand up against the world, if necessary, for his conception of truth and justice.

Unlike so many American political leaders in the last quarter of the nineteenth century, Schurz never capitalized his war record. He seldom used his title of general; he refused to join the Grand Army of the Republic or the Loyal Legion or other similar organizations of veterans; and he made no appeal to the soldier vote, as such. So far as he could do so, he opposed the extension of the pension system, except in cases of disability obviously incurred in military service. Schurz's attitude was refreshing in an era which had to endure "Corporal" Tanner and which became familiar with the titles attached to General Grant, General Hayes, General Garfield, and Major McKinley, to say nothing of Colonel Bryan and Colonel Roosevelt.

CHAPTER XII AFTERMATH

IN LATE May, Carl Schurz, now a plain civilian, went from Bethlehem to Washington to watch the two great armies, the Eastern and the Western, the soldiers of Meade and of Sherman, swing for two long days in impressive, close-packed columns down Pennsylvania Avenue, with countless bands playing and their torn and tattered battle flags fluttering in the breeze, until the spectators had weary eyes and dizzy brains. The inflexible Sherman himself, Schurz's hero, rode at the head of his bronzed veterans of the March to the Sea, a wreath of flowers hanging from his shoulders, with applause greeting him all along the route. It took more than six hours for his "mighty phalanx" to pass General Grant and President Johnson in the reviewing stands. As he gazed upon these men whom he had known, Schurz's heart leaped in the consciousness of having been one of their number; but he was even more moved, as the summer came on, by the astonishing spectacle of demobilization, resulting in the uneventful return of nearly seven hundred thousand soldiers to humdrum peaceful occupations. Hostilities were over. The fratricidal war was finished. But new and grave questions were arising, requiring prompt settlement. What was to be done with the now emancipated Negro? How were the former "rebels" to be treated? In what way could the South best be brought back into the Union? The political struggle which ensued between the two sections was to be prolonged for many years and, even in the twentieth century, has not altogether died out.

It must be remembered that, in 1865, there was no place in the North, except in the five New England states, where the Negro could vote on the same plane as the white man. Nevertheless Schurz joined with the more radical Republicans in urging unrestricted Negro suffrage throughout the "conquered" South. Undoubtedly his motives were commendable. As a newcomer to our shores, he had instinctively become an abolitionist. He had fought for freedom in Germany; now he wanted to help the Negro out of bondage and to procure for him the political rights to which he thought him to be entitled. But, like many well-intentioned idealists, he neglected certain factors of the problem: whether the Negro was ready for the ballot, what the effect of his plan would be on the Southern social system, and what the consequences might be to the black man himself. Although he was actuated by a humanitarian spirit, he was often more philanthropic than wise.

Furthermore, Schurz rather vindictively upheld the use of repressive and coercive measures against the unrepentant South. Admirer of Lincoln that he was, he should have caught something of the Martyr-President's generous and far-sighted tolerance toward a vanquished foe. Instead, he was not unreluctant to insist on the pound of flesh. When General Sherman agreed with General Johnston upon a treaty of surrender, offering to his conquered adversary terms which were liberal as well as comprehensive, Schurz, in his position as Slocum's chief of staff, expressed regret and predicted that trouble would follow. He also felt that Sherman had blundered in inviting the Confederate Governor of North Carolina, Vance, to return to Raleigh and summon his State legislature. Schurz believed that Sherman had exceeded his authority and that his agreement with Johnston would be rejected by the administration. He was right.

As soon as the draft of the treaty reached Washington, it was repudiated, and Secretary of War Stanton telegraphed the disapproval of his department. The quick-tempered Sherman burst into a torrent of vituperation. He had risked his life at the front and, now that the victory was won, he was under the dictation of meddlesome politicians. In a day or two, General Grant arrived at Raleigh, and the two old cronies lighted their cigars and talked matters over. Eventually Johnston accepted the same conditions to which Lee had yielded at Appomattox

—conditions which many Northerners still thought to be too lenient. Schurz, impatient to escape from militarism, handed in his resignation; and, although it was not accepted for several weeks, he felt once more like a free man—free, as he said, "to begin a regulated activity in which there is a future." With calculated energy, he proceeded to Washington, to get in touch with the new President, with whom he had become acquainted in Nashville. On May 4, he wrote to Mrs. Schurz: "I have seen Andie Johnson. He invited me to a long consultation in which I was to lay before him my views on the present situation and the policy to be pursued. So far he seems all right; there are no longer any traces of bad habits, and the hints he gives in regard to policy permit us to hope from him on the whole an energetic and at the same time discreet use of his executive powers." Within a month or two, Schurz was to modify his opinion of Andrew Johnson.

Meanwhile Schurz, so often the volunteer adviser of President Lincoln, continued the practice with the new administration. Jefferson Davis, President of the Southern Confederacy, had been taken prisoner, and a popular clamor demanded his immediate execution. The outcry against "Jeff" Davis in the spring of 1865 was as savage as that against Wilhelm II in 1918, and even conservative newspapers thirsted for his blood, just as the slogan, "Hang the Kaiser!" was raised after the World War. Davis was placed in irons in Fortress Monroe. When Schurz heard that the trial of the "traitor" was to be held before a military tribunal, in secret, he promptly protested, and had an interview with Johnson on May 18, in which it was suggested that he should participate in the court proceedings. The administration postponed any positive action, and Davis was not brought before the Circuit Court of the United States until May, 1867, after he had been incarcerated for more than two years. He was then bonded and released, with the approval of most reasonable citizens.

Johnson, whom Schurz was seeing frequently, seemed "uncertain and perplexed," as indeed he had a right to be, for he was pondering in his mind the extent to which he should adopt Lincoln's plan of reconstruction, and he was being beset by the advocates of unconditional, immediate Negro suffrage. On May 26, Schurz had another long conversation with the President, during which the latter asked whether he would be available for some special investigation; but, although Schurz lingered hopefully in the vicinity of the White House, nothing developed. As the days passed, the President was coming slowly to the conclusion that Negro suffrage might be introduced by the gradual enfranchisement of literate and property-owning blacks, but that complete enfranchisement would produce a terrible race war in the South. On May 29, he issued his Amnesty Proclamation, carrying out policies already laid down by Lincoln; and, on the same day, he promulgated an executive order announcing the appointment of a provisional governor for North Carolina, who should call a convention of delegates for the alteration of its constitution. The President had shown the original draft to Schurz, who had urged him to take no step which could not later be retraced and had ventured several suggestions leading to complete Negro enfranchisement. As soon as the North Carolina Proclamation was published, Schurz, then on the most intimate terms with Charles Sumner, wrote to him: "The President's opinions are quite unsettled on the most vital points. I fear he has not that clearness of purpose and firmness of character he was supposed to have." Johnson, however, knew precisely what he was doing. Soon provisional governors for several of the Southern States had been named, and the work of presidential reconstruction was well under way.

Johnson, slow to make up his mind but very stubborn in his decisions, had resolved that Lincoln should be his guide; but there were obstinate men in Washington who were determined that the Southern whites should be treated as alien, subdued enemies. During the summer of 1865, although Congress was not in session, the battle front was to form, with Thaddeus Stevens, the cynical and sinister old politician from Pennsylvania, heading a motley group of associates; the fanatical patrician, Charles Sumner; the bold and vulgar "Ben" Butler, also from Massachusetts, but with a vastly different background; the rough and outspoken "Ben" Wade, of Ohio; and the ambitious Chief Justice Chase, "caring for no friendship that could not be used for his own aggrandizement." These men were to undertake to overthrow Andrew Johnson, the "Tailor President." The story of the contest has been told more than once in recent years—never more vividly than in Claude G. Bowers's excellent *The Tragic Era*—and Johnson, long reviled as a drunken sot and the most contemptible of our Presidents, has been rehabilitated in a series of interesting biographies by Judge Winston, Lloyd Stryker, and George F. Milton. In the eyes of historical scholars, he now stands out as a firm nationalist who regarded the interests of the entire country, South as well as North, and who resisted courageously the encroachment of the legislative branch of our government upon the executive. Possibly the process of vindication may have gone too far. It has been proved, however, that Johnson, with all his faults, was a patriotic champion of fair play against bigotry. He had little sympathy with the outrageous demands of such extreme abolitionists as Wendell Phillips; but neither had Lincoln. What he was determined to do was to restore the Union. It was a worthy aim, but it was not altogether understood, even by Carl Schurz. Johnson was an obstinate person, deficient in tact and unversed in the gentle arts of conciliation; but he was honest, intelligent, industrious, and conscientious, and he tried sincerely to do what Lincoln, if he had lived, would have done.

Schurz, as his correspondence indicates, hoped to exercise a decisive influence in Johnson's administration, but soon learned that the President had a will of his own. When the North Carolina Proclamation appeared, Schurz warned Johnson that the question of Negro suffrage would soon become a "burning issue" and begged him, in dealing with South Carolina, to stipulate that the task of restoration be placed in the hands of the *whole* people of that State and that "*all* loyal inhabitants of South Carolina without distinction be permitted to vote." Schurz even asked to be allowed to address certain letters which he desired to publish on this controversial topic direct to the President, without, of course, committing the latter in any way. To this somewhat naïve petition Johnson wisely made no answer.

Discouraged and rebuffed, Schurz returned to Bethlehem and his family. "The uniform has been laid aside, the sword hangs on the wall," he wrote Henry Meyer. "The children play with the riding-whip and spurs." Then, in mid-June, the President summoned him to the White House, assured him that the North Carolina Proclamation was not to be construed as laying down a broad rule for reconstruction, but rather as "merely experimental," and asked him to make a tour through the Southern States, especially those along the Gulf of Mexico, to examine conditions and bring back reliable information. Schurz, beset by financial difficulties, asked for a day or two in which to answer, meanwhile consulting Stanton and Chase, who implored him to accept. He also wrote to Sumner, who replied, "You must go," adding, "Of course the policy of the President *must break down*." Schurz agreed to take the trip, but only after notifying Johnson of his feeling that the presidential reconstruction program was "ill-advised and fraught with great danger." Before starting out, he attempted to see the President, but the latter was ill. He also wrote Sumner, "*The President must be talked to as much as possible;* he must not be left in the hands of his old associates that are more and more gathering around him."

To meet his family expenses in his absence, Schurz tried first to hold up his resignation as major general, not yet formally accepted, so that he might travel with the salary of that rank. He also mentioned to the opulent Sumner a large insurance policy which he had been carrying and on which a considerable additional premium would be demanded if he took such a hazardous trip. The Massachusetts statesman generously responded: "Let me know the *extra* premium on your policy. The friends of the cause here will gladly pay. . . . Send me the bill; and do you go at once on the journey." There can be no doubt that Schurz set out under a monetary obligation to Sumner and other ardent Negrophiles. Before leaving, he made an arrangement to sell to the Boston *Advertiser* certain letters which he proposed to write along the way. Sumner repeatedly besought him to advocate "complete justice to the Negro." "Preach this doctrine," he reiterated. "Talk it wherever you go." It can hardly be claimed that Schurz undertook this expedition in the mood of a non-partisan observer. He wished, no doubt, to be unprejudiced, but all his affiliations made him hopeful that the attitude of the radicals could be justified by conditions in the South.[1]

On July 15, Schurz arrived at Hilton Head, South Carolina, by steamboat. For two weeks he visited places in that State, beginning with Beaufort, on one of the sea islands, where he saw a plantation operated by free Negroes and was favorably impressed by the result. He was naturally eager to ascertain what the feeling of the Southern people would be on the matter of substituting a free labor system for the long-standing method of slave labor, and whether the whites would permit it to be established and adopt it themselves. Charleston, once a flourishing port, he found to be "desolate and melancholy," with grass sprouting up between the paving stones and turkey buzzards flapping their wings lazily from the roofs. The once magnificent Charleston Hotel, formerly the center of social life, "made the impression of a dreary solitude."

Starting with well-formed theories, Schurz announced that all his preconceived opinions were "verified most fully." Writing on July 26, to his wife, he said, "I have come to the firm conviction that the policy of the government is the worst that could be hit upon." Although he had then seen only South Carolina, he was persuaded of the necessity of the presence "of

[1] For a fuller discussion, corroborating the views here expressed, see Beale, *The Critical Year*, 70–73.

a restraining and guiding higher authority." To put it plainly, the Northern troops must remain in the South to protect the Negro from the outrages of his former white masters.

As the month closed, he was in Savannah, to which city he was accompanied by General Gilmore, military commander of the district, who had greeted him officially at Hilton Head and had made arrangements for him to see the people with whom he wished to converse. Here he wrote that, while there was as yet no guerrilla warfare, the whites were unquestionably planning to subject the Negroes to "some kind of slavery" after the withdrawal of the Union army. He asserted that the adoption of a system not far from peonage was inevitable unless the federal government protected the black man in his newly attained freedom. "I see many a new thing," he added, "which strengthens me in the conviction that the restoration of civil government is not yet possible." In reporting with regard to South Carolina, Schurz advised the President to suspend his plans for reconstruction until things had quieted down. Meanwhile he was corresponding with Sumner and writing newspaper articles under an assumed name. "I do not wish it known that I am writing for the *Advertiser*," he told Sumner. "You will easily divine the reason."

On August 9, after a tedious voyage up the Savannah River, he reached Atlanta, which, suffering from the recent depredations of Sherman, made upon him a "sorrowful impression." He found the inhabitants "as bitter as ever." From Macon five days later he sent in his report on conditions in Georgia. After a week in Alabama, he proceeded to Jackson, Mississippi, and from there to Vicksburg, where he visited the headquarters of his old friend, General Slocum, then in charge of the Department of the Mississippi, and promptly got himself into trouble. W. L. Sharkey, appointed by President Johnson as provisional governor, had issued a proclamation calling for the organization of a State militia for the suppression of crime; and Slocum, two days before Schurz's arrival, had signed a general order directing his district commanders not to allow the formation of local militia companies. Schurz, although he had no authority, telegraphed Johnson defending Slocum's action. Speedily a long telegram came back from the President to Schurz, upholding Sharkey and announcing that military men were not to block the civil government. Schurz told his wife that General Slocum had welcomed him "as a rescuer in the hour of need"—but the rescue which he achieved was only temporary. On August 29, Schurz wrote, urging the garrisoning of Negro troops upon the Southern whites, on the ground that this would impress upon the latter the fact of the black man's freedom.

In New Orleans, the next city on his schedule, Schurz found political conditions "much confused." He himself, after riding hundreds of miles over dilapidated railroads and enduring sweltering nights made even more uncomfortable by ravenous swarms of mosquitoes, was worn out and irritable, and suffered an attack of what was called locally "break-bone fever," which he attempted to relieve by short trips to Mobile and Bayou Teche. In the midst of the "blistering heat," he read in a newspaper a paragraph, alleged to emanate from Washington, stating that, because the course which he had followed had not met with the approval of the President, he was soon to be recalled. The article said also that Schurz had published his impressions in Northern newspapers and that he had voiced positive views as to the policy which should be pursued toward the Southern States—both of which he had unquestionably done. Schurz at once sent Johnson a long letter, rather lamely defending his conduct and requesting an explanation, leaving it to the President to decide whether he was not entitled to some manifestation which would clear him of "these damaging imputations" and set him right before the American public. Again the President maintained an ominous silence. Schurz's illness continued, and when he was advised by his physician that he could not recover in that climate, he went north, stopping at Natchez and Vicksburg for additional information.

On his return to Washington in mid-October, Schurz, although not easily rebuffed, found himself in disfavor. When he first reported at the White House—so often open to him in the past—he was told that the President was busy, and he could secure no definite appointment. After one more vain effort, he was received by Johnson, who, however, met him with "demonstrative coolness," without even a smile of welcome. When Schurz announced that he wished to supplement his official letters by an elaborate report, the President looked up sardonically to say that Schurz need not go to the labor of preparing any report on his account. To Schurz's rejoinder that it would be no trouble, merely a duty, the President made no reply. As the silence then became awkward, Schurz bowed himself out.

Working at his report with his customary assiduity, Schurz sent the unsolicited document to the President on November 22, 1865, with a request that he be allowed to publish it on his own responsibility. Johnson did not answer. When Congress opened on December 4, its temper was at once apparent. The Republicans, recollecting that "Andy" Johnson, of Tennessee, had been a Democrat before the Civil War, proceeded to take charge of government policies and aimed to undo all that the President had accomplished during the summer and early autumn. Even before the President's message had been received, Thaddeus Stevens, the Republican dictator, introduced in the House a bill providing for a Joint Congressional Committee on Reconstruction, numbering fifteen; and it was promptly passed. The insult to the President was apparent—and intentional. It was to be a battle to the finish—a fight between the dogs and the bear.

A motion by Sumner on December 12 led the Senate to demand a copy of Schurz's report. The President forwarded it on December 18, together with a statement from General Grant, who, also at Johnson's request, had been traveling through the South, investigating conditions and had reached conclusions pleasing to the administration. With these two documents, Johnson sent a brief message of his own, declaring that he was convinced that "sectional animosity was surely and rapidly merging into a spirit of nationality" and that the disorders were "local in character, not frequent of occurrence, and rapidly disappearing." Sumner, in spite of objection, insisted that Schurz's report should be read to the Senate, and the Clerk began and proceeded until Senator John Sherman, obviously bored, rose in protest, and the reading was discontinued.[1] The radicals in Congress accepted Schurz's report as conclusive, and Sumner, on December 20, delivered an impassioned diatribe against Johnson, declaring that the President was deliberately trying to "whitewash" conditions in the South.

The report itself, printed in Schurz's *Speeches, Correspondence, and Political Papers,* fills approximately ninety-five printed pages, exclusive of the various supporting documents by which it was accompanied. Schurz himself felt that it was the best paper he ever wrote on a public question. After an analysis of the sentiments of the incongruous elements of the Southern population, he showed that outside protection was needed for those who had been or were Unionists. If the Northern troops were suddenly removed, the resident loyalists would not be safe. Furthermore, he thought it to be a mistake to allow it to appear that "treason" could be readily forgiven. He found everywhere among the whites a belief that Negroes would not work without compulsion. Everybody was acutely sensitive on the race issue. Indeed outrages on the colored people were still being perpetrated, even in the more civilized centers, and there was a strong opposition to any project for educating the Negro. The vital problem, as Schurz saw it, was the establishment of some workable system of Negro labor. Negro suffrage would certainly never be extended to the blacks by the "voluntary action of the Southern whites themselves";

[1] When Sumner asked to have Schurz's report read, several Senators cried, "It is very long." Johnson, of Maryland, formally protested but Sumner insisted that it was "a very important document." After the Secretary had read the opening paragraphs, Senator Sherman moved to dispense with the further reading, saying that he could not hear it while so much conversation was going on. Evidently the reading was perfunctory, and there was a "hum and confusion" on the floor. Nobody really wanted to listen.

yet it was absolutely necessary, if the ends of justice and equality were to be attained. The Negro must be made "a true freeman and an intelligent and useful citizen"; and the North, as a logical corollary, must rule with a firm hand until the Southern whites, especially those who had been in arms against the Union, showed a disposition to yield to more enlightened ideas. In conclusion, Schurz entreated Johnson "to take no irretraceable step toward relieving the States lately in rebellion from all National control, until such favorable changes are clearly and unmistakably ascertained."

Johnson had undoubtedly hoped that Schurz's report would support the generous policy of reconstruction upon which he had already determined. Instead, Schurz had given his powerful aid to the radical Republicans, the advocates of "blood and iron," who were planning, in the words of Thaddeus Stevens, to "humble the proud traitors" of the South and to treat the Southern States as conquered provinces.[1] Writing to his wife on December 6, Schurz said, "Sumner tells me the President is not at all favorable to me on account of my Report." He also heard that Johnson had told a Senator, "The only great mistake I have yet made was to send Schurz to the South." The report is full of interesting material, and its sincerity is apparent in every line. Nevertheless, its influence was less than Schurz boasted it to be. By the autumn of 1865, the two sides, equally resolute and obstinate, were lined up against one another: the President, insisting that the Southern States had never really been out of the federal compact and that a magnanimous policy would soon bring them into what Lincoln termed a "proper practical relation with the Union"; Charles Sumner and his associates believing that the "rebels" had lost or forfeited their legal rights within the Union and ought not to be taken back until the granting of Negro suffrage had

[1] Beale, in his book, *The Critical Year,* says, "The South described was not the South Schurz saw, but the South that he and his Radical friends determined in advance it would be expedient to picture." This judgment, though harsh, is not far from the truth.

made the Republican Party secure in the South. In this dispute, the issues of which were clearly drawn, Schurz, although taking no official part after submitting his report, was identified with the radicals, with Sumner and Stevens, against President Johnson.

CHAPTER XIII INTERLUDE

After ten years of almost continuous excitement in politics, diplomacy, and war, Carl Schurz was now confronted with the prosaic necessity of earning a living for himself and his family, who had made a temporary home in Bethlehem, Pennsylvania.[1] Mrs. Schurz's patrimony was now apparently exhausted; Carl had lost rather heavily in a speculation in land; and, in 1866, one of the mortgages on his Watertown farm was foreclosed. Without financial resources, he was obliged to hunt at once some method of earning money. In November, 1865, Horace Greeley offered him a position as Washington correspondent of the New York *Tribune*, and Schurz accepted it as a temporary solution of his difficulties. Journalism was congenial to him, for he liked to write, and he did not undervalue the opportunities which it presented for keeping in touch with political leaders. His duties not being onerous, he was able to accept lecture engagements in Boston, Poughkeepsie, Jersey City, and Brooklyn during the winter. He was in the capital when President Johnson, on February 19, sent to Congress his veto of the bill extending the powers of the Freedmen's Bureau —the first of several vetoes which aroused the wrath of the radicals. It proved to be impossible to pass the measure over the veto, and Johnson won a victory over his foes. Schurz was also on the White House lawn three days later when, by the light of a "guttering candle," the President addressed several thousand of his supporters, deploring the attempt "to concentrate all power in the hands of a few" and naming Stevens, Sumner, and Phillips as among those who were endeavoring to overthrow the fundamental principles of democratic government.

[1] When the Watertown farm had to be given up, Schurz's parents, who had been acting as managers of the place, moved to Monee, Illinois, to live with their eldest married daughter, Mrs. August Schiffer. See Schafer, *Carl Schurz*, 173.

Johnson's courageous veto and his subsequent speech constituted a preliminary skirmish in his battle with the radicals. On March 18, Congress submitted to him the drastic Civil Rights Bill, declaring all persons born in the United States, except Indians not taxed, American citizens. Again he exercised his veto, but this time both the Senate and the House overrode it. It was the first occasion in our history when a really important matter of legislation had been passed over the presidential veto, and showed that sentiment was turning against the Chief Executive. Soon the Fourteenth Amendment to the Constitution, penalizing any State which did not grant Negro suffrage, was debated at length in Congress and finally passed by the necessary two-thirds vote for submission to the States.

Still seeking an opening which would lead to something permanent, Schurz, as early as January, 1866, was negotiating with friends in St. Louis and Detroit regarding a newspaper in one of those cities. Senator Zachariah Chandler was insistent that Schurz should not reject the Detroit offer, but the latter preferred St. Louis. The proposals from Detroit, however, were more alluring, and he accepted the editorship of the *Daily Post* in early March of that year. Detroit was then a community of approximately 75,000 people, of whom about 20,000 were Germans. In May, Schurz assured his parents that he had found a field in which he could make a "secure living."

Hard upon Schurz's monetary losses came another disaster. His household goods, shipped from Watertown, were destroyed by fire in the Detroit railroad station, including a large number of intimate letters from him to his wife, together with a diary covering fourteen years—ever since he had been in the United States—correspondence with prominent people, including Lincoln, his division flag and sword, and all his books. In August, his wife and children rejoined him in Detroit, and the family was again united.

The Congressional campaign of 1866 was regarded by both administration and anti-administration forces as a test of strength. Johnson himself set out in late August with a large party, including Grant and Farragut, for Chicago, where, on September 6, he was to deliver the chief address at the unveiling of a monument to Stephen A. Douglas. Speeches were planned at focal points along the route, both going and returning, and the "Swing Around the Circle," as it was called, received ironic comments from anti-administration newspapers, including the Detroit *Daily Post*. In its early stages, the trip was not unsuccessful, but at Cleveland the radicals began hostile demonstrations, which provoked Johnson to replies. The President's retorts, blunt and sometimes undignified, made him vulnerable to criticism, and he lost ground with the country at large.

Schurz could not, of course, keep out of the campaign. He wrote scathing editorials and finally, busy though he was, contrived to go to Philadelphia in early September as a delegate, with Senator Chandler, from Michigan, to the Unionist Convention. Called to order on September 3, it was attended by many Northern radicals as well as by a scattering of Southerners. "Of all political demonstrations in which I have ever participated," Schurz wrote, "this is the most magnificent." The audience, however, seemed to want to do little but shout. He himself refused to speak at open-air meetings, although tumultuous cheers greeted the mere mention of his name; but he did address a great gathering on Saturday evening, September 8, in National Hall. As usual, Schurz was satisfied with his reception, saying, "I have not spoken with so much applause since my Douglas speech."

Schurz, always a good hater, had grown to dislike Johnson intensely. This address, later printed under the title "The Logical Results of the War," and circulated as a party pamphlet, was a vitriolic attack on the President. Schurz at the moment was like those who wanted to "crush" Germany after the World War, and could not understand the motives behind a policy of magnanimity. Denying that Johnson was following Lincoln's ideas, he declared that the President had been "promenading his bad grammar and clownish egotism across the country to bully a brave and noble people into acquiescence." It was a stirring speech, probably as plausible a defense of radical Republicanism as could have been made. Because of it, he was invited to speak in various other eastern cities, but refused all but a few requests. As the election drew near, he wrote to Meyer: "Johnson is a very narrow man, obstinate and stubborn to an unscrupulous degree. . . . He is a born demagogue, and if he were a man of great talent, he might in his present position become a menace to the Republic." [1]

With the results of the elections, Schurz was well pleased. The Republican victory was unusually complete, leaving that party with 42 in the Senate, opposed by only eleven Democrats; while the ratio in the House was 143 Republicans against 49 Democrats. "Well, we have succeeded in mastering Johnson at the right moment," wrote Schurz, "and during the rest of his administration Congress will rule the country without paying much attention to him." But "Andy" Johnson, whatever his deficiencies, was not the kind of President who would capitulate without a fight. There was still something to be done before he would be subdued.

Carl Schurz had watched the Austro-Prussian War of 1866 with the keenest interest, his sympathies being entirely with the Prussians; indeed he secretly hoped for a quarrel between Prussia and France, out of which German unity might be achieved. He had ceased to long for a revolution in Germany. The extent of his transformation may be judged from a sentence which he wrote to his wife on July 24, 1866, "Bismarck can now be more useful to Germany than any other man if he can only be forced into the right track." In December, Schurz prepared a lecture on Germany and arranged to deliver it in more than thirty places during that winter. This speaking tour, undertaken during a cold and dreary season, was far from pleasurable. "My sole delightful moments," he wrote, "are those in which I put the money earned into my pocket and think, 'Something more for wife and child.'" The schedule of his lectures cannot be traced day by day, but he had many

[1] *Writings,* I, 417.

engagements in Illinois and Wisconsin, where he was well known, and he covered a wide territory.

At the request of Ticknor and Fields, Schurz wrote an article for the *Atlantic Monthly* (published in the issue for March, 1867), under the title "The True Problem," in which he proposed as a workable scheme for reconstruction a Fifteenth Amendment compelling the Southern States to give suffrage to the Negro, and to provide for him a system of common school education. The actual Fifteenth Amendment was not passed by both Houses of Congress until February 26, 1869, and, when adopted, gave the elective franchise to Negroes in the North as well as in the South.

The Detroit project had been burdensome and not altogether agreeable to Schurz, who therefore welcomed a renewal of the proposal formerly made to him by the owners of the St. Louis *Westliche Post*, one of the leading German newspapers of the country, offering him the editorship and a half interest in the company. Although he was virtually without funds, a plan was submitted by which he could repay his share of the purchase price by installments over a period of three years. The original suggestion came from Dr. Emil Preetorius, the chief editor, who, a few years older than Schurz, had also been a "forty-eighter" and had distinguished himself as an anti-slavery leader in 1861. In April, 1867, Schurz met with Preetorius and his associates in St. Louis and signed the contract. He soon became a citizen of Missouri.

The Schurz family seem to have been all their lives rather unregretfully nomadic, never really settling down in a permanent home. Mrs. Schurz now moved to St. Louis; but their youngest daughter, Emma Savannah, died quite suddenly, and the mother was so prostrated that it was thought best for her to return to Germany with the two remaining children while Carl endeavored to rehabilitate his fortunes. There was a prospect of a hot summer in the city; Marianne, the second daughter, needed a good school; and there was reason to believe that Mrs. Schurz, who never quite overcame her longing for her parents and her Fatherland, would be better off in Germany than in sultry St. Louis. She, with Agathe and Marianne, sailed on board the *Allemania*, June 15, 1867, for Southampton and Hamburg, waving Carl farewell as he stood on the dock in New York.

Schurz now accepted the hospitality of Preetorius's house in St. Louis, and the two settled down in a bachelor existence. For the first time, he was prospering financially, and he predicted that a few years of journalism would make him independent. But he complained that he had to scatter his best ideas in innumerable articles, without being able to work them out as a complete whole, and he found himself at the end of each day very much exhausted. Undoubtedly he was overworked, and he wrote rather plaintively to his wife: "It is a pity—is it not?—that I am not rich and able to work as I should like. I should accomplish much more." In midsummer the heat increased. Schurz wrote on August 12 that the temperature at two o'clock reached one hundred degrees. On those warm evenings, Schurz resorted frequently to the German outdoor theater, where he saw Edwin Booth as Hamlet, Richard III, and Iago. He also went on excursions with Preetorius to some of the German colonies in the Missouri countryside, where he found the older citizens preserving the spirit of their childhood traditions, but the boys and girls thoroughly Americanized in language, costume, and conduct. He was himself by this time a perfect specimen of the completely Americanized German.

Schurz carried with him to St. Louis his contempt for the President, and the *Westliche Post* was aggressively Republican in tone. He wrote on August 27: "Politics would be terribly stupid if Johnson did not entertain us with his capers. He is a madman." Four days later he said of the President, "He now bites at all about him like a wounded and anger-crazed bear." On September 8, when General Sheridan, recently removed by Johnson as Governor of Louisiana, visited St. Louis, Schurz turned the official reception into a demonstration against the administration, making a fiery speech of welcome in which he condemned Johnson bitterly. Schurz also published at this period a letter expressing the opposition of the German-Americans of the Middle West to the temperance agitation then finding favor among a certain group of reformers. He himself, like nearly all his friends of German descent, drank wine and beer in moderation all his life, and could not comprehend the Puritanism which wished to interfere with his personal liberty. He warned the Republicans that, if they adopted prohibition as an issue, they could count on heavy defections from the German-Americans.

It was, as usual, impossible for him to keep out of politics. Urged from many quarters to accept a nomination for Congress and promised that his election would be a certainty, he refused to commit himself, desiring to become better acquainted with conditions in Missouri. He did, however, speak on October 4, in Chicago, before "a great and enthusiastic gathering," and he went to Wisconsin to deliver several speeches and help to ensure a Republican victory. For a day or two, he was in Watertown, among his old friends, where he saw sadly that his farm was occupied by an American, who had planted the flower beds with potatoes and onions. . . . In the country at large, the Republicans suffered reverses. The Democrats won in New York and elsewhere, and the omens indicated a reaction in favor of Johnson, whose followers raised what Schurz described as "wild cries of rejoicing." Schurz evidently regarded the defeat as a necessary rebuke to the "wire-pullers and speculators," as well as the temperance agitators, who had seized control of the Republican Party in many sections. "A few stabs this fall will not injure us if they do not come too strong," he wrote. He had already reached the conclusion that Grant should be the nominee for President in 1868.

On December 5, Schurz sailed on the *America* from New York to Bremen, to join his wife for the Christmas holidays. Before embarking, he spent a few days in Washington, equipping himself with a passport and other credentials and getting into touch with political leaders. Schurz shrewdly never permitted himself to become isolated. Wherever he was located, he did not allow his party to forget him, and he considered it well worth while to let himself be seen at headquarters.

Schurz was in Europe nearly three months, and did not sail for home until March 4, 1868. He first rejoined his wife in Wiesbaden, where she had gone to take the water cure and where they, with their children, had a lively and joyous Christmas celebration. Unwilling to become involved in political complications, Schurz had written in advance to the American Minister in Berlin, inquiring whether the Prussian Government would object to his spending a few weeks on German soil. To his amazement, he was welcomed wherever he went, and the President of the Police District in which Wiesbaden was situated called upon him personally and introduced himself as a former university acquaintance. He found himself regarded, not as a rebel or a traitor, but as an expatriated hero.

The climax was reached in late January, when Schurz, having gone with his wife to Berlin for a week's visit, met there some of the leading Prussian statesmen, including the Chancellor, Count von Bismarck, who invited him to call at his palace on the Wilhelmstrasse. During the interview, Schurz felt that Bismarck was trying to persuade him to return to his native land and enter its diplomatic service. The Chancellor spoke with the most engaging frankness on the difficulties of his position and impressed Schurz as being a man who knew exactly what he wanted. He asked many questions regarding political conditions in the United States, especially the quarrel between the President and Congress, which puzzled him very much.

On the following evening, Schurz went to a formal dinner with a group of be-ribboned and be-starred German jurists, and lingered after the other guests had gone in order to answer more of Bismarck's queries. It was an interesting meeting—the former revolutionist, the rebel against monarchical authority, sitting opposite the famous upholder of autocracy. Bismarck realized the humor of the situation, for he said at one point: "It is really funny that we sit together here so peacefully and smoke cigars. Fifteen years ago neither of us would have dreamed of it." The two discussed nearly every weighty question of foreign and domestic policy, even Bismarck's plans for the future of Germany. Schurz, much impressed, wrote a day or two later: "Whatever evil characteristics he may have, Bismarck is at all events an extraordinary person. I have seen many statesmen, but none who speaks his mind on all matters with such complete freedom."

From the recent biography of Amalie Dietrich, by Charitas Bischoff,[1] we get a delightful picture of the Schurz family as they appeared to a contemporary observer at the Meyer family home not far from Kiel. Fräulein Dietrich, then a young girl, after being introduced to Mrs. Schurz and her two daughters, "Handi" and "Pussy," rashly said, "Oh, I wish that I could just shake Mr. Schurz's hand!" Later, when she met him, he stretched out both arms to her and said, "I am delighted to take your hand, my dear little girl." She recalled him as very tall and very thin—almost too thin—with reddish hair and beard, sharp features and clever eyes. "His whole bearing had the stamp of great naturalness and simplicity," she wrote. Mrs. Schurz was an imposing, elegant woman, with large brown eyes and an open countenance. Schurz, at the dinner table, regaled the little girl with dramatic stories of his early adventures in the Rhine Valley, until her breath almost stopped. "And now," she continued, "he sits here highly honored, recognized and talked about both in the old world and the new. Isn't such a life a great wonder?"

While Schurz had been absent, President Johnson had been impeached by the House of Representatives on February 24, 1868, for "high crimes and misdemeanors," the principal charges being concerned with his removal of Stanton as Secretary of War. The trial before the Senate opened on March 13, while Schurz was on the ocean, but the case was not presented by "Ben" Butler, for "the people of the United States," until

[1] *Amalie Dietrich, Ein Leben von Charitas Bischoff*. Berlin, 1929.

March 30, ten days after Schurz landed in New York. By that date, after a brief visit to New Haven, he was in Washington and sat in the Senate Chamber when Butler, the "evil-looking demagogue," began his argument. Prejudiced as he was against Johnson, Schurz was not pleased with Butler's remarks, which he described as "a commonplace lawyer's speech, strong in its arguments, to be sure, but without any higher implications." Schurz listened, filled with impatience over the opportunity lost, and actually suffering while the charlatan Butler "labored one point after another with uniform aridity."

Eager for the conviction of the President, Schurz felt that the entire case for the prosecution was presented "in a very weak way." Although he was obliged to leave for St. Louis on April 2, he followed the developments attentively, and, shortly before the decisive vote, told his wife that they were all looking forward to the outcome "with throbbing hearts." "Fortunately," he declared, "the case of the prosecution was so strong as to compensate for the defects in its presentation." But some Senators thought otherwise. On Saturday, May 16, came the balloting, with both sides excited and uncertain. In the end, in spite of the most unscrupulous tactics on the part of radicals, the much maligned President was acquitted by the margin of a single vote, thanks to the incorruptibility of a small group of Republican Senators, including William Pitt Fessenden, Lyman Trumbull, and John B. Henderson, who, refusing to be cajoled or driven into voting against the evidence, sacrificed their immediate political futures, but won enduring fame for their honesty. Later, when he was preparing his *Reminiscences* after his wartime emotions had cooled, Schurz confessed that the "violent excitement by which many good citizens permitted themselves to be taken off their feet" was deplorable, and even praised highly those Republican Senators, the "faithful seven," who "maintained their convictions of right and justice." Like many reasonable Republicans, he came to believe that the impeachment was a mistake.

At the Republican State Convention in early May, Schurz

was chosen a delegate-at-large from Missouri to the National Convention, which opened on May 20, in Chicago. When he arrived in the city, he was astonished to learn that he was slated to be temporary chairman—an honor which he appreciated as a tribute to himself and to the German-American element in the party. After calling the delegates to order, he made a ringing speech, which was tremendously applauded, and then handed over the gavel to General Joseph R. Hawley, of Connecticut, the permanent chairman.

During the sessions of the convention at Crosby's Opera House, Schurz was a conspicuous figure. His one real contribution was made after the Committee on Resolutions presented its report. Noticing that nothing had been said in the proposed platform regarding an amnesty to former "rebels," he drew up and read an article favoring "the removal of the disqualifications and restrictions imposed upon the late rebels in the same measure as the spirit of disloyalty will die out, and as may be consistent with the safety of the loyal people." It was, of course, nothing but a gesture, but it was adopted with virtual unanimity and it had some psychological effect on the country. It indicated also a modification of Schurz's views, a disposition to be less harsh in his attitude regarding the South. He was to progress even further towards a policy of leniency.

While Schurz was not enthusiastic about Grant, he supported him for the presidential nomination with his influence and his vote; and, after Logan's brief but stirring speech, "the whole great assembly broke into never ending applause." For Vice President, Schurz favored "Ben" Wade, but Schuyler Colfax, described by Schurz as strong because of his "happy mediocrity," was finally named. The Democratic candidate, selected in early July after a prolonged contest, was Horatio Seymour, of New York.

Soon Schurz, "head over ears in politics again," was undergoing once more the ordeal of 1860—receptions at railroad stations, interminable processions, serenades, and unceasing noise from brass bands. But, although he complained to his wife, he really enjoyed the applause and the approval of masses of men. During the early autumn, he went into States where the German vote might be doubtful, such as Indiana, Ohio, Illinois, and Pennsylvania, showing the same fervor which he had displayed eight years before. A typical trip took him from St. Louis to Bloomington, Illinois, from there to Chicago, Indianapolis, and Lafayette, and then across Indiana to Madison, on the banks of the Ohio. This journey, as he describes it, was a continuous ovation, including at Bloomington the singing of an original ode in which he was heralded as the champion of liberty in two hemispheres, and a torchlight parade in Indianapolis.

Underlying all Schurz's activities during this campaign of 1868, was the half-defined hope that he might be elected United States Senator. He had thought of that office as the chief goal of his political ambition. In 1865, on his trip from Bethlehem to Washington to confer with President Johnson, he had supper in Philadelphia at the home of his friend, Dr. Tiedemann.[1] During the evening, the family held a spiritualistic seance, at which one of the daughters, a charming fifteen-year-old girl, acted as a "writing medium." In the course of the proceedings, some of which, as Schurz related them, were "passing strange," he called up the spirit of Abraham Lincoln, who, after answering questions about the reasons why the President had summoned Schurz to the capital, finally announced that the latter was to be a Senator of the United States. "From what State?" queried Schurz, suppressing a desire to laugh. "From Missouri," came the positive reply; and there the ghostly interview ended. At that time, Schurz, officially a citizen of Wisconsin, had no intention of moving to Missouri. The incident had elements of mystery,[2] and seemed more inex-

[1] Dr. Henry Tiedemann, who married the sister of the revolutionist, Friedrich Hecker, and was the brother of the Colonel Tiedemann who had commanded the fortress of Rastatt, became one of Schurz's closest friends in the United States.

[2] Schurz was reluctantly credulous regarding the power of spiritualistic mediums to read the future. He was obliged, after this and other similar ex-

plicable in the autumn of 1868.

So far as can be discovered, the earliest mention of Schurz as a possible candidate for the Senate was made in the LaGrange *American*, on July 30, 1868. In a letter to his wife, dated August 9, he said that some voices had been raised in his favor. John B. Henderson, whose term was soon to expire, had voted courageously for Johnson's acquittal, thus satisfying his conscience but ruining his political career. The other Senator, Charles D. Drake, was, like Schurz, from St. Louis, and it seemed unlikely that the Republican Party would choose two Senators from the same section of the State. Schurz, however, was not without assurances of support. "I shall wait quietly and see what fate may decide," he wrote. Actually he did his best to create a favorable impression by his speeches for Grant during the autumn.

Although the suggestion of Schurz as a candidate was generally well received, Senator Drake, then the Republican "boss" of the state, was not receptive to it, having settled upon General Benjamin Loan, of St. Joseph, as Henderson's successor. But Schurz, even when on his campaigning trips, did not lose sight of his aim. On August 16, at Valparaiso, Indiana, he confided to his wife: "Preetorius writes me that the Americans in Missouri are talking more and more about putting me in Henderson's place in the Senate and that several papers have already formally placed my name at the heads of their columns. . . . I shall not be a candidate, but if the thing settles itself, as is not wholly impossible, it would not be so bad—what do you think?"

With this pleasing dream to cheer him, Schurz left Indiana for Pennsylvania on a "march of triumph." On September 5, he spoke in Cooper Union, before a "colossal meeting," at which several hundred veterans of his old Twelfth Corps leaped to their feet, swung their hats, and cried "Lebe Hoch," so that even his self-assurance yielded to confusion. In Chicago, on

periences, to conclude that "there are forces active in and upon the human mind the nature of which we do not know."

September 19, he delivered one of the best known of his addresses, published under the title, "The Road to Peace—a Solid, Durable Peace." He then, as the campaign drew to a close, returned to Missouri, where he canvassed the rural districts, driving about over rough roads, in a miserable carriage, behind slow horses. The election itself went off quietly, Schurz being chosen as first elector-at-large on the Republican State ticket. The national contest proved to be one-sided, and Grant had a large majority of the popular and electoral vote.

Schurz, no tyro in political matters, had a watchful eye on possibilities for his own future. On November 2, the day preceding the elections, he wrote from St. Louis, "The demand for me to become Senator grows daily." In the same letter he mentioned the rumor that Grant might offer him a place in the Cabinet, but confessed that Grant had given no intimation of it and added that he would rather be a Senator than have any portfolio except that of Secretary of State—which he was unlikely to get. "Do you recall that a seat in the Senate was from the first the highest position we desired for me?" he asked his wife; and then he concluded, "Let us wait patiently for the good things fate may present to us." It was, of course, impossible for Carl Schurz to wait patiently for anything. The senatorial election was fixed for January 20, 1869, and, although he at no time announced himself openly as a candidate, he was soon in the midst of plots and intrigues, which became more complicated and serious as the day drew near.

On December 1, he was at Jefferson City, the state capital, where the Missouri electors met to cast their vote for Ulysses S. Grant as President. Two weeks later he went to Chicago for a widely advertised Soldiers' Reunion, culminating in a great banquet in the hall of the Chamber of Commerce, where he responded briefly to the toast, "The Loyal and Patriotic Press." Here he had a conversation with Grant, who aroused little enthusiasm, but sat at the banquet "with his impassive, stony countenance" and, regarding the Cabinet, was "as dumb as a fish." On Christmas Day, Schurz was back with the Preetorius family, lonely, but looking forward to a new triumph.

The struggle for the senatorship was to be a bitter one, for "Boss" Drake, not wishing to abandon his dictatorship of the Republican Party, even came back from Washington to "mend his fences" and supervise personally the opposition to Schurz. "You see," wrote the latter to his wife on the day after Christmas, "my life is a continual battle and will doubtless remain so." Little by little, the Schurz forces gained strength. Early in the new year, he estimated that thirty-eight English and ten German newspapers had openly come out for him; while Loan had only thirteen. It was a campaign of vilification. Schurz was assailed as a "German infidel," a drunkard, a professional revolutionist, a coward, and a foreign upstart; but his manager, Colonel Grosvenor, editor of the St. Louis *Democrat*, the leading Republican paper in that city, was exceedingly energetic and skillful in turning these denunciations to Schurz's advantage.

As soon as the legislature met, on January 6, Schurz went to Jefferson City, where he cleverly lured Drake and Loan into a public debate, to be held on two successive evenings. It was Missouri's "battle of the giants," and was really to settle the party leadership in the State. On Monday, January 18, General Loan spoke, "weakly and tediously," for he was no orator. He was followed by Drake, who stepped upon the platform with the utmost confidence, but was obviously disturbed by some of the "heckling" from the audience. Continuing on the next evening, he committed the tactless blunder of denouncing the Germans of Missouri. After he had declaimed in his best manner for two hours, the crowd shouted for Schurz, who rose and made a stirring defense of German-American loyalty to their adopted country. The excitement was intense as Schurz, with barb after barb of sarcasm and logic, stung the audience into laughter at his antagonist. Drake was humiliated. As soon as the debate was over, he hurried to his hotel, packed up his clothes, and made an ignominious retreat. His autocracy was over. At a midnight caucus, Schurz was nominated by the

Republicans on the first ballot, and one of his opponents moved to make the choice unanimous. There was a noisy jubilation at Schurz's hotel. His rooms were packed with people, and a band serenaded him from the street outside his window. His right hand was so crushed after the first hour that he had to bandage it and use his left one for shaking hands.

On Wednesday, it was announced that, at a joint session of the Senate and House, Carl Schurz had been elected Senator, and he made a brief speech of response, urging that the Republican Party remain a united force for good. Drake sent him a congratulatory note from Washington, saying that he had no reason for desiring any relations between them except those "of respect, good-will, and cordial coöperation"; and Schurz, a week later, replied with equal courtesy that his conduct as Senator would be governed "entirely by considerations of public interest without any ingredient of personal resentment." But there was no question as to who had won. When he had returned to his desk in St. Louis, Schurz, in a mood of exultation, wrote his wife, "I believe I can tell you without exaggeration that I am today the most powerful man in Missouri."

There had been moments during and after the Civil War when Margarethe Schurz, depressed by financial worries, had hinted to her husband that he was losing his grip, that his best days were over. Now he had an effective reply. From Washington, on February 16, immediately after his arrival there from St. Louis, he sent her a letter which was like a pæan of victory. Greeted by all his friends in the capital as a statesman with a promising future, he had much reason to be complacent. Only a little over forty years of age, he had arrived at what he regarded as the highest position which a foreign-born citizen could reach—a position which, as he boasted, "No German before me has attained." It was just fifteen years since he had visited Washington for the first time, a stranger who could speak the English language only imperfectly. Now he was one of the rulers in his adopted land.

CHAPTER XIV SENATOR OF THE UNITED STATES

ON THE fourth of March, 1869, Carl Schurz, escorted by his rival, Senator Drake, walked down the aisle of the Senate Chamber [1] shortly after noon to be sworn into office by the new Vice President, Schuyler Colfax. In a few moments, the President-elect entered and was conducted to a seat in front of the Secretary's desk. Schurz then marched in the procession through the rotunda to the east front of the Capitol, where he watched Chief Justice Chase administer the oath to Ulysses S. Grant—a man who, a decade before, had been an obscure "ne'er-do-well," apparently without ability or hope, but whom the accident of war had transformed into a national hero. Andrew Johnson, sullen and unforgiving, had gone out of the White House alone, refusing to ride with his successor to the inauguration or to attend any of the ceremonies. The inaugural address, brief and noncommittal, inaudible to all but a few, aroused little enthusiasm, although Schurz thought that it "breathed a rugged honesty of purpose." When it was over, the Senators returned to their Chamber for a short session. Thus Schurz began his senatorial career—described correctly by James Ford Rhodes as "the brightest and most useful part of his very useful and interesting life." [2] It lasted only one term, until 1875, and, before it closed, Schurz was a political "free lance," out of sympathy with the administration and the "regu-

[1] The Senate Chamber, in the North Wing of the Capitol, is a large rectangular room which has been occupied by the Senate since 1859. The famous bronze doors, by Crawford, had in 1869 only recently been hung. The general appearance of the Chamber, with its rich furniture, its decorations by Brumidi, and its semicircular rows of desks, divided by an aisle down the middle, was much the same in 1869 as it is today. Here the trial of President Johnson had been held only a few months before.

[2] Rhodes to Frederic Bancroft, June 10, 1906, printed in Howe, *James Ford Rhodes,* 131.

lars" in his party; but it gave him a place in history as an intelligent, independent, and honest legislator.

Schurz had come to Washington untrammeled by pledges, with lofty ideals and ambitions. "I have decided to be a distinguished Senator," he wrote his wife shortly after his election, "and that involves a great deal." Later, in his *Reminiscences*, he expressed the feeling with which he entered the Senate:

> I recorded a vow in my own heart that I would at least honestly endeavor to fulfill that duty; that I would conscientiously adhere to the principle *salus populi suprema lex;* that I would never be a sycophant of power nor a flatterer of the multitude; that, if need be, I would stand up alone for my conviction of truth and right; and that there would be no personal sacrifice too great for my devotion to the Republic.

He at once took up the study of international law and requested his brother-in-law, Adolph Meyer, to send him from Europe a selected list of works on economics and diplomacy, together with volumes dealing with East India, China, and Japan. In his committee work, Schurz was conscientious and reliable, and could be depended upon to complete an assigned duty promptly. Fortunately, he had prospered in his journalistic ventures, and, by the autumn of 1869, had paid off his original obligation to the *Westliche Post* and accumulated a surplus. Although he was a Senator, he could still continue as an editor, and was thus freer from financial embarrassment than he had ever been before.

Schurz entered the Senate as a marked man. He was recognized as the leading German-American, whose good will was worth cultivating. He had been temporary chairman of the Republican convention. His recent contest with Drake in Missouri had attracted the attention of the country, and he was favorably known in many sections through his political speeches and lectures. When he was allotted seat Number 2 in the front row, second from the wall on the Vice President's left, many appraising glances were turned in his direction. On his right was another new member, "Parson" Brownlow, of Tennessee, whom he described as "a half-paralyzed old man, who shakes continually"; on his left was the shrewd John Pool, of North Carolina. As he looked around, Schurz could see many faces already familiar to him: Charles Sumner, handsome, egotistical, fanatical, humorless, who was to be his staunchest friend on the floor; Roscoe Conkling, the floridly pompous New York politician, with his blond beard and theatrical manner; Oliver H. P. Morton, of Indiana, the spokesman of the Grant administration, physically disabled, but autocratic, driven on by his iron will; the bluff and practical Zachariah Chandler, of Michigan, another champion of the President, who understood and practised the doctrine that every man has his price; Lyman Trumbull, from Illinois, a bespectacled, scholarly-looking personage, dignified and incorruptible; and a group of experienced leaders, including Simon Cameron, Hannibal Hamlin—who had been Lincoln's first Vice President—Henry Wilson, and the two Vermonters, George F. Edmunds and Justin S. Morrill. Among the Democrats, the chief were Allen G. Thurman, of Ohio, with his shaggy whiskers, firm lips, and massive leonine figure, and Thomas F. Bayard, of Delaware, tactful, cultured, and sagacious, a gentleman even when party passions flamed highest. A few weeks later, in February, 1870, the conservatives were to be startled by the entrance of a Negro, Hiram R. Revels, elected by an ironic touch to fill the seat once held by Jefferson Davis as Senator from Mississippi.[1]

Charles Sumner, chairman of the important Committee on Foreign Affairs, exerted all his influence to have Schurz appointed to that committee, but there was no immediate vacancy. "It was generally recognized that I belonged on that committee," Schurz wrote to his wife, "and there is no doubt

[1] In what was the first of many cartoons with Schurz as a principal figure, Thomas Nast showed Revels sitting at his desk, with Wilson, Schurz, Morton, and Sumner gathered around him, while "Jeff" Davis, in the costume of Iago, laments that the "lusty Moor" has leaped into his seat.

that as soon as a place is open I shall be given it." When the high-minded William Pitt Fessenden, of Maine, died in September, 1869, Schurz took his assignment on the Foreign Affairs Committee, where he was associated with Cameron, Morton, Harlan, of Iowa, Patterson, of New Hampshire, Casserly, of California, and Sumner. Schurz was also appointed to three other standing committees: Military Affairs, under Wilson, as chairman; Pensions, headed by Edmunds; and Territories, the chairman of which was James W. Nye, of Nevada. On the whole, Schurz had nothing to complain of in his assignments, which were rather better than a new man could expect to receive. Soon, moreover, he was to be named as a member of the Joint Select Committee on Retrenchment, which was to have much to do during the session. Inexperienced in legislation, he was astonished at the amount of work to be done. Before ten o'clock in the morning, he sometimes received twenty-five or thirty callers, most of them hungry for offices; letters came to him "in heaps" three times a day; and he often had to sit up until two o'clock in the morning, in order to avoid being swamped by his correspondence.

Schurz had every reason for being well disposed towards Grant, but it was not long before the two men, so different in their philosophies and aims, were to be openly at odds. The causes of friction were soon apparent. Although Grant's nominee for Secretary of the Treasury, the merchant, Alexander T. Stewart, was ratified promptly by the Senate, someone discovered that he was disqualified through an act of Congress, dated September 2, 1789, providing that anybody engaged in commerce should be ineligible to that office. Grant, much annoyed, sent a special message asking that Stewart be exempted, by joint resolution of the two Houses of Congress, from the operation of the troublesome measure.[1] Sherman promptly introduced a bill to meet the situation. At that moment, Charles

[1] Schurz, calling on Grant on March 6 to present him a congratulatory message from some of his St. Louis constituents, found him drafting this message on half a sheet of note paper, and soon withdrew.

Sumner rose from his seat to object to its immediate consideration, and nothing could be done. The incident seemed unimportant, but it was the preliminary skirmish to a prolonged battle. For the first time, the administration had faced opposition, and Henry Adams wrote to his brother, Charles, "Grant has made Congress madder than the devil." [1] There was a consultation in the Senate ante-chamber, and someone rushed hastily off to urge Grant to yield. Eventually Stewart withdrew, and the President named George S. Boutwell as Secretary of the Treasury.

Writing of the President's attitude in this affair, Schurz said, "He seemed to imagine that the republic could be governed somewhat like an army." Schurz felt, nevertheless, that Grant was "honest enough to see his mistakes, and manly enough to correct them at once." In the early winter, Schurz was often at the White House and was sure that he and the President would "get along well together." But conditions were soon to change. By the following spring, Henry Adams, worried because everything had "gone wrong," wrote to Gaskell, "My hopes of the new administration have all been disappointed; it is far inferior to the last." It was not long before Carl Schurz was ready to confirm this judgment.

In the Senate, Schurz had, for the first time, an opportunity to turn his passion for reform into workable channels. Instinctively he desired all his life to improve conditions around him, and he was untiring as an advocate of basic principles of humanity, equality, and justice. Only at rare intervals, however, was he allowed to put his theories into practice. Some idealists waver lamentably when confronted with definite problems, but Schurz did not quail or evade responsibility. We find him, from 1869 to 1875, insisting on a liberal policy towards the South, upholding sound money, protesting against a misguided imperialism, condemning an unduly severe protective tariff, and demanding honesty in government administration. In each one of these aims he accomplished something, both

[1] *Letters of Henry Adams*, 152.

then and later; but he was even more closely identified with the movement for civil service reform, which first took definite shape during Grant's administration.

The so-called spoils system, by which, with each change of party domination, a large number of public offices were distributed to victorious party workers, had existed since the days of Andrew Jackson, as a curse to all those who had any control over patronage. President William H. Harrison had been harried by insistent office seekers into his grave. Daniel Webster complained bitterly in his letters of the ordeal to which he was subjected by importunate and deserving Whigs. Lincoln himself, pointing out to a friend the greedy mob of office seekers in the White House corridors, said, "There you see something which in course of time will become a greater danger to the Republic than the rebellion itself." Schurz had seen how, in 1861, when Democrats gave way to Republicans, thousands of politicians had marched on Washington to secure jobs for themselves and their friends. The situation was probably even worse in 1869, a period of which Horace White wrote, "The civil service was honeycombed with whiskey rings, custom-house frauds, assessments on officeholders, nepotism, and general uncleanness."

Some attempts to eradicate the abuses of "rotation in office" had been made by Representative Thomas A. Jenckes, of Rhode Island, "the father and pioneer of civil service reform," who, as early as 1865, had proposed certain corrective measures in the House, only to have them derisively swept aside by practical politicians. In 1866, through his insistence, a Joint Select Committee on Retrenchment had been created to investigate the operation of the patronage system, and had presented two excellent reports, one on January 31, 1867, the other on May 14, 1868. Broadly speaking, it was suggested that appointments should be made on the basis of examinations, that partisan influence should be minimized and eventually eliminated, and that the tenure of office should be during good behavior.

As Schurz listened to the office seekers who swarmed around him "like grasshoppers," allowing him no time to read the newspapers or to meditate, he asked himself whether such an ordeal was inevitable. "If I have ever been convinced of the necessity of civil service reform, I am so now," he wrote on March 12. Thus it came about that his first speech in the Senate was made on that cause with which, during the remainder of his career, he was to be especially identified.

The Tenure of Office Act, passed during the heated controversy between President Johnson and the Senate, had forbidden the President to remove officials named by him with the Senate's advice, except by the consent of the Upper House. It was naturally distasteful to the somewhat dictatorial Grant, who, conceiving himself to be the leader of his party, requested its repeal. A measure to that effect quickly passed the House, but opposition developed in the Senate, which was jealous of its prerogative. Schurz, feeling that complete repeal would at that moment be unwise, spoke in the Senate on Friday, March 19, following Scott, of Pennsylvania, and urging the suspension of the Tenure of Office Act. He did this mainly, he explained, in order to gain time for the formulation of a comprehensive plan which would do away with the spoils system, and supersede it by a scheme of appointment on the basis of merit only. Schurz's remarks, covering less than half an hour, were received with courteous attention. As usual, he was complacent after the event. "When I closed," he wrote, "the Senators, particularly the old ones, pressed about my seat to shake hands with me." On that very day, Schurz was appointed by the Vice President as a member from the Senate of the Joint Committee on Retrenchment, which had the civil service under its jurisdiction. "Here is a great field," he wrote Mrs. Schurz on April 12, "and I hope to become the leader of reform in the Senate."

The session adjourned on April 10, but Schurz was obliged to remain in Washington while the Senate convened in executive session for confirming appointments, and he was not back in St. Louis until late in the month. Schurz had made a credit-

CARL SCHURZ IN 1871

able debut in a legislative body which is often cold to new members. Although he had delivered only one speech, that had demonstrated his ability, and he was now resolved to draft and put through a bill which would correct the evils which he had seen in Washington. By May 30, he had almost completed a plan the purpose of which was "to deal out offices according to ability and deserts, instead of personal and political favoritism."

While Carl Schurz was sweltering in St. Louis during the summer of 1869, there occurred in New York the conspiracy of two notorious speculators, Jay Gould and James Fisk, Jr., to make a corner in gold, with the aid of Corbin, Grant's brother-in-law, who hoped to delay or block the President's interposition. At the critical moment, however, Boutwell, Secretary of the Treasury, ordered a sale of gold from the government deposits, and the sinister plot collapsed, after a panic on what has ever since been known as "Black Friday"—September 24. The affair was of such a nature as to shake the confidence of a man like Schurz in Grant and his associates.

Congress reopened on December 6, for a long and stormy session lasting until July 15, 1870, during which the breach between Sumner and the President widened, Schurz, of course, supporting the former. On December 20, Schurz introduced a carefully framed bill embodying his ideas on civil service reform, based largely on the earlier recommendations of Congressman Jenckes, but covering a larger number of offices. It provided for a civil service board, whose business it would be to examine the qualifications of candidates for positions; for a year of probation for appointees, in order to determine whether they possessed practical ability; for a lengthening of the tenure of office so that there would not be a clean sweep with each incoming administration. In presenting his proposals, Schurz made a brief but effective speech, in the course of which he said, "The obstacles which such a reform will have to encounter and overcome are not unknown to me." He was supported on the floor by Sumner, Thurman, and Bayard, but they could not cope with the inertia and selfishness of many of the other members, who suspected Schurz's motives and sneered at "snivel service reform." Schurz's bill was referred in due course to the Joint Committee on Retrenchment and was finally, on June 10, "passed over."

The seed had been sown, however, and was soon to germinate and bear fruit. In his annual message of December, 1870, Grant, possibly influenced by heavy Republican losses in the autumn elections, recommended some change in the methods of civil service appointments; and Senator Lyman Trumbull inserted a provision in one of the appropriation acts authorizing the President to appoint a commission to regulate the entire system. Schurz, making a most interesting speech on January 27, 1871, painted a dramatic picture of the way in which the whole machinery of government had to be taken to pieces after the accession of a new administration, but objected to Trumbull's bill on the ground that it was not sufficiently comprehensive and moved as a substitute his own measure of the previous session.[1] The Senate, however, preferred Trumbull's bill, which was passed on March 3. On the following day, the President named seven members of a Civil Service Commission, headed by George William Curtis, and the machinery was established for improving conditions. As Schurz well knew, however, the practical politicians by whom Grant was surrounded and controlled had no intention of parting with one of their strongest weapons—their patronage. The commission submitted on December 18, 1871, a thoroughgoing report, suggesting rules for competitive examinations, which were approved by the President and formally promulgated in April, 1872.[2] By that date, some of the most zealous reformers, including Schurz himself, were enemies of the Administration,

[1] Schurz did not expect that his plan would pass. Writing on February 3, 1871, to Jacob D. Cox, he said, "Of course, there is no hope of carrying a plan like that which I propose in the present Congress, but we can in any event work on public opinion." *Writings,* II, 177.

[2] One of Nast's cartoons of this period shows Grant handing a spoonful of "Civil Service Broth" to a group of reformers—Schurz, Sumner, Trumbull,

and the supporters of the spoils system were able to block and nullify the work of the commission by declining to vote the necessary appropriations for putting its plan into operation, and the rules so carefully drawn were, as Curtis admitted, never made really effective. Grant was himself at heart a spoilsman, and the patronage was employed for the benefit of the Republican Party so long as he remained in power.

Schurz's serious quarrel with the Grant administration arose in connection with the desire of the President to annex Santo Domingo to the United States. It was primarily this issue which ultimately thrust Schurz into a position as leader of the "Liberal Republicans," in revolt against the regular party organization, and won him the title, which he never lost, of an "Independent in Politics." Shortly after Congress adjourned in the spring of 1869, Grant sent as his agent to Santo Domingo a somewhat indiscreet and not altogether incorruptible army officer, General Orville E. Babcock, who, although unauthorized to do so, eventually executed treaties with agents of the Dominican Republic, dated December 3, 1869, providing for its annexation to the United States. There was an element of comedy and opera bouffe about the affair, but its humorous aspects were not apparent to men like Schurz, who felt that, on general principles, all extension of our territories into the tropics should be avoided.

Although the suggestion was coldly received by the Cabinet, Grant, who was loyal to his subordinates and eager to gain prestige for his administration, made up his mind to insist on the adoption of the Babcock treaties and openly exerted all his influence to secure their passage in the Senate. It was essential, of course, to make sure of the fidelity of the Senate Committee on Foreign Relations. Accordingly, early in January, 1870, the President called on Senator Sumner, the chairman, while the latter was at dinner with two notoriously gossipy journalists—John W. Forney, whom Andrew Johnson had characterized as

Fenton, and others—dressed as small boys, saying as he does so, "If you can stand it I can."

a "dead duck," and Benjamin Perley Poore. After an adjournment to the library, Grant, undisturbed by the presence of guests, brought up the subject of the treaties, saying that, as they would shortly come before Sumner's committee, he wished to urge the latter to support them. His language was vague and general; and the interview closed by Sumner's saying, with equal lack of definiteness, "Mr. President, I am an administration man, and whatever you do will always find in me the most careful and candid consideration." Sumner undoubtedly thought that he was reaffirming his Republican allegiance but not committing himself in details. Forney, however, had some question as to what Sumner had actually promised; and Grant, believing that he had the Massachusetts Senator's backing, was later all the more angry when he imagined himself betrayed.

By sending the treaties to the Senate on January 10, 1870, the President gave them his official sanction, and the regular Republicans, fearing another controversy between the executive and legislative branches, set to work to secure their ratification. But when Sumner laid them before the Committee on Foreign Relations, to which they had been referred, only Morton favored them. The President, always obstinate under opposition, now did his best to subdue it. In late January, at a reception at the house of Colonel Forney, Grant walked across the room to greet Schurz, saying "Senator, you have not called to see me at the White House for some time, and I have been wanting to speak to you." Schurz made a conventional reply, but, when the President repeated his remark, the Senator could not ignore the invitation. On the following evening, Schurz was ushered into the President's library, where Grant, sitting beside him on a sofa, urged him to support the Santo Domingo treaties. It was an embarrassing moment, but Schurz, never a coward, came out frankly with his views, declaring that, while he wanted to act with the administration whenever he could conscientiously do so, he was convinced that the annexation of Santo Domingo would be "against the best interests of the republic." More explicitly, he stressed the dangers involved in the acquisition of territory in the tropics, with its perilous racial problems; and he expressed the opinion that, since the treaties could not command the necessary two-thirds vote in the Senate, the administration would blunder by committing itself irrevocably. It was sound advice, to which the President listened for a few moments attentively; but soon his eyes wandered, and he looked restless, even bored. Grant did not like to be admonished or preached at. After Schurz had finished, there was silence. Then the President, as if all was harmony between them, said, "Well, I hope you will at least vote for the confirmation of Mr. Jones, whom I have selected for a foreign mission." [1]

Although the annexation project seemed to unprejudiced observers to be hopeless, the President was exasperatingly pertinacious; nor, on the other hand, were Schurz and Sumner willing to yield. Grant accused Sumner of having broken a pledge to support him, and the two men, so wide apart in birth, education, and culture, were soon open foes. Sumner, enraged, would follow a guest to the door of his home, bellowing "like a bull of Bashan" in denunciation of the President. Schurz once later, leaving the Arlington Hotel, looked up at the second story of the house which Sumner had formerly owned and said: "Ah, how many long evenings I have passed with Sumner up there in his library! It was there we planned the defeat of Grant's plan to annex Santo Domingo." On the other hand, Grant, strolling one evening with Senator Hoar past Sumner's residence, shook his clenched fist at the silent windows and burst out, "The man who lives up there has abused me in a way which I have never suffered from any other man living."

For the delay in the Senate committee, Grant, not altogether

[1] During this period two White House emissaries separately approached Schurz to tell him that, if he would aid the President on the Santo Domingo annexation project, he could have all the patronage he wanted. Apparently this naïf attempt at bribery was made at Grant's instigation and with his full approval. Schurz, *Writings,* II, 403. Schurz also said of Grant, "He actually did descend to the role of lobbyist. I have seen him in that capacity myself." Schurz, *Writings,* II, 418.

justly, blamed Sumner, who was now marked for sacrifice. On March 15, the Foreign Affairs Committee reported adversely, Harlan being the only member to join Morton in favor of ratification. The debate which followed, held in secret session, was opened by Sumner in a brilliant speech four hours long. Schurz also spoke eloquently in opposition, although his words were not taken down. During the next few weeks, every conceivable kind of pressure was brought to bear by the Chief Executive, who, in his last extremity, even sent another message, on May 31, dwelling on the advantages to be gained from annexation. After an interval, discussion was resumed on June 29,[1] and a vote on the next afternoon resulted in a tie, 28 to 28. Sumner and Schurz had successfully resisted the presidential will. On the following morning, Grant took a shameless revenge by asking for the resignation of Sumner's close friend, Motley, from his post as Minister to England.

It was not Schurz's fault that his once amicable relations with the President were ruptured. On July 17, 1870, two days after this stormy session closed, he wrote to Grant, saying, "I am painfully sensible of the change which our personal relations have suffered in consequence of our difference on the Santo Domingo treaty," and declaring that rumors that he had attacked Grant in the secret sessions of the Senate were "unqualifiedly untrue." Pointing out that the outbreak of the Franco-Prussian War had brought to him many invitations to address gatherings of German-Americans, he stated that he wished to have a fair understanding between the administration and himself, and he reaffirmed his loyalty to the President. Schurz's request for an interview was promptly granted, but no record of what was said has been preserved. The two men were so far estranged that no permanent reconciliation was

[1] On this day Schurz made a personal explanation to his colleagues. A Washington correspondent had said that the protocol preliminary to the Santo Domingo Treaty had been inserted in the report of the investigating committee in a mysterious way, and accused Schurz of having shown the protocol to the committee "with the deliberate purpose of stabbing the President." Schurz was able to exonerate himself completely.

possible.

Other factors also were tending at this time to make Schurz dissatisfied with the policies of the administration. A theoretical free trader, he had joined with William Cullen Bryant, E. L. Godkin, Horace White, David A. Wells, and others in establishing the American Free Trade League, in 1869; and he had been greatly disappointed by the passage in 1870 of the Schenck Bill, which, although adding several articles to the free list, was really a measure for high protection. Schurz's innate liberalism made him object to any plan which tended to foster one industry or interest at the expense of another. The administration had approved the Schenck Bill, and Grant showed no desire to reduce duties.

Still another basic issue was reconstruction, on which, oddly enough, Schurz showed himself more liberal and generous than Grant, thus reversing conditions in 1866. Influenced by radicals like Morton and Conkling, the President cared more for establishing Republicanism in the South than for conciliating the Southerners, and insisted on a vigorous repression of Southern discontent. Schurz, meanwhile, had become a champion of amnesty and of the restoration of home rule in the South. In December, 1869, Virginia, Mississippi, and Texas, the only three Southern states still outside the Union, made formal application to Congress for readmission. When the question of Virginia was taken up, Schurz, although he had intended to be silent on the reconstruction program, spoke in the Senate on January 14, 1870, urging the restoration of good feeling by the reinstatement of former "rebels" in their political rights. Here was the true Schurz—not the bitter irreconcilable who had opposed Andrew Johnson in 1865, but the enlightened liberal who was now able to see that the Negro question was more complex than he had thought. In this Virginia matter, Schurz was opposed to Sumner, who, as usual, tried to make the readmission of that state as difficult as possible.

Two months later, when the radicals in Congress attempted

to interfere with affairs in Georgia by prolonging the legislature for two more years, in defiance of the state constitution, Schurz spoke (March 18, 1870) contending that, if the laws could not be enforced otherwise, the only proper remedy was to hand Georgia over to military rule—a policy which, in his opinion, would needlessly alienate public sentiment in the South. He returned to this theme on April 19, in a plea for constitutional government, and an appeal to loyal citizens in the South to accept peaceably the results of the war. Broadly speaking, Schurz had progressed to a point where, while insisting that the Negro must be protected in his newly acquired rights and privileges, he was convinced that the wisest attitude towards the former Confederates was "forgive and forget." His position was halfway between that of Sumner and that of such a Southern adherent as Thurman.

The opposition to Grant, even among good Republicans, had grown rapidly among free traders, tariff reformers, and advocates of a liberal policy towards the South. The Santo Domingo incident had alienated others, and the President's ignorance of public affairs had disgusted some of his former supporters. He had proved to be an unswerving partisan, the easy tool of self-seeking politicians, and had made many scandalously unfit appointments. "All administrations, I suppose, are more or less corrupt," wrote Whitelaw Reid to John Bigelow. "Certainly the depth of corruption this one has reached is scarcely suspected as yet, even by its enemies." [1] Schurz, however, knew what was going on, and, by the late summer of 1870, was prepared for a fight to the finish with Grant.

It was in Missouri, and largely at Schurz's instigation, that the revolt against Grantism first took definite shape. The main question at issue in the state election of 1870 was that of the removal of political disabilities from those who had recently been in arms against the Union. The Republican Party had pledged itself to the removal of all disqualifications and disabilities just as soon as pacification should be complete. That

[1] Cortissoz, *The Life of Whitelaw Reid,* I, 204.

stage had, Schurz felt, been reached in Missouri. The Republican State Convention, held at Jefferson City, on August 31, was a radical body, unwilling to declare itself unequivocally for the enfranchisement of those concerned in the rebellion. When the state of affairs was evident, Schurz, with two hundred and fifty delegates of liberal views, withdrew, organized a separate convention, and, refusing all overtures for compromise, nominated B. Gratz Brown, a veteran anti-slavery man who had served from 1863 to 1867 as Democratic senator from Missouri, for governor, and issued a forceful *Address to the People of Missouri*, with Schurz's name heading the list of signers. The regular convention, in the meantime, had renominated Governor Joseph W. McClurg. In the campaign which followed the Democrats had no candidate, but lent their support to Brown.

Schurz evidently hoped not to antagonize the national administration, but it was soon apparent that Grant meant to exert all his influence in favor of McClurg. Pressure was brought to bear on all federal officeholders to support the regular organization by cash contributions and other aid. Writing to the Collector at St. Louis, the President expressed his disapproval of the liberal movement, adding, "I hope you will see your way clear to give the regular ticket your support." Schurz, explaining to Senator Matthew H. Carpenter why he could not go to Wisconsin, said, on October 20: "You do not seem to be aware that Grant has read me out of the Republican Party and is vigorously at work chopping off the official heads of those who are suspected of sympathizing with me. Under such circumstances I have to fight right here."

Despite the interference of the administration, Brown was elected by a majority of more than forty thousand, and the amendments to the State constitution giving the suffrage to former "rebels" were passed by a large vote. Brown himself wrote to Schurz, "I, more perhaps than any one else, realize that in this great victory in Missouri you were the true hero, and that for our success we were more indebted to your prudence, sagacity, and indomitable canvass than to all other causes combined." In the same letter, Brown declared, "Our fight . . . was for State reform, revenue reform, and civil service reform, and we had the right to make those issues as Republicans." [1] Senator Morrill wrote to Sumner, begging him to restrain Schurz from breaking with the Republican Party. But Schurz knew that the breach could not be mended. When he called at the White House in December, 1870, he was refused admittance. Political ostracism had begun.

Once back in Washington, Schurz seized the earliest opportunity for a public declaration of his independence. He introduced, on December 12, 1870, a resolution calling for the removal of "the disqualifications and disabilities imposed upon persons lately in rebellion against the Government of the United States"; and, three days later, he edified his senatorial colleagues by a summary of the events in Missouri during the preceding summer and autumn. Frankly avowing that he had as much as any one man to do with the party schism, he blamed the President for the administration defeat in Missouri, defended his own conduct, and presented an eloquent justification of political independence. In phrases which must have annoyed Morton and Conkling, he asserted: "I recognize objects in political life superior to the immediate advantage of party. . . . I have never been able to look up to a party as a deity that has supernatural claims upon my veneration." He even declared that he did not regard the possibility of organizing a new party as anything "particularly criminal." He warned his senatorial colleagues that "the only way to preserve the vitality of the Republican Party is to make it the party of progressive reforms," announcing that, unless this were done, he was prepared to head a revolt. It was a courageous, even an audacious, speech, under the existing conditions, promulgating doctrines with which Schurz was to make his countrymen more familiar before he dropped out of public life.[2]

[1] *Writings,* I, 521–22.

[2] To Moses Coit Tyler, who called on him on December 27, 1870, Schurz

It needs no subtlety to understand Schurz's motives in breaking thus sharply with the Grant administration. Louis A. Coolidge, one of Grant's eulogists, has insisted that Schurz had "an insatiate appetite for opposition"—a charge which James G. Blaine had earlier made against him. But this is not an explanation. Schurz's liberal philosophy, his repulsion at political corruption, his sensitive moral nature—all these triumphed over party regularity. To him, a party was a means "of promoting the execution of certain measures of public good." When it ceased to do this, he had no longer any desire to be affiliated with it. Carl Schurz was neither a prig nor a hypocrite. He was a political idealist, with the passion of a crusader. It is not astonishing that Ulysses S. Grant did not understand him or approve of him.

talked freely of his political troubles saying, "I have taken my political life in my hand. I have resolved to act as if I were to end my career with this term in the Senate; be independent, true to my real convictions, and not hesitate to say and do what I think to be right on account of any regard for a reëlection. . . . I am going to have the luxury of doing what I think to be right." Of this conversation, Tyler declared, "This was said with a beautiful simplicity and sweetness of tone. He carried my heart. I think him quite sincere."

CHAPTER XV A LIBERAL IN REVOLT

WE MUST picture Carl Schurz at this phase of his career as a very busy legislator, presenting scores of petitions—often of a trivial character, dealing, for instance, with pensions—introducing more than his share of bills, attending committee meetings with punctuality, speaking frequently on all sorts of questions, and, in his rare leisure moments, corresponding with his fellow liberals and building up sentiment against Grant. He spent long hours in reading and research, adding to that store of information on American history and economics which made him so formidable in debate. By sheer persistence he had developed into a clever extemporaneous speaker, with an easy colloquial style quite different from the somewhat florid rhetoric of his earlier memorized orations. Only self-restraint kept him from indulging too freely in sarcasm and abuse, which he could on occasions employ with telling effect; but he did, we are told, avoid "mere personalities and unreasoned invective" except when exasperated by the thrusts of his opponents. In the heat of controversy, he was alert, unperturbed, corrosive, never losing sight of the thread of argument and always ready with some convincing or withering retort. Unlike Sumner, he was never solemn or pompous, and he did not exaggerate. A gift of crisp and vivid phrasing held the interest of his listeners. Finally, behind all that he said was a sincerity, a deadly earnestness, which gave him an advantage over time-serving or hypocritical adversaries.[1]

He had won recognition as the outstanding spokesman of the German-American population of America and as one of the uncompromising liberal thinkers of his generation. Prac-

[1] Charles A. Dana, editor of the New York *Sun,* who disliked Schurz's aims and policies, once heard him deliver an oration and wrote afterwards, "Few persons know that this red-bearded Teuton has the eloquence of Demosthenes and the fire of Kossuth."

tical enough as a political manager, he could not be ignored by those whom he criticized; but he refused to make concessions on matters which seemed to him vital. He still continued his work for a reformed civil service, for a generous plan of reconstruction, and for sound money; but always in the back of his mind was the hope that he might be able to overthrow the Grant regime, which he believed to be a corrupting scourge in American life. He was undoubtedly ahead of his time in his zeal for reform. He was, however, the herald of improved conditions and a better attitude toward government. What he was thinking for the moment is well expressed in a letter written on February 3, 1871, to Jacob D. Cox, for some months Grant's Secretary of the Interior. After pointing out that the Republican Party was "drifting into great dangers," he added, "There is an attempt being made to create the impression that the Republican Party can be successful only if General Grant is nominated. Tell me, do the people of Ohio think that the fortunes of the party depend on one single individual?" This was obviously a hint, and more than a hint, that Schurz was to support another candidate in 1872.

Grant was never convinced that the brute persistence which had been so successful against General Lee in the Wilderness would not be equally effective in political affairs. In his annual message in December, 1870, after the Democrats had won sweeping victories in New York and Indiana, he reiterated his belief that Santo Domingo should be annexed. To pacify him, it was agreed to introduce a resolution authorizing the appointment of a commission of inquiry. Then Charles Sumner, still implacable, rose to deliver his famous philippic, beginning, "The resolution before the Senate commits Congress to a dance of blood." He declared that the President had planned to reorganize the Committee on Foreign Relations—removing Sumner himself from the chairmanship and dropping Schurz—but had learned that the elimination of the latter would lose the administration many German supporters. Sumner's bitter eloquence was quoted everywhere but changed no votes. The resolution was passed in the Senate, with many of that body deliberately absent, and was approved by the House with an amendment providing that such action must not be construed as expressing a desire on the part of Congress for annexation. When this was returned to the Senate, Carl Schurz, on January 11, 1871, made a ringing speech, ridiculing the proposed commission and ending with the warning, "Do not touch a scheme like this; do not trifle with that which may poison the future of this great nation; beware of the tropics." Congress passed the measure by joint resolution. The commission, composed of Andrew D. White, Benjamin F. Wade, and Samuel G. Howe, made a report favorable to annexation. But the matter was quietly shelved when it was ascertained that a sufficient number of votes could not be commandeered for the administration plan. Sumner, Schurz, and their adherents had defeated the President, but the Massachusetts Senator was to pay a heavy penalty.

The Forty-first Congress died on March 3, 1871, but the Forty-second Congress assembled immediately in special session. Sumner had been growing more and more arrogant and abusive, and Grant insisted on his punishment. When the slate was prepared for the Republican caucus in the Senate, Sumner's name did not appear on the Committee on Foreign Relations, Simon Cameron being designated in his place, as chairman. Schurz protested, moved in vain for a postponement, and insisted that Senator Howe make an explanation. The reply was that Sumner had ceased to represent the views of a majority of his party in the Senate and that he was no longer on such terms with the President and the Secretary of State as would permit the proper attention to government business. This answer had some justification; indeed such an authority as Charles Francis Adams has defended the removal of Sumner on grounds of expediency. But it did not please Carl Schurz. The final vote, taken on March 9, was 26 to 21 in favor of the substitution of Cameron for Sumner. Grant was that night "in high glee." It was his turn to rejoice.

The ill-fated Santo Domingo scheme was to raise its head

once more. In late March, Sumner, returning to the attack, introduced resolutions condemning the action of the administration in using the American navy to sustain Baez, the Dominican revolutionist, in power, in anticipation, apparently, of the ratification of the Babcock Treaties. Sumner's speech—a masterpiece of vituperation—was delivered before an audience of more than two thousand people, who cheered him noisily as he entered the chamber. It was answered by Morton and Howe; and then Schurz came to Sumner's aid in a speech which covered two days—March 28 and 29—and which was later entitled, "Grant's Usurpation of the War Powers." Interrupted by questions from his opponents regarding details of the history of the United States, Schurz showed himself remarkably well informed and amazingly quick in repartee. Although of foreign birth and education, he was at no disadvantage in disputing with Morton, Stewart, Frelinghuysen, and Howe. When Morton, the administration whip, advanced a precedent from President Tyler's procedure prior to the annexation of Texas, Schurz was able to show that the utmost Tyler had done was to inform the Mexican Government that certain acts would be regarded by our country as unfriendly gestures. Grant, on the other hand, had ordered an American rear admiral to take belligerent measures against Hayti, a foreign and friendly power. Schurz's speech did not accomplish the passage of Sumner's resolutions, and merely widened the breach between himself and the President, already so wide that the two men never met afterward except in very casual and formal ways.

On another matter arising out of the difficulties of reconstruction, Schurz found himself, oddly enough, out of touch with both Grant and Sumner. He had already in Missouri constituted himself the champion of amnesty toward former "rebels." When, on March 28, the so-called "Ku-Klux Act" was introduced in the House, authorizing the President at his discretion to declare in rebellion any sections infested by the Ku-Klux Klan and granting him the right to suspend the *habeas corpus* and to suppress disorders by calling upon the army,

Schurz was horrified. The bloody shirt, then so potent in stirring loyal Republicans to rally around the party standard, was waved again. Grossly extravagant statements were being made, and all the old familiar hatreds were aroused. Schurz, thinking the proposed act to be both impolitic and unconstitutional, hoped to modify some of its worst features, and, to this end, made, on April 14, a speech which Horace White described as "a masterpiece of political philosophy." The situation in the South, as Schurz saw it, was "one of those second fermentations which almost uniformly follow great civil convulsions"; and he was willing to trust, for its amelioration, "to that natural process which will gradually develop and educate public sentiment in the South, as to the true interests of Southern society." To us today the measure seems despotic and unnecessary, but it was defended by Charles Sumner. The fanatical Senator from Massachusetts has sometimes been called a great statesman, and his official biography stretches over four volumes; but Carl Schurz, the German emigrant, was, during this period, far superior to Charles Sumner in those attributes of mind which appeal to reasonable men. It was not a period, however, when reason held sway. What Schurz called "the insane Ku-Klux legislation" was made by the radical leaders a test of party loyalty, and was passed on April 20, 1871, just before Congress adjourned.

With the most important matter of this session, that of the attempt at adjustment of the *Alabama* claims, Schurz apparently had little to do. Sumner, while chairman of the Committee on Foreign Relations, had absurdly insisted that no arrangement could be made with Great Britain for the settlement of the damage caused by the *Alabama* and other cruisers during the Civil War which did not involve "the withdrawal of the British flag . . . from this hemisphere, including provinces and islands." This ridiculous, indeed almost insane stipulation, had resulted, naturally enough, in a clash between Sumner and Hamilton Fish, the Secretary of State, who had the vision and good judgment which Sumner lacked. The Presi-

By Thomas Nast in Harper's Weekly, *1872*

THE DISAFFECTED SENATORS—SCHURZ, FENTON, TRUMBULL, SUMNER AND TIPTON—CONSIDER THE SELECTION OF MR. GREELEY AS THEIR PRESIDENTIAL CANDIDATE

dent and Fish decided virtually to ignore Sumner; an agreement was reached with England for a joint high commission, which met in Washington on February 27, 1871; and, as the outcome of these friendly deliberations, the Treaty of Washington was signed in May and quickly ratified by the Senate, Schurz voting in its favor.

The special session of the Senate was over in late May, 1871, and Schurz devoted the ensuing summer to the arduous task of organizing and directing the group who had come to be known as "Liberal Republicans." He could not count on the support of many federal office holders; but the critics of the administration were ready to rally at his call. He could rely on some of his senatorial colleagues, including Lyman Trumbull, of Illinois, Orris S. Ferry, of Connecticut, and Thomas W. Tipton, of Nebraska. There was much dissatisfaction among leading liberal newspaper editors, represented by Horace Greeley, of the New York *Tribune,* Murat Halstead, of the Cincinnati *Commercial,* Horace White, of the Chicago *Tribune,* and Samuel Bowles, intrepid head of the Springfield *Republican.* E. L. Godkin, of the *Nation,* was also one of Schurz's correspondents and advisers. It was Schurz's hope at first that he might be able to bring about some concerted action among these leaders which would block Grant's nomination for a second term by the Republicans. He had not as yet abandoned the party, but he wrote Sumner on August 14, 1871, that it could be saved only "by making it the party of reforms and by suppressing the bad influences governing it." Two days before this letter, he had made at Chicago a brilliant speech declaring that he would not vote for Grant for a reëlection and outlining the liberal creed to which he proposed to adhere.

By September 20, when he spoke at Nashville, he had crossed the Rubicon and, in a frank and forceful address, later published under the significant title, "The Need of Reform and a New Party," summarized the evils of Grantism and urged the formation of a third party, drawing its strength from the better elements among Republicans and Democrats. As a possible program, he suggested a general amnesty to Southerners, the encouragement of local self-government in the South, a reform of the civil service, a reduction in the tariff, a return to specie payments, and a more effective control of corporations. Schurz's correspondence indicates that he was aiding in the establishment of liberal clubs at several strategical points, especially in the South and Middle West. He spoke at Louisville and Cincinnati in October; and, when he visited New York City in November, he was hailed by the *Herald* as "the great political missionary, laboring for the defeat of General Grant next year." He found obstacles, of course; timid souls, who shrunk from deserting the regular organization; selfish men, who asked only what they were to get out of a repudiation of Grant; and, worst of all, the Laodiceans, held back by inertia or indifferentism from any positive activity. But Schurz returned for the reopening of Congress on December 4 in a very optimistic mood. Of all the liberals in Congress, he was perhaps the only one at that time definitely committed to the policy of a new party. There was then still a possibility that some of the regular organization leaders might be converted. As the winter passed, however, it was clear that the administration had its henchmen well under control and that Grant could not possibly be beaten as the Republican nominee.

During this session of 1871–72 the insurgent movement steadily gained momentum. The atmosphere of the Capitol was "heavily charged with cynicism and corruption," and Schurz and his coterie were alert for any opportunity of discrediting the administration spokesmen. The situation was clarified when, on January 24, 1872, the Liberal Republicans of Missouri, in their convention at Jefferson City, adopted a platform recommended by Schurz, including tariff readjustment, civil service reform, and a general amnesty, and issued a formal call for a national convention to be held on May 1, at Cincinnati. Here was something definite to build on. Schurz, with this date in mind, could devote himself now chiefly to bringing the more influential leaders of liberal thought to the convention.

Schurz had, meanwhile, plenty to do in the Senate besides his routine responsibilities. On January 30, he rose to speak at length in connection with a bill for the removal of legal and political disabilities imposed upon certain classes of Southerners, stating that "the reasons which make it desirable that there should be amnesty granted at all, make it also desirable that the amnesty should be universal." He made a cogent plea for the revival of a truly national spirit on the ruins of sectionalism, and for a genuine friendliness on the part of the North toward the South. This speech, though not often quoted, shows Schurz's natural tolerance and generosity of heart. It was thus that Lincoln would have spoken if he had lived.

Schurz received far more publicity, however, from the debate arising from a resolution presented by Sumner—aimed at the administration—asking that an investigation be instituted regarding the charge that American government officials had violated the rules of neutrality during the Franco-Prussian War by selling arms and munitions to France—a matter upon which Schurz, as a former Prussian, was very much aroused. After Sumner's introductory speech on February 13, several Senators rushed to the defense of the War Department, including the ostentatious Roscoe Conkling, who, in spite of his idiosyncracies, was no mean antagonist in debate. At Sumner's insistence, Schurz retaliated, supporting the resolution with an array of facts which dazzled his auditors.

On the 19th, Conkling, having made careful preparation, came forth once more as champion for the administration, and his rotund phrases stirred the galleries to applause. An oratorical duel was in progress in the tradition of Webster and Clay. Aware that he must assume the leadership of the Liberal Republicans, Schurz secured the floor for the following day. Mrs. Schurz, very much depressed by the fear that her husband might not be equal to the ordeal, refused to accompany him to the Capitol; [1] but we may be sure that he did not lack con-

[1] By this date, Mrs. Schurz had returned from Europe, but in poor health, and was settled with her family in Washington.

fidence. As he entered the corridors, he saw that every available space was occupied, and felt inspired. Never did he speak with more fire and fluency. When Mrs. Schurz, too nervous to remain quietly in her lodgings, walked to the Capitol to hear his concluding remarks, she found the great crowd pouring out through the doors; and Sumner, noticing her in the lobby, rushed up, seized her hand and shook it, and burst out: "Oh, madam, I congratulate you. Your husband has just made the greatest speech that has been heard in the Senate for twenty years."

There was an undertone of bitterness about this debate which indicated that the rival orators regarded it as the opening skirmish of the presidential campaign of 1872. Conkling asserted that no one owned the German-Americans; whereupon Schurz replied, "No politician owns them, no Senators do; not even the President of the United States; but least of all are the Germans of this country owned by that class of politicians who desperately cling to the skirts of power through whatever mire that skirt may be trailed." This was the clash of sword against sword. The climax came a little later, when Conkling accused Schurz of having secured secret information from the emissary of a foreign power, presumably Germany, and asserted that Schurz was "indulging in cowardly insinuations that the President was corrupt." In his irritation, he exceeded the bounds of good taste and ridiculed Schurz for "strutting about on the floor of the Chamber." This left an opening which Schurz, with all his self-restraint, could not neglect, and he responded:

If I did or said anything yesterday that looked like strutting, then I most sincerely beg the Senate's pardon; for I certainly did not want to encroach upon the exclusive privilege of my honorable and distinguished associate from New York. If I did and said anything like boasting, let me assure you, sir, that it was not the remark that "even if I met a thousand of his kind I would not quail"; for I would not consider that a striking demonstration of courage.

It was clear from this episode that the participants were "on edge." Half a century before a similar interchange of personalities often ended in a meeting on the "field of honor." As it was, the excessively vain Conkling was deeply hurt and never spoke to Schurz again. Aside from this estrangement, very little resulted from this clash of opposing leaders. A committee of investigation, from which Schurz, by what the *Nation* called "a scandalous piece of trickery," was excluded, held a number of hearings and eventually acquitted government officials of any wrongdoing. Not satisfied, Schurz made another speech at the end of May in the Senate, reiterating his previous accusations. But this affair, which was simply a means of discrediting the administration and of stirring up the German vote against it, had by that date ceased to interest anybody. When Congress adjourned on June 10, the average American citizen was absorbed in speculating how many votes Horace Greeley would poll for President against Ulysses S. Grant.

It was at this period that Thomas Nast, a naturalized German-American who had been born in 1840, at Landau, began caricaturing Schurz in *Harper's Weekly*, a periodical with which he had been associated since 1862. Nast's reputation had been made by the ferocious attacks which, since 1869, he had been making on Boss William M. Tweed and his coterie of Tammany grafters in New York City. When Tweed was arrested in the autumn of 1871, Nast's work in that field was over, and, with an irony quite unconscious, he became the defender of Grant and his administration against the assaults being made upon them. In spite of the protests and appeals of George William Curtis, the political editor of *Harper's*, Nast began the systematic ridicule of the anti-administration Senators, especially Sumner, Trumbull, and Schurz, increasing his boldness as their plans for forming a Liberal Republican Party became apparent. The course of events for the year 1872 may be traced in Nast's drawings in *Harper's*. On March 9, he showed Carl Schurz as Mephistopheles trying to arouse Sumner, as Faust, against the administration on the matter of the sale of war supplies to France. On April 6, he portrayed him as Don Quixote, attended by Senator Tipton, as Sancho Panza, tilting unsuccessfully against a windmill represented by the Capitol and being thrown from his donkey. On April 20, he depicted him as Man Friday, trying to persuade Sumner, as Robinson Crusoe, to go to the Cincinnati convention. When the investigation of the selling of arms to France was over, Nast printed, on May 11, a sketch called "Carl's boomerang," showing him being injured by the bursting of the gun with which he had expected to injure others. As the campaign of 1872 got under way, Nast's humor became more and more bitter, culminating, perhaps, on August 24, in a picture of Carl Schurz at the piano, the music of *Mein Herz ist am Rhein* before him, while Uncle Sam says to him, "Look here, stranger, there is no law in this country to compel you to stay." This was based on a statement published in the *Frankfort Gazette*, to the effect that Carl Schurz was "disgusted with American politics." In all the cartoons representing the anti-administration forces, Schurz was a conspicuous figure, easy to identify because of his long thin body, his bushy hair and whiskers, his spectacles, and his prominent teeth.

According to Nast's biographer, Albert Bigelow Paine, Schurz was infuriated by the caricatures of himself in *Harper's*. In March, 1872, when Nast was in Washington, he was introduced to Schurz, as a fellow German-American.

"You will not be allowed to continue your attacks on me," Schurz said, rather fiercely.

"Why not, Senator?" asked Nast.

"Your paper will not permit them!"

"Oh, I think it will," replied the artist pleasantly.

"Well, then, I will not!" declared Schurz, with a threatening air. "I shall publicly chastise you!"

As a matter of fact, Nast's caricatures made Schurz's strong and individual features known the country over, and probably injured him very little among people who knew him. Even *Harper's Weekly*, although denouncing his policies, spoke of him always with respect and conceded his own incorruptibility. He was dangerous; and that is why Nast did his best to annihilate him.

A series of incidents during the spring of 1872 provoked a rapidly heightening interest in the approaching campaign. Everywhere among politicians was an air of mystery, of suppressed excitement, of wild rumors and gossipy murmurings. Nast, on February 10, showed "Cincinnatus" Greeley, the farmer at the plough, receiving the presidential nomination from Greeley, the editor, while Schurz and Tipton look on with eager expectancy. On March 16, again, he sketched the "Liberal Conspirators"—Schurz, Sumner, Trumbull, and Tipton—in a scene from *Julius Cæsar*, trying to attach "Brutus" Greeley to their cause. All sorts of questions were being asked. What candidates were available for the Liberal Republicans? What would Sumner do? How far could Grant hold his followers together? What might be expected from the Democrats? A careful reading of *Harper's Weekly*, defending the Administration, and of the *Nation*, strongly against Grant, will prove that both sides were puzzled, like two chess players each awaiting an aggressive move from the other. All was uncertainty. Many of the regular Republican organization men were tempted to join the Liberals, but would not commit themselves until they were surer of their ground. A few had more courage and announced their defection. Even Horace Greeley himself was, in the early winter, uncertain of his course; but, on March 12, he wrote, "You see that I am drifting into a fight with Grant," and, on March 20, he issued a letter fully endorsing the third party movement. The culmination of the preliminary agitation was reached on April 12, at a mass meeting in Cooper Union. The principal speakers were Trumbull and Schurz, whose address, according to the *Nation*, was distinguished by "that powerful and *telling* rhetoric of which he is now the greatest master in America." Greeley made some extemporaneous remarks, declaring that he was going forward with the "non-office holding Republicans" to the Cincinnati convention, whatever its consequences. So alarmed were the regular Republicans that they called a similar gathering five days later, at which General "Dan" Sickles, as the chief orator, reviewed Schurz's career, referring contemptuously to his war record and calling him a foreigner "by profession."

In the spring of 1872, Carl Schurz was leading a rich and stimulating life, corresponding with scores of political leaders, keeping in close touch with all that was occurring, and doing what he enjoyed most—revolutionizing existing conditions. This Liberal Republicanism was his child, and he was its sponsor before the country. He had been the first important Republican to announce that he would not support Grant; the call for the Cincinnati convention had emanated at his suggestion from his own state; and he was recognized as the one who would dominate it. It pleased Carl Schurz to be regarded as a party chieftain. Once again he was Don Quixote, swept along by a crusader's zeal—a gallant, romantic knight, battling against the forces of reaction and corruption.

CHAPTER XVI GREELEY VERSUS GRANT

THE scene now shifts to Cincinnati, the "Queen City of the Ohio," where the drama of Liberal Republicanism was to reach its crisis—a crisis which was both farce and tragedy. Carl Schurz had seen party conventions and was familiar with their pageantry—the blare of bands, the waving of banners, the shouts of the multitude, the sudden outbursts of mob psychology, and, behind all the noise and color, the little groups of practical men, sitting in smoke-filled hotel rooms, directing the machinery, as a general and his staff send regiments from one position to another. Now, less than twenty years after setting foot on American soil, he was himself to manage a convention formed largely through his influence and intended to form a new party voicing "a general revolt against privilege and corruption." [1] The story of the rise and decline of Liberal Republicanism is also the sad tale of an idealist's disillusionment —a tale repeated only too often in a land where theoretical democracy has frequently been thwarted by sordid intrigue and the exigencies of political compromise.

More than anyone else in the United States, Carl Schurz was identified with and responsible for the Liberal Republican movement. He was its "leader and master mind," and, if he had been eligible under the Constitution, could doubtless have been named as its candidate for President. He himself favored Charles Francis Adams,[2] of Massachusetts—a gentleman of

[1] Bowers, *The Tragic Era,* 376. Mr. Bowers, using contemporary newspapers freely, has drawn in this book a vividly dramatic picture of the revolt against Grantism.

[2] Adams had sailed for Europe in late April, to complete his duties as American arbitrator at Geneva for the adjustment of the *Alabama* claims. Before leaving, he had written several letters to friends, disclaiming any desire to be President but saying that he would accept the nomination if it came to him unconditionally. His utterances were considered by many to be cold and unresponsive. See Henry Adams to Gaskell, April 27, 1872, in *Letters of Henry Adams,* 223–25.

culture, with a background of fine traditions, who had been first a Democrat and then a Whig, but was at heart, like Schurz, non-partisan—a dignified and wholly honorable figure, who, furthermore, would be likely to appeal to the Democrats, from whom Schurz hoped to get support.

Leaving Washington on April 27, Schurz was in Cincinnati on the following afternoon, and was given a tremendous greeting that evening by the German Branch of the Cincinnati Reunion and Reform Association. Cincinnati had a large population of Germans, who regarded Schurz as their hero. At this gathering he made a brief speech replying to the charge that he pretended to carry the German vote in his pocket.[1] "This amounts to nothing further," he said indignantly, "than that those making that assertion do not carry that vote in their own pockets." On the morning of Tuesday, April 30, he journeyed to Covington, to speak at the Kentucky Liberal Republican State Convention.

The Cincinnati convention was called to order on Wednesday, May 1, in the huge Exposition Hall, erected originally three years before to hold the performances of the National Saengerfest—a frame structure, with two wooden towers, looking inside like a "whitewashed depot" but facing the green oasis of Washington Park. It had been remodeled for the occasion, the stage having been thrown one fourth of the distance into the auditorium. A huge sounding board helped in some degree to enable the proceedings to be heard by the two or three thousand guests in the galleries. The delegates were, of course, all volunteers, with no party organization behind them; and the first step was to bring harmony out of bedlam by allotting to each state two representatives for each Senator and Congressman to which it was legally entitled. The convention then adjourned to permit the states to choose their delegates.

[1] On April 20, only a few days before, Nast had published a cartoon in *Harper's Weekly,* showing Schurz as a Lilliputian figure looking at a very large person labeled "German Vote," with the legend underneath, "Which is the better able to pocket the other?"

On the following afternoon, Judge Stanley Matthews turned over the gavel, rather to the astonishment of some observers, to Carl Schurz, as permanent chairman, and the latter, taking his place on the stage "amid a perfect whirlwind of cheers and applause," delivered his "keynote speech." He brought the delegates to their feet by his first sentence, "This is moving day," and then continued with his prepared address, setting forth his own noble aims, emphasizing the opportunity for overthrowing a "pernicious system" and eradicating "flagrant abuses," and ending by saying that they must forget "availability" and select not merely an "honest and popular man," but a statesman. Deploring the slogan, "Anything to beat Grant," he announced, "I do not struggle for the mere punishment of an opponent, nor for a temporary lease of power." The hall was very quiet as he drew to a close, saying:

We know that not every one of us can be gratified by the choice of his favorite; many of us will have to be disappointed; but in this solemn hour our hearts should know but one favorite, and that is the American Republic.

Schurz's words of warning were rightly interpreted as favoring Adams. After all, he was simply restating what the *Nation* had said only a few days previously, in an article on "The Work before the Cincinnati Convention," in which it had demanded as a candidate "a first-rate man, a distinguished man, a man versed in affairs, and who has filled places of trust and difficulty with ability and fidelity." Schurz's speech was universally praised, even by such a hostile newspaper as the New York *Times*, which called it an utterance "of which any public man might reasonably be proud." [1]

But there were other persons at Cincinnati besides Carl Schurz—persons less visionary and scrupulous than he. The gathering was made up, for the most part, of orderly, middle-

[1] The Cincinnati *Commercial* declared on May 5, "The conduct of Carl Schurz in the Cincinnati Convention was that of a statesman and a gentleman, standing above the petty intrigues and aloof from the smart schemes of small politicians."

aged men; but, with these, were many "rascals and bummers," who had descended, like vultures, in quest of prey. There were the usual "cranks." Susan B. Anthony and Laura de Force Gordon, enthusiasts for woman suffrage, seized conspicuous seats on the floor, and the latter even stirred up a tempest by claiming to be a delegate from California. Henry Watterson later described the motley gathering as including "long-haired and spectacled doctrinaires from New York, spiced by short-haired and stumpy emissaries from New England." There was danger from the first that a movement which had been initiated largely by amateurs, reformers of respectability and prestige, if not of experience, would drift into the control of professionals—disappointed office seekers, shameless adventurers, and party hacks—who would manipulate it for their own selfish purposes. The delegates, made up of all classes and types, had little coherence except in their opposition to the administration; indeed they represented certain diverse elements which, under other circumstances, might have been disputing among themselves. Schurz, the only leader who could have dominated them, had, by accepting the post of permanent chairman, deprived himself of the opportunity of guiding their actions from the floor. This was soon to be a serious handicap to him.

The serious problem of a suitable platform was settled by a committee headed by Horace White, the only real difficulty arising over the tariff. Schurz's followers were mainly free traders, violently and openly opposed to a protective tariff. On the other hand, Horace Greeley, one of the foremost candidates for the presidential nomination, was the most influential exponent of protectionist doctrines in this country. The issue was clearly one which would have to be ignored or evaded; and the committee finally reported a paragraph in which the tariff was declared a question which should be settled by each Congressional district, "wholly free of executive interference or dictation." This method of escape was so obvious as to be ridiculous; but the extreme free traders undoubtedly perceived that some concession was necessary if the delegates were not to break up in a riot. The other resolutions were those favored by Schurz—universal amnesty, civil service reform, the restriction of the President to one term, a renewal of specie payments—the whole bound together and spiced with a denunciation of the Grant administration.

This source of controversy having been weathered, attention was concentrated on the nominations. Schurz's candidate, described by him as a man whose character would "appeal to the loftiest instincts and aspirations of the patriot-citizen," was Adams, who, in addition to being the ablest of those suggested, was also probably the most available. Another possibility was Senator Lyman Trumbull, who, although not personally magnetic, was most respectable, and would have been agreeable to all but a few Democrats. Horace White felt that either Adams or Trumbull, if nominated at Cincinnati, could have been elected; [1] but Adams had no organization working for him, and Trumbull was too honest to engage in underhand intrigues. Less meritorious, perhaps, was Judge David Davis, the friend of Lincoln, already the nominee of a so-called Labor Party, a large flabby man of wealth and ambition whose henchmen were spending money freely on beer and railroad transportation. In the background always was Horace Greeley, the picturesque editor of the New York *Tribune,* a high protectionist in a nest of free traders, with whose abolitionist record before and after the Civil War no Democrat could possibly be in sympathy; honest but unsteady, intelligent but erratic, with a large, moon-shaped countenance like that of Samuel Pickwick, bespectacled eyes, and a valance of neck whiskers, resembling those of some ancient mariner—a perfect victim for the caricaturist. What observers saw in Greeley were his old, white, broad-brimmed hat, his trousers tucked in his boots, his faded cotton umbrella, his crumpled clothes. In character, he was kind-hearted, vindictive, emotional, arrogant, and simple—a

[1] Horace White, *Lyman Trumbull,* 402. George F. Hoar thought at the time that either Adams or Chase would have had a good chance of beating Grant.

jumble of inconsistencies. At Cincinnati, however, he was supported by experienced political managers, who watched every turn of events with sagacious eyes.

Before the convention opened, a little group of newspaper editors,—including Samuel Bowles, the ablest journalist-politician of his day; Murat Halstead, a vivacious reporter with a wide acquaintance; Horace White, outwardly cold as marble, but a shrewd analyst of men and affairs; and the exuberant "Marse Henry" Watterson, of the Louisville *Courier-Journal*, then only thirty-two, but sophisticated beyond his years,—engaged headquarters at the St. James Hotel, their inner sanctuary being a drawing room between the chambers occupied by Watterson and Schurz. Calling themselves the "Quadrilateral," after the four fortified towns of Northern Italy, they conceived of themselves as President-makers and talked far into the night, with plenty of Bourbon whiskey to loosen their tongues and keep them awake. Schurz sat with them at these convivial conferences, and they were later compelled to invite Whitelaw Reid, who represented both the New York *Tribune* and Horace Greeley. It was the members of the Quadrilateral who, when the "boom" for Judge Davis assumed alarming proportions, expressed their opposition both privately and publicly, thus eliminating him from the list of possibilities. This early victory doubtless gave them self-confidence and led them to treat the Greeley candidacy with an indifference which it did not deserve.

The Quadrilateral could have accomplished the nomination of either Adams or Trumbull on Friday morning if it had not been for the activities of B. Gratz Brown, who emerged unexpectedly from Missouri, Schurz's own state, to thwart most of what the latter had planned and to ruin the Liberal Republican protest. In 1870, as we have seen, Schurz had zealously espoused Brown's campaign for Governor of Missouri, and had been largely responsible for his election. But, when a Senator had to be chosen from Missouri to fill the vacancy caused by the resignation of Drake—who had been appointed

Chief Justice of the Court of Claims—Schurz, distrustful of Democrats, opposed the fusion of Democrats and Liberal Republicans which, in January, 1871, elected Francis P. Blair, Jr., a Democrat, as Drake's successor. As Brown, by previous arrangement, had supported Blair, Schurz was popular with neither; and when the two learned that Schurz was likely to bring about the nomination of Adams at Cincinnati, they promptly took the next train east out of St. Louis with the avowed intention of frustrating the scheme. Horace White thought, in the retrospect, that Blair and Brown were jealous of Schurz's power in Missouri. They were typical machine politicians, who looked upon any election as a game in which the shrewdest trader wins. They arrived on Thursday evening, the news of their coming being spread through the corridors of the Burnet House by Colonel Grosvenor, chairman of the Missouri delegation, who beat on doors and awakened the sleeping delegates. The arch-conspirators at once went into conference with the Missouri delegation. Before morning dawned on that ill-omened Friday, a working agreement was reached and a slate decided upon with the Greeley managers. The plan as there devised was carried through almost without a hitch.

The Quadrilateral, as well as Trumbull and Schurz, heard the rumors which were being spread abroad, but the latter, who might, through the exercise of his influence, have compelled the nomination of Adams, resolved not to interfere. Very little secrecy seems to have been observed about these midnight conferences. The Cincinnati *Commercial* announced on Friday that Brown had turned over his strength to Greeley and that the ticket would be either Greeley and Brown or Adams and Trumbull. Long after the election of 1872 was history, Schurz confessed to Grosvenor: "Blair's appearance and intervention at Cincinnati destroyed, at the decisive moment, with the character of that great enterprise, also its chances of success. He was the evil genius whose very touch was destruction." But this does not explain why Schurz, if he knew of their plot, did not act promptly to circumvent the plotters. The truth is that he was perplexed and confused by the sudden entrance of Blair and Brown. In critical emergencies, he was not always quick in his resolutions. There was some truth in the comment of Joseph Pulitzer, one of the delegates, "Carl Schurz was the most industrious and the least energetic man I have ever worked with." Furthermore he had no well-oiled political machine through which to operate—nothing but his moral and intellectual supremacy, difficult to exert as chairman.

It was, furthermore, not so apparent on Friday morning that Adams was to be defeated. Nominating speeches having been dispensed with by a ruling of the convention, the first ballot was taken, showing Adams in the lead with 205 votes, Greeley second with 147, Trumbull third with 110, and B. Gratz Brown fourth, with 95. When the roll had been called but before the result was announced, Brown, although not a delegate, sent up a small piece of paper to Schurz asking to be allowed to address the delegates. Schurz, visibly disconcerted, was hesitating whether or not to invoke the parliamentary rule against such a procedure, when Brown himself, the sun from the upper windows shining with a fierce light on his red beard and hair and pallid features, slowly mounted the platform. Having secured a hearing, he made a brief but spirited speech, withdrawing his own name as a candidate and pleading with the delegates to turn to Horace Greeley. This attempt to stampede the convention resulted in some confusion, which Schurz could not altogether control. Although Brown's conduct was impudent and mischievous, it was not the decisive factor in the result. Actually the shifting of votes had already been secretly agreed upon between representatives of Brown and Greeley, although probably without the connivance of the New York editor. On the second ballot, Greeley went to the front, with 245 votes, Adams receiving only 243. A third trial placed Adams again in the lead. Even at this late moment, many keen observers felt that, if Trumbull had been willing to withdraw, Adams might still have been chosen. But Schurz, adhering to his policy of non-intervention, would not counsel his friend to drop out, and

Trumbull's managers were not prepared for the emergency.

On the sixth ballot, although both Adams and Greeley had gained, it was evident that the latter's adherents were in control. Even before the tellers had finished tallying, delegates asked to change their votes. Soon there was a landslide, impossible to stem, for Greeley. Schurz, in desperation, ruled that the roll call was defective, but was shouted down. He even neglected to announce the result until a friend reminded him of his duty. Then, with ill-concealed reluctance, he shouted the figures—Greeley, 482; Adams, 187. The underlying bitterness was disclosed for a few seconds when a motion to make the nomination unanimous could not be carried. The bargain was completed when B. Gratz Brown was nominated for Vice President on the second ballot. "It was understood," said the Cincinnati *Commercial*, "that the Blair and Brown party, having handed over their goods, were to receive their pay."

"The Quadrilateral," wrote Henry Watterson, "had been knocked into a cocked hat." The professionals had beaten the amateurs. That evening, at the home of Judge Stallo in Walnut Hills, the reformers met to commiserate with one another. There was reason for their gloom. Most of them free traders, they had nominated a high protectionist; idealists, they had been circumvented by the least responsible and reputable elements in the convention; hoping for Democratic support, they had selected the candidate least likely to appeal to that party. It seemed as if all their high aims and purposes had amounted to nothing. Schurz, according to Watterson, "was as a death's head at the board." As they sat together, he turned to the piano, which he had not forgotten how to play, and touched the keys so mournfully that many of those present wept. He knew only too well, as Henry Adams wrote in 1876, that he had been "made the slave of the monster he was fighting." [1]

Schurz left Cincinnati, to which he had come with such optimism, a chagrined and irritated man. Samuel Bowles wrote him that the two men who "gained most character out of Cin-

[1] Adams to Lodge, February 27, 1876, *Letters of Henry Adams*, 282.

cinnati" were himself and Adams; but Schurz, in reply, could only lament that the whole Liberal Republican movement had been "dragged down to the level of an ordinary political operation." He attributed the failure of his hopes to "a combination of politicians striking and executing a bargain in the open light of day." It could not have pleased him to read in the *Nation* that the Cincinnati convention "must, so far as the general aims and objects of those who called it are concerned, be pronounced a failure." But a failure it unquestionably had been, from any point of view.

Schurz himself seems to have been honestly at a loss what to do. Before returning to St. Louis, B. Gratz Brown told a reporter from the Cincinnati *Commercial* that he had talked with Schurz, who, although he preferred another ticket, could be "relied upon." It is a pity that the circumstances of that conversation have not been preserved. Schurz's own *Westliche Post* announced on May 5 its adherence to Greeley and Brown, stating that, although the ticket was "not entirely satisfactory to many persons," Greeley was, after all, better than Grant.[1] On Sunday, May 6, after some meditation, Schurz wrote Greeley from Washington, giving him a succinct history of what had happened at Cincinnati and saying frankly that, although he believed in Greeley as a "pure and honest man," the latter's nomination was "a successful piece of political huckstering" and intimating that, under him as a candidate, the Liberal Republican movement could "no longer appeal to that higher moral sense which we had hoped to evoke in the hearts and minds of the people." He added significantly that the prominent German leaders of the West were determined to oppose the ticket, refusing to be "the victims and tools of Frank Blair and New York politicians." He himself regretted that a protest, so hopefully begun, should be thus "stripped of its

[1] Consulted by his partners by telegraph as to whether they should come out for Greeley and Brown, Schurz had replied in the affirmative. Later they notified him that it would probably not be possible to continue this support if the paper were to retain its influence. Schurz, *Writings*, II, 365.

moral power," and hinted that it might be well to "begin again at the beginning." It was a typical Schurz letter—candid and straightforward, but blunt and tactless, and exceedingly irritating to the recipient. It was the same type of communication which had once so much annoyed Lincoln.

Greeley, who was fluent and enjoyed controversy, replied in two letters, dated May 8 and 10, declaring in the first that he had had nothing to do with any "bargains or arrangements of any kind," admitting that many Germans disliked him because he was a protectionist and a total abstinence man, but showing himself most optimistic regarding his prospects. Advising Schurz, to "take time for reflection and consultation," he expressed the view that sober second thought would bring them together—or rather, would bring Schurz over to Greeley. Undiscomfited, Schurz continued the correspondence, suggesting, on May 18, that there would probably be "another Liberal Republican ticket" and that Greeley would do well to postpone acceptance. Two days later, Greeley spoke decisively and, after thanking Schurz for his frankness, ended, "I shall accept unconditionally." Both Schurz and Greeley were good letter writers, but in this case the tactical advantage lay with Greeley.

The attitude of the leaders of the Liberal Republican movement had not been unanimous. The *Nation* called Greeley a candidate "of undoubted personal honesty who is and has long been associated intimately with the worst set of politicians the State contains—excepting the Tammany Ring." Samuel Bowles and Horace White had accepted the inevitable and were advocating Greeley's election in their respective journals—the Springfield *Republican* and the Chicago *Tribune*. Stanley Matthews, on the other hand, at once repudiated the ticket; and Schurz was disposed to join him. On May 20, he wrote Godkin that he had been urged to lend his support to a movement for another nomination and asking him to come to Washington for a consultation. "I would do anything," said Schurz, "to escape from the necessity of supporting Greeley against Grant." Godkin, who had already written Schurz that Greeley's election would be "a calamity of the first magnitude," and had said editorially that the Cincinnati nominations were "amusing and melancholy," was sympathetic—but was unwilling to take the responsibility of leadership.

Meanwhile discreet intermediaries were trying to bring about a reconciliation between Schurz and Greeley. On June 5, more than a month after the Cincinnati fiasco, Schurz was writing to Grosvenor, "I do not think that, as things now run, success is certain or even very probable," and was arranging to hold a conference in New York at which representative men "of the different opposition elements" could get together. He would espouse Greeley's cause only if it could be proved that there was no other means of beating Grant. Until that question was settled, he refused to ratify Greeley's nomination or to come out publicly for him.

During the interval the tactful Horace White had extracted from Greeley the form of an apology, or explanation, for the latter's offensive letter to Schurz. When the conference met at the Fifth Avenue Hotel, in New York City, Schurz, who had been one of the signers of the letter of invitation, was in a less belligerent mood. Congress had closed its session ten days before, and he was free for the summer. At the meeting, which was secret and unattended by reporters, Jacob D. Cox, one of Schurz's most intimate friends, presided, and there were about sixty present, including William Cullen Bryant, Trumbull, Watterson, Horace White, Godkin, and Parke Godwin. They discussed the situation in all its phases, reaching a general agreement that Greeley's nomination was most unwise and inexpedient. But when it was moved that a new ticket, headed by Adams and Groesbeck, be placed in the field, Schurz, his political sanity regained, declared that it would only increase the confusion; and he terminated the meeting with a speech indicating that nothing was left but to endorse Greeley. Before he left New York, Schurz had a satisfactory interview with Greeley, securing his pledge to carry through certain specific measures for civil service reform; in return Schurz promised to make several speeches for the Liberal Republican ticket. Some of the strong anti-Greeley men at the conference held another gathering the next day, repudiated the acts of the Cincinnati convention, and called upon voters to cast their ballots for William S. Groesbeck for President. This, however, was merely a futile gesture. Carl Schurz was undoubtedly right. It was too late to do anything but accept Horace Greeley.

The situation was already absurd, but it was to become even more ridiculous. The Democratic Convention, assembling on July 9, at Baltimore, was compelled to face the necessity of concurring in the nomination of an editor who for years had denounced all Democrats as villains. A gathering dominated largely by Southerners actually nominated, by a vote of 686 to 46, Horace Greeley, of the New York *Tribune,* for President—a man who, according to Senator Voorhees, was "an older and a far abler Republican than Grant." It is no wonder that a story was evolved of David Livingstone, returning to civilization after five years in Central Africa and listening to such marvelous news as the Franco-Prussian War, the fall of Napoleon III, and the execution of Maximilian, and accepting all this as authentic; finally, when he was informed of the action of the Baltimore convention, he said, "You have told me stupendous things, and with a confiding simplicity I was swallowing them peacefully down; but there is a limit to all things, and when you tell me that Horace Greeley is become a Democratic candidate, I will be hanged if I believe it." [1] When the Democrats had adjourned, it was obvious that the intelligent voter must choose between Grant and Greeley; and Carl Schurz had already adopted the lesser evil. As the *Nation* said caustically, the Liberal Republican candidate was, to the Democrats, "boiled crow"; but he was more palatable than Grant. It is to be noticed, however, that both E. L. Godkin's *Nation* and Bryant's New York *Evening Post,* preferred Grant to Greeley; and Godkin, in a letter telling Schurz that the latter was "the one man in American politics who inspires

[1] *The Nation,* Aug. 8, 1872, quoted in Rhodes, VI, 430–31.

me with some hope about them," also accused Bowles, White, and the other reformers of "accepting blindly a grossly unfit candidate at the hands of a bellowing convention"—a candidate representing quacks, charlatans, ignoramuses, and sentimentalists.

Schurz had promised to speak for Greeley. On July 22, in the Temple, in St. Louis, before his own constituents, he made a vigorous defense of his conduct. He had remained silent for some weeks after the Cincinnati convention in the hope that it might be possible, by selecting another candidate than Greeley, "to make the movement all that it could be desired to be." That had proved to be impracticable and now, after a period of "painful anxiety," he proposed to come out publicly for the "old white hat." Schurz spent much of his time in a survey of the shortcomings of the administration. Sumner's notorious philippic delivered before the Senate on May 31 had been the most scathing rebuke of an American President ever spoken in Congress. Schurz, more moderate, and therefore more effective, did not think Grant to be a "monster of iniquity." He was rather "a man who makes use of his high official position to suit his own convenience, regardless of other interests," and his administration had been "simply dull and heavy, stupid and stubborn in its selfishness." Schurz had no intention of becoming a Democrat. But he did feel that they were living in "a period pregnant with new formations, which need but the electric spark of opportunity to spring into shape." Schurz's later speeches in the campaign of 1872 had the same tone of explanation, if not of apology, although he did grow slightly more enthusiastic as summer slipped into autumn.

After the battle was over, Schurz, writing to Horace White, said, "We designed it to be a campaign of ideas, and it became a campaign of personalities." "Matt" Morgan, in *Leslie's Weekly*, published each week a cartoon assailing Grant and his satellites,[1] showing him as a drunken sot, leering on the presi-

[1] A typical Morgan cartoon portrayed Grant as a drunken military tyrant, in a cocked hat, attended by "Boss" Tweed, Secretary Fish, and others, being

dential throne; as Belshazzar, cowering before the writing on the wall; as an embezzler, guilty as the notorious "Boss" Tweed; and as a military despot. Morgan was excelled, however, by Nast, who published picture after picture of Greeley's "old, lunar, bespectacled face," with the unforgettable neck whiskers, and always in the old white hat and coat. By a happy inspiration, Nast, unable to secure a photograph of the vice presidential candidate, merely attached a tag, labeled "Gratz Brown," to Greeley's coat tails.[1] Schurz himself was always included by Nast in the group around Greeley, and was attacked frequently as a foreigner, interfering in the domestic concerns of his adopted country.

In these days so remote from the stormy passions which tore the hearts of Grantites and Greeleyites, it is a diverting pastime to turn the yellow disintegrating pages of *Harper's Weekly* and study the Nast cartoons. Even before the Cincinnati convention, Schurz, recognized as hostile to Grant, was, in spite of protests from George William Curtis, depicted in ridiculous postures and costumes.[2] On May 4, for example, before the Liberal Republican nominations had been announced, Nast portrayed Schurz as a very irate and feathery rooster, perched on a rifle and gazing sadly down at a box labeled "Cincinnati," in which reposes Greeley as a motherly hen upon a nest. When the ticket was named, the artist drew Grant as the helmsman of the Ship of State, very benign and honest, whom Greeley and Schurz, with sinister expressions, were preparing to throw overboard. The legend underneath read, "Liberal Gratitude." After the party conventions, the caricatures became more abusive. Greeley and Schurz, with other reformers, were revealed

weighed in the scales against a very benevolent looking Greeley, with Grant saying, "Well, who'd have thought that the old white hat, boots and axe would have more weight than all these hangers-on of mine?"

[1] Brown had a very large head and amazingly bushy red whiskers, giving him a distinctive appearance almost as unusual as Greeley's famous neck whiskers. This Civil War period might be called the "Bearded Age."

[2] See J. H. Harper, *The House of Harper*, 301–304, for Curtis's protests against the cartoons by Nast ridiculing Schurz.

bending over and watching the Liberal Mountain bring forth a tiny mouse—B. Gratz Brown; while Schurz was sketched as handing to the goddess Columbia a fool's-head, representing Greeley, on a stick, meanwhile covering his mouth to keep from bursting into laughter. Schurz was shown as reaching into his pocket for the German vote and saying, "Perhaps I've lost it," and as a professional "Carpetbagger," moving from Wisconsin to Missouri.

The conspicuous place assigned to Carl Schurz in these cartoons is an indication of the respect which Nast had for his influence. Oddly enough, *Harper's Weekly*, in its editorials of this period, treated Schurz very kindly as an honest, high-minded, but misled reformer—a visionary, victimized by unscrupulous politicians. When Schurz, at the end of June, sent a letter to the Illinois State Convention saying that it was necessary to defeat Grant in order that thus "a free field be opened for a reformatory movement," *Harper's* declared, "Mr. Schurz began by demanding reform, and in the second month of the canvass he declares himself content with change." But Curtis, as editor, was careful to avoid scurrilities. Nast, however, was less fastidious. It was, of course, unfair that idealists like Greeley and Schurz should be ridiculed because of physical peculiarities; and Curtis was right in asserting that it was not playing the game "to represent as morally contemptible men of the highest character with whom you politically differ." Such, however, are the risks which any honorable man assumes when he enters actively into American politics. Fortunately Schurz was not abnormally sensitive and could proceed on his way undisturbed by malice.

From the beginning, there was very little chance for Horace Greeley. The American people admired, but did not trust, the eccentric editor of the New York *Tribune*. He was on occasions an effective political speaker, who drew crowds to hear him; but public sentiment did not turn in his favor. He had to overcome not only the sentimental affection which people felt for Grant as a military hero, but also the inertia which keeps citi-

By Thomas Nast in Harper's Weekly, *1872*

CLASPING HANDS OVER THE BLOODLESS (SAR)C(H)ASM

zens away from the polls; and he did not have sufficient magnetism to lure the stay-at-home vote. In September, he made a series of speeches in Indiana, Ohio, and Pennsylvania which aroused much enthusiasm by their simplicity and argumentative force, as well as their good temper. But the average man trusted Grant. The early elections, in Vermont and Maine, showed large Republican majorities; and in October the Republicans won their state contests in Pennsylvania, Ohio, and Nebraska. It was evident that very few Republicans could be seduced from their party allegiance. On October 26, Nast showed a tidal wave overwhelming the Greeleyites, carrying with it Carl Schurz and the German vote as well as Trumbull, Sumner, and the mysterious Gratz Brown. The final figures showed that the "Sage of Chappaqua" had been, as he confessed, "terribly beaten," winning only six out of thirty-seven states. Mrs. Greeley had died a week before the election; and, on November 29, Greeley himself, after an attack of brain fever, followed her to the grave. It was a pitiful ending to a career which had many noble aspects.

On November 10, Greeley had sent to Schurz a letter marked "private forever," containing these few words, "I wish I could say with what an agony of emotion I subscribe myself, gratefully yours, Horace Greeley." Early in the campaign, on June 15, Nast had drawn a striking full-page cartoon for *Harper's*, showing Schurz at the piano, his long spindly legs tied in a knot beneath the stool, with various song sheets strewn about bearing such titles as "Down with Grant" and "The Germans will vote for H. G.," and underneath the words, "Played Out." Now at the close the artist showed Grant and Uncle Sam shaking hands, while below, in various moods of dejection, lie in a chasm all the leading followers of Greeley —Trumbull, Bowles, Henry Ward Beecher, and others, with Schurz, completely disgusted, in the foreground. The Liberal Republican movement had come to naught, and the reformers, as Schurz wrote to Horace White, had been defeated in their best aspirations.

CHAPTER XVII MARKING TIME

CARL SCHURZ is identified with no one spot, as Washington is with Mount Vernon, Clay with Ashland, or Webster with Marshfield. His life was one journey after another, a succession of transitory residences, each one rented for a few months and then left behind. He had, during these years following the Civil War, no place of permanence where his books could be accumulated. He seemed to be constantly on the move, coming from one city or going to another, looking up time-tables or packing traveling bags. It was a feverish, nerve-racking existence, but he did not complain. Perhaps it filled a demand in his soul for action; for, thinker though he was, he craved always to be doing things. His boundless energy, even at forty, needed an outlet. Even when he was with his family in what they for the moment called home, he would sit for hours at the piano, his fingers twinkling restlessly over the keys in improvisation. There was nothing languid or lazy about his impetuous active body and mind. So, too, even while he was out of Republican favor in the Senate, he continued his battle for reforms. Always, even to the day of his death, he was planning how society and the world could be improved.

The Schurzes did not enter with any ardor into the gaieties of Washington society.[1] The birth of their first son, Carl Lincoln Schurz, on February 28, 1871, made them very happy, but kept Mrs. Schurz busy in the nursery. The capital, during Grant's administrations, was very lively and extravagant, the pace being set by the wealthy rather than by the aristocratic. The Schurzes were certainly not rich, and their tastes were

[1] According to Dr. Frederic Bancroft, an authority on Schurz, the Schurzes lived during this senatorial period for a time in a house on the south side of F Street, N. W., between 19th and 20th Streets, and later on West Jackson Place, a few doors north of Pennsylvania Avenue.

what are sometimes known as "middle-class." Carl, who was a very serious person, was indifferent to the frivolity and aimless eating and drinking around him. As for Mrs. Schurz, she was a stately matron, always simply dressed but dignified—not at all likely to be taken up by Kate Chase Sprague or the second Mrs. Belknap. To many persons, including young Henry Adams, the capital offered "a brilliant sort of butterfly existence . . . with prancing and flirting every night"—but not, we may be sure, to Senator and Mrs. Schurz. Their simple forms of entertainment were quite different from those to be found at the British Embassy, where Lady Thornton presided so gracefully, or at the beautiful home of Madame Catacazy, wife of the Russian Ambassador.

Unfortunately the existing letters of this period do not help greatly in reproducing the daily routine of the Schurzes in Washington. Thomas Nast recorded in his diary seeing them at a reception given by the Blaines in February, 1872, and being told that they were watching him carefully because of the cartoons which he was beginning to draw about Carl. Once Margarethe Schurz, standing in a corner at a ball, saw "M. Mori standing motionless, his arm tight around a young lady's waist." "Imagine it," she said, with disgust—and the tone of her remark showed what she felt about such improprieties. We do not hear of the Schurzes being invited to the White House to meet Mrs. Grant, of whom Henry Adams wrote, "She squints like an isosceles triangle, but is not much more vulgar than some Duchesses." Even if nothing else had happened, Carl's estrangement from the administration would have effectually blocked any intimacy between him and the President or Secretary Fish.

That estrangement was now open and complete. When Congress reopened on December 2, 1872, Senator Schurz found himself dropped from all committees except that of Foreign Affairs. Grant's administration had, according to Henry Adams, "outraged every rule of common decency," but it had been vindicated at the polls by the American people, and

Schurz, who had denounced it, was in a political eclipse. After 1872, Schurz was an Independent, voting now with one party and now with another, whose movements could not always be predicted. He still called himself a Republican, but it was difficult for him to demonstrate his party loyalty to men like Conkling and Morton. His votes in the Senate were determined entirely by considerations of public welfare, not by fidelity to any organization.[1]

There will always be a difference of opinion among intelligent men as to how far a political leader is justified in adhering to a party with the policies of which he temporarily disagrees. Senator George F. Hoar, one of the most high-minded and incorruptible of public servants, was frequently not in accord with the Republican Party—notably on the issue of imperialism. But he maintained that, by continuing as a party man, he was able "to accomplish . . . ten-fold the good that has been accomplished by men who have ten times more ability and capacity for such service, who have left the party." Commenting specifically on the Liberal Republican movement of 1872, Hoar declared that Sumner, Schurz, Greeley, and the others who left the Republican Party were "so long as they maintained that attitude, absolutely without political influence from that moment." [2] This is, of course, an exaggeration. Schurz was always a person to be considered by the party managers because of the widespread influence which he exercised, particularly over German-Americans. He himself felt that "the overthrow of party despotism is the condition precedent of all reform." But there must have been periods, especially from 1873 to 1875, when he felt isolated and lonely. He had no intention of becoming a Democrat, and the Republicans refused

[1] Schurz was often at odds with the party leaders. On Jan. 16, 1873, he recommended that the United States take part in the international exposition at Vienna and appropriate $300,000 for our exhibition. Senator Chandler vigorously opposed the proposal, saying that foreigners merely took advantage of our inventions and paid nothing in return. The fact that Schurz was of foreign birth was often mentioned by his opponents.

[2] Hoar, *Autobiography,* I, 197.

to accept him as one of themselves. But his conscience was clear. Speaking on September 24, 1874, at St. Louis, he said:

> I have now been well-nigh twenty years more or less active in public life, and so often have I seen the same men cover me with obloquy one day and with lavish praise the next, so often have I been killed stone-dead politically and risen up again fully alive, that I can speak from experience; He who walks his path with unswerving fidelity to his conviction of right has nothing to fear.

Schurz was still in Washington on that fearfully cold March day in 1873 when Ulysses Simpson Grant was inaugurated for his second term, and, drawn triumphantly by four horses and escorted by cavalrymen in gaudy uniforms, proceeded from the White House to the Capitol. If there was any moral to be drawn from Grant's success, it was that the American people like to be bamboozled and robbed. From this second administration, Carl Schurz expected nothing—and received nothing. He was an outsider, ignored by the Republican Party, which, as a reward for its sins, had secured not only the Presidency, but also a two-thirds majority in both House and Senate.

The Senate, with certain executive business to transact, held a special session from March 4 to March 26. Schurz spoke at some length on March 14, on the question of the validity of the election to the Senate of Alexander Caldwell, of Kansas, which had been effected, it was claimed, by fraud and bribery. Schurz upheld a resolution declaring Caldwell's election to have been null and void, and maintained that it had been accomplished "by the corrupt use of money." Caldwell wisely resigned without forcing the issue, became a manufacturer of wagons and carriages at Leavenworth, Kansas, and lived until 1917. The matter is of importance in Schurz's career because it shows him taking a positive stand against "the invasion of men who purchase with money their way to the highest legislative dignity of the greatest of republics."

During the late spring and summer of 1873, Schurz was

mainly in St. Louis, busy with his editorial work and conferring with progressives on certain policies which would in some degree neutralize the evils of the Grant administration. It was a period when one scandalous revelation followed another. The President reappointed as Collector of the Port of New Orleans his brother-in-law, Casey, whose record was notorious. Discouraged at the lack of congressional coöperation, George William Curtis resigned as chairman of the Civil Service Commission, and Grant himself soon openly abandoned all efforts to promote civil service reform—Schurz's favorite project. The country was horrified by charges of corruption involving the Vice President, members of the Cabinet, and several of the Republican leaders, in connection with the operation of the Crédit Mobilier, a company formed by Oakes Ames and his associates for constructing the Union Pacific Railroad. An investigating committee, while finding Ames and his colleague, James Brooks, guilty, exonerated such conspicuous figures as Blaine, Colfax, and Garfield; but the taint of suspicion clung to them throughout their political careers. A flagrant "salary grab," passed at the close of the session, did not tend to conciliate public opinion. Charges of "graft" were frequent everywhere among government employees, from low to high. Grant's administration had indeed justified Carl Schurz's saddest apprehensions.

To add to the gloom of those who already were despairing of the republic, the autumn of 1873 was distinguished by an industrial and financial crisis—the consequence of several factors, one of which was over-speculation in railroad enterprises. In September, the supposedly impregnable banking house of Jay Cooke and Company closed its doors, thus precipitating a panic in Wall Street. The Treasury provided some emergency relief, and the Stock Exchange was closed for eight days. Still securities continued to decline, and many insolvencies were reported each week. As a matter of fact, business was not really to revive until 1878, and the Republican Party had to endure five years of much unemployment, of reduced wages, of bankruptcies, and of general depression.

Congress reopened on December 1, 1873, with a hard winter ahead. The usual panaceas based on a policy of inflation were suggested by irresponsible experimenters with finance; and William H. Richardson, the Secretary of the Treasury, had audaciously reissued on his own responsibility several millions of greenbacks, apparently with Grant's approval. The question now reached Congress in a bill proposing to reissue the entire "reserve" up to a total of $400,000,000—an increase of approximately $44,000,000.

Problems relating to the currency are certainly unromantic and are ordinarily hard to explain, even by an expert. During the seventies, a group of Westerners, representing for the most part agrarian interests, and including such politicians as Morton, of Indiana, and Logan, of Illinois, committed themselves to a plan for increasing the amount of greenbacks, or paper money, and for making it on a par with gold. Into the arguments for enlarging the supply of legal tender paper it is not essential to go here. But Schurz, like most of the accepted authorities on economics, regarded such a procedure as unwise. He was what was known as a "sound money" man—one who believed that the government should discharge its obligations in specie and should keep the amount of greenbacks as low as possible. He did not wish to increase the volume of Treasury legal tender notes—then considerably less than $400,000,000. In resisting the clamor for inflation, Schurz performed a genuine service to the nation, a service less spectacular than some of his other achievements, but which reacted to the permanent benefit of the Treasury.

On his speeches relating to this subject, Schurz spent long hours of study. The West asserted that an expansion of the paper currency would lower prices and stabilize economic conditions. Schurz, in the course of a debate on January 14, 1874, demonstrated that an irredeemable paper currency unnecessarily stimulates speculation, causes prices and interest rates to rise, and would, therefore, be disastrous to the farmer and plantation owner. In ringing words, he maintained that the government was morally obligated to redeem legal tender notes in gold as soon as it was in a position to do so. The *Nation* said, January 28, 1874, that he had "propounded and supported a series of propositions which contain the sum and substance of all sound finance."

It was natural that Morton and Cameron should call Schurz a theorist, unfamiliar with practical finance. When they fell back on this argument, he replied with his famous story of "Old Tatum," the illiterate Southern farmer, with a lofty contempt for book-learning, who, when told that the earth revolved around the sun, would fairly roll over with laughter and cry: "There again, from the books. The earth moving around the sun! And don't I see every day with these, my own eyes, the sun moving around the earth? Don't I see it rise there in the morning, and don't I see it go down yonder every evening? Ah, you book-men can't fool Old Tatum." So, when economists would tell Mr. Tatum that greenbacks were not money at all, but merely promises to pay money, he would smile in their faces and answer scornfully: "Do we not call these paper notes dollars? Cannot I read it with my spectacles in big print upon them, 'one dollar,' 'ten dollars,' 'one hundred dollars'? Ah, you can't fool Old Tatum, I tell you." This story was effective as a retort, but, to those acquainted with the basic principles of economics, his reasoning was even more conclusive.

Unfortunately, logic and common sense counted for little in the discussion. Schurz was in the minority, and the bill eventually passed both House and Senate. But Grant, who had been supposed to agree with the inflationists, now, to the astonishment and delight of Schurz, vetoed the measure,[1] and the "greenbackers" were foiled at the very moment when they thought victory to be theirs. This veto, rightly described by Rhodes as "a brave and noble act," brought back to the President some of his lost popularity and did much to encourage

[1] For an interesting discussion of Grant's position, see Hoar, *Autobiography,* I, 206, ff.

business. It proved to be impossible to pass the act over his veto. A compromise measure, passed on June 20, validated Richardson's earlier unauthorized measures, but forbade any further issue of greenbacks. This, although not approved by Schurz, received the presidential signature. The "hard money" men had held their ground.

Charles Sumner, deserted by his wife, condemned by the radicals for his bill to remove from the regimental colors the names of "battles with fellow citizens," had returned from a trip to Europe worn out, and had settled down, lonely and debilitated, in his house on Lafayette Square. Still retaining his seat in the Senate, he spoke for the last time in the chamber on March 6. Four days later he appeared for a few minutes at his desk, but on the following day he had another attack of *angina pectoris* and died, with former Attorney-General Hoar at his side, just as Schurz was entering the bedroom. At the funeral services in the Senate on Friday, March 13, Schurz sat nearest the foot of the coffin. He was one of the Senate Committee of Arrangements and served as an honorary pall bearer. He was also selected by the city government of Boston to deliver a eulogy in Music Hall on April 29.

Carl Schurz had been very close to Charles Sumner. In certain respects, the two men were much alike. Both were scholars, both were independents, both were vitally interested in reform. Schurz, however, had tact and a sense of humor—two qualities which Sumner did not possess. Schurz had worked with Sumner, but had not been subservient to him. He had admired him without being his satellite. His eulogy on the Massachusetts statesman is probably the best of his occasional addresses. While he did not shrink from dealing with his hero's weaknesses, he gave it as his conviction that Sumner's was a life "wholly devoted to what was good and pure," and described him as "the stalwart, brave old champion, whose face and bearing were so austere, and whose heart was so full of tenderness." In words which might have been applied to himself, Schurz said: "He always remained in morals while in politics. He never was anything else but a Senator with a conscience."

On the evening following the eulogy, Mrs. John Ellerton Lodge, mother of Henry Cabot Lodge—then a young Harvard graduate of twenty-four—gave a dinner for Senator and Mrs. Schurz, Longfellow, Emerson, and Holmes. Lodge, who was then the editor of the *North American Review*, was present and remembered that Holmes drew Schurz into a very interesting discussion on debating. At one point in the proceedings, Lodge asked Longfellow whether he did not think Schurz's address very fine. "No," the poet replied, "It was a clever speech, but I do not believe in proceeding by negation. I did not wish to have him tell us what Sumner was not, but what he was." [1]

The repudiation of Grantism at the elections of 1874 was virtually nation wide. Schurz went on the stump in Missouri, making his most notable address on September 24, at the Temple, in St. Louis, in which he denounced scathingly the Crédit Mobilier scandal, the Sanborn contracts, and the recent outrages in the South, presenting a convincing case against the administration. It was a forceful statement of what many thoughtful Americans, Republicans as well as Democrats, were feeling. When the returns were in, it was learned that the Democrats, in addition to controlling the Senate, would have a majority in the House for the first time since 1861. It was almost a political revolution.

In 1873, when a Senator was to be elected from Missouri, Schurz absolutely refused to favor "Frank" Blair, who was a candidate to succeed himself. As a result, the Legislature eventually chose a St. Louis lawyer and business man, Lewis Vital Bogy, a Democrat and a nonentity. Schurz's own term was to expire on March 4, 1875, and the overwhelming success of the Democrats at the polls in the previous November made it certain that he could not be reëlected except by a political

[1] Longfellow wrote Mrs. Schurz, May 13, 1874, "I wish you could know the effect this discourse on Sumner has produced on all minds here, and the impression he [Schurz] has left behind him." *Schurz MSS,* Congressional Library.

miracle. When, a few years before, Schurz had been working to abolish the disabilities imposed upon the "Bourbon" Democrats, they had displayed a wild enthusiasm for him and had even, to his disgust, carried him around on their shoulders. Once, with a premonition of what would happen, he said to such a mob, "Oh, yes, you are wonderfully fond of me now; but you will soon choose a Confederate brigadier to succeed me." This is precisely what happened. He had vaguely hoped that the spirit of partisanship might be invoked in the case of one who had been so little of a partisan and that he might be allowed to remain in an office so congenial to him. But the triumphant Democrats proceeded to elect Francis M. Cockrell, who had risen in the Confederate Army from captain to brigadier general, and who was to serve in the Senate for five consecutive terms from 1875 to 1905.

During his last session in the Senate, Schurz took an active part in discussing a bill reported by John Sherman dealing with financial matters, and providing particularly that, after January 1, 1879, the Treasury should redeem greenbacks in coin. Sherman, asked by Schurz whether the greenbacks retired under this measure could be reissued, tried to evade the question, knowing that this matter had been left open in order to pacify the inflationists; but Schurz finally compelled him, through sheer persistence, to answer that the United States notes must be reduced to $300,000,000 before any reissue could be made. In the end, although disapproving of some of its provisions, Schurz voted with a majority of the Republicans for the bill, and it was signed by the President on January 14, 1875. It was, on the whole, a good measure and did much to stabilize financial conditions.

On January 11, 1875, Schurz delivered his last formal speech before the Senate—a speech entitled, "Military Interference in Louisiana,"[1] dealing with a resolution introduced by

[1] Regarding this speech, Chas. F. Adams made the following entry in his *Diary:* "Went to the office after reading a report of the speech of Mr. Schurz in the Senate on the Sheridan outrage. It is very seldom I am envious of any-

him a few days before calling for an inquiry by the Committee on the Judiciary into the matter of the legislation needed to secure to the people of Louisiana their "rights of self-government under the Constitution." With more than his wonted seriousness, he warned Congress against "the insidious advance of irresponsible power" and begged them to discover a method of undoing "the usurpations that have been perpetrated." A few days before his term closed, he characteristically said a few words in opposition to an increase of the tariff. And so he withdrew unostentatiously from the Senate, mourned by only a few intimate friends and associates. He was disappointed about losing his seat, but entirely philosophical. "No man of experience," he had written a few months before, "will look for anything like gratitude in politics."

In this account of Schurz's senatorial career, two interesting matters with which he had to deal have not yet been taken up. On the question of a liberal naturalization policy, he had occasion to speak early in 1870, in opposition to a bill amending the naturalization laws so that every naturalized citizen might be subject at any time to the call of a district attorney if the latter received information that the papers were in any respect doubtful. Schurz objected on the ground that this would be a source of unnecessary inconvenience to every possessor of naturalization papers and might lead desirable immigrants to decide not to become naturalized. Schurz also protested against the exclusion of the Chinese from naturalization, contending that the dangers of an overwhelming influx of Chinese had been much exaggerated. A naturalized citizen himself, Schurz was the defender of just legislation toward others who might follow him to the "land of promise."

Twentieth century Americans will, of course, be interested to know how Carl Schurz felt on prohibition. That he was opposed

body, but I should like to have something on the record which must stand permanent like that. I could not help sitting down, and writing a note signifying my opinion. I could not have expressed my own convictions more fully, not to speak of the style, which is the more remarkable that he is a German."

to it goes almost without saying. On February 25, 1874, he spoke briefly against a bill for the appointment of a commission to inquire into the economic, moral, and scientific aspects of the liquor traffic, pointing out that legislation on that subject was a State, not a Federal matter, and that any attempt to force temperance on the American people was misdirected zeal. One sentence from his speech, although rather clumsily expressed, sums up his point of view— "When you absolutely prohibit, or by force of law attempt to suppress, an indulgence which, when moderate, people will not consider morally wrong, then you will always fail."

Two of Schurz's utterances, with the quality of epigrams, ought also not to be forgotten. Once, in a controversy with Senator Carpenter, of Wisconsin, the latter, maintaining that Schurz, in trying to prove that the United States had blundered in selling firearms to France, was false to the sentiment, "My country, right or wrong," said that he was unpatriotic. Schurz responded with his revised version of this doctrine, "My country, right or wrong: if right, to be kept right; if wrong, to be set right." At a later session, when Senator Morton accused Schurz of inconsistency, the latter answered:

I want him to point out in my record a single principle that I have ever betrayed. I want him to show that in the platforms of policy I have favored a single contradiction. He will not find one. He has never left his party. I have never betrayed my principles. That is the difference between him and me.

Such incidents as these give some idea of Schurz's quickness of wit and facility of expression. It is true, as Rhodes has said, that he was "almost an ideal Senator." It is a pity that our political system does not permit a distinguished statesman who happens to belong to the minority in his own district to seek a constituency in another section of the country.[1] In Great Britain, an arrangement would be made by the party managers

[1] Charles Francis Adams declared that there was never a period after 1881 when Schurz could not have found a large constituency which would have been glad "to place him and keep him in Congress as its representative."

which would allow a man of Schurz's type to retain a seat in Parliament virtually for life. But Schurz, one of the most intelligent of legislators, one of the most brilliant of debaters, and one of the most high-minded of Americans, had to give up a place in which he was performing important service to the nation and gratifying also his own personal desires. He should have been a Senator in perpetuity—if not from Missouri, from Pennsylvania or New Jersey or New York.

ON THE evening of April 28, 1875, Carl Schurz, lately Senator of the United States but now a private citizen, was the honored guest in the ornate ball room of Delmonico's Restaurant in New York City, at a "German Dinner," given by more than two hundred friends. The scandalous Beecher-Tilton trial was then going on, but the newspapers found space for long accounts of the banquet. The bill of fare included only German dishes and wines, and the speeches were all in the German tongue. After Dr. Krackowizer, the chairman, had introduced him, Schurz responded, confessing that on him "the sun of the administration had ceased to shine." Referring reminiscently to a similar gathering in the same hall six years before, when sixty of his compatriots had assembled to congratulate him on his election to the Senate, he declared that he had done his best to keep the faith. He ended by exhorting his hearers to be, first of all, Americans. "I love my Fatherland," he asserted, "but that does not lessen my love for America." Other speakers followed, including Bayard Taylor, all of them Schurz's eulogists. Finally a brass band appeared outside, heading a procession from Turner Hall, and members of the German singing societies serenaded Schurz and compelled him to say a few words to them. There had been another dinner on the night before, more distinctively American, at which William M. Evarts presided and Charles Francis Adams spoke; [1] but this German festival was the most dramatic of the many evidences of esteem which he received after his retirement from Congress.

[1] The earlier dinner, also at Delmonico's, included two hundred guests, representing all political beliefs, including Whitelaw Reid, Henry Adams, Peter Cooper, and Francis W. Bird. Schurz made a brilliant address, and was followed by Parke Godwin, David A. Wells, Charles F. Adams, Jr., and Murat Halstead. The *Tribune* commented, "The chief significance of last night's utterances lay in the obvious desire of men of all parties to do honor to the statesman who had declared and maintained his independence of party."

For the moment, Schurz's occupation was gone. He had been President-maker, Ambassador, General, and Senator; he had been on intimate terms with Lincoln and Sumner, Adams and Greeley, with the great and the near-great; what was there left for him now at forty-six? A reformer's lot does not provide bread and clothes for a family, and Schurz had children who were growing up—Agathe, Marianne, and Carl Lincoln. It was Agathe, indeed, who had become the manager of his household as well as his secretary. He was, of course, constantly in demand on the lecture circuit, and, before the opening of his last congressional session, he filled a lyceum schedule in New England and New York. He was also meditating a *Political History of the United States* and revolving in his restless mind the advisability of devoting himself solely to a "literary career." At this period, he thought of leaving St. Louis—which his family never really liked—and moving to Massachusetts, where he would be in a "cultural atmosphere." In this plan he was encouraged by Samuel Bowles, who, however, recommended Springfield or Northampton, adding that Boston and its vicinity were "somehow very provincial and narrowing." Bowles even hinted that Schurz might later be elected Senator from Massachusetts.

Schurz had not retired into seclusion. Toward the close of April, he attended a private dinner with a little group of avowed reformers—Godkin, Cox, Halstead, Henry Adams, Bowles, Nordhoff, and others—at which plans for the coming presidential campaign were discussed. Then, fulfilling a promise to his wife, who was far from well, he sailed with her for Europe. In May, he was in Hamburg, remote from even the echoes of American politics. Everywhere in Germany he was greeted with enthusiasm. He had audiences with many important persons, including the Kaiser himself, and his tour resembled a triumphal progress.

But Schurz was not allowed to forget the impending contest. Consulted by his friends, he urged them to declare openly for Charles Francis Adams as the only possible Republican candidate having the great merits of "absolute independence of party dictation and entire absence of ulterior ambitions." Furthermore, in the centennial year, with a notable celebration to be held in Philadelphia, the name of Adams, reminiscent of the splendid traditions of the republic, would be one to conjure with. Meanwhile events in the Middle West were shaping themselves in a way to bring Schurz back to the United States far earlier than he had planned. In Ohio, the gubernatorial battle had brought out a "sound money" Republican, General Rutherford B. Hayes, to run against the venerable Democratic incumbent, William Allen, and the fight was sure to be close. With both candidates honest and able, the deciding issue was likely to be the resumption of specie payments, to which the Democratic platform was positively opposed. As Ohio was a doubtful state, the result there would have some influence on the national election in the following autumn.

Things were not going well for the Ohio Republicans; and, as their position became critical, Charles Francis Adams implored Schurz to return and help to smash "old Bill Allen" and "rag money." The German vote in Ohio would probably be the determining factor at the polls, and Adams significantly pointed out that Schurz's intervention, if successful, would undoubtedly "give the whole shape" to the approaching presidential campaign. Adams's appeal was supplemented by Halstead and Nordhoff, and later, more desperately, by Whitelaw Reid and Henry Cabot Lodge, then a budding Bay State politician with reforming tendencies.[1] Schurz, in reply, maintained that the Independents should not attach themselves to either Republicans or Democrats in the local contests of that year.

Finally, after repeated entreaties, Schurz wrote on August 18 that he would come home. Reaching New York in mid-September, he conferred with Reid and then proceeded post-haste to Ohio, where, in a series of powerful speeches in both

[1] Writing to Lodge, Jan. 7, 1876, Schurz said, regarding a possible political conference, "You have to represent 'Young New England,'" *Schurz MSS*, Congressional Library.

English and German, he devoted himself to the "sound money" issue, declining to commit himself as between the two national parties and reserving complete freedom of judgment in 1876. His most widely advertised appearance was on September 27 at Turner Hall, in Cincinnati, in a speech entitled "Honest Money." Alphonso Taft, trying to reach the hall, found all the entrances blocked by people and had to remain outside, thus missing Schurz's scathing analysis of the iniquity of the inflationist Ohio Democrats. His argumentative eloquence helped to gives Hayes a majority, on October 12, of rather more than five thousand. "I got home this morning," wrote Adams gleefully, "serene in the knowledge that 'old Bill Allen's' grey and gory scalp was safely dangling at your girdle." Schurz's share in the victory was recognized by the Republican organization, which thanked him profusely and wished to compensate him for his services; but he refused to accept even money to defray his expenses. Schurz was one public man who always kept his skirts clean.

Schurz was not unwilling to return to the Republican fold in 1876 if only a reform candidate could be named. He was, of course, irrevocably opposed to a third term for Grant, and he cared even less for James G. Blaine, who seemed to him to be tainted by corruption. Writing to Cahoon on March 3, 1876, he declared that the republic was in a condition "of unprecedented humiliation and shame," adding, "Of all the men who have been mentioned as the possible Republican candidates, Adams and Bristow are *the only ones* I would trust and accept." Bristow, the Secretary of the Treasury, who had recently uncovered the notorious "Whiskey Ring," thus incurring Grant's displeasure, was a man of integrity and ability; but it was Adams whom Schurz really desired. Schurz's early warning that he would support the Republican ticket only if an honest candidate were chosen undoubtedly had a salutary influence on the party leaders.

It was a period when Schurz was saddened by a succession of domestic calamities. His beloved Margarethe, who had returned from Europe in the early winter, died on March 12, 1876, from illness following the birth of her son, Herbert, just a week before. Mrs. Schurz had been a semi-invalid from lung trouble for some years and had frequently taken the cure in sanitariums. She was, moreover, in her forty-fourth year, and the strain of childbirth was too much for her exhausted physique. Henry Holt is the authority for the story that, on the night of her death, Schurz sat until morning over the piano, expressing his grief through music. To his friend, Bird, Schurz wrote: "The loss of the wife of one's youth is unlike any other bereavement. It is the loss of the best part of one's life." His father had died only a few weeks before, in Monee, Illinois, where he had been spending his declining years with his married daughter.[1] Schurz's mother then came to St. Louis to live with him—"a keen-eyed, practical-minded old lady, with soft wavy auburn hair framing her strong features"—and there died in February, 1877. Writing to Hayes, Schurz described these disasters, coming within a twelvemonth, as "staggering blows from which it was not the easiest thing to rally." Oppressed by a sense of gloom, he sought relief by throwing himself with renewed vigor into political affairs.[2]

As everybody knew, Schurz was the head and front of the Liberal Republican coterie, and much depended on his decisions. In the late winter and early spring Henry Adams and Henry Cabot Lodge were in active correspondence regarding the situation. Both had leanings toward Bristow; and Adams had an arrangement with Lodge by which, if it became necessary to telegraph, Schurz and Bristow were to be disguised un-

[1] Mrs. Marie Jüssen Monroe, his granddaughter, remembers Christian Schurz as "a white-haired, blue-eyed old man, removed from all practical duties of life," busy among his flowers and birds or in his primitive chemical laboratory, or "seated on the piazza of his home in his dressing gown and skullcap, smoking his meerschaum pipe." He was inordinately proud of his distinguished son and liked to talk of the latter's achievements. See Schafer's *Carl Schurz, Militant Liberal,* Introduction, viii.

[2] Writing to Henry Cabot Lodge, March 20, 1876, Schurz said, "The beauty of life is gone, but I may still make an effort to make myself useful." *Schurz MSS,* Congressional Library.

der the names of Smith and Brown.[1] A plan was formed by which the Boston *Post* was to be purchased and placed under Schurz, as editor; but Henry Adams, who had agreed to furnish $5000 toward the project, made his contribution contingent on Bristow's nomination. Adams wrote Schurz on March 6, asking him whether he would accept the editorship "of one of our chief daily papers here, with a fixed salary of say $5000 a year, and a percentage on the profits over and above a certain sum." Schurz's reply cannot be found, but the plan fell through when the party nominations were made.

Schurz was beset by Republicans who pleaded with him to support Blaine, then regarded as the logical candidate of the regular organization. A delightful story is told of how the magnetic Maine statesman once tried his blandishments on Schurz. Once, when the latter was calling on Charles Nordhoff in Washington, Blaine appeared and walked home with him. As they drew near Lafayette Square, Blaine became effusively friendly and finally, throwing his arms almost around Schurz's neck and looking at him appealingly, said, "Carl, you won't *oppose* me, will you?" It is evident that Blaine was, in those days, very active in his own behalf. There were moments when he felt very confident, for he despised Charles Francis Adams, and did not fear Morton or Conkling. "Is there anybody you are afraid of?" asked Judge Jeremiah Black. "Yes, there is," answered Blaine, very seriously. "The Great Unknown."

Carl Schurz certainly had no intention of supporting Blaine, whom he considered thoroughly untrustworthy, especially after the scandal of the Mulligan Letters was carried into the House of Representatives in late April. On May 3, he expressed himself vigorously on this topic, pointing out that Blaine, although he had for years exercised great power and influence, had never used it "to uncover and put down corruption." Meanwhile he was busy with a definite plan. On February 14, 1876, Henry Adams wrote him a long and important letter, saying that Bristow was the ideal candidate of the In-

[1] Adams to Lodge, February 20, 1876, *Letters of Henry Adams,* 279.

dependents but that he could not be nominated by the regular Republican Convention. He therefore recommended that Schurz and half a dozen other reformers write a circular letter to "about two hundred of the most weighty and reliable of our friends," calling a meeting one week after the Republican Convention to decide whether they would support the regular candidate or nominate a candidate of their own. If the convention did not name Bristow, it would be the duty of the reformers to place another nominee before the people,—thus founding a third party.[1]

The plan was eventually modified by the sending out, on April 6, of a call for a conference to be held in New York City on May 15. Schurz met Brooks Adams and Henry Cabot Lodge in late March in New York to make the preliminary arrangements, and the invitation was signed by William Cullen Bryant, President Theodore Woolsey, of Yale, Alexander H. Bullock, Horace White, and Carl Schurz. Replies were to be addressed to Henry Cabot Lodge, in Boston.[2] The names of the endorsers of the conference were a sufficient guarantee of its respectability, and it had the approval of liberals who had been shocked by recent disclosures of the corruption of the Grant administration.

Nearly two hundred men appeared at the Fifth Avenue Hotel on Monday, May 15, when Henry Cabot Lodge, as secretary, summoned the meeting to order and called the roll. It was a gathering of brilliant people—college professors, clergymen, lawyers, publicists—all of them patriots and most of them reformers.[3] Their object, as stated in the invitation,

[1] Henry Adams to Schurz, February 14, 1876, *Letters of Henry Adams,* 273, ff. Adams enclosed a draft of the proposed circular letter, and suggested that the conference be held at Cleveland or Pittsburgh.

[2] Schurz was unquestionably the leading spirit in the movement, but he relied on Lodge to raise the necessary money. On April 26, 1876, Schurz wrote Lodge, "I have tried with several persons to have a business committee formed but it seems that nobody can be got to work except myself." *Schurz MSS,* Congressional Library.

[3] Among those present were Thomas Wentworth Higginson, Charles Francis Adams, James Freeman Clarke—all from Boston; Franklin MacVeagh, later

was to consider what could be done "to prevent the national election of the Centennial Year from becoming a mere choice of evils." Woolsey was at once elected president, and, on Schurz's motion, a committee of five was appointed to meet and determine upon a program. While this committee was in session, several leaders made brief addresses, for the encouragement of the delegates.

On Tuesday morning, the gathering was called to order at ten o'clock, in a room so small that only the invited guests could be admitted. Here Schurz read an "Address to the People," which he had prepared over night, declaring that the Independents would support no candidate, "however conspicuous his position or brilliant his ability, in whom the impulses of the party manager have shown themselves predominant over those of the reformer," or who "is not publicly known to possess those qualities of mind and character which the stern task of genuine reform requires." This was adopted without discussion. When Sidney Thomas moved a resolution committing the conference to Adams as a candidate, it was not well received, and, in the interests of harmony, he withdrew it. It was clear that the gathering would not support Blaine, Morton, or Conkling—then the chief contenders for the Republican nomination. A permanent committee was constituted, with Schurz as chairman, to take care of emergencies, and the conference adjourned in the evening, *sine die*, many members remaining to sign the address. The New York *Tribune* said editorially on May 17 that, although the meeting had been called derisively a conclave of "soreheads" and "college professors," its members belonged to "the saving element in American politics," and added, "It is the parties that have failed; not these men." Another point of view was expressed by a typical Tammany

in Taft's Cabinet; Theodore Roosevelt (not the future President, who this year became a Harvard undergraduate, but his father); and several German-American friends of Schurz, including Dr. Tiedemann, Dr. Jacobi, and his cousin, Edmund Jüssen, of Chicago. Among the college professors were Mark Hopkins, William G. Sumner, Julius H. Seelye, David A. Wells, and Perry, of Williams.

ward leader, who, when asked what Schurz and his colleagues had accomplished, replied, "Oh, they have reënacted the moral law and the Ten Commandments for a platform, and have demanded an angel of light for President."

The Republican Convention, so eagerly awaited, was called for June 14, at Cincinnati, in the immense auditorium where the Liberal Republicans had met in 1872. Schurz was present and conferred with Murat Halstead and others, but kept himself carefully out of the limelight. Blaine, during the preceding months, had held the center of the political stage. In January, he had delivered in the House a "bloody shirt" speech, denouncing Jefferson Davis, reviving quite unnecessarily all the bitterness of the Civil War, and deliberately stirring up sectional animosity. In April, caught in the Union Pacific Railroad scandal, he had daringly turned on his accusers and had temporarily discomfited his enemies. On the Sunday morning before the convention, he had succumbed to the heat, thus leading some of his supporters to believe that he might not be physically equal to the demands of the Presidency.

The reformers entered the convention prepared to support Bristow, for Adams had slipped into the background. It was evident, however, after the Grant men had held consultations with Morton and Conkling, that Bristow was the one candidate to whom they and the regulars were unalterably opposed. Hayes, apparently neutral, remained astutely quiet, but his campaign was being cleverly directed by General Edward F. Noyes and Stanley Matthews, and he was being groomed as a compromise candidate. Noyes presented Hayes's name in a convincing speech; General John M. Harlan nominated Bristow, as Kentucky's "favorite son"; but the climax came when the silver-tongued Robert G. Ingersoll, from Illinois, presented James Gillespie Blaine as the "plumed knight," who had "marched down the halls of the American Congress" and had thrown "his shining lance full and fair against the brazen forehead of every traitor to his country and every maligner of his fair reputation." Most of his speech was nonsense—but it was eloquent nonsense, carrying a thrill, and it so swept the delegates off their feet that, if a ballot could have been taken that evening, Blaine might have won the coveted prize.

But it was, after all, Blaine against the field. Behind the scenes, the party managers were meeting. The convention adjourned at 5.15 in the afternoon. The night was spent in conferences behind closed doors, but, on Friday morning, those "on the inside" knew that Rutherford B. Hayes, who had no foes to block him, was the man of the hour. The first ballot, as had been expected, showed Blaine at the front, followed in order by Morton, Bristow, Conkling, and Hayes. The movement toward Hayes began on the fifth roll-call. On the seventh, the trend could not be resisted, and he received 384 votes, six more than was necessary for a choice. Rhodes felt that Blaine would unquestionably have been nominated "had not the charge of personal corruption been fastened on him." It must be added, also, that the announced refusal of the Liberal Republicans to accept him as a candidate had something to do with the decision of the party managers—just how much will probably never be known. Hayes, on the other hand, was not vulnerable. His very weakness, as H. J. Eckenrode has suggested, proved to be an element of strength. No one was really displeased. Blaine sent him a telegram of congratulation, promising him his support; the regular politicians believed that Hayes was one of them; and, as we shall see, Carl Schurz and a considerable number of Independents were willing to accept and trust him.

On June 28, Carl Schurz received from Harvard University, at the hands of President Charles W. Eliot, the honorary degree of Doctor of Laws. Henry Adams had made the original suggestion to President Eliot, who at first expressed some hesitation because two other men had already been awarded a similar honor for that Commencement. Some judicious pressure, however, accomplished what was desired, and Schurz stood up with Governor Alexander H. Rice, Edward Lambert Cushing, and Daniel Coit Gilman. On the same day, Henry

Cabot Lodge received the degree of Doctor of Philosophy for his excellent thesis on Anglo-Saxon Law.[1] On the same day, also, the Democratic National Convention, assembled in St. Louis, nominated for the Presidency the New York lawyer and reformer, Samuel J. Tilden—undoubtedly the wisest choice which could have been made.

The Democratic platform satisfied Schurz, in that it arraigned the Grant administration scathingly and demanded a change in both measures and men. He had already, however, written Hayes on June 21, acknowledging that he would work for him if the Republican candidate would give pledges on the questions of civil service reform and sound money, and urging him to speak out boldly on these matters in his letter of acceptance. He intimated that such action would rally to Hayes "a large majority of the independent element, especially of the independent Germans." Two days later, without waiting for a reply, Schurz wrote again, stating that he had called for June 30 a meeting of the executive committee appointed by the Conference of Independents and adding that Hayes's letter of acceptance would furnish a text for a future letter from that committee to its constituents. To put it plainly, Schurz brought every form of pressure at his command to bear on Hayes; and the latter, who had already, during his gubernatorial campaign of the previous year, seen something of the influence exerted by Schurz, was in a conciliatory mood.

Hayes answered with unaffected cordiality on June 27, and Schurz responded with a draft of two paragraphs, one on the civil service and the other on the currency, for the letter of acceptance. The two men, who had never met up to this time, were brought together early in July, and reached complete agreement on nearly every subject. Hayes's letter, dated July 8, was clear, straightforward, and specific in its statements on the civil service, the currency, and reconstruction—the matters

[1] Schurz was Lodge's guest while he was in Boston. The two men were at this period on terms of intimacy, Lodge evidently regarding Schurz as the proper pattern of the idealistic statesman.

in which Schurz was chiefly interested. I have found it impossible to ascertain to what extent Hayes adhered to the language of Schurz, but it is unquestionable that the candidate was guided by what his adviser had to say.

Schurz now wrote to Charles Francis Adams, Jr., most significantly, saying that he had corresponded with Hayes and had conferred with him twice, that the letter of acceptance would be agreeable to all the reformers, and that the Cincinnati convention had nominated "our man without knowing it." He added, "It will be our fault, I think, if we do not gain a decisive influence in his administration." At the meeting of the executive committee, however, it soon became evident that the members did not wish to have their body take sides, and the Independents tacitly agreed to go each his own way. Some of them, including the Adamses,[1] Ottendorfer, and Koerner, came out openly for Tilden, feeling that his past record was better than that of Hayes; and indeed Schurz confessed that "a certain measure of reform is promised on either side." [2] But he felt that Tilden was "too much of a wire puller and machine politician," and preferred Hayes, with whom he had already worked. Not unnaturally, he was condemned by some of the Liberal Republicans,[3] who feared that he would henceforth be

[1] Henry Adams wrote Henry Cabot Lodge, June 30, 1876: "Before the result, I thought I should be perplexed between Tilden and Hayes, but to my great amusement I found that my mind decided the matter without any need of calling on the will. I have no ill-will to Hayes. If he is elected I shall support him loyally. But I can no more resist the pleasure of voting for Tilden than I could turn my back on a friend. . . . Schurz may do what he will. I advise him to do nothing." *Letters of Henry Adams,* 293.

[2] Lodge wrote Schurz, Aug. 16, 1876, "I reserve the right in voting for Hayes to give the fullest support to Tilden if he prove himself a real reformer,—which he never will." Later, however, Lodge wrote, Nov. 23, 1876, "I finally abandoned Mr. Hayes and voted for Mr. Tilden and believe him to have been fairly elected. But I care very little for either candidate and a great deal for my country and its institutions." *Schurz MSS,* Congressional Library. Lodge was influenced in his final decisions by the Adamses.

[3] Regarding Schurz, Henry Adams wrote Lodge, September 4, 1876: "I am not angry with him, but of course his leadership is at an end. Well! we knew what he was! The leader who treats his followers in that way is a mere will-o'-the-wisp. I hope he will get his Cabinet office, and I hope he will forget that

back, a repentant straggler, in the regular fold. A study of Schurz's correspondence during this period indicates, however, that he had convinced himself that Hayes would offer the most to the causes in which he was most deeply concerned. The outcome showed that he was not mistaken.

Having secured Hayes's adherence to his pet reforms, Schurz never relaxed his pressure on that candidate. It was a difficult situation; for Hayes, himself an absolutely honest man, was under the control of managers who were much less scrupulous. The Republican chairman, Zachariah Chandler, when Grant's Secretary of the Interior, was not likely to be restrained by ethical inhibitions; and Schurz, his ideals overcoming his tact, now denounced Chandler as an unworthy manager and urged Hayes to repudiate him. Hayes respectfully declined this invitation to cut his own political throat. Furthermore, Hayes, much to Schurz's disgust, was driven, as the contest waxed closer, to resort to the familiar and previously efficacious argument of the "bloody shirt";[1] and the Republicans, on the defensive, revived the Civil War enthusiasm, attempted again to identify the Democracy with the Confederacy, and appealed to the slumbering passions of fifteen years before. This invocation of the God of Hate was still effective, for the Grand Army of the Republic was in its early prime, and Tilden, who had not enlisted, could not match Hayes's fine military record. But Schurz did not like this method of persuasion. As usual, he preferred to rely on the corruption of his opponents and on his own consciousness of superior rectitude. But if these had been the only issues, Hayes would have been overwhelmed, and the Republican Party would at last have paid the penalty which, in 1872, Schurz had tried vainly to impose upon it. The election of Hayes was made possible largely by the subtle operation of the forces which Schurz most detested.

we ever worked to make him our leader, independent of party." *Letters of Henry Adams*, 299.

[1] Hayes wrote Blaine, September 14, "Our strong ground is the dread of a solid South, rebel rule, etc., etc. I hope you will make these topics prominent in your speeches."

Early in August, Schurz wrote Hayes that, if the voting were to take place immediately, the Democrats would win. He pointed out that Hayes was "loaded down with the discredit incurred by the administration and the old party leaders," and that Hayes's letter of acceptance, excellent though it was, was regarded by many influential Independents as "a bundle of well-meant promises" which would not, and could not, be carried out. Accordingly, he pleaded with Hayes to come forth with another statement, guaranteeing once more that the promised reforms would be carried out. The candidate's reply was discreetly noncommittal. Was not what he had done enough? The real trend of his thoughts was brought out by his statement that a majority of the plain people felt that a Democratic victory would "bring the Rebellion into power." A psychoanalyst would have discerned that Hayes, although guided by others as well as Schurz, was quite aware of the prestige in certain quarters of the gentleman from Missouri.

Hayes remained during the summer and autumn at his home in Columbus, making no speeches and conducting himself in a dignified fashion. Meanwhile Schurz, who had not been well, was recovering, and preparing to fulfill the important function expected of him. His first important public utterance was in his favorite Cincinnati, where he was always sure of a warm welcome, and where, on the last day of August, he delivered a speech later published under the title "Hayes versus Tilden," and extensively circulated as a campaign document. It was necessary for him to justify his action in abandoning his old friends and choosing Hayes.[1] With shrewd moderation, he did not overdo his eulogy of the Republican nominee, but he did declare that the latter's letter of acceptance was "the clearest and completest program of civil service reform ever

[1] The attitude of many of the Independents toward Schurz is indicated in a letter from Henry Adams to Gaskell, dated September 8, 1876, in which he said, referring to himself and his friends: "The two parties made their offer for us, and we dissolved like a summer cloud. I am left smiling at the ruins. Our principal leader has returned to his party traces." *Letters of Henry Adams,* 299.

put forth by a public man in this Republic"—a sufficiently modest statement if, as was probably the case, Schurz wrote that section himself. He did not guarantee that Hayes would be able to remedy all the evils by which human society, in that "Dreadful Decade," was oppressed, but he did refer to "the clear, solid, cultivated intellect, the unostentatious but firm force of quiet persistent energy, and the inviolable pledge of a born gentleman." The tone of this speech was such as to make it exceedingly valuable to the Republican cause at that moment. Such an appeal to the consciences of voters was unfamiliar to the Republican Party of the "Tragic Era," which had almost forgotten the crusading zeal displayed by Carl Schurz in 1860.

Schurz spoke at other focal points during the campaign, although a slight accident compelled a cessation of his activities during early September. The result was in doubt, for both sides had managed cleverly and the two candidates were, after all, evenly matched in character—Tilden's brilliancy being balanced by Hayes's reliability. The preëlection omens, such as they were, seemed to favor the Democrats. Four days before the end, Hayes wrote Schurz, "I shall find many things to console me if defeated," and he went to bed on the evening of November 7 thinking that he had lost. As the sun went down, the Democrats, learning that they had carried New York, New Jersey, and Indiana, began noisily to celebrate their victory. Schurz, having returned to St. Louis to vote, could count up 203 votes for Tilden—eighteen more than were necessary—and felt that he had failed.

And then, to the astonishment of the Democrats, came an authoritative statement from the Republican headquarters asserting that South Carolina, Florida, and Louisiana were in the Republican column, and that Hayes with 185 votes, was elected. Even the Republican New York *Tribune* had already conceded Tilden's success; but the New York *Times*, although desperate, did not lose hope, and, on the fateful morning of November 8, printed an editorial headed, "A Doubtful Election." After a careful survey of the returns, telegrams were dispatched to Republican leaders in South Carolina, Florida, and Louisiana, warning them that a Republican victory could be claimed if those states could be secured for Hayes. Within a few hours a plot was planned and perfected which was to place the unsuspecting Hayes in the White House.[1]

Even Carl Schurz, in Missouri, far distant from the real scenes of excitement, could get the thrill that comes from an approaching battle. On November 10, President Grant issued an order to General Sherman, instructing the officers in command in Louisiana and Florida to preserve peace and order. Schurz, a man with a conscience, who tried painfully to be honest with himself, was in an embarrassing position, and it is not difficult to imagine the struggle in his mind. On December 3, he joined John B. Henderson and other Missourians in writing to Senator Thomas W. Ferry, then president pro tempore of the United States Senate (Vice President Wilson having died on November 22, 1875), urging that the problem be referred to the Supreme Court of the United States and thus removed altogether from the realm of politics. Hayes, writing to Schurz on December 6, said that this suggestion struck him favorably, and added, "I have no doubt that we are justly and legally entitled to the Presidency." Schurz told Jacob D. Cox, late in December, that Hayes thought himself to have been "fairly and rightfully elected."

Schurz himself, although he had his doubts, was able ultimately to quiet his conscience, largely because he distrusted "the character and purpose of the leading men on the Democratic side." Writing in December to his fellow reformer, Henry Cabot Lodge, Schurz declared, "I never had any confidence in Tilden but now I have less than ever." "What I fear most," he went on to say, "is not a civil war—for I think neither party is prepared for that—but a condition of things completely upsetting our political morals." By the close of the year, Schurz had reached the conclusion that nothing but the

[1] See H. J. Eckenrode, *Rutherford B. Hayes: Statesman of Reunion*, 176, ff.

decision of some tribunal outside of Congress could give Hayes an unquestioned title to the presidency, and that any ruling based on the Louisiana Returning Board would be most unfortunate. Even when the Constitutional Amendment referring the whole matter to the Supreme Court failed to pass, Schurz continued to exert his influence to have it settled "by some tribunal standing above party interest and ambition."

The situation in its chief phases was already clarified. The disputed states were South Carolina, Louisiana, and Florida, with a technical detail confusing the result in Oregon—and all of these four States must be counted for Hayes if he were to be declared elected. The Republicans, holding the reins of government and with the Civil War veterans to back them, could, through the employment of force or corruption—or both—seize and retain the presidency. Some of the Republican managers had few scruples. But Carl Schurz wanted to be sure that Hayes was not elevated to the highest office in the land by "a proceeding of a doubtful character"—as he wrote Hayes on January 12, 1877—and the latter, to do him justice, had the same feeling. The vital problem was how the electoral vote should be counted. Some of Hayes's most devoted friends were insisting that Senator Ferry, the Republican President of the Senate, should claim and exercise the right of counting the votes and settling controverted points. To this proposal, Schurz objected, and expressed his feeling vigorously to Hayes. The latter wisely replied that he would have nothing to do with the matter but should "quietly await the event." He did, however, in anticipation of a decision favorable to the Republicans, go ahead with the preparation of his inaugural address and with the choosing of a Cabinet; and on these two subjects he asked Schurz's advice. Tilden, meanwhile, vacillated, showing himself far from eager for the presidency. Watterson believed that the "missing ingredient" in his personality was "the touch of the dramatic discoverable in most of the leaders of men." Either Blaine or Roosevelt, said "Marse Henry," would, in Tilden's place, "have carried all before him." Rhodes too emphasizes

Tilden's "infirmity of purpose"; but the latter's mood was rather the equanimity of the philosopher. After all, as Mr. Eckenrode has recently pointed out,[1] the dice of the Gods were loaded in 1877, and it would have been a national catastrophe if any authorized commission had declared for Tilden. It was possibly a premonition of this fact which led the Democratic candidate to endure his destiny without a struggle.

Various proposals for the settlement of the crucial questions were introduced in Congress, culminating in the Electoral Count Act, providing that the decision in the case of States from which there had been more than one return should be made by a tribunal consisting of five Senators, five Representatives, and five Justices of the Supreme Court of the United States. The Congressmen, by agreement, were to be evenly divided between the two parties, and the four Justices—two Republicans and two Democrats—were to select a fifth. At first, Hayes objected to this project for an outside commission; but Schurz urged him to accept the plan, and the Republican candidate finally yielded. Abram S. Hewitt, who was Tilden's exceedingly able manager, accepted for the Democrats. The bill was signed by Grant on January 29, in the faint hope on the part of many—including Carl Schurz—that the Electoral Commission would approach its important task in a spirit of non-partisanship, but with the tacit assumption by practical politicians that it would divide along partisan lines. It had been expected by the framers of the commission that the fifth Justice would be David Davis, who leaned toward the Democrats. But Davis, who at precisely this juncture was suddenly elected Senator from Illinois, felt that it would be an impropriety for him to sit on the commission; accordingly Justice Joseph P. Bradley, a Republican, was named, and the ultimate decision

[1] Eckenrode, *Rutherford B. Hayes,* 210, ff. Mr. Eckenrode's account of the "Crime of '76" is clear and fair-minded. As the ablest and most recent biographer of Hayes, he believes that the decision of the Electoral Commission was "the most spectacular act of injustice in American history" but that, for the good of the country, and especially of the South, "the seating of Rutherford B. Hayes was fortunate."

really rested in his vote. It turned out, as the prophets expected, that he was for Hayes.

A good deal of bargaining was discussed, and some was carried out, by both Republicans and Democrats. The evidence is practically conclusive that certain agents made a bargain for Hayes to the effect that the latter, if inaugurated, would agree to withdraw the Northern troops from South Carolina, Louisiana, and Florida, and leave the whites to reëstablish their government there. Although Hayes later asserted that assurances were given without consulting him, his papers indicate that he was informed of every step in the proceedings and that he definitely committed himself. It is equally clear that representatives of Tilden were negotiating at one time for the bribery of the corrupt Returning Board in Louisiana. The election of 1877 is not an episode of which any American can be proud.

When the Electoral Commission opened its sessions on February 2, in the Supreme Court Chamber, the first State which it had to consider was Florida. If an absolutely fair election had been held, Florida would probably have gone for Tilden. But this was not the question at issue. After counsel had presented the arguments of the respective parties, the Electoral Commission, by a strict party vote of eight to seven, refused to go behind the certified return. When Justice Bradley joined the Republicans on the first test vote, all knowing Democrats perceived that the battle was over. On February 12, when Congress again convened, the vote of Florida was announced for Hayes and Wheeler.

It is true that Louisiana was still to be considered, that the Returning Board in that state was corrupt, ready apparently to sell itself to the highest bidder, and that shameless fraud blackened all its proceedings; but it was evident that the Republicans, with victory within reach, would hesitate at nothing. On March 2, all the questions were settled, and Rutherford Birchard Hayes was declared to have been elected President of the United States. A few days later, Samuel Bowles wrote Schurz, "The Louisiana steal is a dreadful one, but if the

Republican party can follow President Jackson's example and get religion, they may yet cheat the devil!" Tilden and his supporters, though convinced that they had been the victims of fraud, preferred four years of Hayes to fratricidal strife. Tilden had received a considerable majority of the popular vote and probably was entitled to a majority in the Electoral College. Yet each party had a plausible case, and, now that the affair had been legally settled, the country returned to normal. After all, Hayes turned out to be fully as good a chief executive as Tilden would have been.

During the winter, Carl Schurz had made short lecture tours in the Middle West,[1] but had, at Hayes's expressed wish, carried on with him a copious correspondence. On January 25, for example, Schurz wrote out some ideas for the inaugural address, saying that Hayes should seek the support of public-spirited citizens by making a "bold and strong statement" of his political aims, with specific reference to civil service reform, the Southern question, and the need for sectional peace, concluding with a declaration that he would not accept a second term. To these suggestions, Hayes answered that he could vote "aye" on them all. On January 30, Schurz, at Hayes's request, made some recommendations for the Cabinet: Evarts for Secretary of State, Bristow for the Treasury, Cox for the Interior, Edmunds for Attorney-General, Hawley for the War Department, Henry L. Pierce for the Navy, and Jewell as Postmaster-General—with second and third choices in nearly every instance. It was typical of Schurz that he should mention for Secretary of State George William Curtis, whom he described as "a very pure, patriotic, and able man."

From the opening of his campaign, Hayes had kept Schurz in mind for a Cabinet position—and indeed the latter had earned substantial recognition. Murat Halstead, Jacob D. Cox,

[1] *Harper's Weekly*, September 1, 1877, announced that Schurz was paid at the rate of $1200 a week by a Boston lecture bureau, and that a handsome profit resulted to the promoters of the tours. I have been unable to verify these figures.

and others did not let Schurz's interests suffer, and it was generally assumed that he would not be ignored. On February 19, Schurz wrote to Halstead the conventional deprecatory letter, saying: "Office for its own sake is of no value to me at all. I can afford to remain in private life, and in many respects it would be best for me." But—if the President felt that Schurz could render essential service, the latter was "willing," and, if consulted regarding a department, preferred either the State or the Treasury, as covering fields regarding which he knew something—international affairs and finance. He added, "The Interior would not be a very interesting department to me, as I have never given much attention to the Indians, patents, pensions, and public lands. But it does offer some opportunities for useful work, and a seat in the Cabinet council."

Halstead sent to Schurz on February 20 an interesting confidential letter, explaining that he had talked for three hours with Hayes, who thought that Schurz would have more scope for civil service reform in the Interior than in the State Department. But he inserted one significant paragraph: "Is there some danger that if you went into the Cabinet you would be a disturbing element? How would you get along with Sherman, if Evarts, Hawley, and Harlan were in?" Evidently Hayes had hinted to Halstead that Schurz had the reputation of being a meddler. Halstead ended: "And now I will not conceal from you that I have misgivings. Blessed are those who expect nothing, for they shall not be disappointed."

Five days after this interview, however, Hayes sent Schurz a short note, offering him a place in the Cabinet and saying: "The Interior Department is my preference for you. The Post Office would come next." Schurz lost no time in accepting, and added, "Of the two Departments you mention, there is one, the Interior, the business of which I should, with diligent application, hope satisfactorily to master." Hayes answered on February 27, "Your choice of Department is also my choice for you."

Although not yet officially elected, Hayes set out from

Columbus on March 1, reaching Washington on the morning of the following day and going at once to call upon President Grant. Some hours previous to his arrival, before daylight had dawned, Senator Ferry, after the final vote in Congress, had announced that Rutherford B. Hayes, of Ohio, had been elected President of the United States for four years. On Saturday evening, March 3, just before an elaborate state dinner at the White House, Hayes privately took the oath of office, and, for the next few hours, the United States had two Presidents. On the following Monday, before an enormous but undemonstrative crowd, he delivered his inaugural address—a document couched in noble and vigorous language, indicating that a new era had begun. To Schurz's delight, many of his own ideas had been embodied in an idealistic statement of the President's purposes: a "wise, honest, and peaceful self-government" for the South; a civil service reform which should be "thorough and complete"; an "early resumption of specie payments." It was a strong but conciliatory paper, almost universally praised. It was felt, even by Democrats, that "an honest man had come to the presidency." As for Carl Schurz, who had been denounced in 1872 as a renegade and assailed repeatedly in Congress as a traitor to the Republican Party, he was back in its councils, with the supreme satisfaction of knowing that he had yielded nothing but that its leaders had been converted to his own viewpoint. He had long been recognized as a civil service reformer; now, in one of the most important Cabinet positions, he was to have what every theorist desires most—an opportunity to put his ideas into practice. Many of his friends sent him their felicitations, but none was more welcome than that from Frederick Billings, who wrote:

> I can hardly believe my eyes! The reform-element square at the front and you in the Cabinet! What a Reformation! I cannot help congratulating you—and, much more, congratulating the country. Now, for a resolute Forward!—in the spirit of the Inaugural—and in harmony with the Cabinet, and the better days of the Republic are close at hand.

CHAPTER XIX SECRETARY OF THE INTERIOR

CARL SCHURZ was the first United States citizen of German birth to fill a seat in any President's Cabinet. He was, in appearance and manner, almost completely Americanized, but, although he wrote flawless English and spoke with only the slightest trace of a foreign accent, he was regarded in many quarters as an alien; indeed he once complained to Henry Watterson, "If I should live a hundred years, my enemies would still call me a Dutchman!" His foes, when actively annoyed, employed even less complimentary epithets, such as "Dutch viper" or "Mephistopheles with whiskers." When arguments failed, they could always stigmatize him as a Prussian, trying to import European practices into our uncontaminated country, and tell him to go back to the Rhine where he belonged.

What had originally given Schurz his potency in politics was his voice. As an orator he was undeniably superb. Thoughtful judges, comparing him with others, have maintained that he was the greatest platform speaker of his generation, not excluding Wendell Phillips and Robert G. Ingersoll. Still under fifty years of age, he was physically vigorous, with a tall and slender figure, thick and very conspicuous wavy hair, a firm mouth beneath his neatly clipped moustache and beard, and hawk-like eyes which could gleam with amusement or flash with indignation. Taught by experience, he had discarded the sonorous and often inflated rhetoric of his youth, and now spoke simply, directly, and incisively, with gestures fitted to his mood. His voice was melodious and could, in a large hall, he raised in pitch until it carried his words to the far corners. The secret of his success as an orator, however, lay chiefly in his sincerity—a trait in which he resembled Lincoln. He convinced others because he believed what he said.

Like Woodrow Wilson, whom in temperament and philosophy he somewhat resembled, Schurz had about him always the faint aroma of the pedagogue, shown especially in his bookishness, his idealism, his fondness for bestowing advice, and his difficulty in working with others. In some aspects he was a doctrinaire, drawn from his library by circumstances into the wider world of affairs. When he was disappointed in politics, he would seek solace at the piano with his favorite composers, the romanticists Schumann and Chopin. But he was no mere theorist. He could hold his own in the give and take of debate, and his occasional sentimentalism did not soften his intellectual and moral fiber.

Practical politicians, accustomed to devious methods of promoting their interests, could not understand Schurz. His indifference to the claims of party seemed to Conkling and Platt to result from instability and disloyalty. Tricksters, like "Ben" Butler, and cynics, like Zachariah Chandler, looked upon him as an enigma. He was not ostentatious in parading his moral standards, yet he was impervious to all the usual forms of political seduction. Although he had his ambitions and worked hard to achieve them, he must realize them legitimately, or not at all. Like most reformers, he could be, under certain conditions, extremely irritating, but he was never so bigoted as Garrison and Sumner.

Schurz was a tower of strength to a reform administration. His inclusion in the Cabinet was a proof that a new era had dawned. Soon it was apparent that the long dominant congressional oligarchy—Blaine, Conkling, Cameron, and their satellites—were to be shorn of their power, for Hayes, in choosing his advisers, deliberately ignored them and followed his own inclinations. He proffered his declaration of independence in his letter of acceptance, to which Schurz had contributed suggestions. He reiterated it in his inaugural address, in his famous sentence—the only one with which his name is associated—"He serves his party best who serves his country best." And now, as President, he selected for his Cabinet, in every case except one, men not closely identified with the Grant regime. Of these, Carl Schurz was the one on whom he most relied. Lean years had arrived for the "practical politicians."

In the large high-studded room, with the map of the United States on the wall, where the Cabinet gathered at noon on Tuesdays and Fridays, sat an interesting group of men, the President at the head of the long table and Carl Schurz at the foot. Hayes himself, methodical, industrious, and thoughtful, but not brilliant, was a tactful presiding officer. At his right was William M. Evarts, the Secretary of State, cadaverous and smooth-shaven, with an intellectual countenance, a Yale graduate who had become one of the great lawyers of his generation. Now after defending Andrew Johnson in the impeachment trial, representing the United States as counsel at the Geneva Tribunal, and serving as attorney for the Republicans before the Electoral Commission, he was to bring his learning and his wit to the support of the administration. On the President's left was John Sherman, of Ohio, brother of General Sherman, a Senator since 1861 and long chairman of the Senate Committee on Finance, intensely partisan and once a guiding spirit in the senatorial inner ring, but now, as Secretary of the Treasury, important to Hayes because of his staunch championship of "sound money." Hayes owed much politically to Sherman, who, despite his former intimate relations with Morton and Conkling, was, next to Schurz, the counsellor whom the President most trusted.

Evarts, Sherman, and Schurz were the really important members of the Cabinet. General Charles Devens, of Massachusetts, associated with Schurz fifteen years before in the disaster at Chancellorsville, had been designated, at the recommendation of George F. Hoar, as Attorney-General. He was a Harvard graduate, of aristocratic antecedents, who had sat since the war on the Supreme Bench in his native state. To the astonishment of the Grand Army of the Republic, Hayes appointed as his Postmaster-General David M. Key, of Tennessee, a Confederate veteran, a jovial man with a massive head, a heavy mane of hair, and a flowing beard, who kept his colleagues laughing with his jokes. The Secretary of War was George W. McCrary, a somewhat ponderous ex-Congressman without military experience, whose chief asset was his authorship of the Electoral Commission plan. Richard M. Thompson, the oldest of the group, was Secretary of the Navy. A lawyer in Terre Haute, he had been named as a concession to Senator Oliver P. Morton, of Indiana. In a government which had virtually no navy, his ignorance of ships and sailors was a subject for jest rather than for criticism.[1] Schurz, the youngest except McCrary, was also the most active and resourceful. Although they represented different elements in society and politics, they were very congenial, and dissension among them was almost unknown.[2] With only slight exceptions, they were agreed on the important principles of governmental policy.

When the Cabinet announcements were disclosed, there was indignation among the Republican "Stalwarts." Conkling disliked Evarts; Blaine was angry because his suggestions had not been followed; and Cameron was annoyed because his son, Don Cameron, had not been retained as Secretary of War. All three, furthermore, were opposed to Schurz, who had openly refused to be restricted by Republican orthodoxy and had been foremost in denouncing "Grantism." He was assailed in the Senate as a renegade; and, when it was feared that he might be rejected, some of his friends were driven to move about among the Democratic Senators asking for their aid. Sherman was confirmed first. Finally, after the other nominations had been favorably reported by the various committees to which, contrary to precedent, they had been referred, they were approved,

[1] Thompson later accepted a position as chairman of an American advisory committee for promoting the interests of De Lesseps and the Panama Canal project—a sinecure office with a salary of $25,000 a year—and was asked to resign by Hayes. He was succeeded by Nathan Goff, Jr. McCrary was appointed in 1879 as District Judge of Iowa and was succeeded by Alexander Ramsey. In 1880, Horace Maynard, of Tennessee, took the place of Key, who had been made District Judge for Eastern Tennessee.

[2] See the Washington *Star,* July 14, 1879.

Evarts, Key, and Schurz with only two dissenting votes, and McCrary, Devens, and Thompson unanimously. Thus Carl Schurz, who had spent the preceding four or five years in damning a Republican administration, was now endorsed for a Republican cabinet.[1]

Grant had not been altogether successful in his Secretaries of the Interior. Jacob D. Cox, his first appointee, had been an excellent man, one of Schurz's closest friends, but he had resigned in December, 1870, to be succeeded by Columbus Delano, a Congressman from Iowa, under whom various scandals developed, especially in connection with Indian affairs. Eventually Delano was bitterly attacked by Professor Othniel C. Marsh, of Yale University, for rascality and corruption in the distribution of supplies to the Red Cloud tribe, and resigned before the official investigation was concluded. In his place, Grant named Zachariah Chandler,[2] who, having been defeated for reëlection to the Senate, was in need of a salaried position, and looked upon a place in the Cabinet chiefly as a vantage point from which patronage could be shrewdly distributed. Schurz inherited from the previous administration some unfortunate situations for which he was to be wrongfully blamed but which he did his utmost to rectify.

Schurz had considered inviting Henry Cabot Lodge, who had been secretary of the Fifth Avenue Hotel Conference in 1876, to become his Assistant Secretary. Samuel Bowles wrote Schurz in July, 1877, saying that Lodge would have been glad to accept, and adding:

> Nobody could have been better for you. We need to import into the Departments, just such men—fellows who have the

[1] Hayes wrote in his *Diary,* March 14, 1877, "The chief disappointment among the influential men of the party was with Conkling, Blaine, Camerons, Logan, and their followers. They were very bitter. The opposition was chiefly to Evarts, Key, and Schurz, and especially Schurz."

[2] Gail Hamilton, in the New York *Tribune* for June 16, 1877, described Chandler as "an old war-horse," a "wire-puller of wire-pullers." When Schurz first took office, he gave out an interview praising his predecessor in a rather conventional way, but soon was obliged to modify his complimentary opinion.

working temperament, as he has, who have high patriotic purposes and while independent of their salaries, will abundantly earn them. With such a man at your right hand, you would have simply doubled yourself, while you could have had the benefit of all the other kind of material in the next places below.

Schurz, however, thinking that Lodge was not available, had already chosen his Assistant Secretary, and thus missed having Lodge as his coadjutor. What might have happened to Lodge's political philosophy if he had been exposed to the contagion of Schurz's reforming zeal is a matter for interesting speculation.

Although Hayes soon lost the backing of nearly all the regular Republican leaders, he was not at all discomfited. Unswerving in his purpose, he insisted on fulfilling his pledges to restore constitutional government to the South, to maintain a sound currency, and to improve the civil service. On March 29, Schurz, who never found it easy to bestow unqualified praise, wrote: "Hayes makes haste slowly but surely. You will soon wake up and find things done." The President was an undramatic person, with no gift for self-advertising, but he was conscientious and courageous. Schurz found in him a hearty supporter of all worthy reform projects.

Hayes conceived his first task to be the pacification of those sections of the South which were still suffering under "carpetbag" rule. Before the inauguration, Schurz had urged upon Hayes the desirability of conciliating the South, not only by naming to the Cabinet some man "of Confederate antecedents," but also by gaining the good will of the Southerners in every other possible way. The President did not need to be convinced that reconstruction, except as a gratification of a desire for revenge, had been a failure. He also realized, as he wrote in his *Diary* on October 27, 1877, that "the pacification of the South is a total departure from the principles, traditions, and wishes of the Republican party." But the fear of criticism was not a deterrent with Hayes. On April 10, he withdrew Northern troops from the confines of South Carolina, and, on April 24, from Louisiana, thus leaving the existing "carpetbag" government in those states without support. From that moment, all the Southern states were free to manage their own affairs. In his *Diary*, on April 22, the President wrote, "The troops are ordered away, and I now hope for peace, and, what is equally important, security and prosperity for the colored people." It had taken him less than seven weeks to settle the long-standing Southern question. Eckenrode has said correctly that Hayes "was a better friend to the South than all its soldiers and statesmen."

In mid-September, 1877, Hayes cemented his policy of conciliation by starting on a tour of the South, in the course of which he visited Louisville, Chattanooga, Knoxville, Atlanta, Lynchburg, and Charlottesville. Schurz was a member of the presidential entourage, which also included Secretaries Evarts, McCrary, and Key, as well as Mrs. Hayes and her two sons, Birchard and Webb. The speeches along the route expressed a sentiment of union; and the Governor of Georgia, in the heart of the district through which General Sherman had made his devastating march, welcomed the President as "the peacemaker between brethren estranged." Schurz was called upon at nearly every public meeting and always spoke effectively. In October, he accompanied Hayes on shorter excursions to Richmond and to Montpelier, the old home of James Madison. Willing to meet Southerners in an affable and liberal way, the President did much to repair the injuries caused by Thaddeus Stevens and the radical Republicans of that post-war era.

With Hayes's Southern policy, Schurz had little to do except to encourage and congratulate its author. But it was different with civil service reform. In any study of Schurz's enduring influence in American life his part in civil service reform must take a foremost place. The evils of the "spoils" system, as it was in operation under Grant, seem obvious enough to us today. Appointments were usually made not because of merit, but because of demonstrated party loyalty. An office and its salary were regarded as the logical reward of fidelity to a political organization. Much of what was called euphemistically "patronage" was controlled by members of Congress, who used it as a means of advancing or consolidating their own interests. As a corollary, any Senator or Representative found, as Schurz did in 1869, that innumerable hours were wasted in talking with applicants for office, who only too frequently brought pressure of various kinds to bear. Even when a man was assigned a clerkship and handled it well, he was not sure of retaining it, for a new administration might come in, and rotation in office was considered normal. Thus, when an employee had begun to "know the ropes" and function efficiently, he might be liable to dismissal. Some government servants, because of peculiar conditions, managed to make themselves indispensable. But nobody felt sure of his future. In addition, federal employees were usually expected to contribute to each campaign a percentage of their salaries and to exert their influence, often very potent, to keep their party in power. George William Curtis exaggerated only slightly when he said:

> Every four years the machinery of government is pulled to pieces. The country presents a most ridiculous, revolting, and disheartening spectacle. The business of the nation and the legislation of Congress are subordinated to the distribution of plunder among eager partisans. . . . The country seethes with intrigue and corruption. . . . Economy, patriotism, honesty, honor, seem to have become words of no meaning.

To any fair-minded observer, it would seem that, if the government is to operate efficiently, it ought to be managed like a private company, and that the country needs a "non-partisan business administration," at least on purely routine or clerical matters. Appointments should be made on the basis of competency; good servants should be retained and unsatisfactory ones discharged, regardless of party affiliation or "pull." Such methods are demonstrably economical. Government service would then become a career, like law or manufacturing, sought out and pursued by able men with the assurance that their positions were permanent during good behavior and that promotion would come solely through faithfulness to duty. This ideal was illustrated by the remark of a "practical politician" regarding Postmaster-General Jewell, "Curse the fellow, he wants to run his department exactly as if it were a factory."

Who defended the "spoils" system? First of all, politicians like Platt and Conkling, who, having built up a smoothly running party machine based largely on the distribution of patronage, naturally did not wish to discard a policy which had placed them where they were. The motives of "bosses" like these, though occasionally disguised, were entirely selfish. Conkling, at the New York Republican State Convention in September, 1877, at Rochester, made a savage speech in denunciation of civil service reformers, describing George William Curtis, who was a delegate, as a "man milliner," the "carpet knight of politics," and shouting out an unforgotten sentence, "When Dr. Johnson said that patriotism was the last refuge of a scoundrel he ignored the enormous possibilities of the word reform." But not all the opposition was corrupt. There were some cautious people who honestly feared the creation of an office-holding class—a bureaucracy which would exercise too great an influence in the republic. And there were also those who could not be goaded out of their inertia. "Things are going along very well," said these good-natured folk. "Why make a change?"

Schurz's attitude on the question was unequivocal. Early in his senatorial career, he had announced his opposition to the "spoils" system and had made speeches analyzing its faults. Although other problems at various periods demanded temporarily more of his attention, he never forgot the civil service. Indeed from 1869 until his death in 1906, one of his main objects was to keep successive Presidents, no matter of which party, alive to their responsibilities. Often he tried to move forward too rapidly—not an uncommon error with reformers —and he received an occasional disconcerting setback. Sometimes he expected, and claimed, too much. But on the whole he made progress.

Schurz suffered at first from a common delusion among idealists that all that is required to make mankind accept the truth is to present it to them. Practical experience ultimately convinced him that some of the best-intentioned of men can be at times strangely perverse and blind. Then it was that he realized that, even to establish a wise and sane project, one has to fight; and, to meet this situation, he became an aggressive and undaunted controversialist. The disillusionment was painful, and, even to the end of his days, Schurz could not get over his astonishment that he should be opposed when he was so thoroughly sincere.

Grant, as we have seen, had honestly tried to accomplish something, but had met with so little encouragement from a greedy Congress that he finally gave up in despair. In the spring of 1875, the rules of the Civil Service Commission were suspended, and, without any appropriation from Congress, it could no longer function. It had already, however, demonstrated the possibilities of a "merit" system, and the reformers, including Schurz and Curtis, undertook a campaign of education. They talked and lectured on the subject, and *Harper's Weekly*, Curtis's organ, became its militant advocate. In 1876, both parties somewhat resignedly pledged themselves in their platforms to some degree of civil service reform. The New York Civil Service Reform Association was established in 1877. And then Rutherford B. Hayes came to the presidency—the first chief executive who took office with the avowed intention of doing something definite on the matter.

Like Grant, Hayes had a Congress which turned a deaf ear to all his appeals.[1] At his first Cabinet meeting, however, he named Evarts and Schurz as a committee to draft rules governing future appointments to subordinate positions. With Evarts's approval, Schurz outlined certain regulations based on the doc-

[1] A good illustration of the spirit of the House of Representatives is its action in naming the notorious "Ben" Butler as chairman of a committee on Civil Service Reform.

trine that efficient service should be the only criterion for retention in office. The head of each department was then made responsible for all appointments under his jurisdiction. All the Cabinet members accepted Schurz's rather advanced ideas. Later, however, John Sherman, whose earlier training and associations made it difficult for him to neglect the use of patronage, reverted to his former practices.

Bristow had warned Schurz, four days after the inauguration, "The Administration must either conquer the machine politicians or surrender to them." Hayes had no intention of yielding. He at once instructed Dorman B. Eaton to prepare a report on the history of the movement for civil service reform in Great Britain—a report which was submitted to Congress with the President's Annual Message of December 1, 1879. On May 26, 1877, he sent a significant letter to Secretary of the Treasury Sherman, approving a partial report of a commission, headed by John Jay, which had been investigating the New York Custom House; and, on June 22, he issued an executive order to all federal officials, declaring that no employee should "be required or permitted to take part in the management of political organizations, caucuses, conventions, or election campaigns," or assessed for political purposes. This order brought consternation to the Republican leaders, and it was never thoroughly carried out in the Treasury Department. It was, however, the writing on the wall.

Reversing Grant's nepotistic tendencies, Hayes consistently refused to appoint to office any of his own or his wife's relatives. He was conservative in his removal of federal officials, and good men were usually undisturbed. He made, on the whole, excellent new appointments, although his tacit approval of the providing of places in the Treasury Department for the ejected Southern Republicans and the members of the Louisiana canvassing board was not to his credit. He recommended measures of civil service reform to Congress in his first annual message and in each successive one; and he considered the preparation of a special message dealing solely with that subject. He repeatedly, but without success, urged Congress to revive the somnolent Civil Service Commission by appropriating the small sum of $25,000 to its support. He refused to allow Conkling to dictate to him with regard to the New York Custom House, and noted in his *Diary*, "This question of senatorial patronage is the salient point in the improvement of the civil service." On the whole, Hayes was a real friend of the movement. At the close of his administration, *Harper's Weekly* said editorially, "We think that Mr. Hayes has done more for a reform of the civil service upon sound principles than any President in our history."

Carl Schurz made the Department of the Interior, with Hayes's full approval, a demonstration station, where the experiment of the merit system could be observed in operation. At his first meeting with his subordinates, he said firmly, "Gentlemen, I desire to say to you that I intend to conduct this department upon business principles." Resisting the importunities of patronage mongers, he at once instituted competitive examinations so far as possible as the primary basis for admission into the service; and promotion was based upon similar tests, joined with a comparison of efficiency records. With relentless justice, he sought out incompetents and filled their places with industrious and faithful officials. Within a year, he had won the praise of such an ardent reformer as Benjamin F. Bristow, who congratulated him on the quiet but effective manner in which he was wielding a new broom.[1]

Schurz was, of course, assailed by Republican politicians seeking sinecures for their henchmen. Callers haunted his footsteps, hoping that he might be induced to yield to their persistency, and the more subtle exercise of "pull" estranged him from

[1] For Schurz's own statement as to his aims and accomplishments, see *Writings,* VI, 138, ff. Schurz selected his private secretary from the force already in the Interior Department. Schurz left the Cabinet feeling that the work of the department would be done more efficiently and economically if every position in it were subjected to civil service rules. The only obstacle to doing this was "the pressure of political influence for patronage, and the lack of resisting power among appointing officers to stand firm against that pressure."

Courtesy of the Estate of Carl Schurz

PRESIDENT HAYES

© 1904 by Pach, N. Y.

PRESIDENT CLEVELAND

some of his friends. Stories were circulated to his discredit. Colonel Thomas Wentworth Higginson heard that Schurz had dismissed women solely on account of their sex, and the latter had to write denying the allegation. He had a quarrel with a well-known editor of an Ohio newspaper because of the reduction in rank of one of its Washington correspondents—a woman who had proved to be inefficient. In this case, Schurz, with exquisite tact, transferred the woman to another branch of the department, thus pacifying both her and the irate journalist. When he was asked to manage the patronage in Missouri to the detriment of his opponents in that state, he answered that he was in duty bound to carry out those principles which he had always advocated. Schurz acted as an honest man might have been expected to do.[1]

On April 21, 1877, Miss Abigail Dodge, a kinswoman of Mrs. James G. Blaine, writing under the pen name of "Gail Hamilton," began a series of weekly Washington letters in the New York *Tribune*. They were, from the beginning, clearly actuated by hostility to the Hayes administration, and especially to its reforming tendencies. Schurz was hardly mentioned in the earlier articles, but, when it became evident that he was actually trying to undermine the "spoils" system, Gail Hamilton made him a conspicuous target of her abuse. On June 16, she ridiculed his efforts to clean up the Interior Department, but, unable to find anything really to his discredit, was obliged to resort to vague irony. Later she accused Schurz of having received money for making political speeches, of "selling his voice at a fixed price per hour in the Republican cause." This charge, which had been made against Schurz before and was to be made again, was not a serious one even if it could have been substantiated. Its only basis was the fact that Schurz had allowed the Republican organization to defray his expenses

[1] When Jacob D. Cox was Secretary of the Interior, he said, "The seekers after places give me only a small fraction of the day to attend to my legitimate work." Schurz so altered conditions that, during the latter part of his term, he needed to devote less than fifteen minutes a day to talk about appointments.

on some of the longer speaking tours which he had taken in the party interests. The very triviality of the specifications indicates how difficult it was for Schurz's enemies to find a vulnerable point in his armor. In the final letter of her series, dated August 25, Gail Hamilton singled Schurz out as a chief victim, but her sarcasm was ineffective.

With Hayes's financial policies, Carl Schurz was in the most complete sympathy. As we have seen, Congress had passed in January, 1875, a bill providing for the resumption of specie payments on January 1, 1879. During the first part of Hayes's administration, congressional inflationists did their best to repeal this resumption act—fortunately without success. When the day of resumption arrived, there was no excitement whatever in the business world. Very little paper currency was presented for redemption, and even that was paid out again almost immediately. The bogey conjured up by alarmists proved to be a complete illusion.

The President, in his first annual message, had dwelt at some length on the evils of a debased silver coinage. Regardless of his objections, however, Congress, in February, 1878, passed the Bland-Allison Bill, authorizing the Secretary of the Treasury to purchase silver bullion to the amount of at least two million dollars and not more than four million dollars monthly, and to coin it into silver dollars. Hayes consulted his Cabinet, including Schurz, who advised a veto, saying that, if successful, it would "save the country from an immoral and dangerous measure," and, even if it failed, its consequences would be less damaging than "the effect of concurrence." The President courageously sent back his veto, but Congress passed the measure over his disapproval.

In the autumn of 1878, Schurz contributed to the cause of sound money by speaking at Cincinnati, September 28, 1878, on the subject, "The Currency Question." He was badly needed if Ohio were to be kept Republican in the autumn congressional elections, and he did not disappoint those who relied upon his voice. His speech, dealing necessarily with unromantic matters of finance, was convincing to those who had any knowledge of the subject, and was published throughout the country. Hugh McCulloch, who had been Secretary of the Treasury under Lincoln and Johnson, wrote Schurz that this address covered the entire field, "leaving nothing for inflationists to stand on"; while Horace White declared that it was the first speech which seriously threatened "the citadel of the anti-specie resumption party."

One of Hayes's biographers has said that Carl Schurz was a man to whom the President, "by reason of mutual intellectual sympathies and political ideals . . . became affectionately attached." Of this there can be no doubt. Schurz, with his simple tastes, enjoyed the informality of the White House as Lucy Webb Hayes managed it, and found himself at home in its atmosphere of domesticity. Unattached men, especially if they are good conversationalists, are always in demand in Washington society, and Schurz actually became a "diner-out." His intelligence, his wit, and his wide experience made him welcome in any gathering. To Hayes, personally and politically, Schurz remained loyal and, long after the administration had become history, he wrote articles extolling the President's virtues.

CHAPTER XX SCHURZ AND THE INDIANS

THE Department of the Interior, even more in 1877 than today, was a complex organization, charged with supervising miscellaneous unrelated phases of government activity. It was like a rambling chateau to which at different periods additions have been made of various incongruous architectural designs. Its routine business, for example, included control over patents and pensions; over geological, entomological, and geographical surveys; over national parks as well as over public buildings and grounds in Washington; over the census and the Bureau of Education; over territories and the General Land Office; over the Columbia Hospital for Women, the Government Hospital for the Insane, the Asylum for the Deaf and Dumb, and the Freedmen's Hospital, not to mention Rocky Mountain Locusts and the Pagosa Hot Springs of Colorado. It had become, in fact, a dumping ground for odds and ends, an *omnium gatherum* for all sorts of commissions which seemed to fit nowhere else; and the Secretary himself, if he attended to his business, had to be a Pooh Bah, a specialist on all the topics in the encyclopedia. Schurz, industrious and intelligent though he was, had to spend several weeks merely acquainting himself with what he called "the vast and complicated machinery of the Interior Department." Of all the problems under his jurisdiction, those relating to the American Indians were the most puzzling and involved him in the most controversy.

Without any forewarning, Carl Schurz, knowing almost nothing about Indians and their troubles, found himself the heir of a disagreeable departmental inheritance. It was only a few months after the uprising of the Sioux under Sitting Bull and the astonishing and overwhelming defeat of General Custer and his troopers on the Little Big Horn, June 25, 1876. At the time when Schurz took the oath of office, Sitting Bull and many of his followers had crossed the border into Canada, where they refused to submit to the authority of the United States. Several separate military operations were in progress against other recalcitrant tribes. Barbaric outrages had been perpetrated on innocent whites, and, in retaliation, scores of red men had been brutally slain. Our Indian policy, to put it mildly, had been short-sighted, unjust, and stupid. A Board of Indian Commissioners, serving without pay and with no ulterior motives, reported year after year that the dealings of the government with the Indians were inexcusable.[1] While misguided philanthropists were indulging in fatuous sentimentalities, greedy agents were exploiting the unfortunate aborigines. Frequent commissions had been appointed, had traveled through the West in search of evidence, and had returned convinced that something must be done. The situation was muddled and shameful. Seldom has any cabinet officer been confronted by more urgent demands for reform.

The almost uninterrupted Indian wars of the seventies were due, not to those homesteaders or farmers who were making permanent settlements, but to the encroachment of white buffalo hunters, traders, and frontiersmen—a large proportion of them horse thieves and desperadoes—on lands where the Indians had lived for many generations and which they naturally thought to be their own.[2] Quite unconsciously and undeservedly, the redskins were the victims of that roving impulse

[1] The Board of Indian Commissioners had been established by Act of Congress in 1869, to be composed of gentlemen "eminent for their intelligence and philanthropy." William Welsh, of Philadelphia, was its first president, and its personnel was of high quality. So long as the members confined themselves to moral suasion, they were tolerated and ignored; but when they tried to effect reforms, they made many enemies. In June, 1874, six members resigned, maintaining that, under existing conditions, it could accomplish nothing. It lacked the power to change the evils which it criticized. Even today, many of the board's recommendations are politely acknowledged and then pigeon-holed.

[2] For many of the facts and some of the opinions expressed in this chapter I am obligated to my friend, Dr. Warren King Moorehead, the present senior member of the United States Board of Indian Commissioners and author of *The American Indian,* who has given me the benefit of his wide experience and knowledge and has directed me to valuable sources of information.

which was driving adventurous Caucasians across the plains and into the mountains in quest of "something lost behind the ranges." The government policy under President Grant had been to establish the various tribes upon their own reservations, in the hope that, if properly guided and rationed, they might abandon the warpath and take kindly to agriculture. This attempt to alter the habits of a nomadic people was not unsuccessful; but it was blocked by the cupidity of white contractors, who stole supplies from the Indians, filled them with bad liquor, and swindled them in the most brazen way. The agents in charge of the posts and reservations were often political appointees under the "spoils" system, more concerned with the enlargement of their bank accounts than with the welfare of the squaws and braves under their charge.

Following the Custer disaster, the United States army, under Nelson A. Miles and others, had, after some exhausting campaigns, brought most of the more pugnacious chieftains to terms. But the circumstances were complicated by a conflict of jurisdiction between the War Department and the Interior Department. During the summer of 1877, while Schurz was trying desperately to mete out justice to the Indians, federal cavalrymen were pursuing White Bird, Lame Deer, and other leaders, suffering heavy casualties, and learning to respect their foe. A joint congressional committee was named to examine in detail the probable consequences of transferring the Indians to the sole authority of the War Department, the theory being that, since they could never be civilized, they ought to be confined under military supervision until, through the beneficent operation of Nature, they became extinct.

Schurz accepted his Cabinet position in the mood of an efficiency expert engaged to reorganize a factory which has been mismanaged. He astonished his department by appearing at his desk before nine o'clock each morning and by remaining there often until six.[1] It was easy for him to ascertain that the

[1] Schurz wrote to Lodge, Dec. 1, 1877, "I thought that I had worked hard in my life,—but I feel now as if I had learned only during the last six months what hard work is." *Schurz MSS,* Congressional Library.

chief responsibility for past errors lay in a wrong policy. Congress, the War Department, and the Board of Indian Commissioners were all somewhat culpable, but the fault was mainly that of the Department of the Interior. It did not take him long to discover the existence of what was sometimes called an "Indian ring," composed of grafters of various degrees of turpitude who had been allowed to exercise their own unscrupulous discretion in their negotiations with the red men. There had been no real supervision of the agents, who were accustomed to make their own rules and decisions. Schurz promptly appointed a commission of three persons—one from the Interior Department, one from the War Department, and one from the Department of Justice. When it opened its inquiries in June, 1877, it had great difficulty in taking testimony. Important documents were found to be missing. Everybody with a guilty conscience ran hastily to cover. The final report, submitted in January, 1878, was a startling revelation, charging the chief clerk of the Indian Bureau, Galpin, with almost every form of arbitrary and unbusinesslike conduct; showing that many Indian agents had cheated and that many contractors had been little better than common thieves; and accusing the Indian Bureau of "cupidity, inefficiency, and the most barefaced dishonesty." [1] The management of the Indians had been, in short, "a reproach to the whole nation."

Schurz acted without delay. He had already removed the Commissioner of Indian Affairs, John Q. Smith,[2] superseding him by Ezra A. Hayt, of New York. He now discharged a considerable number of suspected employees and undertook the reorganization of the Indian agents. Thomas Nast, in a contemporary cartoon, showed Schurz, lanky, bearded, and bushy-haired, opening the drawers of a chiffonier, out of which were

[1] A copy of this *Report of the Board of Inquiry to Investigate Certain Charges against S. A. Galpin,* containing 546 pages in small type as well as a 98 page appendix, is on file in the library of the Department of the Interior.

[2] Smith, originally appointed by Secretary Chandler on December 11, 1875, was discharged by Schurz on September 27, 1877, for what seemed to him good and sufficient cause.

jumping puppet figures, labeled "Fraud," "Dishonesty," "Rascality," and "Corruption," all in a state of great agitation. Underneath was the legend, "The Secretary of the Interior Investigating the Indian Bureau—Give *Him* His Due, and Give *Them* Their Due."

Schurz brought to the Indian problem not only his scrupulous honesty but also a reassuring common sense joined with a warm-hearted sympathy for a down-trodden and much maligned race. In his first annual report, dated November 1, 1877, he declared that he was doing his utmost to have his new broom sweep clean. He was obliged to confess, however, that the general state of Indian affairs was "by no means satisfactory" and that there had been altogether too many collisions between reckless white adventurers and the red men. "We have to deal," he said, "with a population whose character and habits of life are such as to present extraordinary difficulties to civilizing influences."

As a positive program for his department, Schurz had certain policies to suggest, none of them really new, but so linked together as to indicate that a new era was in sight. He would discourage hunting, because it kept alive warlike propensities, and would gather the Indians together upon small reservations, teach them cattle raising and agriculture, and allot to each head of a family a tract of arable land. Over these reservations he would extend the laws of the United States. To the establishment of schools he attached much importance; but he also hoped to use the better farms for instructing the young braves in agriculture, and he planned to employ Indian labor whenever that was possible. Above all, he insisted that absolute faith must be kept with the tribal representatives, especially regarding financial arrangements and treaty regulations. The program thus outlined was entirely practicable and, if it had been carried out, might have done much to alleviate the bitterness of the Indian chieftains.

The main object, as Schurz saw it, was to absorb the Indians by legal means into the citizenry of the United States and, when this had been accomplished, to treat them in all respects like other inhabitants of the country. It has been justly said by Frederic Bancroft that this plan "outlined every feature of the policy which was destined to achieve such signal success in the break-up of tribal life during the ensuing quarter century." One very important preliminary step was taken when, on December 6, 1878, Schurz, before the joint congressional committee, presented his case so effectively that the bill for transferring control of the Indians to the War Department was killed in the House of Representatives. For his decisive aid in blocking all proposals for military supervision, Schurz earned the lasting gratitude of the Indian leaders.

In his successive annual reports for 1878, 1879, and 1880, Schurz reiterated and amplified the opinions originally expressed in 1877. "Only as the Indians progress in the ways of civilization," he declared in 1878, "will they cease to be a troublesome and disturbing element." Each year he was able to announce some advance in the elimination of corruption, in the promotion of efficiency, and in the establishment of peace. It was slow work, for he had to contend with both inertia and depravity. In his valedictory report, however, he said that "on the whole the Indian situation is now more hopeful than ever before."

The most exasperating of Schurz's departmental difficulties, perhaps, arose from the case of the Ponca Indians—a case which caused a mild excitement even in phlegmatic official Washington and which stirred up popular feeling throughout the nation. The essential facts have frequently been repeated and are not today in dispute. The Poncas were a small and comparatively unwarlike tribe living upon a reservation along the Missouri River in southeastern Dakota. Through a congressional error, explicable but not excusable, a treaty had been concluded in 1868 with the Sioux, granting them an area which comprehended the lands where the Poncas had built their village; and when the Poncas persisted in residing upon what they naturally thought to be still their own domain, they were harassed by marauding Sioux. The government took the easiest way out of the quandary by "persuading" the Poncas, innocent victims of a foolish blunder, to move.

After the customary delays resulting from "red tape" and lack of authority, Congress, in an act dated March 3, 1877, provided for the transfer of the Poncas to the Quapaw Reservation in Indian Territory. During the first months of Schurz's term of office, while he was familiarizing himself with his routine duties, the hegira was effected, and the Poncas after some painful vicissitudes and trials by storm and flood, reached their new home.[1] Schurz has been blamed for carrying out the provisions of the obnoxious act.[2] The truth is that he knew nothing about it until the damage had been done. Not until the autumn of 1877, when certain Ponca chiefs journeyed to Washington to protest to the "White Father," were the full details laid before him. Even if he had been acquainted with what was going on, it is difficult to see what justification he could have invoked for deliberately interfering with an act of Congress.

When the truth was brought to his attention, Schurz saw at once that this tribe had been unjustly treated,[3] and, in his first annual report, asked for some redress, saying: "The case of the Poncas seems entitled to especial consideration at the hands of Congress. . . . Their removal from their old home on the Missouri River was to them a great hardship. . . . I urgently recommend that liberal provision be made to aid them in their new settlement." In considering the question of reparation,

[1] The journey of the Poncas lasted from May 21 to July 9, 1877. The change of climate was disastrous, and many of them contracted malaria. The story as told by Howard, the Indian Agent, in his official report, is most pathetic. The total number to arrive at the Quapaw Reservation was 681, including 197 heads of families. For interesting details, see Schurz's letter to Long, December 9, 1880, *Writings,* IV, 50, ff., and Jackson's *A Century of Dishonor,* 186, ff.

[2] Williams, *Hayes,* II, 233.

[3] Writing to John D. Long, December 9, 1880, Schurz said, referring to the Poncas, "I concluded that they had suffered great hardship in losing the reservation originally conferred upon them by treaty, after a so-called consent which appeared not to have been a free expression of their will." *Writings,* IV, 56.

Schurz was guided, as usual, less by sentimentality than by common sense. The Poncas themselves requested permission to be returned to the Niobrara Reservation, in South Dakota, their former home. Meanwhile, however, the pugnacious Sioux had been allowed to settle on the lands from which the Poncas had been removed, and, if they were irritated, it was feared that another bloody Indian outbreak might ensue. In his embarrassment, Schurz directed the Poncas to choose a new and more fertile location within the boundaries of Indian Territory; and, in July, 1878, they migrated to the South Fork of the Arkansas River, which became their permanent residence. It would appear from the testimony that Schurz was the first prominent government official to tell the public about the wrongs endured by the Poncas; that he did everything possible, in view of the Indian situation as a whole, to rectify the initial mistake; and that he repeatedly urged Congress to make amends for its iniquity. That he was unable to satisfy all the complaints of the Poncas was clearly not his fault.[1]

Although Schurz was actuated throughout this affair by the best of motives, he and his department did not escape severe criticism. He who had so long been recognized as a reformer was now the object of attack by other reformers, just as wolves in quest of prey sometimes turn and rend one of their own number. The idealistic but impetuous Mrs. Helen Hunt Jackson ("H. H."),[2] later the author of *A Century of Dishonor* (1881) and *Ramona* (1884), unfortunately gave many people an entirely erroneous impression of the part played by Carl Schurz. In the spring of 1879, several enterprising and nostalgic Poncas, trying to make their way back to their former Dakota

[1] Several independent investigators have arrived at this conclusion. Humphrey, in *The Indian Dispossessed* (1905), says of Schurz's defense, "He shows clearly that the whole scheme involving the Ponca removal was laid by the preceding administration, although consummated immediately after he took office." A similar view is expressed by Leupp in *The Indian and His Problem* (1910).

[2] Helen Maria (Fiske) Jackson (1831–85) was born in Amherst, Massachusetts, but, after her marriage in 1875, spent much of her time in Colorado Springs. She was a poet, a short story writer, and an essayist—a prolific contributer to periodicals.

abode, were arrested by federal troops on the Omaha Reserve. There, however, some Omaha lawyers interested themselves in the case, brought it before Judge Dundy of the Nebraska District Court, and secured a writ of *habeas corpus* which freed Chief Standing Bear. Although Schurz wisely decided not to institute a judicial appeal, Mrs. Jackson raised a fund for defraying the expenses of a possible trial, and also wrote to Schurz, on January 9, 1880, an open letter asking him to approve a plan for aiding the Poncas to bring suit for the recovery of their Dakota lands. Schurz sent back a courteous and temperate reply, explaining the situation as the Department of the Interior viewed it; and an interesting correspondence ensued, superficially polite, but seething underneath the printed words.

With his unfailing common sense, Schurz pointed out that the government had no intention of appealing the case of Standing Bear, and that the money raised for his defense would not have to be used. He also showed that, because the Supreme Court had repeatedly ruled that an Indian tribe could not sue in the federal courts, it would be futile for the Poncas to try legal means for getting back their old reservation on the Missouri River. "It is evidently idle," said Schurz, not without irritation, "to collect money and to fee attorneys for the purpose of doing a thing which cannot be done." He recommended that whatever sum had been secured could be employed most effectively in promoting a project for granting to each individual Indian a title to his own land—a project which would give to the red man a legal property protection which, under the existing system of tribal ownership, he did not possess. As for returning the Poncas to South Dakota, Schurz informed Mrs. Jackson that such a procedure would do more harm than good.

Schurz had not been content with second-hand information. Wishing to investigate conditions for himself, he set out in August, 1879, on a tour of inspection among the various Indian agencies, spending six weeks in traveling over a wide area. He was accompanied by Webb C. Hayes, the President's son, by his own private secretary, and by several newspaper correspondents. Proceeding first to Yankton, in Dakota, he went from there to the Santee and Rosebud agencies, and thence to Red Cloud, Camp Robinson, Laramie, Rock Creek, Denver, and Wichita. He drove by carriage through the less accessible districts of Indian Territory, paying especial attention to the Poncas. After consultation with their chiefs and a study of the methods by which the reservation was managed, he reached the conclusion that most of the Poncas were more contented in their new home than they had been in Dakota, constantly menaced by the Sioux.

Meanwhile a former Indian agent, the Reverend Mr. Tibbles, had organized a systematic campaign for the relief of the Poncas and, accompanied by Standing Bear and an Indian girl named Bright Eyes (Susette La Flesche), was touring the country, trying through lectures to arouse the active interest of humanitarians. A typical gathering was that held on December 3, 1880, at Tremont Temple, in Boston, at which Governor John D. Long presided over a large audience. In his address, Long argued that Schurz's excuses for inaction were paltry; that the Sioux could easily be indemnified; that the expense of returning the Poncas to South Dakota, however large, would be justified; and that an alleged petition from them, begging leave to remain in Indian Territory, had been obtained by fraud. Both Tibbles and Bright Eyes were present; stirring letters were read from Edward Everett Hale and Henry L. Dawes; and, to close the program, the venerable Wendell Phillips, once the champion of the Negro and now the defender of the red man, made an eloquent appeal for contributions.

There was a Sophoclean irony in the spectacle of Carl Schurz, who had been in the past so critical of government policies, now being hounded for sins of omission and commission. He was, of course, much disturbed, but he kept his official temper. With self-restraint, he wrote Governor Long an open letter, protesting that he had studied the Indian problem "patiently, earnestly, and laboriously" and that the thought of any injustice to the red man was revolting to him. A few weeks later, after a bitter speech on the floor of the Senate by Senator Dawes, Schurz sent him a communication, again reviewing the dismal story and matching his critic in fluency of invective. In closing, Schurz urged that the Poncas be allowed to rest:

> Give them the indemnity they justly ask for and which I asked for them years ago. Let them go quietly about their farms and improve their homes and send their children to school, undisturbed by further agitation. That is the best service you can render them. They would probably be in a better condition already had that agitation never reached them.

Throughout this discomposing controversy, Schurz had the unswerving support of the President. In December, 1880, however, Hayes felt obliged to appoint a commission, consisting of Generals Crook and Miles, William Stickney, and Walter Allen, to visit the Poncas, conduct an investigation, and prepare a report. As a consequence of their recommendations, supplemented by the pathetic personal appeal of several Ponca braves who visited the capital, Hayes, on the first day of February, 1881, sent a special message to Congress advising prompt remedial legislation along the lines already suggested by Carl Schurz. The President obstinately insisted that the Poncas should be fully compensated for their losses through Sioux depredations, for the inconvenience which they suffered during their forced removal to Indian Territory, and for the lands which they had relinquished. As a matter of general procedure, Hayes said:

> In short, nothing should be left undone to show to the Indians that the Government of the United States regards their rights as equally sacred with those of its citizens. The time has come when the policy should be to place the Indians as rapidly as practicable on the same footing with the other permanent inhabitants of our country.

The commission had not attempted to palliate the original transfer of the Poncas, considering this action to have been "injudicious and without sufficient cause." Nor did the President proffer any excuses. Without apportioning the blame for what had happened, he simply stated the need for reparation. The tone and spirit of this entreaty were such that Congress could not disregard it. On the day before the session closed, measures were passed appropriating $165,000 to indemnify the Poncas, so far as that could be done by money and land grants, for the injustices which they had endured. The tribe seems to have been satisfied with this belated redress, and the agitation subsided. A few months after Schurz's retirement, the Reverend Mr. Tibbles and his protégée, Bright Eyes—"the maiden and the missionary," as Dr. Bancroft happily describes them—were united in marriage, and a somewhat sordid episode was thus terminated with a romance.

Slander, however, takes a long time to die, and is easily resurrected. Until the close of his days, Carl Schurz was the target of accusations which could have been easily refuted by consultation of the records. As late as October, 1900, when Roosevelt and Lodge, engaged in a political controversy with Schurz, were searching for a vulnerable point in the latter's apparently flawless armor, the Ponca affair was again revived, and, when John D. Long was consulted, he wrote to Lodge: [1]

> Roosevelt may be right about Schurz and the Nez Percés. But the much worse case was the Poncas, whom, as I recall the fact, he took from homes which were as much theirs as yours is yours, and transported hundreds of miles. The suffering was horrible, and I think two or three hundreds perished. There was, as I think, investigation by the Senate which reported with severe condemnation the whole outrage. I am speaking from memory and cannot give details.

The question as to how far any man of prestige is justified in making such charges without substantiating them by ample evidence is one which needs not be discussed here. Lodge, who had the scholar's instinct and passion for fact, looked up the details and wisely decided not to press the matter further. For

[1] Lodge Papers.

historical purposes the vindication of Carl Schurz may be considered complete.

Following out his plan for educating the Indians and bringing them into touch with modern life, Schurz, in 1878, placed a small group of Indian boys and girls in Hampton Institute, in Virginia, under General Armstrong, and was able to prove that they acquired readily the customs of what we call civilization.[1] He then negotiated with the War Department for the abandoned cavalry barracks at Carlisle, Pennsylvania, and opened there under Captain R. H. Pratt the famous industrial school later known as Carlisle Institute. Starting with fifty children, it enrolled nearly one hundred and fifty before the year closed. Schurz had reached the conclusion that, if Indian children could be brought up under the same conditions as white people, they probably would not as adults revert to the barbarism of their parents, and might even become the deputies of culture. There will doubtless always be a dispute as to the type of training most beneficial to the Indians. In some degree, at least, Schurz's hopes were realized, and the school which he founded—although it was discontinued some years ago—did perform a real service. If he had been able to secure the necessary funds, he would have established at least ten similar institutions, but he found it practicable to open only one other—a small affair, located at Forest Grove, Oregon. On the whole, adult Indians regarded these experiments with favor and encouraged the continuance of the policy through later schools at Chilocco, Haskell, and elsewhere.

Writing to Henry Cabot Lodge, December 2, 1877, regarding Schurz, Henry Adams said, "Lumber and Indians are his sole mental food just at present." Indian affairs alone were sufficient to keep him busy—and perturbed. Late in 1879, suspicious of Commissioner Hayt's connection with the San Carlos

[1] When Schurz paid an official visit to Hampton Institute at its Commencement in 1880, he was greeted by the Indian pupils as their "wise and kind friend." Booker T. Washington, then a pupil there, later described Schurz as "a man who had been able to lift himself out of the poisoned atmosphere of racial as well as sectional prejudice."

Agency, Schurz requested the Board of Indian Commissioners to "probe the matter to the bottom." A committee of investigation found Hayt cognizant of corruption, if not actually a participant in it. Schurz at once removed him and in his place appointed Roland E. Trowbridge, of Michigan, on March 15, 1880.[1]

In the same year, a band of Utes, in Colorado, broke out in one of their periodical pillaging expeditions and, inflamed by cheap whiskey, killed the agent, Mr. Meeker, and carried off several white women into captivity. In their justifiable anger, the citizens of Colorado—which had been admitted as a state in 1876—began a movement for the extermination of the offending tribe. Luckily a special agent of the Interior Department intervened, under Schurz's orders, and secured the surrender of the small body of "bad Indians" who had caused the trouble. Schurz's speedy action did not please the more aggressive of the Colorado vigilantes, who wanted to take the law into their own hands; but the Indians appreciated his sense of fair play.

Indeed the red men soon learned that the Secretary of the Interior was genuinely concerned over their wrongs and their welfare. According to Bishop Whipple, Schurz was "the first Secretary to inaugurate the system of Indian police and the employment of Indians in the transportation of supplies." Dr. Schafer relates an enlightening incident involving certain Sioux who had murdered a white man in Nebraska and had stolen some horses. The Indian police, then just organized, arrested six suspects and turned them over to the regular courts for trial. Schurz then received from Chief Spotted Tail a check for $332.80, together with a request that counsel be employed to

[1] Henry Adams wrote Lodge, February 22, 1880: "Schurz seems to have got into trouble with his Indian Commissioner. This must be a blow to him, but as he has ceased to be anything to us, and so long as he is in the Cabinet, never can return to his old importance, I don't know that his mischance affects our interests." *Letters of Henry Adams*, 321. Adams felt that Schurz, by taking a position in the Republican administration, had thrown away all the influence for good which he might have exercised as an independent.

care for the interests of the accused criminals. No better evidence could be submitted to show the confidence which the Indians had in Schurz's sense of justice.

The Board of Indian Commissioners has not always been entirely in sympathy with the Department of the Interior and its policies. In 1880, however, at Schurz's invitation, the board appointed a special committee of three, consisting of Clinton Fisk, chairman, Albert Smiley, and William Lyon, to examine the conduct of Indian affairs. Profiting by the investigations of this committee, the board, in its report dated March 11, 1881—a week after Schurz had retired to private life—declared that it had "the utmost confidence in the integrity of the Secretary" and that he had shown always "a resolute purpose to promote the efficiency and purity of the service." [1] In fact, Schurz had won everywhere the commendation of wise and honest men. James Freeman Clarke wrote to tell him that he had been "the best friend the Indians have had"; Edward Eggleston praised him for his "wise and statesmanlike management of Indian affairs"; and Bishop Whipple, the missionary bishop, bestowed upon him, February 15, 1881, the unsolicited eulogy, "I have never found an officer of the government more ready to examine the wrongs done to the Indians." All this laudation was sincere—and deserved. In his last annual message, President Hayes expressed his own opinion in the sentence, "It gives me great pleasure to say that our Indian affairs appear to be in a more hopeful condition than ever before."

Schurz had the satisfaction of knowing that his successor, Samuel Jordan Kirkwood, followed in his footsteps. Alonzo Bell, Assistant Secretary of the Interior under both Schurz and Kirkwood, wrote, August 5, 1881, "Our Indian policy is substantially yours. In fact, I see no desire to depart from the wise plans laid down by you." As a final justification of his methods, Schurz published in the *North American Review* for July, 1881, an artitle, "Present Aspects of the Indian Prob-

[1] *Twelfth Annual Report of the Board of Indian Commissioners,* Washington, 1881.

lem," in which he recapitulated the broad principles laid down in his annual reports and reiterated certain conclusions drawn from his none too placid experience.

One of Schurz's chief claims to far-sighted statesmanship is his early interest in the preservation of our natural resources. He has rightly been termed the "original conservationist." When he became Secretary of the Interior, he was shocked to discover that miners and settlers had for years unsystematically and wastefully been denuding the national domain whenever and wherever they saw fit to do so. Our forests then seemed inexhaustible, and no one was impressed with the desirability of reforestation. Government standing timber was being cut down and sold by private operators, who set up their own saw mills and had their own methods of ensuring the lethargy of public officials. Schurz appointed timber inspectors, but soon found that, under existing statutes, he was almost powerless to establish any really constructive policy of replanting. He did, however, by invoking an almost forgotten law, succeed in curbing the lumber thieves and in obtaining judgment for more than half a million dollars against some of the more flagrant offenders.

In his first annual report, Schurz, familiar with the scientific procedure followed by Germany in such areas as the Schwarzwald, recommended that the President be authorized to appoint a commission "to study the laws and practices adopted in other countries for the preservation and cultivation of forests." He urged strongly, moreover, the regulation of lumbering operations so that a growth of young trees might be left; the passing of stringent measures to penalize the setting of fires on forest lands; the exemption of timber areas from homestead or preëmption claims; and the regulated sale of wood by the government to settlers and miners. Schurz hoped thus to open and carry through a campaign of education. Knowing that only through a program extending over many years could forests, streams, and soils be conserved, he wanted to tell his story to the public. He could see that a spendthrift people was recklessly wasting its heritage. But he was blocked constantly by selfishness and greed.[1] As soon as his first report was published, he was assailed by telegrams of protest and interviewed by indignant members of Congress. James G. Blaine, allied with the lumber companies of northern New England, did all that he could to hinder Schurz's request for rational forest legislation, and, in the spring of 1878, denounced the Secretary of the Interior for introducing "Prussian methods" into our democratic country.[2] A few days afterward, Senator Timothy O. Howe, of Wisconsin, made a similar attack upon the department. Schurz answered, temperately but effectively, having both reason and economy on his side. But Congress was in no mood to accept his suggestions, and little was really accomplished until President Roosevelt, a quarter of a century later, made conservation a national issue.

In the face of an opposition which was both ignorant and unscrupulous, Schurz maintained an outward imperturbability; but he was really deeply wounded. It seemed to him as if honesty were being punished and cupidity rewarded. Toward the close of his term, in proffering some advice to the incoming chief executive, Schurz wrote Garfield, "I shall never forget the trials I had to go through during the first period of my administration, and the mistakes that were made before I had things well in hand. It is a constant fight with the sharks that surround the Indian Bureau, the Pension Office, and the Patent Office, and a ceaseless struggle with perplexing questions and situations, especially in the Indian service." He pointed out,

[1] For Schurz's own account of some of his troubles, see *Writings,* V, 22, ff. Writing to Herbert Welsh, February 25, 1899, he said, "What I did with regard to the public forests was simply to arrest devastation, in which I partially succeeded, and for which I was lustily denounced, and to strive from year to year to obtain from Congress legislation for the protection of forests, in which I largely failed." *Writings,* VI, 38–39.

[2] An unfortunate sequel to this attack was the reduction to $5000 of the sum regularly appropriated by Congress to the Department of the Interior for the enforcement of the law. This reduction, said Schurz, "rendered the government impotent to enforce the police regulations against lumber thieves." *Harper's Weekly,* April 13, 1878.

furthermore, that, unless the Secretary of the Interior knew his business, the President would be "in constant danger of disgrace." On this matter Carl Schurz was unquestionably an authority.

To all the activities of his complicated department, Schurz imparted his own dynamic and infectious enthusiasm. The census of 1880, for example, was superintended by General Francis A. Walker, and, in its comprehensive statistics, included a vast amount of material never before accumulated. But Schurz aided and encouraged Walker, and advised him on plans and methods. Schurz also kept careful watch over the proper administration of pensions and never relaxed his vigilance against corruption. When his friend, Godkin, sent him some complaints regarding this section of the Interior Department, Schurz made an immediate investigation and, while confessing that his inadequate clerical force was behind on applications, declared that "every possible effort is made to perform the duties imposed upon the Department satisfactorily." Schurz seems to have been very industrious, very conscientious, and very fair-minded.

Of course he made enemies. He always did. Long after he had withdrawn from official Washington, he was pursued by slander. In October, 1881, after receiving an anonymous letter saying that his "rascalities" in handling the contingent fund would soon be exposed, he promptly wrote to George M. Lockwood, the chief clerk of the Department, asking what the latter knew about these charges. "I get such things frequently," he added in a somewhat plaintive tone. In January, 1882, a resolution was passed in the Senate calling upon the Department of the Interior for copies of a ruling handed down by Schurz three years before regarding a land grant to the Northern Pacific Railroad; and certain hostile journals at once accused Schurz of having acted under improper influences. The latter at once requested his friend, Senator George F. Edmunds, to ask for a committee to investigate the transaction. Edmunds, in a sensible reply, said that unless some more specific statement than that in the newspapers could be found, the Senate was unlikely to order an investigation, and reminded Schurz that if he appealed to Congress for a vindication whenever he was assailed in the press, he would have "a pretty busy life."

In the *North American Review* for March, 1883, George W. Julian published an article in the course of which he stated that the Department of the Interior in Hayes's administration had been constantly under the thumb of the railroads. Schurz, unable to resist the temptation of a controversy, replied in one of those open letters of which he was so fond, submitting facts and arguments to refute Julian's allegations. When the latter responded with a rather ineffective reiteration of the original charges, Schurz burst out, "The public letter you recently addressed to me is in point of argument so wild and absurd that it appears more like a joke than a serious thing." Like most reformers, Schurz was abnormally sensitive to criticism. Even his sense of humor, which was in certain other respects rather well developed, occasionally deserted him in public controversy. Very few opponents, however, surpassed him in that form of debate which is based on irony and sarcasm.

Having announced at the time of his election that he would not be a candidate for a second term, Hayes was definitely out of the campaign of 1880. Schurz, at the request of groups of Independents from Pennsylvania and Missouri, urged him to reconsider his resolve; but the President, much as he would have liked to spend another four years in the White House, thought himself bound by his pledge. With Hayes thus eliminated, a plan to nominate Grant for a third term was started and had acquired some momentum by the day he arrived in San Francisco, in September, 1879, after his triumphal trip around the world. He did not forbid his followers to support him, and it was evident as 1880 opened that he was to be a leading figure at the Republican Convention.

To the possibility of Ulysses S. Grant as President Carl Schurz was, of course, irrevocably opposed. Although as a member of the Cabinet he could not participate actively in pre-convention politics, he did not hesitate to let his views be known in quarters where they might do good. But to whom were he and the other Independents to turn? Blaine, again in the field, might be the instrument of thwarting Grant's inordinate ambition; but Blaine was no less repugnant to Schurz. John Sherman, with whom Schurz had been associated for almost four years, was also being advocated; and Schurz could have accepted him with an easier conscience. The main object in Schurz's mind as the convention drew near was to defeat Grant. He wrote to George William Curtis, as the year 1879 closed, urging those who were against a third term to say so openly, and begging him, as an editor, to set in motion a movement "not only to prevent Grant's nomination, but that of any candidate whose record is not clean"—an obvious reference to James G. Blaine. Five days later, he dispatched a similar appeal to Henry Cabot Lodge, saying that those who did not mean to support Grant should make it known "boldly and loudly." With Schurz's approval, a conference was called for May 6, 1880, at St. Louis, at which resolutions were passed against a third term and arrangements were perfected for the appointment of a committee of one hundred to meet in New York in the contingency of Grant's nomination. On May 23, Schurz wrote Lodge that Grant's nomination, while not improbable, was by no means certain. He added with some complacency, "The chances are one hundred to one that Blaine cannot be nominated."

The Republican Convention, held on June 2, at Chicago, was a race between Grant and the field. Roscoe Conkling, the pompous but able Grant manager, had under his control somewhat over three hundred delegates—known traditionally as "the loyal 306"—who made the auditorium resound with cheers when he declared, with his florid rhetoric, that his candidate hailed from Appomattox and its famous apple tree. Blaine was not far behind Grant, but reached his maximum strength on the first ballot. Garfield, the suave and astute Ohio politician, was on the floor directing John Sherman's campaign and, through his unfailing tact, had made a good impression on the followers of both Grant and Blaine. Suggested before the convention opened as a possible compromise candidate, he received one vote on the second ballot; and, as the impossibility of naming either Grant or Blaine became apparent, sentiment turned in his direction. Garfield, as the champion of his friend, John Sherman, felt himself bound not to interfere with the latter's aspirations and rose to protest against the use of his own name. On the thirty-fifth ballot, however, he was given fifty votes, and a stampede toward him ensued, with the customary noise and uncontrolled disorder. Garfield was a candidate with very few enemies—a man of pleasing personality who, although not a reformer, had never antagonized the Independents.[1] Schurz, well satisfied, wrote Lodge, "I have known Garfield very well for many years, and I have full confidence in his integrity."

Through the persistence of the Massachusetts delegation—of which Lodge, in attendance at his first national convention, was secretary—a plank favoring civil service reform, although rejected by the Resolutions Committee, had been carried to the floor and passed without dissent. It was during the debate on this topic that Flanagan, of Texas, acquired a dubious fame by asking, "What are we here for if not for the offices?"—a question which was to be cited by the reformers for many years to come. This victory was gratifying to Schurz, but both he and Lodge were disappointed at the choice of Chester A. Arthur as the nominee for Vice President. In a hitherto unpublished memorandum written on the spot Lodge recorded a justification for Arthur's selection: [2]

That such a nomination on general principles is thoroughly bad and a direct insult to the present administration cannot be questioned, but that it is a strong one politically seems equally certain. No one will abandon Garfield on account of Arthur,

[1] See Robert Granville Caldwell, *James A. Garfield: Many-Sided American.*
[2] Lodge Papers.

and in New York the defeated machine will, instead of sulking, be brought to full play under the direction of the shrewdest political manager in the country.

The Democrats, assembling at Cincinnati later in the month, nominated General Winfield S. Hancock, a distinguished Union officer and a man of blameless character, but not the kind of leader to lure Carl Schurz from the Republican phalanx. There was, however, a difficulty to be overcome. Garfield's letter of acceptance was a very disappointing document. Even his authorized biographer admits that it was a "purely political performance," vague on the matter of the currency, evasive on the tariff, and, worst of all, designed, in what it said on the civil service, to placate the "Old Guard," represented by Conkling, Platt, and their henchmen. On July 20, 1880, Schurz wrote Garfield, voicing his disapproval and warning him that he must choose between two roads—"one running in the direction of reactionary tendencies and machine politics, and the other in the direction of intelligent, progressive, and reformatory politics." This letter was composed on the very day when Schurz delivered a campaign speech in Indianapolis, in which he referred to Hancock as a good soldier and a gentleman, but unequipped by training or experience to be President. He ended with a eulogy of Garfield, not glowing but sincere, and declared that the welfare of the republic demanded his election.

Carl Schurz was not a man whom presidential candidates could ignore. Garfield replied by the next mail to his criticism, saying that he had no intention of letting the party "down from its high standard of recent work"; that he had "stood on the skirmish line against all forms of soft money and bastard silver fallacy"; and that he had "made no terms of concession with the New York wing." Evidently Schurz was pacified, for he spoke for Garfield in several focal points in the Middle West, as well as in New York, New Jersey, and Connecticut. During the campaign, Schurz and Garfield corresponded regularly, Schurz advising Garfield not to revive the issue of sectional warfare and not to resuscitate the "old patronage business." In August and September, Schurz went for the first and last time to the Pacific Coast, stopping at important cities along the route and spending an exciting week in visiting the marvels of San Francisco. On his return, he spoke, at Garfield's special request, in Cleveland and Toledo. Schurz's influence on the German-Americans was no less cogent than it had been in 1876, and helped greatly to bring about a Republican victory. When Garfield, on November 3, was assured of election, Schurz wrote: "I congratulate you and the country most sincerely on your success. . . . Your real troubles will now begin."

When Garfield consulted Schurz regarding his Cabinet, the latter replied without reserve, urging the President-elect to respect the "different elements composing the Republican party," but suggesting that it was far more important to have "a perfectly honest and intelligent management of the public affairs." Whether or not Schurz expected to retain his place in the Department of the Interior cannot be ascertained from his letters, but it is plain that Garfield had no intention of appointing him.[1] The new President had long been close to Blaine, whose counsel was to be potent with him. Schurz was careful to mention only a few names, but he did point out the value of John Sherman in the Treasury and recommend Francis A. Walker for the Interior. In later correspondence he continued to stress Walker's name, feeling that he was a liberal Republican who could be relied upon to continue the policies espoused by the Hayes administration.

Garfield, however, had other plans. As early as November,

[1] In answer to a rumor that he had made an arrangement to give Schurz a seat in his Cabinet, Garfield wrote, October 7, 1880, to Whitelaw Reid, saying that there was no foundation for the story and adding: "It is clear to me that his appointment would displease a large majority of the party. For this and for other reasons, I have never entertained the thought of doing so—and shall not." For the full text of Garfield's interesting letter, see Cortissoz, *Whitelaw Reid,* II, 43.

1880, he had asked Blaine to be Secretary of State—a fact which, in itself, would have been sufficient to prevent Schurz from having any sway with the new regime. Schurz's successor, Samuel Jordan Kirkwood, had been Governor of Iowa and was Senator from that state when he was chosen for the Cabinet. It was an innocuous selection—but undistinguished. On March 8, Schurz turned over his desk and papers to Kirkwood and retired permanently from Washington officialdom.

Of Schurz's private and social life while he was in the Cabinet, there is little to be said. During most of this period, he occupied a large double house still standing at 1719 H Street, N.W. There Agathe, now well along in her "twenties," acted as hostess and also as nurse for her two brothers, one a small boy and the other a mere baby. We hear of Schurz's dining at the home of Henry Adams,[1] with Abram S. Hewitt, Charles Nordhoff, and William Wetmore Story, and of his entertaining these and other friends at simple meals in his own home. To Hayes, Schurz became affectionately attached, and long after his chief had retired to the rural peace of Spiegel Grove, Schurz corresponded with him and defended his administration against its critics. It was an intimacy which endured unimpaired until Hayes's death in 1893 and which was highly creditable to both men.

Two weeks after his retirement, Schurz was invited to Boston as the guest of honor at a great dinner attended by many of the finest citizens of New England. At the head table, besides the chairman, Charles R. Codman, were James Freeman Clarke, President Charles W. Eliot, Oliver Wendell Holmes, Thomas Bailey Aldrich, Colonel Thomas Wentworth Higginson, and Charles Francis Adams; and among those who attended were Ameses and Atkinsons and Cabots and Lodges and Longfellows and Endicotts and Parkmans—the elite of the city. Hailed as a statesman who had remained true to his ideals, Schurz seized the occasion as an opportunity for justifying his attitude as an Independent, explaining that, at a time

[1] Adams to Lodge, December 2, 1877, *Letters of Henry Adams,* 303.

when the two major parties were evenly balanced, it was the unconstrained element among the voters who could determine the outcome. He ended his eloquent speech with significant words, "Ours must necessarily be, in a certain sense, a government of and by political parties; but it will be all the better for the country if it is a party government tempered by an unselfish, enlightened, and patriotic independent opinion."

Schurz was probably even more pleased on the following evening, when the Boston Germans gave him a reception in the Turn Halle, followed by a typical Rhenish *Nachtessen,* or supper, accompanied by much beer drinking and cigar smoking. The three hundred guests, led by Heinrich Reuter, shouted a lusty "dreimal hoch," and sang one after another of the noble ballads which Schurz so loved. In his response he brought them to their feet by saying—of course in German—"It is the duty of a good citizen to be first a patriot before he is a Republican or a Democrat." Schurz's enemies had not ceased their criticisms. While he was in Boston, the *Traveller* said editorially, "Carl Schurz's record as Secretary of the Interior is the cardinal blot that disfigures Republican administration from the days of Lincoln to the days of Garfield." But few, even among the Democrats, really believed such an utterance. The intelligent and high-minded people in the community, Republican or Democratic, had confidence in Schurz.

On June 29, Schurz, as the guest of Professor Charles Eliot Norton, was in Cambridge to deliver the Phi Beta Kappa Address at Harvard—an honor which he regarded as one of the highest he ever received. Introduced by Joseph H. Choate, he spoke in a thoughtful and serious vein on the subject, "Education in America," offering as his remedy for cleansing the republic, "public discussion, with power to act as its result." [1] It was in this oration that Schurz used his famous phrase, "an honorable character, well built up by honest conduct and pa-

[1] The Boston *Herald,* in a leading editorial, June 30, 1881, said of Schurz's address, "There was no gush, no sophomorism, but the tone throughout was that of a man engaged in the serious consideration of affairs."

Courtesy of the Estate of Carl Schurz

CHARLES FRANCIS ADAMS

triotic service"—a description which might have been aptly applied to himself.

Carl Schurz, after all the evidence has been considered, must be placed among our ablest Secretaries of the Interior. Both as Senator and as member of the Cabinet, he had kept the faith. He had proved that he was no mere fumbling idealist, fond of talk and criticism, but incapable of constructive action. Out of power, he had been a shrewd and courageous diagnostician of the maladies of the state: in power, he was a physician and surgeon, with remedies to prescribe and operations to perform. Neither cynic nor scold, he had set diligently to work, with hope in his heart. He had not always succeeded in pleasing others, to say nothing of himself. But he had refused to yield, except to overwhelming arguments; and, in spite of disappointments, he had accomplished enough to entitle him to a position among the great practical reformers. It would be easy, of course, to emphasize his mistakes, but it is fairer to dwell on his achievements. Viewed sympathetically, he stands out for what he was—a clear-headed, persevering, and rather gallant gentleman, battling heroically against corruption and sluggishness and inefficiency.

CHAPTER XXI A "MUGWUMP" LEADER

AFTER 1881, Carl Schurz was never again to hold political office. At the early age of fifty-two, he returned to private life—much to his regret, for he enjoyed as much as any man the sensation of power. During the next quarter of a century, his home during most of the year was to be in New York City, where he was to exercise a large and beneficial influence on contemporary opinion. As editor, orator, and writer, he had opportunities to express his views on current problems. When presidential campaigns were in the offing and rival parties wished to make sure of what was known as the German vote, attempts to cajole him were frequent and usually quite obvious to their intended victim. But he carefully cherished his independence and his prestige as an untrammeled reformer. He was, in the best sense of a much-abused word, a "publicist," a leader and director of thought.

Schurz had had some experience as an editor; indeed he still retained a share in the St. Louis *Westliche Post*. It was natural that, in his quest for a remunerative occupation, he should listen to a proposal that he become editor of the New York *Evening Post*, the journalistic gospel of many independent voters. Henry Villard purchased a controlling share in the paper and, in the spring of 1881, transferred its editorial management to Carl Schurz, Edwin L. Godkin, and Horace White, the first named to be editor-in-chief. On May 26, John Hay wrote Whitelaw Reid, "Schurz begins his editorial work on the *Post* today with a long, serious leader on civil service reform." The New York *Nation*, of which Godkin had been the aggressive editor, became under this new plan the weekly edition of the *Evening Post*. It was predicted that this triple array of talent would set a high standard for American journalism.

Both Godkin and Schurz were reformers, bent on cleansing

a corrupt and maculate world. Born in Ireland of English stock, Godkin [1] was two years younger than Schurz, but he had been connected with the *Nation* since 1865, and it was recognized as his voice. An experienced journalist, the master of a mordant and ironic prose style, he resented criticism, even from an associate; and Schurz himself was not an easy man to handle. Temperamentally the two were unlike, although both were dogmatic and tenacious of their opinions. Godkin was inclined to denounce those whose views differed from his own, and his manner justified the remark that he "made virtue odious"; Schurz's methods were more persuasive and less productive of pain. Henry Holt once said of Godkin that no editor of his time had so much authority over educated people. The contributions of the two men to the *Evening Post* are easily differentiated because of their marked contrast in tone and style. As an editorial writer Godkin, it must be confessed, had much the greater range, incisiveness, and power; indeed, he was such an editor as the world has seldom seen.

Although no open rupture is mentioned between Godkin and Schurz, they were at odds from the beginning as to the proper policies for the *Evening Post* to follow. Both loved to dominate, and neither was accustomed to compromise. Godkin's narrow, not to say reactionary, attitude upon labor and agrarian problems seriously disturbed Schurz; while Schurz's rather limited list of topics and lack of thrust and humor irritated Godkin. A break was merely a question of time. The direct cause for separation was a conflict over the best method of dealing with a strike called by the railway telegraphers in the summer of 1883. Godkin denounced the strikers in harsh and arrogant terms, and Schurz expostulated. As no compromise

[1] Godkin was a thick-set man, with dark hair and close-cropped beard, and an imperious air, looking as if he would brook no opposition. A thorough aristocrat, he was not interested in the common people. Unfortunately he left but three books, now little known, behind him, and only elderly people now recall the withering irony of his pen. For a fine characterization of him, see Villard, *Some Newspapers and Newspaper Men* (1923).

seemed to be possible, Schurz resigned.[1] The full-length history of the *Evening Post* makes it clear that Schurz was on the liberal side in this particular controversy; but it also shows that Schurz was not cut out for a great newspaper editor.[2]

Although Schurz had liked St. Louis, it had never been his real home. It was, therefore, without much regret that he moved his family during the summer of 1881 to New York and took up his residence in that city. At the time of this transfer, he had a moderate but regular income from his investments, and his salary from the *Evening Post* provided him with sufficient money for his modest needs. In 1883, however, he sustained some heavy financial losses and was left in a position which required him to practice the most frugal economy. A group of his friends, chiefly German-Americans, on learning of his misfortunes, undertook to raise a fund of $100,000, to be tendered to him as a testimonial of their esteem. The secret leaked out, as such secrets usually do; and when Schurz learned of the project, he notified Gustav Schwab, treasurer of the committee, that he should be forced to decline the gift. While expressing his gratitude, he said that he could not accept money without returning a proper equivalent. Moreover, he suggested that some contingency might arise in which his opinion in regard to the action of the United States might not coincide with that of other German-Americans; and he must remain independent. He asked, therefore, that the plan be abandoned.[3] It was precisely the kind of donation which Daniel

[1] Henry Adams wrote Schurz, December 12, 1883: "I was extremely sorry to see the announcement yesterday of your withdrawal from the *Evening Post*. . . . In such cases one does not stop to ask the cause of the trouble. I neither know nor care what it was; but I have perfect confidence that it was nothing which would affect my regard for you. I am quite content to leave it there." *Letters of Henry Adams*, 356.

[2] Allan Nevins, *The Evening Post: A Century of Journalism*, 438–457.

[3] Schurz to Schwab, March 21, 1884, *Writings*, IV, 197–98. Schurz's original letter was in German—probably because the fund idea was started by German-Americans—but was published in the New York newspapers in translation. See also George Haven Putnam, *Memories of a Publisher*, 85, ff., on this episode.

Webster had taken unreluctantly less than forty years before.

Before his retirement from the *Evening Post*, Schurz had been asked by John T. Morse, Jr., the able general editor of the "American Statesmen" series, to write the biography of Henry Clay. Henry Cabot Lodge, whose one-volume life of Daniel Webster was to appear in the spring of 1883, in the same series, had recommended Schurz as a suitable person to deal with the "Great Compromiser." Schurz wrote Morse, January 9, 1883, confessing that the pressure of his routine duties would allow him only parts of two or three evenings a week for the project and asking whether, in consideration of the immense amount of research and labor required in writing about Clay, it might not be possible for him to prepare instead a life of Albert Gallatin. No such arrangement could be effected, however, and the *Gallatin*, in accordance with the original plan, was completed by John Austin Stevens and published in 1884. The manuscript of Schurz's *Clay* was delayed month after month, to the disgust of Morse, and the book did not appear until 1887.

Much to Schurz's delight, Garfield had shown some reforming tendencies; indeed he had, perhaps as a warning to Conkling and Platt, appointed Judge Robertson, leader of the New York Independents, as Collector of the Port of New York, thus alienating the "Stalwarts" in that state and bringing about the somewhat theatrical resignations of the two Senators.[1] In his editorials in the *Evening Post*, Schurz treated the President with much consideration, while regretting that the latter did not devote more attention to the improvement of the civil service. As a matter of fact, Garfield, increasingly irritated by the demands of the "spoils" system upon his time, had virtu-

Putnam states that "with some little difficulty" the money was all redistributed to the many original donors.

[1] Garfield and Conkling were temperamentally incompatible. The latter once called on the President and found him out. When he discovered that Garfield was at that moment riding with Schurz, the New York Senator had a fit of the sulks and refused to answer Garfield's letters. Cortissoz, *Whitelaw Reid*, II, 36.

ally decided to press upon Congress the need for enacting a genuine civil service law; but his assassination on July 2, 1881, followed by his long weeks of suffering and eventual death on September 19, left his plans unripened. It was irony indeed that the shot which killed James A. Garfield should have been fired by a disappointed office seeker.

The accession to the presidency of Chester A. Arthur was regarded by Schurz and his friends at first as a calamity. Up to that moment, Arthur had been looked upon as a master of machine politics, with skill and discretion in dispensing patronage. "The new administration will be the centre for every element of corruption, South and North," wrote Henry Adams to Lodge. All the members of the Cabinet but one were changed. Blaine, whose influence over Garfield had been paramount, was superseded in the Department of State by Frederick T. Frelinghuysen and became an avowed candidate for the presidential nomination in 1884. To the astonishment of nearly everybody, Arthur proved to be a supporter of the merit system and emphasized in his first message the desirability of reform.

This conversion won Carl Schurz's sympathy for the new administration. In August, 1881, he had taken a prominent part at Newport in the establishment of the National Civil Service Reform League, of which George William Curtis had been elected the president; and he had promoted in the *Evening Post* the organization of similar societies in several Eastern states. Pressure from various quarters had its usual effect on Congress. Finally George H. Pendleton, an Ohio Democrat, presented and sponsored a bill the main features of which, drawn up by Dorman B. Eaton, embodied the principles so long advocated by Schurz; and this measure, passed early in 1883, became a law on January 16 of that year. It provided for three commissioners to be appointed by the President, for the classification of clerks, and for open competitive examinations of a practical nature. It was sufficiently thoroughgoing, always provided that the chief executive was in sympathy with its operation.

Arthur unquestionably did his best to make the scheme successful. His appointment of Dorman B. Eaton as chairman of the new Civil Service Commission was universally commended. Its first report, submitted in February, 1884, showed that more than fourteen thousand government employees had already been classified and placed under civil service rules. The forward step taken through the Pendleton Act has never been retraced, and each new President has, in his turn, added more places to those under its control. For the benefits which have resulted from thus putting efficiency above partisanship in government management, Carl Schurz is very largely responsible. He helped valiantly to keep alive the agitation which culminated eventually in practical reform.

Schurz had no confidence whatever in James G. Blaine as Senator, Secretary of State, or potential President, and, when the latter's candidacy began to take shape, was out at once in open opposition to it. In the *Evening Post*, he early announced unequivocally that Blaine's personality and public record unfitted him to be the Republican nominee in 1884.[1] When Blaine, in the autumn of 1882, tardily laid claim to being a civil service reformer, the *Evening Post* published an editorial by Godkin savagely denouncing him as one of the most venal of the apologists of the "spoils" system. Under the impression that Schurz was its author, Blaine retaliated on September 19, in the Chicago *Tribune*, charging Schurz with being an impostor who, after a ringing flourish of trumpets, had done little or nothing as Secretary of the Interior to put his noble theories into practice. Schurz promptly wrote to Joseph Medill, editor of the *Tribune*, disclaiming responsibility for the offensive editorial and saying that if Blaine desired to reply to its allegations, he would have to abuse somebody else. The fundamental cause of Blaine's outburst was his resentment because Schurz would not back him for the Presidency.

The principal charge against Blaine, succinctly stated, was

[1] New York *Evening Post*, August 8, 1882.

that, at a period when his financial affairs were much involved, he had used his prestige as Speaker of the House of Representatives as a means of increasing his bank account. There were several separate and distinct accusations, the chief one being based on his mysterious activities, beginning as early as 1869, in connection with the Little Rock and Fort Smith Railroad, with the promoters of which he had engaged in shady transactions which had paid him well. When, in the spring of 1876, while he was a leading candidate for the presidency, the criminations became more specific, Blaine was embarrassed. A Bostonian, James Mulligan, having in his possession certain inflammable letters written several years before by Blaine to Warren Fisher, Jr., one of the railroad officials, appeared in Washington, where Blaine, by methods which did him no credit, obtained possession of them and in self-defense produced and read some of them on the floor of the House in a theatrical speech which was by his friends regarded as proof of his innocence. Careful study of the "Mulligan Letters," however, indicated that he had resorted to evasion, if not to falsehood, and that his connection with the railroad and its affairs was unworthy of an honest man.[1] Before the House Committee of Investigation could report, Blaine was appointed United States Senator, and the matter was not officially pursued further.

The question of Blaine's guilt, so violently debated in his own lifetime, has been settled by the judgment of unbiased

[1] The most recent and, in many respects, the fullest treatment of the subject is in Charles Edward Russell's *Blaine of Maine*. The "Mulligan Letters," with some additional documents later discovered, were printed in 1884 by the New York *Times*, the *Evening Post*, the *Nation*, and *Harper's Weekly*. Read entire in *Harper's Weekly* for September 27, 1884, they contain phrases and sentences which no scrupulous man could have written, such as "I do not feel that I shall be a dead-head in the enterprise," "I see various channels in which I know I can be useful," and "Burn this letter." These became bywords with the reformers during the 1884 campaign and were quoted over and over by Nast in his cartoons. No one should form an opinion without going through these letters with a due regard to the choice of words and the motive of the man who wrote them.

historians adversely to him. No one can examine the "Mulligan Letters" or read Moorfield Storey's pamphlet, *Blaine's Record*, without concluding that the Maine politician was both indiscreet and corrupt. He had his apologists, including Senator George Frisbie Hoar,[1] but even their confidence in him cannot alter the verdict of history. If there was a straightforward explanation of Blaine's conduct, it was never made either by him or by anybody else. James Ford Rhodes, a cool observer, reached the decision in 1905 that Blaine was justly chargeable with moral delinquency; and an even more conservative scholar, H. C. Thomas, has said, "Although actual corruption was not proven, no one can doubt that Blaine was guilty of conduct unbecoming a Congressman."

Schurz was always sentimentally drawn toward the Republican Party. He refused, however, to swallow Blaine. At a dinner of the Brooklyn Young Men's Republican Club, on Washington's Birthday in 1884, he outlined a program for the Independents, making it entirely clear that he would under no circumstances accept Blaine as a nominee. At a meeting held on the following day, a "Conference Committee of Independent Republicans" was formed, which later, at Schurz's instigation, sent out circulars urging all Republicans to vote in the primaries for a man pledged to reform.

The avowed candidates for the Republican nomination, besides Blaine, were President Arthur, who was eager for reelection, Senator John Sherman, General John A. Logan, the favorite of the Grand Army of the Republic, and Senator George F. Edmunds, of Vermont, who, although backed by the reform element, was generally considered too frigid and austere. Schurz wrote Plumb on May 12 that Blaine and Arthur were the two candidates least acceptable to New York, and that Blaine could not possibly carry that state. "I have good reason," he said, "for apprehending that Blaine's nomi-

[1] The authoritative defense of Blaine, prepared by William Walter Phelps, was printed in *Harper's Weekly* for May 10, 1884, followed by a conclusive refutation written probably by George William Curtis.

nation would be followed instantly by a break." He himself was for Edmunds, and he had with him two promising young Republicans, destined to make some stir in the party, Henry Cabot Lodge, of Massachusetts, and Theodore Roosevelt, of New York, both of whom were delegates to the convention which opened in Chicago on June 3.

Although Blaine had some prophetic misgivings, the movement for him had made headway, and his success was assured unless the opposition could unite. Magnetic and astute, he had fostered the impression that he deserved a martyr's vindication. For a brief moment, George William Curtis, chairman of the New York delegation, and his fellow reformers, saw a possible victory when Lodge nominated John R. Lynch, a Mississippi Negro, for temporary chairman, and he was elected over Powell Clayton, a notorious Arkansas carpetbagger, who had been Blaine's selection.[1] Schurz, present as an observer, was in the auditorium when Judge West, the blind orator, delivered his eloquent eulogy placing Blaine in nomination. On Friday, June 6, came the voting. Blaine, clearly in the lead on the first ballot, gained steadily, and was chosen on the fourth trial. Taking out his watch, Schurz noted the time and remarked to his neighbor, "That is the hour and minute which will go down in history as marking the death of the Republican Party." It was an unfortunate prediction, as those who have watched Mr. McKinley, Mr. Roosevelt, Mr. Taft, Mr. Harding, Mr. Coolidge, and Mr. Hoover have good reason to know. But Blaine's nomination did allow the Democratic Party its first President since the Civil War.

As soon as the standard bearers, Blaine and Logan, were announced, the Independent Republicans had to consider what their policy would be. Early in the convention a resolution had been proposed declaring every delegate "bound in honor to support the nominee," but, at Curtis's vigorous protest, had

[1] Roosevelt, then only twenty-six years old, attracted some attention by seconding the nomination of Lynch and by doing some very active work in Edmunds's behalf. See Pringle's *Theodore Roosevelt,* 84–85.

been withdrawn. After the battle, Curtis was in doubt as to what to do, but was induced by Nast and his other colleagues on *Harper's Weekly* to come out openly in that periodical against Blaine. In the issue for June 14, accordingly, appeared a Nast cartoon showing the Republican elephant with his back broken by the weight of the political magnet, Blaine, together with an editorial amplifying the sentence, "The nomination of Mr. Blaine ought to alarm honest Republicans as showing how dangerously far the Republican standard has fallen."

Schurz never wavered in his opposition to Blaine. Writing on June 27 to ex-President Hayes to say that the tariff question had nothing to do with his decision, he continued:[1]

I oppose Blaine because I believe that the election to the presidency of the United States of the man who wrote the Mulligan letters, and who stands before the country as the representative of the practices they disclose, would be a precedent fraught with incalculable evil—a fatal blow at the moral foundations of our republican government. It would be a terrible thing to teach our young people that such a record does not disqualify a man for the highest honors and trusts of the Republic. . . . I solemnly declare my belief that, provided the Democratic candidate be an honest man, nothing a Democratic administration may bring with it can possibly be as bad in its general and permanent consequences, as the mere fact of Mr. Blaine's election.

Henry Cabot Lodge, and later Theodore Roosevelt, took a different attitude. Before the convention, according to Lodge, they had notified Godkin that, if Blaine were chosen, they should support him.[2] Lodge, then chairman of the Massachusetts Republican State Committee, lost no time in declaring publicly that he should stand by the party. When Schurz, on July 12, wrote him a friendly note, saying that Blaine's election would mean "a virtual endorsement of corrupt practices by the American people" and urging him to follow a "noble im-

[1] Hayes MSS.

[2] *Roosevelt-Lodge Correspondence,* I, 11–13.

pulse," even though it might temporarily compromise his party affiliations and obscure "the prospect of immediate preferment," Lodge, in an equally courteous but unyielding reply, answered, "I regard my action as the only honorable course to take." "I may be wrong, but I am firmly convinced on this point," added Lodge, who also confessed that he should accept a nomination for Congress if it came his way. The essence of his argument was: "By staying in the party I can be of some use. By going out I destroy all the influence and power for good I possess."

These diametrically opposite points of view, each obviously sincere and honest, were never better expressed than in these two letters of Schurz and Lodge. For them, as for many others, it was the parting of the ways. Even Theodore Roosevelt was in a dilemma. "There is no possible doubt," writes his biographer, Pringle, "that Roosevelt was disgusted with the nomination of Blaine." He went from Chicago direct to his Dakota ranch, after saying to Horace White, in words which he later repudiated, "I would say that any proper Democratic nominee will have our hearty support." From Dakota he wrote that he could not say that Blaine and Logan were fit nominees and that he should probably be in the West on Election Day. In July, however, he returned hurriedly to the East and, after a conference with Lodge, the details of which still remain mysteriously veiled, declared his fidelity to the Republican Party and even took the stump in the autumn for its candidates,[1] including Lodge, who had been nominated for Congress. Lodge was defeated in his own campaign, but he had remained with his party and was never again in any danger of abandoning it.

[1] Students of United States history, especially of the period following the Civil War, will read with astonishment and amusement the following excerpt from Roosevelt's speech at Winchester, Massachusetts, on October 28, 1884: "I believe, if you take the last twenty-four years, that future historians will hold it to be the heroic period of American history. . . .There never has been a time when so much good has been done and that so much bad has been undone, and it has been done by the Republican Party." *Roosevelt-Lodge Correspondence,* I, 24.

Schurz, avowing that the real issue was "the question of honesty in government," wrote to Lodge, "My convictions are so strong that I should have worked against Blaine under any circumstances, asking only that the opposing candidate be an honest man." In the course of his correspondence with John B. Henderson, furthermore, he said, "I cannot look upon Mr. Blaine as a mere jolly Prince Hal who has lived through his years of indiscretion and of whom the presidency will certainly make a new man." Many hitherto loyal Republicans agreed with Schurz. The Massachusetts Reform Club voted on June 7, after an address by Charles Francis Adams, Jr., to renounce Blaine and Logan. Six days later a meeting of Boston Independents was attended by more than five hundred leading citizens—citizens of whom the *Evening Transcript* said, "Here were men who do not make a barter of their judgment and conscience at the price of winning." Henry L. Pierce called them to order; Charles R. Codman was elected president; and the speakers included James Freeman Clarke, Colonel Thomas Wentworth Higginson, President Charles W. Eliot, and William Everett. The Massachusetts delegation was censured for not opposing Blaine, and Moorfield Storey declared, amid cheers, "We are united to rebuke corrupt men and corrupt methods in politics." Two committees were appointed: an executive committee of one hundred, comprising Eliot, Higginson, Storey, Gamaliel Bradford, William Endicott, Frederick J. Stimson, and many other distinguished Bostonians, some of them still alive; and a smaller committee of twenty-five to attend an Independent conference, on June 17, in New York City.

This New York meeting was of a more private nature, called at the home of Joseph Henry Harper, at 269 Madison Avenue. First to ring the doorbell, according to the reporters, was George Haven Putnam, then and later a force for good government. Close after him came Carl Schurz and his constant companion, Dr. Abraham Jacobi. From Boston had arrived Theodore Lyman, Colonel Higginson, Moorfield Storey,

Josiah Quincy, Richard H. Dana, and William Everett—names representative of the aristocratic liberalism of New England. Curtis was chosen chairman. Schurz presented resolutions asserting that Blaine and Logan had been named "in absolute disregard of the reform sentiment of the nation" and ending: "We look with solicitude to the coming nominations of the Democratic Party. They have the proper men. We hope they will put them before the people." During the discussion, Moorfield Storey again voiced the sentiment of his associates by saying, "Our first duty is to induce the Democrats to put up a good man; our second to help them elect him."

The revolters watched with much trepidation the proceedings of the Democrats at Chicago during the second week of July. To Schurz, the only two candidates who could command the entire Independent vote were Thomas F. Bayard, the distinguished Delaware statesman who had succeeded his father in the United States Senate, and Grover Cleveland, the sturdy and phlegmatic figure who had risen almost out of obscurity in Buffalo, to be elected as Governor of his state by the then unprecedented majority of almost two hundred thousand. Although Cleveland had incurred the hostility of Tammany and its notorious Boss John Kelly,[1] he had lost nothing in the eyes of the common people, to whom his rugged manhood and fearless integrity made a strong appeal. Between Bayard and Cleveland, Schurz probably preferred the former, whom he knew and trusted. But Bayard, with all his probity, was without magnetism; and Cleveland, although no more attractive personally, had the decisive advantage of availability. In the convention, Cleveland, despite all that Tammany could do, had a commanding lead on the first ballot and was easily nominated on the second. Edward S. Bragg's remark regarding Cleve-

[1] Nast drew "Honest John" Kelly in his caricatures as a tough-looking Irishman, wearing a somewhat battered "plug" hat and smoking a clay pipe. Schurz loved to tell the story of how he and Kelly, meeting accidentally on Broadway, recognized one another from their cartoons. "We had been pictorially introduced," said Schurz. "We both laughed simultaneously, touched our hats, and passed on."

land—"We love him for the enemies he has made"—was the watchword of the party. The ensuing campaign was to be a battle between two leaders of very different types. On the one hand was Blaine, nervous, alert, and brilliant, with his amazing memory for names and faces, his impressive bearing, his fluent eloquence, and his seductive charm; on the other was Cleveland, slow, stolid, unimaginative, reticent in speech and clumsy in his movements. Blaine had shown himself to be keen-minded, but unreliable; Cleveland, new though he was in public life, had won a reputation for industry and trustworthiness. Blaine possessed all the wiles and suavity of the politician; Cleveland was tactless, even surly, but never evasive.

Schurz's resolve to support a Democrat was entirely consistent with his political philosophy.[1] Aside from thinking Blaine to have been guilty of prostituting his high office for money, he considered him to be at heart an upholder of the pernicious "spoils system" and a symbol of the venality and insensibility to morals which had attained their culmination under the administrations of President Grant. Blaine's opinion of Schurz may be read in his *Twenty Years of Congress*, the first volume of which appeared in season for the campaign of 1884. Although in this work Blaine was usually generous even toward his enemies, he described Schurz as having "certain unsteady and erratic tendencies," as a man "incapable of attachment to party" and out of touch with "true American feeling." Schurz knew very little, except from hearsay, about Grover Cleveland, but the latter's brief public service had been spotless, and he seemed far more promising than the battle-scarred and vulnerable Blaine of Maine.

Unrestricted by any routine occupation, Schurz was free to devote himself unreservedly to the Independent movement. As early as March, 1884, the New York *Sun* had christened the bolting Republicans by the name of "Mugwumps"; and Schurz

[1] Interviewed on July 11, 1884, by the New York *Morning Journal*, Schurz said, "I am pleased with the nomination of Grover Cleveland and shall give him my support. I think he is the strongest candidate the Democrats could have nominated."

and his followers soon were glorying in an appellation the true meaning of which has never been satisfactorily explained, although etymologically it may be derived from an Algonquin Indian word signifying "Great Chief." Faced with a situation not unlike that of 1872, Schurz was like an old war horse who, retaining much of his youthful ardor, gallops hotly into the fray. He soon showed that he had lost none of his physical or mental vigor. His was the animating spirit behind the "Mugwump Revolt"—a political protest up to that time without a parallel in our history.[1]

Under Schurz's inspiration, a national conference of anti-Blaine Republicans was called for July 22, in New York City,[2] with about four hundred present, including fifty from Massachusetts. Charles R. Codman, of Boston was honored with the chairmanship, and, after his opening remarks, Carl Schurz, who received an enthusiastic greeting, rose to offer a motion providing for a Committee on Resolutions and Address, of which he was appointed chairman, with Curtis, Storey, Williams, and others as his associates. Schurz was also later designated as head of a large National Committee, empowered to conduct the campaign and express the views of the conference. The address, composed by Curtis, denounced Blaine as an "unfit leader . . . unworthy of respect and confidence," and called upon all honest men to vote for Cleveland; but when William Everett offered a resolution declaring that Cleveland and Hendricks were the nominees of the conference, it was laid on the table. The gathering, harmonious in nearly every respect, was completely dominated by Carl Schurz. Everyone deferred to him, consulted him as to the proper procedure, and

[1] A brief but entertaining account of the "Mugwumps" may be found in Frederick J. Stimson's *My United States*. In spite of the credit which has been claimed for others, including Storey, Putnam, Curtis, and Adams, Schurz was the engine which drove the machinery along. Without him, the movement could never have gathered momentum as rapidly as it did.

[2] For an excellent account of this "Independent Republican Conference," called by the *Sun* "only a Democratic annex," see the supplement to *Harper's Weekly* for August 2, 1884.

paid him the honor due to a commanding officer. It was clear that he had nothing to gain personally except the satisfaction of public service. Soon money was provided and a headquarters established at 35 Nassau Street, in New York. With earnest supporters to cheer him on, Schurz devoted the next few weeks to electing Grover Cleveland President of the United States.

Some of the "Mugwumps," such as the Adamses, had already been sufficiently Democratic to vote for Tilden in 1876, and it was not remarkable that they should come out for Cleveland. Others there were, like Schurz himself, who had backed Horace Greeley and the Democratic ticket in 1872. But a large proportion of them were younger men, just starting out in politics, many of them with Republican leanings. Some of them never returned to the Republican fold. Others, like Schurz, came back with McKinley and the free silver agitation. It would be a mistake to regard the Mugwump movement as merely a Democratic manifestation. It was a genuine and almost spontaneous protest by citizens who did their own thinking against a situation which seemed to them intolerable. Its influence was most salutary. Theodore Roosevelt might say in July, "The bolt is very large among the dudes"; but the decision of men like President Eliot, Moorfield Storey, and George William Curtis had to be respected even if it were not approved.

There were moments when the Cleveland "boom" was threatened with collapse. As the delegates to the Independent Republican Conference were leaving the hall, copies of the Buffalo *Telegraph* were handed to them making sensational disclosures regarding Cleveland's connection some years before with a Mrs. Maria Halpin, a "dipsomaniac widow" by whom he was said to have had an illegitimate child. A group of Mugwumps dined that evening at the University Club, Schurz sitting at the head of the table, all of them very gloomy over the probable consequences of the scandalous revelation. As they were sipping their coffee, Curtis, Codman, and others entered, also looking despondent. "How can we possibly continue our support of Cleveland?" inquired Curtis, with a gesture of despair. Finally an anonymous gentleman from Chicago brought hope to the mourners by saying: "From what I hear I gather that Mr. Cleveland has shown high character and great capacity in public office but that in private life his conduct has been open to question; while, on the other hand, Mr. Blaine in public life has been weak and dishonest while he seems to have been an admirable husband and father. The conclusion that I draw from these facts is that we should elect Mr. Cleveland to the public office which he is so admirably qualified to fill and remand Mr. Blaine to the private life which he is so eminently qualified to adorn." [1]

The Republicans made the most of this sordid story, and even started a marching cry, "Ma, ma, where's my pa?" But the unevasive Cleveland's frankness in acknowledging his early indiscretion won him friends among sensible people and was in pleasing contrast to Blaine's attitude toward the charges made against him. I cannot believe that the publication of Cleveland's lapse from virtue lost him many votes. It did not deter Carl Schurz from opening his speaking campaign with an address in Brooklyn on Tuesday, August 5. A few days previous to the meeting, Henry Ward Beecher, who had joined the Mugwumps, wrote asking him to postpone it, on the ground that several eminent clergymen of Buffalo had told him that Cleveland was still "a grossly dissipated man." Schurz responded that some study of the case had made him feel that Cleveland had been "much calumniated" and that he was going ahead. The speech delivered that evening, later entitled "Why James G. Blaine Should Not Be President" and circulated widely in both German and English, was a carefully reasoned and bitter analysis of Blaine's career. Opening with the declaration that the issue of the campaign was "honesty in government," Schurz asserted that the Republicans had nominated a candidate with a

[1] This anecdote was related by Moorfield Storey to James Ford Rhodes and told by the latter in his *History of the United States from Hayes to McKinley*, 221–22.

"blemished public record," and then, quoting verbatim from the Mulligan Letters, proceeded to prove his point. He maintained that Blaine had used his great political influence in order to make money—and had grown rich. He contrasted him with Cleveland, a leader "whose ideas of honest, intelligent, and efficient administration are remarkably clear and correct," and who was likely to become "the representative of courageous conscience in the administration of public affairs." Schurz's speech reads very much like his excoriation of Stephen A. Douglas a quarter of a century before, but was much more personal. He acted like a prosecuting attorney with a disagreeable task, which, however, he was resolved to carry through to the end.[1]

The campaign had already degenerated into a contest in vilification.[2] Thomas Nast, now restored to the staff of *Harper's Weekly*, was, by a strange revolution, enlisted on the side of Schurz and the reformers, and drawing for that periodical caricatures of Blaine as the adroit and oleaginous "Plumed Knight," in grotesque attitudes and disguises. He showed a "Free Republican" as the noble Virginius, about to slay his lovely daughter, "Republican Party," rather than yield her to the embraces of the foul ravisher, Appius Claudius Blaine. Under the caption, "A Roaring Farce—The Plumed Knight in the Clean Shirt," he displayed Blaine, his legs ludicrously protruding through the armholes of a white shirt, trying desperately to get it on correctly before appearing on the stage and crying plaintively to Whitelaw Reid: "Wait a minute! *There's something wrong!*" He depicted a perplexed Blaine, one arm around a bibulous hobo labeled "Free Whiskey" and the other encircling a clergyman carrying "Prohibition Laws" under his arm. Blaine was sketched always as sleek and furtive,

[1] Commenting on this Brooklyn speech, *Harper's* said editorially, "It was very effective in delivery, and yet is entirely free from clap-trap." Curtis wrote Schurz that it was "a model of the best political oratory and a masterly presentation of the case." He added, "There will be nothing so good said by either side during the campaign.

[2] For an amusing summary of the current scandals, see Adams's letter to Gaskell, September 21, 1884, *Letters of Henry Adams*, 360.

trying to divert the issue to the tariff or whispering to Evarts, "Let's talk about the weather." Cleveland, on the other hand, was revealed as blunt and resolute, unpolished but veracious, a plain man of the people. Another clever artist, Bernhard Gillam, was meanwhile caricaturing the Maine statesman as "The Tattooed Man," spotted all over with "Little Rock," the "Mulligan Letters," and similar legends—one of several freaks in a national dime museum. It is not strange that Mrs. Blaine was filled with what Blaine's biographer calls "an uncontrolled and almost hysterical terror."

It was indeed an exciting summer and autumn, long remembered by those who lived through it. One sensational tale after another flared out in large headlines in the metropolitan dailies. Cartoon after cartoon tickled the risibilities of the public. There were colorful parades, with long lines of men chanting monotonously, "Blaine, Blaine, James G. Blaine." It was a campaign unprecedented for its animosities, its unscrupulousness, and its filth. Among the important newspapers of Republican leanings which turned openly against the party candidate were the Boston *Transcript* and *Herald*, the New York *Times* and *Herald*, the Springfield *Republican*, and the Chicago *News* and *Times*. Whitelaw Reid's *Tribune* remained faithful, but the *Evening Post* came out for Cleveland. Carl Schurz watched all these developments with observant eyes. Under his direction the Independent National Committee published fourteen separate pamphlets, started many subsidiary organizations in other communities, and raised and spent more than twenty-five thousand dollars—a sum which seems small in these days, but which probably decided the outcome.

With real enthusiasm, Schurz also lent his voice to the movement. Early in September he left New York for a long "stumping" trip in the familiar Middle West, where every person of German ancestry knew him by sight. On September 6, in Schlitz's Park, in Milwaukee, he spoke before six thousand German-Americans, who, on an intensely hot night, listened to him for two hours. He wrote from Dayton, Ohio, on September

21, that he was traveling from one hundred to one hundred and fifty miles a day and was constantly surrounded "by crowds of people." In Ohio alone he delivered twenty-two speeches,[1] several of them in both German and English, causing so much alarm to the Republican managers that Blaine was brought to that state in person to offset Schurz's stirring eloquence. Blaine ignored Schurz's charges, emphasized the need of a protective tariff, waved the "bloody shirt" once more, and carried Ohio by a plurality of eleven thousand.

On September 29, Schurz was back in the East at a great gathering of German-Americans in the Academy of Music, in New York, presided over by Oswald Ottendorfer, of the *Staats-Zeitung*. Here he won rounds of applause by crying, "*Wir opponiren Blaine am hefigsten wegen der Freunde, die er sich gemacht hat,*" and saying that, just as there had been no German rebels and no German repudiationists, so there would be no German defenders of dishonesty. On October 11 he was in Chicago, and two days later in Buffalo, Cleveland's home. A whirlwind tour through the state brought him to New York City for another rally on Sunday evening, October 19. He was certainly doing all that it was humanly possible for one speaker to do. Always he stressed the "Mulligan Letters," and Frederic J. Stimson recalled how, in quoting the correspondence between Blaine and Fisher, Schurz, after repeating the substance of what Blaine had written, would read "in a delicious accent" the postscript, "Kind regards to Mrs. Fisher."

When his enemies accused him of taking $250 from the Democratic Central Committee for each speech, he answered indignantly, "The facts are that I am not receiving one cent from any source for my speeches in the contest, and that I am paying all my own traveling expenses."[2] There were moments

[1] Schurz's schedule on this trip began with Indianapolis, on September 15, included Detroit, Toledo, Cleveland, Mansfield, Dayton, Cincinnati, Portsmouth, Marietta, Columbus, Wooster, and Canton, and kept him away from New York until September 27.

[2] In January, 1885, when George W. Folsom, Treasurer of the Independent Republican Committee, sent him a check for $600, Schurz said that he had kept

when he complained with some reason that he was being given no help. "Is nobody available?" he asked Bowker. "I must say that I begin to feel a little lonesome in this struggle. Where is Curtis? And where are the able speakers from Massachusetts?" It seemed as if he were being forced to carry on his missionary work alone. Fortunately his strength held out, and he was as tireless as he had been in 1860. He fought valiantly until the eve of the election. And then came victory!

The exceedingly close result was affected by various factors, the relative importance of which will probably never be positively determined. The popular vote was larger for Cleveland than for Blaine, but the decision rested in the final analysis on New York, where Cleveland had a plurality of only 1149 in a total of almost 1,200,000. Without New York, Cleveland could not have won; with it, he had 219 electoral votes against 182 for his opponent.

Historians have been busy ever since explaining Blaine's defeat. Nast's cartoons undoubtedly influenced many people through their cumulative exposure of Blaine's weaknesses, and his biographer, Albert Bigelow Paine, believes that the "Little Lad of Landau," as Nast was called, really made a President. The incredibly stupid speech of the Reverend Samuel Burchard in the Fifth Avenue Hotel, in which, addressing Blaine as the spokesman for a delegation of clergymen, he said, "We are Republicans, and don't propose to leave our party and identify ourselves with the party whose antecedents have been *Rum, Romanism, and Rebellion,*" undoubtedly had disastrous consequences in alienating the Irish Catholic vote from Blaine. The equally unfortunate "Boodle Dinner," at Delmonico's, a few days before the election, at which millionaires like Henry Clews, Russell Sage, Jay Gould, and Cyrus W. Field were seated at the table with Blaine, was heralded by the Democrats

no detailed account of expenses, expecting to bear them all himself, but that he was willing to accept $300, if the committee had any surplus funds. He had actually expended from his own pocket about $450, but he wished to consider $150 of this as his cash contribution to the campaign. Schurz, *Writings,* IV, 308–9.

as the occasion for raising a large fund for last minute use by the Republicans, and did not help that party. The Prohibition issue doubtless led many orthodox Republicans to vote for St. John, the "dry" candidate. The indifference, if not the actual hostility, of former Senator Roscoe Conkling to Blaine had an effect on the result not only in Conkling's own bailiwick of Oneida County, but also throughout New York State. In some sections, furthermore, the rainy weather may have been unlucky for the Republicans. But, when all these elements have been considered, one must conclude that Carl Schurz and the despised Mugwumps settled matters. If the Independent Republican movement had not been started, Blaine would certainly have been President. Schurz had set himself the duty of blocking the ambition of James G. Blaine. He succeeded.

The victory of the Democrats in 1884 was a triumph for clean politics. The country refused to accept a man with Blaine's tarnished public record. It has been the fashion among certain conservative Republicans to refer to the Mugwumps rather sneeringly, as hypocritical, as "dudes" and "saints" and "gentle hermits." Blaine himself had at an earlier date described the Independents as "noisy but not numerous, pharisaical but not practical, ambitious but not wise." This is an unfair judgment upon them. Among them were men unexcelled in our annals for high ideals, clean living, and good citizenship. They had nothing of the "holier than thou" attitude. They merely believed that moral standards should be upheld and maintained in public life. If James G. Blaine was culpable, these men, including Schurz, deserve the highest praise for the position which they took. No one can study the last quarter of the nineteenth century with an unprejudiced, open mind without reaching the conclusion that the Mugwumps were, on the whole, a power for good.

CHAPTER XXII SCHURZ AND CLEVELAND

CARL SCHURZ's position in New York in the eighties and nineties was not unlike that of William Cullen Bryant at an earlier and Elihu Root at a later period. He was a leading citizen of whom the city was proud and whose utterances on controversial topics were awaited with eagerness, especially just before Election Day. He had a large following of voters who formed their judgments on his, knowing that he had no selfish ambitions to gratify. To the younger generation, he seemed the embodiment of a modernized Stoic virtue. Was he not a man who had walked untainted where scores of political leaders had bowed to Mammon? The sleuths employed by his enemies had been unable to find any stain upon his character. He was a popular member of that exclusive literary and artistic club known as the Century Association, which his position as a lonely widower justified him in frequenting. He was a familiar "first-nighter" at plays, as well as an habitué of concerts and operas and a constant "diner-out." Once at a fancy dress ball, some one called Henry Holt's attention to a peculiar looking figure, exclaiming, "By Jove, what a make-up as Carl Schurz!" It turned out to be Schurz himself, renewing his youth.[1] He met old age gracefully, with his enthusiasm only slightly abated, his faculties unimpaired, and his energy undepleted.[2]

His chief activity more and more centered in the improvement of governmental methods. The Pendleton Act of 1883 had marked the abandonment of the old "spoils" system. It became Schurz's business, as the self-constituted "Watch Dog of the Civil Service," to see that there was no retrogression. His eye was the first to detect any concession to expediency; his

[1] Henry Holt, *Garrulities of an Octogenarian Editor,* 140.

[2] In February, 1887, when he was nearly sixty, he broke his thigh bone and was in bed for two months, but made a satisfactory recovery and was only slightly lame thereafter.

voice was the first to praise any wise appointment. His preference for admonishment and reproof was often exasperating to officials who were trying to do their best. Nobody really loves a schoolmaster, and Schurz was always a bit of a pedagogue. But he could ignore unpopularity if he thought that, by becoming censorious, he could accomplish any good.

He opened fire at once on Grover Cleveland—a slow-moving, phlegmatic, thoroughly sincere figure, resolved to keep the faith; not a dreamer, but a man of shrewd common sense; a sagacious opportunist, who disdained gestures unless something could be accomplished by them. *Harper's Weekly* appeared on November 15, 1884, in jubilant mood, with a full-page Nast drawing showing Columbia as a female figure pointing to an inscription reading in part: "VICTORY. GROVER CLEVELAND. PUBLIC OFFICE IS A PUBLIC TRUST. THE UPRISING OF A GREAT PEOPLE TO MAINTAIN THE HONEST BUSINESS PRINCIPLES OF OUR GOVERNMENT." On the same day, Carl Schurz, congratulating Cleveland on the opportunity before him of "striking a decisive blow at the spoils system," wrote that the crucial question of the incoming administration would be, not the tariff, but the civil service. Schurz added that, if he could assist as friend and adviser, he should be glad to do so. When George Fred Williams inquired whether he would accept a seat in the Cabinet, Schurz replied, "My circumstances do not permit me to go into official life again. . . . Public life has kept me poor; I am growing old, and I have to think of my family."[1] Doubtless Schurz would not have declined had a department been offered to him, but he was only too well aware that, as a Democrat, Cleveland was unlikely to choose for his Cabinet one who had so long been identified with the opposing party.

Cleveland responded to Schurz's advances with a courteous, but noncommittal letter, suggesting that there were obstacles to a real conference. At this date, apparently, the two men had not

[1] *Writings,* IV, 295.

met. Replying to Cleveland's intimation of his receptiveness to ideas, Schurz now produced a long letter of advice, pointing out that "the Democratic Party won under its banner of reform" and that Cleveland's own strength with the people lay in his "character and reputation as a reformer." He emphasized the necessity of selecting as heads of the three great "patronage" departments—the Treasury, the Post Office, and the Interior—men who believed in, and were willing to fight for, reform. Without mentioning specific persons, he said, "The only really important thing is to get the right man." [1]

Between the election and the inauguration, Schurz scrutinized events day by day to get a clue as to Cleveland's policies. The President-elect, on Christmas Day, answering a letter of inquiry from the National Civil Service Reform League, announced to George William Curtis his intention of enforcing the Pendleton Act "without evasion" and stated that certain other officials not covered by this law would not be removed until the expiration of their terms, except for incompetence or offensive partisanship. This sensible decision, although Schurz wished that it had gone further, pleased him very much, and he wrote to Cleveland a letter of commendation.[2]

Schurz had much to say regarding the cabinet. Replying to a query from Silas W. Burt, he expressed only lukewarm approval of Daniel Manning as Secretary of the Treasury, saying that the appointment could be defended but would require much explanation. On February 23, he had a conference with Cleveland in Albany at which the latter submitted to him the names of possible Cabinet members. To the choice of William C. Whitney as Secretary of the Navy, Schurz was strongly opposed, writing to Lamar that Whitney's only recommendations were that he was Senator Payne's son-in-law and had contributed $25,000 to the Democratic campaign fund. Lucius Q. C. Lamar, of

[1] Schurz to Cleveland, Dec. 10, 1884, *Writings,* IV, 297, ff.

[2] Horace White wrote to Schurz, January 24, 1885, "The impression I got of Governor Cleveland is that he is an honest, true-hearted, single-minded man, who has mastered the civil service question and is inflexible to carry out that reform in the spirit of his recent letter." Schurz, *Writings,* IV, 351.

Mississippi, Cleveland's selection as Secretary of the Interior, was a civil service reformer and one of Schurz's trusted friends. It was to him, on March 2, that Schurz poured out his soul, complaining about the appointments of Manning and Whitney and saying that, while the Mugwumps had declined any reward for their efforts during the campaign, everything which they had especially recommended had been refused. "If the Cabinet is formed as intended," he said warningly, "a majority of the rank and file of the Independents, disappointed and distrustful, will, I apprehend, quietly find their way back to their old associations."

After the inauguration, Schurz, with the best of intentions, became to Cleveland a good deal of a nuisance. Like every President before and after him, Cleveland sometimes found himself in situations where he had to balance one benefit against another; and there were occasions when it seemed wise to yield on an appointment in order to gain on a matter of far greater importance. In politics and government, as in other fields, it is often difficult to determine the proportion of right or wrong in two different courses. It would be very easy to choose if one selection were obviously bad and the other as obviously good. But problems do not present themselves in that form. Cleveland generally tried to weigh the evidence and reach an honest conclusion. Schurz, who had usually in the past paid some attention to the demands of practical politics, was growing less responsive to broader considerations; and his letters to the President were not soothing to the busy and often weary Chief Executive.

The case of Henry G. Pearson, the Republican Postmaster of New York City, was one in point. Although he had apparently been an honest and capable incumbent, his term had expired without a reappointment by the President; and, even before the date of expiration, Schurz had warned Cleveland that the continuance of Pearson in office would be regarded by the reformers as a test of the administration program. The President's reply indicated, in its tone, a patient desire to restrain his temper despite much provocation. He pointed out that he was studying certain documents and papers on file in the Post Office Department and that, while endeavoring to "do just the right thing," he did not wish to be hurried. "I take up my burden every morning and carry it as well as I can till night," he added, "and frequently up-hill." [1]

The first Democratic President since Buchanan could hardly have been expected to exclude from public office all members of his own party. He refused to admit that the federal government was to be conducted, as he phrased it, "merely for the purpose of promoting civil service reform." He did, however, believe in the broad principles advocated by Schurz and Curtis, and ultimately, although threatened by Democratic defections, reappointed Pearson as Postmaster of New York City. He took pains, nevertheless, to make it clear that this deed must not be construed as indicating "that in other cases those opposed to the party of the President will either be appointed or retained after the expiration of their terms of office." To put it more bluntly, Cleveland, although conceding to the wishes of the reformers, did not propose to commit himself irrevocably to their doctrines.

All the evidence indicates that Grover Cleveland was extremely conscientious in trying to place the best men in the vacant posts. He was increasingly exasperated by what he called "the damned everlasting clatter for offices," and terribly hurt when former friends and allies, aggrieved at not receiving remunerative sinecures, turned against him. But he was also harassed by men like Carl Schurz, who were ignorant of the difficulties which he was confronting. When Cleveland reappointed Pearson, Schurz sent him a note of appreciation, but could not refrain from condemning, in the same letter, the naming of Eugene Higgins as appointment clerk in the Treasury Department. A few weeks later, Schurz congratulated the President on the selections made for the marshalships in Chicago and Cincinnati; but he also spoke out against some

[1] *Writings*, IV, 363.

"sweeping changes in the internal revenue collectorships," especially in Boston and New York. It seemed impossible for Schurz to use praise without nullifying it by censure. And yet, as he told Cleveland, the general feeling among high-minded men regarding the administration was one of "satisfaction, confidence, and hope." When Dorman B. Eaton resigned on July 28, 1885, as Civil Service Commissioner, he commended the President for his faithful carrying out of the Pendleton Act. As a matter of fact, Cleveland, in his first message to Congress (December 8, 1885) made some very practical observations regarding the extension of the civil service rules, endorsing it whole-heartedly, but also rebuking some of the over-zealous reformers who were making his life miserable.

A quarrel between the President and the Republican Senate, which broke out early in 1886, almost brought about an open rupture between him and Schurz. Cleveland had refused in several cases to give reasons for removing officers whose places he expected to fill; and the Senate, in retaliation, had declined to confirm his nominations. The dispute came to a head in January, when Senator Edmunds, chairman of the Committee on the Judiciary, asked for the papers relating to the removal of George M. Duskin, a federal attorney. The Attorney General replied, "I am directed by the President to refuse your demand." Though Edmunds was perfectly sincere, to most Republicans the affair was really a political game, and Cleveland refused to submit to party dictation.[1]

Schurz, as usual, could not keep out of the controversy. On January 16, he sent a letter arguing that the President ought to present to the Senate his reasons for all removals, and adding that a statute making it the duty of the Executive to do this would be "a great help to a reform administration." He followed this with another communication on February 5, in which, while protesting how distasteful it was to him to say "unpleasant things," he declared that there was much open and

[1] An excellent account of this incident will be found in Peck, *Twenty Years of the Republic,* 84, ff.

secret criticism of Cleveland's removals and warned him that the chief danger of any reform administration was that it would "sit down between two chairs"—pleasing neither one party nor the other. Schurz begged the President to yield, and, through his influence, the National Civil Service Reform League passed resolutions recommending publicity in all matters connected with appointments and removals. Cleveland's reply was his message of March 1, 1886, assuming full responsibility for his conduct and defying the Senate. The Upper House was powerless to do anything except pass a vote of censure on the Attorney General. The affair resulted in a strong reassertion of the independence of the Executive.

On May 6, not having received from the White House any acknowledgment of his previous letters, Schurz wrote to his friend, Bayard, evidently hoping thus to reach the President. Recapitulating many of the opinions earlier expressed, he urged that Cleveland abandon the policy of "gaining small points by management of the patronage," and asserted that, because of the President's vacillation and timidity, his party was losing ground. It was a peculiar charge to bring against Grover Cleveland, but Schurz felt that his methods were justified by the emergency.

With characteristic pertinacity, Schurz also assailed Secretary of the Interior Lamar, indicating cases in which the civil service regulations had been flagrantly violated and imploring him to advocate a rule putting on record the reasons for every suspension or removal. Finally, on December 15, 1886, he again addressed the President directly, prefacing his remarks by saying that, as he saw it, the Democratic Party had only one chance of salvation—the nomination and reëlection of Cleveland. In this letter, somewhat presumptuous and rather critical in tone, he dwelt on the shortcomings of the administration, especially in its reinstatement of United States District Attorney Benton, who had been dismissed for "offensive partisanship," and in the mistakes and weaknesses of members of the Cabinet. Again he warned the President that the latter could be saved only "by a strong reform policy, commanding general confidence." The letter was certainly sincere, but not one which any proud and well-meaning Chief Executive could read without some degree of resentment.

Cleveland still remained discreetly silent. Charles R. Codman, who saw the President in January, 1887, told Schurz that the latter's letters sometimes irritated Cleveland, though he acknowledged their disinterestedness. "The impression made upon me," wrote Codman to Schurz, "was that he thought you did not allow for the difficulties of his position in the immense variety of questions and subjects to which he is obliged to give attention." When Schurz heard this, his hot temper led him to say of Cleveland, "His mind seems to be controlled by irritation at his critics rather than by an intelligent endeavor to disarm their criticism." Peculiarly annoyed when he learned that the President could not find three or four hours to answer his letters, Schurz asked Codman, "Might I not say that he could possibly find those three or four hours where I found three or four months to advocate his election?" [1] These details are worth recording, perhaps, as indicating Schurz's methods of achieving his desires and the persistence with which he pursued his aims.

After this interchange, the relations between Schurz and the President could no longer be described as intimate. Cleveland was not a dummy or rubber stamp, but a strong and obstinate Chief Executive who liked to do his own thinking and had his reasons for every step which he took. Through inexperience and ignorance, he occasionally committed serious blunders in his appointments; but he resented deeply criticism based on a misunderstanding of his motives. Schurz, well acquainted though he was with the entanglements and inconsistencies of official Washington, seems to have thought that the millennium could be reached in a few months.

Annoyed by the aggressiveness of the reformers and dismayed by the lukewarm support which he received from the

[1] For the Schurz-Codman correspondence, see *Writings,* IV, 470, ff.

Democratic Senators, Cleveland, perhaps unconsciously, relaxed his vigilance as his term of office drew to a close, with the inevitable result that a few of his influential subordinates felt free to make appointments and removals on a purely partisan basis. In New York State, furthermore, Cleveland's rival, David Bennett Hill, was gaining ground through denunciation of the President's independent policies. Many factors conspired to make the President petulant, and, when the National Civil Service Reform League held its annual meeting at Newport in the summer of 1887, Cleveland, suspecting that it was about to assail his administration, warned a government official in the New York Custom House not to attend the gathering on the ground that it would be considered an interference in politics. The President of the National Civil Service Reform League did, in his opening address, point out a discrepancy between what had been hoped for and what had been accomplished under Cleveland and evinced a disposition to be uncompromising in the demands of his organization. Cleveland merely complained mildly that this Newport speech had made his difficulties "a little harder" and continued patiently on the course which he had resolved to follow. Schurz, for his part, remained uncompromising in his public and private comments on the errors and neglected opportunites of the administration.

At heart, however, Schurz was aware that Cleveland, considering the problems which he had been obliged to confront, had been a serviceable friend to reform. As the campaign of 1888 drew near, Schurz was fearful lest Blaine might again be nominated by the Republicans; and, although he planned to spend the summer in Europe, he promised that, to prevent the disaster of Blaine's election, he would even return to the United States and go actively on the stump for the Democrats. Schurz felt that Benjamin Harrison, nominated by the Republicans in late June, was really one of Blaine's tools, from whom much less was to be expected than from Grover Cleveland. Accordingly, when he was urged by Thaddeus C. Pound to "recross the ocean and take the field for Mr. Harrison," he sent back a long letter of explanation saying that, if he reached home by the date of the election, he should vote for Cleveland. In his decision, Schurz was undoubtedly much influenced by Cleveland's public declaration against a high protective tariff. A free trader himself, he favored the tariff policy advocated by the Democrats. But he also rather grudgingly confessed that Cleveland had been, on the whole, the friend of reform and had won the confidence of the people by the ability, the energy, and the wholesome conservative spirit of his administration. Such an admission from Carl Schurz was high praise indeed.

Schurz was unquestionably disappointed in the result of the election. The complications of politics in New York State and Indiana, joined with the vigorous efforts of the protectionists, gave Harrison the victory by what was actually a very small margin. It was the first presidential campaign since 1856 in which Carl Schurz had not taken an active part.

The unremitting agitation of the reformers during Cleveland's first administration was displeasing to many men who, in theory, agreed with them. We find young Theodore Roosevelt for example, writing to Lodge, April 16, 1886, "What perverse lunatics the mugwumps are anyway," and referring, on February 15, 1887, to "those political and literary hermaphrodites, the mugwumps."[1] Roosevelt's instinctive dislike of Schurz and his friends was not mitigated by their refusal to support him during his campaign for mayor of New York City in 1886 against Abram S. Hewitt and Henry George. Schurz spoke in favor of Hewitt at a large meeting of German-Americans in late October, thus doing much to assure Hewitt's ultimate success in a contest in which Roosevelt ran a poor third.

The most intense dislike of Schurz, however, came from the practical politicians of both parties, who saw in him the implacable foe of the system on which their power was built. Leaders like Platt and David B. Hill, whose strength lay in political machines put together through patronage, always

[1] *Letters of Theodore Roosevelt and Henry Cabot Lodge,* I, 39, 51.

spoke sneeringly of the reformers; and quotations could be culled from scores of "bosses," large and small, condemning the baneful influence of Carl Schurz. Most spectacular of all, perhaps, was the famous speech delivered in the United States Senate on March 28, 1886, by a Republican, John J. Ingalls, of Kansas. Ingalls, who has been described by Professor Peck as "a tall, thin, cynical-looking man, with a power of emitting words which scorched like drops of vitriol," displayed all his gifts of sarcasm in characterizing reformers as belonging to a "third sex," "effeminate without being either masculine or feminine; unable to beget or to bear; possessing neither fecundity nor virility; endowed with the contempt of men and the derision of women, and doomed to sterility, isolation, and extinction." Invective like this admits of no reply in kind. Now, nearly half a century after the event, we can see that Ingalls belonged to a passing generation, and that his theories were destined to oblivion.

While promoting the cause of civil service reform, Schurz had taken up certain literary work which gave him some reputation, especially as a biographer. He was importuned repeatedly by Thomas Bailey Aldrich to write for the *Atlantic Monthly* on political topics. During the winter of 1884–85, in order to replenish his pocketbook, he made a lecture tour through the South, speaking chiefly on Benjamin Franklin, whom he considered to be "the greatest of Americans." Starting in Charleston, South Carolina, on January 21, 1885, he visited all the Southern States except Mississippi. Not having traveled in that section for some years, Schurz was much struck by the changed conditions, and prepared a pamphlet called *The New South*, in which he summed up the results of his observations, prophesying that eventually, through the normal evolution of politics and economy, the color line would virtually disappear. This startling prediction, which does Schurz's reputation as a seer no credit, was accompanied by the statement that the Southern people, two decades after Appomattox, were as loyal to the Union as the residents of any other section of the country.

In August, 1885, Schurz, at the solicitation of his Boston friends, seriously considered moving to that city and becoming the editor of the Boston *Post*. Negotiations were carried on with George Fred Williams, and Schurz, who wished to hold the controlling interest in the corporation, actually sent his check for $15,000 and was ready to provide a similar amount when it was necessary. Some discussion arose, however, regarding his editorial salary, and no agreement could be reached satisfactory to the business men who were backing the project. Meanwhile Schurz sprained both ankles badly and was confined for several weeks to his bed, during which period he made up his mind not to pursue the matter further.[1]

The project which most absorbed him, however, was the biography of Henry Clay, which, as we have seen, he had agreed to prepare for the "American Statesmen" series. Schurz's researches for this book were frequently postponed by the exigencies of politics or lecture trips; and John T. Morse, Jr., the general editor, tried to goad him into greater celerity. But Schurz, regarding his task as worthy of his best thought, refused to be hurried. He wrote on April 30, 1885, to Morse, "I hear the growl of the impatient editor, and I appreciate his feelings too." "The book would have been finished long ago," he added, "had I not been interrupted by calls upon my time of various kinds, which I could not possibly disregard." He insisted, furthermore, that Morse should allow him two volumes, although Lodge's *Webster* and Von Holst's *Calhoun* had filled only one.[2] The period devoted in part to the work was rather more than four years—not too long a time

[1] The full correspondence between Schurz and Williams is contained in the *Schurz MSS,* Congressional Library.

[2] Roosevelt, then writing the *Thomas H. Benton* for the same series, wrote Lodge, August 20, 1886, "How ridiculous to have Clay in two volumes; just like that Dutchman to go off on such a tangent." Mr. Morse has given his recollections of his relations with Schurz in an entertaining paper on the "American Statesmen" series, read before the Massachusetts Historical Society in November, 1931.

when one considers that it is probably the best biography in the series. As finally published in the spring of 1887, it comprised two volumes of approximately four hundred pages each, and containing twenty-seven chapters.

The *Henry Clay* was favorably received, even by those pedagogical historians who are most likely to fix an eagle eye on minor blemishes, and still stands as the most complete and accurate treatment of Clay and his career. Sound critics noted at once that it was the product of wide and discriminating reading, of careful research, and of wise judgment. Schurz's method was conservative. He followed a chronological order in his narrative and avoided irony and paradox. Although Clay, a magnetic and frequently inconsistent party leader, was very different from Schurz in temperament and ideals, the latter, with a tolerance which he did not always display in the practical affairs of the world, painted a portrait which does full justice to the Kentuckian's virtues. To Schurz, Clay was brilliant but imprudent, a daring leader but an unsafe guide, whose weaknesses in character and errors in diplomacy were counterbalanced by his "glowing national spirit." Although he emphasized the importance of the Compromise of 1850 as postponing the inevitable conflict until the North had an overwhelming advantage in men and material resources, Schurz felt that Clay never learned "that no compromise about slavery could last." The style of the book is lucid and forceful, with no attempt at "fine writing." In its combination of thoroughness, fairness, and charm, the *Clay* is a first-class biography—possibly the best written up to that moment in the United States and still ranking among the classics in its own field.

Among those who praised the biography at the date of its publication were men of widely divergent political affiliations. Rutherford B. Hayes sent Schurz a cordial note; so too did Senator Henry L. Dawes, of Massachusetts, who had been his annoying adversary in the disputes over the Poncas. The reviews were almost uniformly laudatory. For Schurz, the book had been no cut-and-dried affair. He had read deeply in the

Courtesy, Hellingers, New York

CARL SCHURZ IN LATER LIFE

congressional debates from 1810 to 1850; he had visited most of the early haunts of Clay and had consulted original documents hidden in the Washington archives. It had hitherto been Schurz's destiny to spend more time in making history than in writing it; but he had a literary gift not far below that of his friend, Henry Adams, and, if leisure had permitted him to proceed with that political history of the United States the plans for which he was always mulling over in his mind, he might have stood beside Rhodes and Channing.

In the *Atlantic Monthly* for June, 1891, Schurz published an essay on Abraham Lincoln, which was soon reprinted as a little volume something more than a hundred pages long. Although it is not in any sense a comprehensive biography, it offers a better estimate of the martyr President than can be found in the massive volumes of Tarbell and Barton. Schurz had known and understood Lincoln—his faults as well as his excellences, his weakness as well as his strength—and he depicted him, without sentimentality or myth-making, as a very human figure. The style of this essay shows an amazing mastery of the subtleties of English prose rhythm. With consummate ease, Schurz weaves his way through long and complicated sentences. The closing sentence, containing 256 words, is a summary of Lincoln's career and character, in phrases distinguished by clarity, vigor, and beauty. Schurz's literary style is based on no one author and has no conspicuous idiosyncracies. It is peculiarly his own—terse, simple, and vivid, without the slightest vagueness or obscurity. Theodore Roosevelt thought so highly of the article that he at once recommended Schurz to Morse as the best man available to write the *Lincoln* in the "American Statesmen" series, but the latter had already made other plans.[1]

[1] Roosevelt wrote to Schurz, December 29, 1892, "By the way, I can never help regretting that you would not do the Lincoln for the Statesmen series. It ought to have been a crowning piece of what really on the whole is a pretty good series. We do want a comparatively short biography of Lincoln written by a master hand. I think your sketch of Lincoln is by far the best thing that has ever been published about him." *Schurz MSS*, Congressional Library.

Encouraged by the approval of his friends, Schurz began to contemplate a volume of personal reminiscences, and, in order to revive the memories of his period of *Sturm und Drang,* sailed in April, 1888, for Europe, to be away until after the November elections. In London, John Bright secured for him a seat in the House of Commons to hear Disraeli speak. He spent most of the summer at Kiel, on the Baltic Sea, where he and his four children were the guests of Mrs. Schurz's uncle, Professor Meyer, who had there a beautiful estate. During his sojourn in Germany, Schurz was warmly received by leaders in politics and literature, among them Bismarck. Tradition has asserted that Bismarck's secretary, Dr. von Rottenburg, had instructions, after a visitor had remained fifteen minutes with the Count, to send in a red portfolio indicating urgent business, and, if this device failed to expedite the caller's departure, to announce the arrival of a special messenger from the Kaiser. When Schurz was closeted with the Prime Minister, the red portfolio was duly sent in once, and then again. But the bearer, returning after his second entrance, said to von Rottenburg: "Don't trouble yourself any more. Even the direct messenger from the Emperor will have no effect. The Chancellor has just ordered hock and cigars, and the two gentlemen are enjoying themselves immensely."

Bismarck, who admired although he did not always understand Schurz, once asked Andrew D. White to account for Schurz's success in American politics. White replied that Schurz had begun by discussing slavery in a new way "showing, not merely its hostility to American ideas of liberty and the wrong it did to the slaves, but, more especially, the injury it wrought upon the country at large, and, above all, upon the slave states themselves; and that, in treating all public questions, he was philosophic, eloquent, and evidently sincere." It was in this interview with White that Bismarck made the oft-quoted remark, "As a German, I am proud of Carl Schurz." [1]

[1] White, *Autobiography,* I, 586.

Schurz's brother-in-law, a partner in the prosperous firm of Meyer Brothers, in Hamburg, had been concerning himself with Carl's financial welfare. Through his intervention, Schurz was now offered a position as American representative of the Hamburg-American Packet Company, with a salary far larger than any he had hitherto received. It was obviously an experiment, for Schurz had had no business experience and knew nothing whatever about transportation. It was expected, of course, that the glamour of his name would compensate for any deficiencies in his office management. He turned out, however, to be a conscientious, practical, and reliable executive. He commenced his duties on January 1, 1889, shortly after his return from Europe, and for a few months all went well. But soon the routine of his Broadway office became irksome to a man who had long been foot-free. Engagements of various tempting kinds crowded in upon him. He found that he could not write lectures and give speeches without impairing his usefulness as a business man. Furthermore, the affairs of the company did not prosper under his direction. There were certain causes of friction, apparent enough to both Schurz and the Hamburg-American directors, but difficult now to ascertain and elucidate. Schurz went again to Europe in the summer of 1891. On his return in September, it was announced that he would cease to be American Manager on January 1, 1892. The German directors were resolved to come themselves to New York to study what could be done to increase their dividends.

Actually Schurz retained his position until July 1, 1892, on which date he definitely retired from business. From that moment he was his own master, able to choose his activities as he preferred from week to week. He evidently had saved some money, for we find him in August lending an acquaintance the sum of $5000. In confirming the loan, however, he said that his fortune was very limited and that his hour for acquiring wealth was past. The truth is that Schurz, like many otherwise brilliant men, was lacking in the money-getting instinct.

The faculty for making money is a peculiar endowment, often completely dissociated from the other qualities which indicate intelligence, and often, too, existing in persons who appear witless and dull. Schurz was not a good business man. He was far happier freed from the bonds which held him to his office desk.

As a good Cleveland man, Carl Schurz could hardly look upon the inauguration of Benjamin Harrison with enthusiasm. The fact that Harrison was chilly in manner and almost devoid of personal charm would not in itself have prejudiced Schurz against him. But the new President presently appointed Blaine as Secretary of State, following this by naming as Postmaster General John Wanamaker, a wealthy Philadelphia merchant of whom Schurz wrote that "the only distinction he ever achieved in public life was won as a contributor and collector of campaign funds." [1] As the administration continued, Schurz was annoyed by Blaine's aggressiveness in our foreign affairs; he did not approve the McKinley Tariff Bill of 1890, with its increases in duties on important commodities; he was disturbed by the persistent efforts of Congress to pass Lodge's "Force Act"; and he objected to the "Dependent Pension Bill," enlarging immensely the scope of pensions for Civil War veterans. Schurz never became at all intimate with "the little grey man in the White House."

Harrison's record on the civil service was, like Cleveland's, not altogether consistent. He unquestionably rewarded certain Republican editors by installing them in lucrative positions under the government; but he partly counteracted this in 1889 by naming young "Teddy" Roosevelt as a member of the Civil Service Commission, although he did not allow him complete freedom to carry out his policies. Roosevelt, who had no fond-

[1] At an address before the Commonwealth Club, in February, 1889, Schurz declared that, for the first time in our history, a Cabinet appointment had been bestowed "for a pecuniary consideration." This led to a correspondence between Wanamaker and Schurz, terminated by a letter written by the latter on April 9, in which he declared that "the use of money in elections . . . has really become a great evil—probably the greatest danger now threatening the vitality of republican institutions." *Writings,* V, 20.

ness for what he called the "loud-mouthed advocates" of civil service reform—among whom he included Carl Schurz—was, nevertheless, a mighty factor in extending its application. "I have made this commission a living force," he wrote Lodge, with characteristic self-appreciation, "and in consequence the outcry among spoilsmen has become furious." Sometimes, however, even he was foiled. A dramatic story is told in Bishop's *Charles Joseph Bonaparte* of Roosevelt's unexpected appearance at a meeting of the National Civil Service Reform League in New York, at which Dorman B. Eaton, Schurz, and other leaders were present, and of his disgust because Harrison had refused to listen to evidence indicating corruption among postal officials in Baltimore. "Damn John Wanamaker!" shouted Roosevelt, crimson with rage. When he heard the details, Schurz suggested that an investigation by the House Civil Service Committee be demanded; but Harrison had no desire to annoy his millionaire Postmaster General, and nothing was ever done to correct the Baltimore scandal.

David M. Matteson, after a thorough examination of the facts, concluded: "There was little choice, after all is said, between the records of Cleveland and Harrison. Cleveland's action outside the law had been better than Harrison's, though less consistent. Harrison's upholding of the law and its advance was superior to Cleveland's." [1] George William Curtis asserted in April, 1892, that the Reform Law had been "as faithfully observed as by the preceding administration, and the scope of the reform service had been greatly enlarged." Roosevelt, however, confessed, as Harrison's term drew to a close, "Frankly I think the record pretty bad for both Cleveland and Harrison, and it is rather Walrus and Carpenter work choosing between the records of the two parties, as far as civil service reform is concerned." [2]

It was a period when Schurz, sufficiently absorbed with columns of figures and financial reports, had very little time

[1] From a letter quoted in Rhodes, VIII, 336, n.

[2] *Letters of Theodore Roosevelt and Henry Cabot Lodge,* I, 122, 123.

to devote to public affairs. He was well aware that he had nothing to expect from Benjamin Harrison. Schurz did, however, speak on October 15, 1889, in Philadelphia, before the American Forestry Association, on the subject, "The Need of a Rational Forest Policy." In an earnest plea for the conservation of our national resources, he referred scornfully to "a spendthrift people recklessly wasting its heritage" and pointed out the necessity for preserving and restoring the forest lands and opposing "short-sighted greed." With equal vigor he talked on October 20, 1890, before the Massachusetts Reform Club, on the protective tariff, objecting to it mainly because it tended to create a dangerous money power, of the type represented by Senator Matthew S. Quay, of Pennsylvania, bent on using politics for private ends.

As the campaign of 1892 approached, Schurz was sure that he did not want four more years of Harrison. Accordingly he wrote, on November 1, 1891, to Moorfield Storey, maintaining that the Independents should do everything possible to promote Cleveland's candidacy and suggesting the calling of a conference. In the following February, he had a "good talk" with Cleveland, who had resumed the practice of law but who, in spite of the opposition of the wily David B. Hill, was not averse to running again for the presidency. While the politicians among the Democrats were doing their utmost, both secretly and openly, to thwart the plan for renominating Cleveland, he was gaining steadily among the great mass of voters, who had learned to respect his rugged integrity. The Republicans, meeting on June 7, in Minneapolis, settled without much difficulty on Harrison, although Blaine resigned from the Cabinet three days before the convention and apparently was willing to be drafted. When the Democratic Convention met at Chicago two weeks later, it seemed possible that the adroit David B. Hill might, with the backing of Tammany Hall and the support of his own state, wrench the nomination from Cleveland; but the popular demand could not be withstood, and the latter was named on the first ballot. Toward this result, Schurz had contributed something, for he had entrusted to Cleveland's manager, William C. Whitney, an address and a series of resolutions which could be used if it became desirable to pledge some of the state delegations formally to Cleveland. But they were unnecessary. Whitney wrote to Schurz: "It was a grand, mad, enthusiastic rush over the whole field. You never saw anything like it before." In congratulating Cleveland, Schurz said, "You have been nominated *by the people* over the heads of the politicians." This, to Schurz, was the finest kind of victory.

The ensuing campaign, while lacking the combativeness which had been so conspicuous in 1876 and 1884, was also pleasantly free from vicious personalities. The tariff issue was stressed by the Democrats, and the Homestead strike, in the Carnegie Steel Mills, near Pittsburgh, probably turned some votes away from the Republicans. After all, each candidate had served one term in the presidency, and each could be judged on his record. Schurz, whose health was not good, spent most of the summer with his intimate friend, Dr. Abraham Jacobi, at the latter's cottage at Bolton Landing, on lovely Lake George; but he did contribute a leading editorial to each issue of *Harper's Weekly*, discussing some phase of the campaign. On July 30, for example, he analyzed Harrison's record on civil service reform, finding him weak in several respects, and followed this by a strong plea for a tariff for revenue only. These articles, naturally enough, were unsigned. On September 8, replying to an invitation to address a Democratic mass meeting in Brooklyn, he declared, over his own name, his satisfaction in the "moral qualities" which Cleveland had displayed in the presidency. He said of the Republican Party that, although it had a glorious past, it had, in its National Convention of 1888, given itself over "body and soul to the money-power, interested in the protective tariff, expecting from it substantial aid in the election." He had no illusions regarding either the Democratic Party or Mr. Cleveland, but he said of the latter: "He has a conscience. He has a will. He has a patriotic heart.

He has a clear head. He has a strong sense of right. He has a good knowledge of affairs. He is a party man, but not a party slave. He is true to duty regardless of personal interest."

While this letter was being prepared for publication both in English and in German, Schurz heard a rumor that Cleveland had met with certain Tammany leaders in New York and had made important concessions to the demands of the Democratic machine. We now know, from full reports of this conference, that Cleveland came down from his cottage, Gray Gables, on Buzzard's Bay only at the insistent appeal of William C. Whitney, and that, seated at dinner in the Victoria Hotel with the Tammany chiefs, Murphy, Croker, and Sheehan, Cleveland had banged his huge fist on the table and said: "Gentlemen, I will not go into the White House pledged to you or to any one else. I will make no secret promises. I'll be damned if I do."[1] We know, furthermore, that the dismayed Croker finally agreed to stand by Cleveland. But Schurz, unacquainted with the facts, wrote to Edward M. Shepard, requesting him to suspend the publication of his letter until the proof sheets could be shown to Cleveland for his concurrence in the ideas there expressed. Shepard was able to assure him that the Democratic candidate had not surrendered to the politicians, and Schurz's letter was duly printed and widely circulated, with its usual influence on the opinion of the Independents. On October 27, having recovered from a throat ailment which had troubled him since spring, Schurz spoke before a gathering of German-Americans in New York, urging them to vote for Cleveland and saying, "I never gave you advice which I did not myself hold to be good." When the news of Cleveland's victory was confirmed, Schurz wrote a long editorial for *Harper's Weekly*, in which he predicted, "The Republican Party sinks to the level of a mere opposition, to live mainly on the faults committed by the party in power." As an analysis of the situation, it was not altogether accurate.

Schurz at once congratulated Cleveland, saying, "Next to

[1] McElroy, *Cleveland*, 352.

the justice of your cause it was your personal character, commanding the confidence of the people beyond the boundaries of the party, that made such a result possible." It was indeed a personal victory for Cleveland, who had insisted, as he wrote Gilder, that he would "have the presidency clean or not at all." What had been accomplished, as Schurz saw it, was brought out on December 10, at the annual dinner of the Reform Club, at which Cleveland made an address and Schurz spoke on "Moral Forces in Politics," insisting that the determining factor in electing Cleveland had been voters who saw in him a leader actuated by the highest motives. It was, he contended, the Independents who were responsible for making a Democratic President, and he expressed the wish that, under Cleveland's guidance, they might be welded with the Democrats into a powerful political instrument. At this dinner, Cleveland told Schurz of his desire to extend the principles of civil service reform even further than had ever been done before.

Before Cleveland's election, Schurz rather unexpectedly had been thrust into a position where his opinion was even more worth regarding than it would have been if he had been merely a private citizen. In the early summer of 1892, George William Curtis, long one of Schurz's dearest friends and the editor of *Harper's Weekly*, was so ill that he could no longer carry on his duties; accordingly the publishers asked Schurz to write, at least for a few weeks, the leading editorial in that periodical. After Curtis's death on August 31,[1] the arrangement was continued, until both the Harper family and Schurz came to accept it as permanent. It gave Schurz what he passionately craved—an opportunity to express his views on current questions as they arose. Until January, 1897, he prepared each week an article on some topic, usually political, and it appeared without his signature. The secret, if, indeed, it was intended to be one, could not long be kept. Schurz's trenchant style and

[1] *Harper's Weekly* for September 10 printed a picture of Curtis as a frontispiece, together with a long laudatory editorial by Schurz and a eulogy by William Dean Howells.

favorite obsessions mark nearly everything he wrote. When it became known that he was directing the policy of *Harper's*, he became a figure of importance in journalistic circles.

Curtis's death resulted also in Schurz's election as his successor in the office of president of the National Civil Service Reform League, charged with the responsibility of determining the attitude of that organization. Curtis had presided brilliantly over the annual meetings, enlivening them with his extemporaneous wit and stirring eloquence. Schurz, while more effective in argument, lacked the humor, the lighter touches, which so often make such gatherings entertaining as well as profitable to the delegates. But he was even more vigilant than Curtis in keeping alive the principles for which the League had been established.[1]

Supported by the consciousness that he represented, not only himself, but also the League, Schurz urged Cleveland so to outline his program that the civil service regulations might be extended into all government departments. He also advised him on other matters, often on his own initiative. In late February, 1893, in a letter requesting advance sheets of the inaugural address that he might prepare a comment on it for *Harper's*, he hoped that the impending annexation of the Hawaiian Islands might be avoided and asked that a man of "high culture" be appointed as Minister to Berlin. There can be no doubt that Schurz would have been glad himself to return to Germany in a diplomatic capacity; but Cleveland, who could never get over the feeling that Schurz was over-presumptuous, had no intention of selecting him. Just before the inauguration, Schurz recommended the calling of an extra session of Congress for the repealing of the Sherman Silver Law, passed in 1890, which had directed the Secretary of the Treasury to purchase 4,500,000 ounces of silver bullion a month and issue legal tender Treasury notes in payment.

[1] Charles Dudley Warner asked Schurz, Sept. 10, 1892, to write the life of Curtis for the American Men of Letters Series, but the latter declined the invitation. *Schurz MSS,* Congressional Library.

Cleveland, like Schurz, was definitely opposed to what was described as "the dangerous and reckless experiment of free, unlimited, and independent silver coinage," and ultimately called a special session for August 7, 1893, as a consequence of which the objectionable measure was repealed. As soon as the inauguration was over, Schurz wrote again, enclosing the advance copy of an article, "The Annexation Policy," which he was about to print in *Harper's*, and suggesting for the German mission either President Angell, of Michigan, or Professor Sloane, of Princeton.

Since his appointment by Harrison as a member of the Civil Service Commission, young Theodore Roosevelt had been restlessly but usefully active, stirring his colleagues from stagnation into turmoil. Disregarding consequences, he had dashed from city to city on whirlwind tours of inspection, arousing the wrath of local politicians but bringing glee to the hearts of the reformers. When it was intimated in the press that Cleveland would not retain Roosevelt, Schurz arranged for a meeting between the two men on January 17, 1893, at the same time assuring Cleveland that, in dealing a blow to the "spoils" system, he could hardly find "a more faithful, courageous, and effective aid than Mr. Roosevelt." Schurz also implored Roosevelt, if he were requested to remain, not to say "No." Later, when he learned of Cleveland's wisdom in giving Roosevelt free rein, Schurz described the latter's retention on the Civil Service Commission as "a great event, and in itself a large program for the next four years." For Curtis, Godkin, Schurz, and others whom he regarded as professional reformers, Roosevelt seems to have felt a kind of contempt, and his letters contain several references to Schurz as a vague and futile idealist, helpless in the hands of practical men. Schurz, for his part, regarded Roosevelt as rash, impulsive, and not altogether reliable. It is probable that Roosevelt could never quite forgive Schurz for opposing him in his campaign for the New York mayoralty in 1886.

Carl Schurz had had very little to say to President Harrison, with whom his relations had been entirely formal and only coldly amicable. Now, with Cleveland again in the White House, he could resume his habit of criticizing presidential appointments. On March 30, 1893, he wrote protesting against the selection of a man named Burke as United States District Attorney in Indiana, drawing attention to the newspaper condemnation of this choice, and asking Cleveland to send a trusty friend to "make a searching inquiry into Mr. Burke's antecedents and standing." In the same letter, he complained that the removals in the Post Office Department had become a "national scandal and disgrace." Most of us can sympathize with the patient, rather slow-thinking, but absolutely upright Chief Executive as he listened to these protests from the persistent Schurz, who, however well-intentioned, could not be familiar with all the facts and who acted, perhaps unconsciously, as if he were suspicious of the President's motives. Cleveland's reply was direct and sincere, declaring that Burke, so far as he could discover, was a well-qualified lawyer. When Schurz a week later made a rash statement that "the guillotine in the General Post Office is lustily at work and that the heads are falling at the rate of a hundred or a hundred and fifty a day," Cleveland answered at once, citing figures which utterly refuted these charges. The irrepressible Schurz, undaunted, replied that "the question of numbers is, after all, not the important one" and that the President must be careful to make removals only "for cause." [1]

More than once during the spring of 1893, Schurz let the President know that he was preparing his first address as president of the National Civil Service Reform League, in which he would have the opportunity of voicing the attitude of that organization toward the administration. When the meeting was held, on April 25, in New York City, Schurz praised Cleveland effusively, stating that he might be expected to "cause the spirit and purpose of civil service reform to be observed in all executive appointments" and, at the end, apostrophizing him in a

[1] *Writings,* V, 138, ff.

paragraph of inspiring eloquence, closing, "As Abraham Lincoln stands in our annals as the liberator of the slave, you may stand there, if you will, as the regenerator of our political life."

In an important letter sent on May 13 to Cleveland, Schurz besought him to put the division chiefs under civil service rules and to have the Civil Service Commission supplied with necessary funds. "You have," he declared, "these problems before you—the financial question, the tariff question, and the abolition of the spoils system. With regard to the first two, your success is uncertain, for it depends upon Congress. As to the third, your success is in your own hands." He then explicitly warned Cleveland against the use of patronage as a means of securing from Congress the financial legislation which the administration desired. Schurz here, as usual, wrote much like a schoolmaster admonishing a pupil, but his sincerity somewhat extenuated his tone of condescension.

As soon as his second administration had opened, Cleveland was again harassed by "deserving Democrats." Just before taking ether for an operation on his throat in June, 1893, he burst out to the surgeon: "Oh, Dr. Keen, those office seekers! Those office seekers! They haunt me in my dreams!" Though his major interest for the moment was the downward revision of the tariff, he spoke in his inaugural address of his wish "to secure the fitness and competency of appointees to office and to remove from political action the demoralizing madness of spoils"; and he devoted long hours to the business of securing honest and efficient subordinates. On May 8, he took the drastic step of declining all personal interviews with those seeking appointments, except when he especially solicited them. Everything considered, Schurz had reason for feeling that his own aims were being rapidly accomplished under Grover Cleveland. There was, of course, a difference between the two men. Cleveland once wrote, "My civil service friends have sometimes seemed to think that the Government was to be conducted merely for the purpose of promoting civil service reform." Looking at the situation from a lofty viewpoint, with other factors to consider, the President refused to turn his administration into what he called a "moral crusade." Schurz, on the contrary, saw only that conditions were bad and needed to be changed, and, broad-minded though he was in most respects, lost for the moment his sense of proportion.

Under the presidency of Carl Schurz, the National Civil Service Reform League did not relax its vigilance. In the late summer of 1893, the President named J. J. Van Alen, a wealthy society man who had made large contributions to the Democratic campaign fund, as Minister to Italy, and the nomination was confirmed by the Senate. At a meeting of the League's executive committee on November 16 a protest was raised, with Schurz in the chair. Roosevelt, who was present, withdrew as soon as the attack on the administration was opened; but a resolution was passed condemning the practice of rewarding campaign fund contributors with appointments to office. W. D. Foulke published in the December number of the *Forum* a short article entitled, "Are Presidential Appointments for Sale?" and New York newspapers, headed by the *Evening Post*, added to the excitement. As a result, Van Alen declined the mission, and, although urged by the President to reconsider his decision, would not be over-persuaded. In this case, the League unquestionably won a decisive victory.[1]

Not all of Schurz's hopes for progress were realized. Josiah Quincy, Assistant Secretary of State, incurred the opposition of Schurz, who, in his presidential address before the League in 1894, pilloried him as a spoilsman. In the office of the Postmaster General, the changes among fourth-class postmasters were larger than those made by Harrison. James Ford Rhodes concluded that Cleveland did not hesitate to employ government patronage in order to further his plans with regard to the tariff and finance. Nevertheless, Cleveland was not unfaithful to his promises to Schurz. By the close of his administration, the policy of levying assessments on officeholders had been vir-

[1] For fuller details of this interesting, if almost forgotten incident, see Foulke, *Fighting the Spoilsmen*, 99–103.

tually abandoned by both parties. By a blanket order, dated May 6, 1896, he, with one stroke of the pen, extended the civil service classification to some 31,373 places, including all chiefs of divisions, chief clerks, and disbursing officers. Under him, the number of offices under the civil service rules was increased from 42,929 to 86,932. This order, according to Schurz himself, "was the most effective blow the spoils system ever received."

Although he occasionally grumbled, Schurz was well aware that much was being accomplished. In an article in *McClure's Magazine* for May, 1897, when Cleveland had been back in private life for some weeks, Schurz awarded him the highest praise. "He was," said Schurz, "a civil service reformer, not as a theorist, but as a practical administrator. . . . When he became President the first time in 1885, he would have wiped out the spoils system at once, had he not feared by breaking too brusquely with long-established habits, to alienate his party. . . . While he has not done for the reform of the civil service all that could and should be done, he has done far more than all his predecessors together, and he will ever stand preëminent among the champions of that great cause."

With several important features of Cleveland's program, Carl Schurz was openly or tacitly sympathetic. In his first annual message, the President had bravely attacked the question of a reduction in the tariff. The House of Representatives, rallying to his support, passed a measure honestly conceived to carry out his wishes; but the Senate, dominated by the bland but self-seeking Arthur P. Gorman, of Maryland, made 634 amendments to the House bill and, regardless of Cleveland's protests that this modified act was an abandonment of principles, compelled the lower body to yield. The result was a patched-up affair which, although in some features an improvement on its predecessor, the McKinley Bill, was, nevertheless, protectionist in spirit. Cleveland, disdaining to sign such a flagrant abandonment of his hopes, allowed it to become a law without his name attached to it. Schurz, a theoretical free trader, was behind the President in the battle for rational tariff reform and lamented that what he called the "capitalistic Democrats" should thus have ruined the administration's plans.

Cleveland, like Schurz, was an advocate of sound money and of a gold standard. He unfortunately inherited a financial panic which probably nothing could have averted, but which he himself attributed to the baneful influence of the Sherman Silver Purchase Act. Urged by Schurz and other advisers to call an extra session of Congress, the President was obliged to hold up his plans because of an operation for the removal of a malignant growth on the roof of his mouth, performed with the utmost secrecy on board the yacht *Oneida* in the East River. During his convalescence, he prepared a message asserting that "the alarming and extraordinary business situation" was due principally to "the purchase and coinage of silver," and advocated a prompt repeal of the Silver Purchase Act. The Senate, however, would not give way until after a protracted debate, only slightly hastened by the President's judicious dispensing of patronage to win over certain vacillating statesmen. It was a temporary triumph for Cleveland, but he was not to have his will on financial matters as his administration went on.

The conspicuous problem in foreign relations under Cleveland was the Venezuelan Question, in which both he and Richard Olney, who succeeded Gresham in June, 1895, as Secretary of State, participated. It was essentially a dispute over the boundary line between Venezuela and British Guiana, in which Cleveland, insisting that the rights of the United States were concerned and invoking the Monroe Doctrine, demanded that Great Britain submit the case to arbitration. When Lord Salisbury, the British Premier, replied on November 26, 1895, denying that the Monroe Doctrine was applicable, Cleveland sent to Congress one of the most vigorous documents ever issued by an American President, practically making the Venezuelan cause our own and issuing an ultimatum to Great Britain. Congress, in a belligerent mood, at once voted the necessary authority for the appointment of a commission to investigate the disputed boundary line. The British press was war-like in its tone, and lovers of peace in the Anglo-Saxon nations were very much concerned. On January 2, 1896, Schurz, speaking before the New York Chamber of Commerce, pointed out that the matter, originally insignificant, had grown to be "a question of honor," fraught with peril to the two proud peoples involved. Schurz, while conceding that the United States should preserve its credit in the world, declared that it should not, "as our boyish jingoes wish it to do, swagger about among the nations of the world, with a chip on its shoulder, and shaking its fist in everybody's face."

After discussing the situation in a temperate and judicial manner, and pointing out that the commission to be named by the President was "a one-sided contrivance," Schurz suggested that an equal number of Englishmen, designated by the British Government, be joined with the American commissioners, the two groups to agree upon some distinguished outsider to preside over their deliberations. Eventually Great Britain, faced with possible trouble from another quarter over the Jameson Raid in South Africa, wisely accepted the facts. After some negotiations, a board of arbitrators was named which reported on October 3, 1899. Investigation showed that the boundary line was so puzzling and tortuous that it would have been absurd for the English speaking countries to have resorted to arms over it. Opinions of historians have differed astonishingly regarding Cleveland's conduct. His straightforward, blunt language helped, no doubt, to bring the controversy to a head. But, to win this triumph, he took dangerous chances. If, as might easily have happened, a long and costly war had ensued, Cleveland would not have gone blameless down to posterity.

In an address delivered on April 22, 1896, before the Arbitration Conference in Washington, Schurz took the Venezuelan incident as a text for an exposition of his political philosophy. He himself had known what war, at its worst, is like; and he felt that it should be "only the very last resort even in contending for a just and beneficent end, after all the resources of peaceful methods are thoroughly exhausted." To him, arbitration was "not only the most humane and economical method of settling international differences, but also the most, if not the only, certain method to furnish enduring results." Instead of an elaborate system of coast fortifications, he preferred to rely on "Fort Justice, "Fort Good Sense," and "Fort Arbitration." It was, he felt, the duty of the United States, if an international court of arbitration could not be created, to conclude at once an arbitration treaty with Great Britain.

Any attempt to summarize, or even to catalogue, the public utterances of Schurz during this period would too much enlarge the scope of this volume. We find him, as usual, participating in discussions on many subjects—on the forests and on the tariff, on prohibition and on Sunday observance. He was once the victim of a strange mistake. On April 29, 1893, the New York Chamber of Commerce gave a dinner at the Hotel Waldorf to some visiting naval officers. Schurz had understood that he was to respond to the toast, "The President," and had prepared for the newspapers in advance twenty-five copies of his speech, in accordance with his customary forethought. The Chairman, Alexander B. Orr, did not, however, call upon him. He first waited in patience, then left the table and paced restlessly up and down the corridor behind the banquet hall, but his name was never mentioned. He felt that he had received "a direct or an indirect snub," but an apology on the following morning indicated that there had been some confusion among the committee of arrangements.

On June 15, 1893, at the World's Fair, in Chicago, he was the honored guest on "German Day," and gave a noteworthy address in his native tongue before a vast throng of sympathetic German-Americans, who cheered him as he proudly pointed out how the extensive German exhibit at the exposition revealed the industrial vigor of the young empire. In early November of that year he spoke at a rally of German voters in Cooper Union, protesting against the candidacy of Isaac H.

Maynard as Judge of the Court of Appeals, on the ground that he was corrupt. "It was easy to see from the reception," said the *Tribune*, "that Mr. Schurz is the idol of the German-American heart." During that autumn, also, he published in *Harper's Magazine* an article headed "Manifest Destiny," in which, referring to Harrison's unsuccessful effort to attach Hawaii to our Union, he reiterated his old arguments against "indiscriminate territorial aggrandizement," especially in the tropics. In January, 1894, he attended in Philadelphia the first session of the Good City Government Conference, representing the Yonkers Civil Service Reform Club. Schurz himself spoke on "The Relation of Civil Service Reform to Municipal Reform," denouncing Tammany Hall with a vigor almost libelous. Schurz's address was printed in a magazine called *Good Government*, of which he, in 1893, was Chairman of the Committee on Publication. He participated during the summer of 1895 in a dispute regarding the excise, defending Mayor Strong and Police Commissioner Roosevelt [1] for enforcing the Sunday laws. On this issue he was opposed by the *Staats-Zeitung*, but maintained his ground courageously. In December of that year, he represented the Heine Monument Committee in an appeal to the Park Board to urge the acceptance of a proposed memorial to the German poet.

Carl Schurz never approached more closely to literature than in two funeral addresses given during this period. On June 13, 1890, he spoke briefly at the burial of little Henry Hilgard Villard, the son of his friend, Henry Villard, saying simply and gracefully all that any mother and father could wish to have said about their lost son. A few sentences will show the quality of Schurz's style:

According to the ancient saying, those who are beloved by the gods die young. And this dear little boy certainly could be

[1] Theodore Roosevelt had been appointed by Mayor William L. Strong as Public Commissioner of New York City, in the spring of 1895—a position which he really wanted very much and which soon absorbed even his prodigious energies.

counted among those beloved. He was the late child of a most happy union. His birth was to his parents like the breaking of a fresh morning in the advanced day. Upon his cradle nature and fortune seemed to shower their choicest favors. That cradle stood in the lap of the purest and most beautiful family life. All that surrounded him was love and concord and goodness.

Quite a different occasion was the funeral, on December 2, 1896, in Liederkranz Hall, of William Steinway, a German-American who, beginning as a simple workman, had become, through the manufacture of pianos, a millionaire, and a benefactor to thousands. Schurz praised him felicitously as a friend and comrade, as an artist, as a good citizen, and then continued, "Is it too much to say that in this man every human being has lost a brother?"

In still another strain was a beautiful address in German at a banquet held on January 9, 1897, at the fiftieth anniversary of the Deutscher Liederkranz. His subject was *Die Muttersprache*—"The Mother Tongue." Something of the spirit of the original is bound to evaporate in translation; but Schurz dwelt on the emotion, on the sincerity, on the sonority of the language which he had spoken as a child. "Whatever may resist German intellect and German enterprise," he declared fervently; "nothing can withstand German song"—and the audience shouted its delight. It was, he felt, a mistake for Germans to abandon their native language. "I have always been in favor of a sensible Americanization," he went on to say, "but this need not mean a complete abandonment of all that is German." Schurz himself was a model to his hearers, for he usually spoke German to his children in their own home and wrote his letters to them in that language. He ended, poetically, "The German mother tongue, the dear, strong, noble, tender, sacred mother tongue—may it live everlastingly here and all the world over!"

For almost six years, beginning in the early summer of 1892, Carl Schurz was the leading editorial writer for *Harper's*

Weekly,[1] with an influence which cannot be precisely estimated but was indubitably very great. Through the countless topics which he discussed the real man can be discovered. Issues appear and go, recur and vanish, and it is only rarely that one is decisively settled. The tariff, for example, returns to plague successive generations, and one's opinion regarding it may conceivably vary as conditions alter. What a man does is, after all, less significant than what he is. What does matter is the point of view, the philosophy which underlies his conclusions. If he thinks clearly and honestly and fearlessly, he is likely to be an example to others. This Carl Schurz unquestionably was.

In his contributions to *Harper's*, Schurz was likely to fall back at intervals on his pet subjects—civil service reform, sound money, and anti-imperialism—with an occasional excursion into foreign politics. Beginning on January 5, 1895, for illustration, he treated in successive numbers the following matters: "The Government and Banking"; "The Cardinal Point"—a criticism of the "greenback" as a form of currency; "What Can Be Accomplished"—a discussion of the financial situation, ending in the suggestion that a monetary commission be appointed; "The Crisis in France"—an analysis of conditions which had led to the abdication of Casimir-Perier as French President; "The Platt-Lexow Scheme of Municipal Reform"—a declaration that certain proposed bills would deliver the whole police force into the hands of "Boss" Platt; "Civil Service Reform in State and City"; "The People versus the Politicians"—an elaboration of one of his favorite themes; "Reed-Cleveland"—an exhortation to Thomas B. Reed to take a more decisive stand if he expects to be nominated and elected in 1896; "Partisan Aspects of Municipal Reform"; and "Two Years of Cleveland's Administration"—in which he lauds the President's "sterling qualities," saying that he has failed whenever he tried to play practical politics but has succeeded when-

[1] Schurz's articles were unsigned until January 30, 1897, after which date his name was used, apparently in order that the other editors might disclaim responsibility for some of his beliefs.

ever he has risen above them. It will be seen, from a survey of these topics, that Schurz regarded himself as an unofficial director of public opinion. Had he lived thirty years later, he would have welcomed a position like that of Dr. S. Parkes Cadman, with its opportunity for disseminating by means of the radio the doctrines which he thought to be salutary for people to hear.

In his articles, Schurz, for reasons best known to himself, said nothing on the fine arts or on religion, and almost nothing about social reform. He confined himself almost exclusively to finance and politics, and always with regard to specific or practical matters. Schurz was seldom ostentatiously virtuous, but he did give the impression of rugged honesty. Like every reformer, he was something of a missionary at heart, but his zeal for converting the heathen was tempered by a recognition of the complexities of human nature. It was not strange that he was disliked, for he kept hammering away relentlessly at "grafters" and corruptionists and faddists until they cringed under his blows. Carl Schurz well earned, as editor of *Harper's Weekly*, the title of the "Good Citizen."

CHAPTER XXIV FREE SILVER AND IMPERIALISM

As THE campaign of 1896 drew near, Carl Schurz found himself in another perplexing dilemma. The Democratic Party, with which he had been allied since 1884, was now split asunder. The mid-administration congressional elections had given the Republicans a majority in the House of Representatives of more than two to one. The President, a believer in sound money and the gold standard, found himself at odds with the "Silver Democrats" from the West and South. The question of free silver was, almost through an accident, to become the dominant issue between the two long-established parties.

The Republicans, on the other hand, were committed to a protectionist policy, which, to Schurz, was highly obnoxious; and the Republican Convention, meeting on June 16, 1896, at St. Louis, nominated on the first ballot William McKinley, of Ohio, the author of the notorious high tariff bill of 1890. Before the results of the convention were known, Schurz, writing in *Harper's Weekly,* said that McKinley had "an uncertain, uninformed, and thoughtless mind." Commenting on the situation, he added, "American politics will reach a low ebb when Mr. McKinley is nominated for President, but the Republican Party has it in its power to leave some hope to the country." Schurz's one source of satisfaction lay in the clause of the Republican platform declaring for the maintenance of a gold standard—a clause inserted only after long discussion in committee and probably against the real wishes of the candidate. On June 27, therefore, Schurz comforted himself by saying: "The Republican Party has pledged itself to the maintenance of the gold standard. This is a great preliminary victory for those who have made constant and vigorous war upon the silver heresy. . . . It is a victory for intelligence and honesty, gained over greed, ignorance, discouragement, and all the causes of discontent."

Developments within the Democratic Party, meanwhile, were such as to shake Schurz's confidence in its leaders. Cleveland's adherents had no control over the situation. Writing before the Democratic Convention had met on July 7, in Chicago, Schurz stated that the worst elements of the party were in the ascendant. Coming under the oratorical spell of William Jennings Bryan, then in his prime as a spellbinder, the delegates first adopted a free silver platform and then nominated its great avatar as their standard bearer. A small group of seceders opposed to free silver nominated Palmer and Buckner, but it was obvious that their gesture was futile. The real issue was to be sectional—East against West, capitalism against agrarianism, the rich against the poor. Schurz called the Democratic Convention "the triumph of sectionalism and communism."

Schurz, then, was under the necessity of choosing between two evils: McKinley, the apostle of a protective tariff, which Schurz hated; and Bryan, whose constant theme was the free coinage of silver, which Schurz thought to be financial heresy. Feeling that Bryan and his followers were the more dangerous, he promptly repudiated them. But he did not underestimate the forces behind the Democratic candidate. In *Harper's Weekly*, he warned readers that Bryan was "a man of respectable private character and some brilliant qualities" and that the "widespread feeling of discontent and unrest in the West and South" could not be put down with "epithets, sneers, and jibes."

As Schurz studied the situation more carefully, he conquered his early reluctance to support McKinley. He remembered that Bryan had been no friend of civil service reform, but had spoken out against "life tenure in office" and what he called "a permanent office-holding class." When Bryan, through his extraordinary speaking campaign—reminiscent of what Schurz himself had done as a younger man—seemed to be gaining ground, Schurz, although his health was poor, responded to an invitation from ex-Senator Powell Clayton, went to Chicago, and, on September 5, delivered an address under the auspices of the American Honest Money League. He did not mention McKinley's name. His aim was to defeat Bryan, and his speech was a scathing denunciation of the advocates of bimetallism, joined with a defense of a gold standard. His arguments brought comfort to the Republicans, who knew that where Carl Schurz led, many an Independent, many a German-American, would follow. Governor John P. Altgeld, of Illinois, undertook to reply to Schurz; and the latter, his fighting blood at fever heat, appeared at Peoria in late October and completely demolished Altgeld's sophistry.

Meanwhile Schurz was helping in other ways to counteract Bryan's specious eloquence. *Harper's Weekly* for August 15 published a full page of pictures of Bryan and his prominent adherents, including Eugene V. Debs, Coxey—of the notorious "Coxey's Army"—Mrs. Leach, Watson, and Sewall, with the legend underneath, "Enemies of the Nation's Honor, of the Country's Prosperity, of the Wage Earners and Farmers, of Thrift, and of Law and Order"; surely a comprehensive indictment. For the first time in its history the National Civil Service Reform League took official cognizance of a presidential campaign and, in October, 1896, published an address to the voters written by Schurz and cautioning them against Bryan's wiles.

As Election Day approached, the conservative forces rallied. Bryan seemed to gather around him the elements of discontent; while McKinley was heralded as the "Advance Agent of Prosperity," the guarantee of a "full dinner pail." The election itself, giving McKinley 271 electoral votes against 176 for Bryan, was sufficiently decisive. To this result, Carl Schurz contributed materially. Doubtless Bryan would have been checked under any normal conditions, for the conservative sentiment of the nation was made fearful by his heterodox economic theories. But Schurz, in supporting McKinley rather than Palmer and Buckner, led the way for a large number of Cleveland Democrats who wished to cast their votes where they would count. He was gratified at receiving a note from President Cleveland, praising him for the position which he had taken and commending the "best Democrats" for turning away from mere partisanship to serve their country. Schurz's conduct in 1896 was the consequence of a deep-rooted aversion to political claptrap, demagoguery, and captiousness.[1]

As soon as the result was known, Isaac N. Seligman, with good intentions, approached Mark Hanna, the Major Domo of the coming administration, with the suggestion that Schurz be made a member of the Cabinet. When Schurz learned of this kindly intervention, he at once wrote Hanna, telling him that he himself had not been consulted, that he had no desire to reënter public life, and that he should regard it as a mistake for McKinley to form his Cabinet of "heterogeneous elements." He did, however, suggest that McKinley, if he wished to pay off the Independents who had rushed to his aid, might very well "give friendly consideration to their views," especially by retaining "a number of especially efficient and meritorious officers now in the national service." Later a rumor spread through the American and European press that Schurz was to be appointed Ambassador to St. Petersburg, and certain Republican newspapers entered a protest against the award of such a diplomatic "plum" to a man who recognized no party ties. Writing later in the administration, Schurz declared that he should not have accepted the place, even had it been offered to him, his chief reason being that he could not hold an office of that sort under a President "the main object of whose economic policy was certain to be a protective tariff of the extreme kind."

Although Schurz had done much to elect McKinley, he was distrustful of what the latter's course would be. As president of the National Civil Service Reform League, he wrote McKinley on inauguration day, urging him to keep the United States Civil Service Commission as a non-partisan body and

[1] Schurz was not yet unreservedly a Republican. At a victory luncheon on Nov. 10, 1896, at which both Hanna and Roosevelt were present, Schurz occasioned some astonishment by proposing, in the midst of Republicans, a toast to President Cleveland, "a bulwark against all financial heresies." Some orthodox Republicans felt that Schurz's toast was not in good taste. See Pringle, *Roosevelt,* 157–8.

requesting him, if he found it necessary to give it a Republican majority, to make only the one change in personnel necessary to achieve that result. McKinley replied with his usual courtesy, speaking in rather vague generalities, but expressing a genuine interest in what the reformers wished. Pressed though he was by applicants for office, McKinley displayed unexpected powers of resistance and, in July, 1897, issued an executive order restricting removals on political grounds and insisting on the recognition of merit.

Pleased with the attitude of the President, Schurz gave him during 1897 the support of *Harper's Weekly*—with reservations. Before the inauguration, he discussed, on February 6, "The Campaign against Civil Service Reform," and he was ready, on March 6, with an article, "The Quadrennial Disgrace," in which he predicted the troubles which McKinley was certain to have with office seekers. On March 27, he chose as his topic, "Republicanism and the Civil Service." On May 1, in an editorial headed "A Burning Shame," he exhausted even his fertile gifts of vituperation in assailing the League of Republican Clubs for their action in calling upon the President to revoke Cleveland's order placing forty thousand offices under the civil service rules. On July 24, he attacked what was known as "The Senatorial Prerogative," exposing the dangers which it involved to the merit system. Convinced of McKinley's good intentions and achievements, Schurz, on August 14, wrote an article, "The President and the Civil Service," in which he commended the Chief Executive for all that had been accomplished, and followed this on September 18 with "Spoils and Statesmanship," in which he exhibited Senator Wellington, of Maryland, as an illustration of the repudiation of a corrupt boss. It will be seen from this brief summary of Schurz's views that he was convinced that progress had been made. He was even more gratified when, in his first annual message, McKinley, although stating that some offices might well be exempted from the operation of the civil service rules, declared his faith in competitive examinations.

As a rule, Schurz was courteous in argument, observing the amenities customary between opponents who respect one another. During the summer of 1897, however, he was involved in a controversy with Senator Jacob H. Gallinger, of New Hampshire, a reactionary politician who regarded all reformers with undisguised contempt and who aroused in Schurz all his superb powers of disputation. Gallinger had publicly criticized the existing civil service regulations, both in their conception and in their operation; whereupon Mr. George McAneny, then secretary of the National Civil Service Reform League and no feeble antagonist in debate, replied, citing statistics and incidents which completely overthrew Gallinger's thesis. Enraged at being thus thwarted, the New Hampshire Senator published in the Exeter *News-Letter*, for July 23, an intemperate denunciation of Schurz and his associates as "traitors," "political hermaphrodites," "renegades," and "worshipers of Grover Cleveland," displaying the same spirit which had once led Roscoe Conkling to assail "man milliners" and "political eunuchs."

Having been dragged into the fray against his will, Schurz now wrote a letter, dated August 16 and printed in the Exeter *News-Letter* for August 27, in which he revealed a gift for irony and sarcasm worthy of John Milton. He explained his attitude during previous presidential elections, pointing out that he had originally joined the Republican Party as an anti-slavery man; that he had abandoned that party when, as in 1872 and 1884, the question of "public morals in government" had seemed to him a paramount issue, or when, as in 1888 and 1892, the battle was waged over the protective tariff. When, as in 1896, "honest money" was in danger, he had reverted to the Republican fold. Schurz's defense and counter-attack were restrained and in good taste; [1] but, at the end, he gave Gallinger warning of his willingness to "continue this conversation"—a warning

[1] Charles S. Smith wrote Schurz of this letter, "It is the most polite and gentleman-like flaying of a selfish and ignorant politician that I have seen or known of since the days of Junius." Schurz, *Writings,* V, 411.

which the latter was not wise enough to heed.

Gallinger responded with three columns of personal diatribe, and a reassertion of his doctrine that obedience to party is the only sure test of party loyalty. It was a document filled with misstatements and exaggerations, most of them readily exposed. This Schurz did in another letter printed in the Exeter *News-Letter* of October 1. And then, having completed his factual reply, Schurz allowed his ironic bent full rein in the following masterpiece of satire:

> But, Senator, is it not cruel on your part to taunt me with my "obscurity"? Nature and fortune are sparing with their choicest gifts. On you they have lavished a rare combination of genius and success. The great and powerful of this world should at least be generous enough not to scoff at the feeble and insignificant. You are a genuine celebrity. Your noble defiance of General Harrison on account of a consulship, of which your biographers tell us, and your valiant battles for post offices and revenue places, have carried your fame into the remotest corners of New Hampshire. . . . No wonder you are proud. But do not let the pride of your greatness, however just, harden your heart against ordinary mortals. Everybody loves fame. You have it in abundance. Why do you blame me for coveting a little of it? Do not grudge me that passing gleam of notoriety which comes to me through the reflex of your renown, in having my name mentioned for a few days together with yours, in this public discussion.

In controversy of this kind, Gallinger was no match for Schurz. The New Hampshire Senator was almost apoplectic in his reply, and Schurz prepared a third communication, very dignified in tone, which was published in the *News-Letter* for November 12. Gallinger, his vocabulary of vituperation exhausted, now wisely withdrew from a discussion in which he had nothing to gain.

In his own state of New York, civil service reform was having its troubles. The Republican Governor, Frank S. Black, undertook as one of his first measures in 1897 to jam hastily through the Legislature what was described as a "starchless" civil service bill, permitting the head of any department, if he so desired, to select the lowest "merit" man on the approved list. It was decidedly a step backward, and Schurz did his utmost to block it. In May, after the Legislature had passed the bill, Schurz headed a delegation to Albany, made the chief address to the Governor, and introduced the other speakers. He himself warned the Governor not to become the "Buchanan of New York." But Black, who had himself instigated the drafting of the measure, sat with a bored expression during the hearing and refused to interpose his veto. The new bill was an offensive return to most of the practices which good citizens had learned to abhor.

The New York mayoralty campaign of 1897 was one of the most exciting in the history of that turbulent city. A new charter for the metropolis had been passed by the Legislature, providing for several unnecessary new offices, all well paid, and calculated to open a new field to spoilsmen. It was really in the interests of Tammany, but it had been planned by "Boss" Platt, a Republican, and Governor Black did not dare to veto it. As soon as it was in operation, the Citizens' Union, an organization of "good" citizens, persuaded Seth Low to become a nonpartisan candidate for Mayor, in opposition to Tammany, who nominated Judge Robert A. Van Wyck. A third factor in the contest was Henry George, the advocate of the "single tax," who was put forward by a group of independent Democrats, but who died before election day. Low was precisely the type of candidate that Schurz most admired—honest, high-minded, and intelligent—and he entered heartily into his cause. On October 23, at the Clermont Avenue Rink, in Brooklyn, speaking in German before a German-American audience, Schurz declared that Tammany as a political organization existed solely "for the purpose of preying upon the public treasury." At a great mass meeting six days later in Cooper Union, Schurz arraigned Tammany and its leader, Richard Croker, in an address full of passionate invective. Unfortunately Senator

Platt, preferring even a Tammany Mayor to the incorruptible Low, decided to name a Republican candidate, Benjamin F. Tracy, thus dividing the anti-Tammany forces. In this four-cornered contest, Van Wyck won easily, with Low second and Tracy third. The political intrigues of this campaign were so flagrant that Schurz was left discouraged and despondent. There were moments when he felt that the principles for which he had battled so stoutly were being abandoned, even by their friends.

Although Schurz was openly against "Boss" Platt, one of McKinley's advisers, he did not break with the President. The latter actually requested Schurz to assist him and the Republican Party in the Ohio campaign in the autumn of 1897. Schurz, however, declined, ostensibly on the somewhat ironic ground that he was working for the election of Low as Mayor, but actually because he was disgusted with the passage of the Dingley Tariff Bill, which had become a law in July, as the most important act of the special session called by the President shortly after his inauguration. Schurz was too shrewd to break with McKinley while there was any possibility of promoting civil service reform. "As you know, my dear Mr. President," he wrote on October 24, "we do not agree on all points; but I am all the more anxious to coöperate with you to the best of my ability as to those things on which we do agree, especially as to the cause of civil service reform which we both have so warmly to heart." In his presidential address at the annual meeting of the National Civil Service Reform League, in December, Schurz gave McKinley his hearty commendation; and a week later he wrote him, urging him not to yield by making any further exemptions in the cases of positions supposed to be "confidential" or "fiduciary."

To Schurz, identified with the movement to the exclusion of many other reforms, it seemed as if progress were very, very slow. He consoled himself at times with a perusal of Clough's poem, "Say not the Struggle Nought Availeth," especially with the stanza:

For while the tired waves, vainly breaking,
Seem here no painful inch to gain,
Far back, through creeks and inlets making,
Comes silent, flooding in, the main.

But, before the century closed, a blow fell which made him temporarily pessimistic. A senatorial investigation culminated in a report recommending certain specific reductions, numbering approximately ten thousand, in the number of places covered by the "merit" system. Even then, McKinley, less pliable than his sponsors had supposed, delayed action until after the Spanish War had begun. Finally yielding to pressure, the President, on April 29, 1899, issued an executive order removing 3693 offices from the classified service and transferring about 6500 appointments from the jurisdiction of the Commissioners to that of the Secretary of War. This action, Schurz later said, "dealt the merit system the most vicious blow it had ever received." It was unquestionably a step backward, and, as such, was severely criticized by George McAneny, secretary of the National Civil Service Reform League. In his annual address as president of the League, delivered in December, 1899, at Indianapolis, Schurz spoke out his feelings in a long and important analysis of the events of the year. The President's conduct, he declared, had "opened new opportunities for circumventing the civil service law," and was "indicative of a generally receding tendency."

In commenting on the McKinley administration, Schurz pointed out that the Republican platform of 1896 had promised that the civil service law should "be thoroughly and honestly enforced," and even "extended whenever practicable." He then demonstrated that the inauguration had been followed by a distinct lowering of the prevailing standards. The influence of Congressmen in distributing patronage had been increased rather than curtailed; plans for the census of 1900 had been made without regard to the merit system; and the Executive Order of May 29, 1899, had done incalculable damage to civil service reform. Assessments upon government employees for campaign expenses had been revived, and many officials had resumed what Schurz called "pernicious partisan activities." Behind this retrogression could be detected, in each instance, the baneful greed of politicians. And yet, when Schurz came to the conclusion of this address—one of the most effective he ever delivered—he was bound to confess that condtions had really improved since 1883. Civil service reform was no longer "superciliously sniffed at as a whimsical notion of some dreamy theorists." Public opinion had learned to understand and approve of it. The advocates of the merit system were finding their task easier each year. Most sensible people had come to recognize that it was using methods "which every intelligent business man standing at the head of a large establishment and exposed to constant and promiscuous pressure for employment would adopt for himself as eminently businesslike."

Carl Schurz's popularity and the respect which he had won through his labors for the public welfare were given vocal and tangible expression at the time of his seventieth birthday in 1899. Some four hundred of his admirers, headed by Gustav H. Schwab, arranged for a dinner at Delmonico's on the evening of March 2. Senator Gallinger was not among the number. Neither was "Boss" Platt nor "Boss" Croker. But the guests represented the finest elements in American life, the lawyers, physicians, teachers, editors, and statesmen who are the supporters of worthy causes. Charles Francis Adams, who presided, said in his preliminary remarks, "I regard Mr. Schurz as incomparably the best equipped man in the country of whom I have any personal knowledge for effective and brilliant parliamentary life—I mean parliamentary life of the highest order." Close upon this compliment came a letter from Grover Cleveland, saying of Schurz, "His life and career teach lessons that cannot be too often or too impressively emphasized. They illustrate the moral grandeur of disinterested public service, and the nobility of a fearless advocacy of the things that are right and just and safe."

The speakers, all persons of distinction, divided among them the successive phases of Schurz's achievement. Dr. Jacobi responded to the toast, "Young Germany in the Storm and Stress Period"; Professor William M. Sloane to "The Champion of the Slave"; John T. Lockman to "The Soldier in the Civil War"; Congressman William H. Fleming to "The Statesman in Reconstruction"; Moorfield Storey to "The United States Senator"; Herbert Welsh to "The Member of the Cabinet"; and Edward M. Shepard to "The Civil Service Reformer." Thus, in words of judicious praise, the whole varied field of Schurz's activities was covered by authoritative critics.

When Schurz, after this flood of eulogy, was called upon, he was so overcome by emotion that he could hardly raise his voice. His confidence regained, he declared proudly, "I have, doubtless, sometimes committed grave errors of observation or of judgment, but I may affirm that in my long public activity I have always sought to inform myself about the things I had to deal with, and that in my utterances on public interests I have never said anything that I did not conscientiously believe to be true." Then, in retrospective mood, he contrasted the scene before him with that bleak September day in 1852 when, an exile, without friends and ignorant even of the English language, he had wandered despondently through the streets of lower New York, eventually sitting down on a bench in Union Square, the future before him "like a mysterious fog bank" and his mind "in a state of dismal vacuity." He ended his brief response by sounding a note of optimism and reiterating his confidence in democracy and his conviction that a large majority of the American people really mean to do right.

Six days later came another celebration perhaps even more gratifying to Schurz. His German-American friends, more than six hundred in number, assembled in Liederkranz Hall, where L. F. Thoma, the chairman, handed him an enormous volume bound in calf, containing an address of congratulation signed by more than seventy thousand American citizens of German descent from all sections of the United States. The Liederkranz

Society presented him with a large punch bowl and ladle, of solid silver, appropriately inscribed. Henry Villard announced a plan for raising twenty thousand dollars to found a library and endow a Schurz Chair of Literature at Columbia University. Speeches were made by George von Skal, Professor Kuno Francke, and Dr. F. W. Holls; songs were sung in the good old German fashion; and Schurz responded in the tongue of the Vaterland. By universal consent, he was toasted as the greatest of German-Americans.

One more honor was to be his before the year was over. At the Columbia University Commencement in June he was awarded the honorary degree of Doctor of Laws and accorded an ovation hitherto unprecedented on Morningside Heights. He seemed then in the best of spirits and stepped to the platform in his usual jaunty manner, with a rosebud in the lapel of his coat. In the citation read to President Seth Low, the eminent legal scholar, Professor Munroe Smith, said in part: "I am charged with the honorable and grateful duty of presenting . . . a man who, for more than half a century and in two hemispheres, has been making law—not in one or two of the ways, but in all the ways in which the law is really made. . . . He has written and spoken and fought, in the old world and in the new, for the great causes of our century—for national unity and for individual freedom; and what his youth longed for, his age has seen fulfilled. . . . Mr. Schurz is an American; he has held that title longer than most of us who are assembled today, and he has illustrated it by worthy deeds. But in becoming an American, he has not ceased to be a German; and the pride which Germany feels in his American career is one of the bonds that unite his original and his adopted countries."

Several of his acquaintances felt that Carl Schurz was never again quite so vigorous as he was on that June afternoon. It was, in a sense, the crowning episode of his career. That degree was a symbol, the fitting reward of a long and useful life.

CHAPTER XXV THE ANTI-IMPERIALIST

IN THE spring of 1897, the newly inaugurated President McKinley came to New York City to take part in the dedication of General Grant's Tomb, on Riverside Drive. He invited Carl Schurz to call upon him at the Windsor Hotel; and the two men sat for an hour and a half, discussing current problems while they smoked cigars. They touched on many subjects, disagreeing on the tariff, but reaching the same conclusions on sound money and civil service reform. When Schurz questioned the advisability of appointing Sewall, of Maine, as Minister to the Hawaiian Islands, McKinley, of his own volition, said that, if he did select Sewall, it would be with the distinct understanding that there was to be no scheming for annexation. When Schurz congratulated the President on having taken this position, McKinley replied, "Ah, you may be sure there will be no jingo nonsense under my administration. You need not borrow any trouble on that account."

Although Harrison had encouraged a plot for the annexation of the Hawaiian Islands to the United States and had approved a treaty drawn up for that purpose, Cleveland, advised by Schurz, had reversed this policy and promptly repudiated a bargain already struck with Judge Dole, an American resident of Hawaii who had headed a revolt against the monarchy and had established a provisional republic. Our Minister to Hawaii had openly sanctioned plans for annexation and had written to the Department of State, just before Cleveland's inauguration, "The Hawaiian pear is now fully ripe, and this is the golden hour for the United States to pluck it." But Cleveland had sturdily resisted temptation, and Congress went on record in 1894 as opposed to our intervention in Hawaiian affairs. The situation when McKinley took office remained unaltered, and Schurz, after his conversation with the President, had no reason for thinking that any change would be made in our policy.

In June, 1897, however, President McKinley, without any warning or preliminary discussion, sent to the Senate a treaty recently concluded with the Hawaiian Government arranging for its annexation to the United States. On July 1, Schurz, at McKinley's invitation, went to Washington to discuss with him certain problems relating to the Civil Service Commission. Schurz dined that evening with the entire Cabinet, and with some other Washington people whom he knew, at the White House. When the guests had departed, the two finished their civil service business; and then Schurz, who had faced many Presidents in his lifetime, introduced the matter of Hawaii, recalling the talk which they had had at the Windsor Hotel. McKinley was a trifle embarrassed, but, after a moment's hesitation, answered, "Yes, yes, I remember now. You are opposed to that annexation, aren't you?" "Indeed I am," replied Schurz, "as you seemed to be opposed to it at that time." Schurz then stated briefly the objections which he had to the acquisition of tropical territory. McKinley, after a few moments of uncomfortable silence, confessed that there was no possibility of the treaty's being ratified by the Senate during the summer and that he had sent it to that body mainly to get an expression of popular opinion in advance of the first regular session in December. Schurz left the White House that evening "with a heart heavy with evil forebodings." He was later told that McKinley's conversion to an annexation policy had been brought about by the arguments of "a gang of sugar speculators in pursuit of profit"—and evidently did not altogether discredit the story.

Schurz had been willing to admit that McKinley was a man of kindly disposition, good nature, and agreeable manners. He had not agreed with him on the tariff, and he felt that McKinley's rather sudden espousal of the gold standard had been forced upon him by the exigencies of the Republican campaign. But Schurz had never dreamed that the new President would become the ardent advocate of the doctrine of "Manifest Destiny." It was McKinley's foreign policy even more than his attitude toward civil service reform which made Schurz his political foe. The time soon came when Schurz was to make imperialism the burning question of the day.

In spite of his war record, Carl Schurz was a pacifist at heart, with a deep distrust of militarism, especially when it was connected with "expansionist" ambitions. He had deplored Cleveland's Venezuela Message, thinking it altogether too truculent and provocative. He rejoiced when the Hawaiian Treaty of 1897 was rejected by the Senate. When a strong sentiment developed in the United States for our intervention in Cuba, Schurz did his utmost to turn public opinion in the opposite direction. McKinley took office at a moment when Spain, through her Governor General, Valeriano Weyler, was doing her utmost to suppress the Cuban rebellion; and the Republican Party in its platform had shown its interest in the achievement of Cuban independence. More and more as the months wore on it became apparent, even to Carl Schurz, that certain aggressive Americans, represented by Henry Cabot Lodge and Theodore Roosevelt, were getting impatient, and that a sudden impulse might at any moment precipitate us into war with Spain. Schurz wrote editorials for *Harper's Weekly*, trying to appeal to reason. In an article headed "National Honor," he dwelt on the uselessness of shedding blood in order to settle a dispute between a strong nation, like the United States, and a decadent one like Spain. But Schurz, without knowing it, was out of touch with the spirit of the age. The United States, full of unreleased energy, eager to demonstrate its strength, was highly nationalistic in its mood. The sufferings of the Cubans had undoubtedly aroused a real sympathy among our humanitarians, but there were many other factors, including business interests which were demanding protection, driving us toward an "inevitable conflict." For the actual war, some have blamed the Hearst newspapers; some have blamed Theodore Roosevelt, McKinley's Assistant Secretary of the Navy; and some have blamed McKinley himself. The historical truth is that the declaration of war was received with very little disapproval, and that most Americans while it was in process believed that their country was engaged in a kind of modern crusade against the powers of evil.

The culminating incident was, of course, the destruction, on February 15, 1898, of the splendid American battleship *Maine* in Havana harbor. Despite all that cool heads could do, the press, especially in New York, became more bellicose in tone. A court of inquiry was appointed to examine the causes of the disaster, but meanwhile Congress, on March 8, voted fifty thousand dollars as "an emergency fund for national defense." Schurz did all that he could to avert what seemed to him to be a ghastly mistake. On April 1, he wrote McKinley, begging him not rush too hastily into hostilities, and telling him that he would gain "imperishable honors by every effort to save even a last chance of honorable peace at this moment of the decisive crisis." Our government, meanwhile, had much provocation. The Spanish diplomatic policy of delay and procrastination was not calculated to soothe a people who believed that the God of Battles was on their side. When finally the Spanish Government ordered a suspension of hostilities in Cuba, it was too late. On April 7, at a meeting of the New York Chamber of Commerce, Schurz drafted resolutions declaring that war with Spain would be not only a calamity but a crime, and, after their adoption, sent them personally to McKinley, with a letter begging him to pause before the final decision; and he delivered at the same gathering a short, impressive speech, portraying the horrors of Gettysburg and announcing that he was not in favor of what he called the policy of "war at any price." The President, however, had already made up his mind. He sent a message to Congress on April 11, presenting the facts and saying, "I await your action." A few days passed, while Congress engaged in debate. Schurz published in *Harper's Weekly* on April 16 a solemn editorial, headed "Patriotism," ending with the query, "Can true patriotism possibly be eager to rush our country into war while there is a chance for honorable peace?" But his protests were futile. Congress issued an ultimatum and directed the President to employ the military and naval forces of the United States in compelling Spain to withdraw from Cuba. The Chief Executive called for 125,000 volunteers, and, on April 25, Congress formally declared war. This declaration cleared the atmosphere. For the moment, a mood of patriotism swept the nation. The country unquestionably was behind the war. Carl Schurz, discouraged, recognized that he was in a minority and resigned as chief editorial writer on *Harper's*. He confided to his old friend, Bayard, his opinion that "the reckless passions and ambitions of unruly spirits have acquired a sway which bodes ill to the country."

The ensuing war was short and, from the American point of view, highly gratifying. A succession of brilliant victories by Admiral Dewey at Manila Bay, May 1, by our soldiers near Santiago, and by Admiral Schley in Santiago Harbor, July 3, compelled the Spaniards to seek terms of peace. On August 12, less than four months after the opening hostilities, a protocol was signed at Washington preliminary to a formal treaty. Spain, much weaker than had been expected, was humbled on both land and sea, and her possessions in both the Atlantic and the Pacific were at our disposal. The administration of our troops had betrayed many shortcomings on the part of the War Department, and the conduct of our military operations might have been disastrous against a first-rate power. But the ordinary American citizen saw only that Dewey and Roosevelt and Schley were heroes. Their exploits were magnified. At last, according to the "jingo" press, we were a "world power." For good or for evil, we were about to embark upon a policy of "imperialism."

Against such a policy, Carl Schurz struggled manfully. On May 9, he warned the President not to allow the war to degenerate into one "of greedy ambition, conquest, self-aggrandizement," and asserted that the annexation of Hawaii then being considered would be regarded by the world at large as a proof that the war had been actuated by selfishness. To this communication McKinley did not reply. There was nothing to be said, for the sentiment of the country had become irresistible. Schurz might as well have attempted to dam the Mississippi with a few bricks and a pail of mortar.

Undaunted by the indifference with which his exhortations were received, Schurz became a militant crusader, whom nothing could suppress. On June 1, he wrote the President advising him to annex none of the former Spanish colonies, to make Cuba and Porto Rico independent, and to dispose of the Philippines to some minor power, such as Belgium or Holland, "not likely to excite special jealousy." He declared it to be an "incontestable fact" that, if the war had been announced in advance as one of conquest, the American people would most certainly not have consented to it; and he expressed his desire to have the United States become "the great neutral power of the world." Schurz was not, perhaps, fully cognizant of the strongly nationalistic spirit which was then sweeping from coast to coast.

A first step in carrying through the policy of imperialism was taken during the summer of 1898 by the passage of the Newlands Resolution annexing the Hawaiian Islands to the United States. Undoubtedly the problems raised by our naval adventures in the Pacific had much to do with hastening a move which the insistence of the Hawaiian people made almost inevitable. Schurz saw this action with regret, but spent no time in lamentation. Rather he waited until he heard a rumor of the conditions to be imposed upon helpless Spain. Then, on July 29, he sent a communication to McKinley, protesting that, as an honorable nation, we were "peremptorily precluded from annexing any of the Spanish islands" and that we could not take any of them for ourselves "without putting a stain of disgrace upon the American name." Meanwhile articles under his signature were published in the *Independent* and the *Century*, the latter appearing in the September issue with the title, "Thoughts on American Imperialism."

With an energy remarkable for a man nearing three score and ten, Schurz undertook to arouse public opinion through his own personal correspondence with influential people, through petitions, and through platform speeches. On August 18, he delivered an address at Saratoga, during the sessions of a national conference on the foreign policy of the United States, his subject being, "Our Future Foreign Policy." The main object of the conference, which included many eminent men, was to discuss, formulate, and present proposals to form a basis for a treaty of peace with Spain. He summed up the considerations against imperialism under three headings: as a question of morals and honor; as a question of institutional policy; and as a question of commercial interests. In this excellent, but not altogether logical, treatment of the issues involved, he closed by quoting the familiar paragraph from Washington's *Farewell Address*, warning the American people not to implicate themselves "by artificial ties, in the ordinary vicissitudes" of European politics.

It is interesting to the historian to find Schurz, in 1898, invoking against Senator Lodge and his "expansionist" associates the very principles which Lodge was to exalt so extravagantly twenty years later during his fight for the modification of the Covenant of the League of Nations. Schurz lamented that the *Farewell Address* was sometimes spoken of "with supercilious flippancy as a bundle of old-fogyish notions," and found in it, rather, the safest guide for our government in a time of alluring temptation. A committee from the Saratoga conference, including Schurz, secured an audience with the President, in the course of which they announced that they "wished the Republic to use this opportunity for exerting civilizing influences upon the populations of the conquered territories, without burdening itself with any political responsibilities in the regions concerned." McKinley, listening politely, responded in his usual suave manner, and then went his way, conscious that he had the nation and the Republican Party back of him.[1]

In the early autumn of 1898, Colonel Theodore Roosevelt, resplendent under the laurels which he had won with his Rough Riders in Cuba, landed with his troops at Montauk Point, and was at once mentioned, without any disapproval on his part, as the most available Republican candidate for Governor of New York. His friend and political mentor, Lodge, urged him to see that his platform took "good ground on our foreign policy" and opposed "returning to Spain any people whom we have freed." Roosevelt, more sagacious than he was given credit for being, was careful not to commit himself; but, at the Republican Convention in late September, he was nominated by a large majority over Frank S. Black, on a platform distinctly favoring the retention of the Philippines. During the ensuing campaign, with Augustus Van Wyck as his Democratic opponent, Roosevelt wore his Rough Rider uniform continuously and turned his whirlwind tours into a prolonged celebration of our victory over Spain. He now declared in ringing words that "to uphold the national honor abroad is the first great principle for this nation."

Up to this period, Carl Schurz, although not always in sympathy with Roosevelt's energetic "jingoism," had been his personal friend, and had occasionally been of assistance to the promising younger man. Roosevelt, although willing to accept Schurz's aid, had long been suspicious of what he once called "excessive mugwumpery," had styled Godkin "a malignant and dishonest liar," and, as early as 1890, had spoken with half-concealed contempt of the "hoary Schurz." In 1896, irritated at the opposition to his preparedness projects, Roosevelt wrote to Lodge, "If we ever come to nothing as a nation, it will be because the teaching of Carl Schurz, President Eliot, the *Evening Post*, and the futile sentimentalists of the international arbitration type bears its legitimate fruit in producing a flabby,

[1] For the Saratoga Conference and the call on McKinley, see Samuel Gompers, *Seventy Years of Life and Labor,* I, 525, 526.

timid type of character, which eats away the great fighting features of our race." Certainly the two men were temperamentally quite unlike: Schurz, highly intellectual, coming to his conclusions chiefly through his reason, and inclined to weigh evidence with a judicial mind; Roosevelt, guided always more by his emotions than by logic, inclined to exaggeration and overstatement, and uncontrollably impetuous. Schurz was often hypercritical; Roosevelt was sometimes rash. Schurz disdained all party allegiances which conflicted with his high ideals; Roosevelt found machine politicians exceedingly useful, making the end justify the means.

Schurz, with his sincere regard for Roosevelt's excellent work in the interests of civil service reform, would undoubtedly have favored him for Governor over the mediocre Van Wyck if it had not been for Roosevelt's violent expression of his aggressive Americanism. The latter's opening campaign speech in Carnegie Hall in early October had been a characteristic glorification of the "strenuous life," in which he had implored his fellow citizens to "live in the harness and strive mightily," had advocated a larger and more efficient army and navy, and had, in general, posed as the representative of what Schurz called a "militant imperialism." Shortly afterward, replying to a request from Roosevelt that he write an article in the latter's behalf, Schurz regretted that he could not consistently support the Republican nominee. "I cannot tell you," he added, "remembering our long and sincere friendship, how painful it is for me to be obliged to say this." Three days later, he sent an open letter to the *Evening Post*, giving his views more in detail. He did not like Roosevelt's "exceptionally bellicose temperament"; he felt that the Rough Rider was "dangerously deficient in that patient prudence which is necessary for the peaceable conduct of international relations"; and he feared that, in the latter's case, the governorship of New York might prove "the stepping-stone to the nomination for the presidency." Accordingly Schurz, convinced that there were even "worse things than free silver and Tammany," said that he should vote for the Independent state ticket headed by Theodore Bacon, although, as he admitted, it had no possible chance of winning.

A few days later, he wrote Senator George F. Hoar that the only hope of saving the republic "from being rushed over the precipice in the coming election is the defeat of all, or nearly all, of the Republican candidates . . . who have conspicuously come out in favor of that expansion policy." "This," continued Schurz, "is the *main* reason for my opposition to Roosevelt."

Carl Schurz was quite accustomed to battling with corruption. The fight in which he was now engaged was different. His opponent was an absolutely honest man, as honest as Schurz himself, and just as staunch a gladiator. Furthermore, the sentiment throughout the country, even with high-minded statesmen, was not, in general, condemnatory of Roosevelt. There was something decidedly appealing, even magnetic, in his enthusiasm, his sheer physical exuberance, and his boyish fervor. Senator Hoar, as ardent an anti-imperialist as Schurz, wrote to declare that, if he were a New Yorker, he should be on the side of Roosevelt. Jacob H. Schiff sent him a note expressing his admiration for Roosevelt and his "profound regret" at Schurz's decision; and in reply Schurz, with an arrogance in which he sometimes indulged, said: "Perhaps at some future time you will see that in my present position I was right after all. In my public life I have not seldom seemed to stand alone, and deserted, but never long." Through his repudiation of the Republican candidates, Schurz undoubtedly added to his list of enemies. On Election Day, furthermore, Roosevelt was victorious by a plurality of almost eighteen thousand.

Defeated in one contest, Schurz, gallant warrior that he was, continued the struggle on another front. The issue of imperialism was clearly drawn by the signing, on December 10, of the Treaty of Paris, by the terms of which Spain relinquished Cuba; ceded to the United States Porto Rico, Guam, and the Philippines, for the last of which we were to pay the sum of twenty million dollars; and, in general, parted with most of her far-flung colonial possessions. All that Schurz most dreaded had come true. He had now reached an age when most men are content to rest from their labors; but for him there could be no repose until the issue was settled.

On January 4, 1899, Schurz delivered at the University of Chicago a long and closely reasoned address entitled "The Issue of Imperialism," intended to answer every argument which could possibly be advanced by proponents of an imperialistic policy. To those who asserted that our territorial expansion in the nineteenth century had been advantageous, and that Louisiana, Florida, Texas, California, and even Alaska, had been rapidly assimilated, Schurz declared that the proposed new acquisitions were different in several respects: they were not on the North American continent; they were situated in the tropical zone; they were thickly populated in many sections; their population was heterogeneous and not Anglo-Saxon; and they would require, for their subjugation and retention, to say nothing of their protection, a material increase in our army and navy. Schurz did not take very seriously Kipling's version of the "White Man's Burden." He could not feel that we were taking over the Philippines in order to civilize the Filipinos. Rather he believed that a loudly heralded war of liberation and humanity had been turned "into a land-grabbing game and an act of criminal aggression." This speech, as Schurz had hoped, was printed as a pamphlet and widely circulated through the generosity of Andrew Carnegie, who wrote him: "You have brains and I have dollars. I can devote some of my dollars to spreading your brains."

Schurz, who was vice president of the Anti-Imperialist League, actually believed at one time that the Treaty might be rejected. He wrote Charles Francis Adams, on January 16, that the imperialists in Washington were "in full retreat." But he was deceived. Senator Lodge, a master of parliamentary methods, was busy behind the scenes. Mr. Bryan, in quest of an issue for 1900, was secretly urging his Democratic followers not to oppose ratification. It is not astonishing that outsiders were puzzled as to what was going on. On Monday, February 6, to conclude a long and acrimonious debate, the Senate passed the treaty with one vote to spare. "It was," confessed Senator Lodge, "the closest, hardest fight I have ever known." A war with the Filipino insurgents, under General Aguinaldo, had already broken out, and it was not until July 4, 1901, that the islands were officially "pacified" and Judge William H. Taft became Civil Governor.

Still Schurz did not consider himself beaten. There was the presidential campaign of 1900 to be prepared for, when the broad issue could be submitted to the American people in a national referendum. When the imperialists asserted that it was necessary for the United States to retain the Philippines in order to protect them against seizure by Germany, Schurz wrote a long letter to the New York *World*, defending Germany against the persistent charge of hostility to the United States and saying that any attempt to stir up ill feeling between the two countries should be "frowned down by every patriotic citizen as peculiarly wicked and abominable." On April 7, 1899, he read an address before the American Academy of Political and Social Science in Philadelphia, later entitled "Militarism and Democracy," in which he came out in defiant opposition to the Rooseveltian doctrine of "preparedness," saying, with reiterated emphasis, "History shows that military glory is the most unwholesome food that democracies can feed upon." Schurz urged that we restrict our standing armaments "to the narrowest possible limits," pointing out that, "in the peculiar position we occupy among the nations of the world, we need not have any war unless, without any compelling necessity, we choose to have it." In October, he spoke before the Anti-Imperialistic Conference, in Chicago, referring in scathing language to the war of subjugation then going on in the Philippines and to the difficulties of American administration in the islands. Again, on Washington's Birthday in 1900, he was the principal speaker at the Philadelphia Anti-Imperialist Con-

DR. ABRAHAM JACOBI

ference, his subject being, "For the Republic of Washington and Lincoln." In this stirring address, he accused President McKinley of a "breach of faith" with the Filipinos and even of "downright perfidy," and made a scathing indictment of our government policy. "If we permit the great wrong attempted by the administration to be consummated," he declared, "our moral credit with the world will be gone forever." He closed with the famous quotation from George Washington, enjoining his countrymen to "observe good faith and justice towards all nations."

To Carl Schurz at this period, every other issue seemed unimportant compared with that of imperialism. That he was something of a monomaniac was apparent even to himself. Thinking that his anti-imperialism might prove embarrassing to the National Civil Service Reform League, he announced on September 22, 1899, his intention of resigning as its president. The general and executive committees requested him unanimously to reconsider his decision, but he persisted, saying that his position with regard to other policies of the national administration would be bound to cause "practical inconveniences." At the annual meeting in December, President Daniel C. Gilman, of Johns Hopkins University, was chosen to succeed him.[1]

The presidential campaign of 1900 was to place Schurz in another difficult situation. McKinley, the high protectionist and Imperialist, was certain to be nominated by the Republicans to succeed himself, and Schurz could hardly support him without stultifying himself completely. On the other hand, the Democratic candidate was apparently to be Bryan, the apostle of free silver. "A plague on both their houses," Schurz might have exclaimed. As early as November 5, 1899, he wrote Charles Francis Adams to confess that the alternative before them was dreadful, but also to announce his intention, if a choice had to be made, of swallowing his personal disgust and voting for

[1] Later presidents of the League have been Charles W. Eliot, Richard Henry Dana, and Joseph H. Choate.

Bryan. In other words, he believed that imperialism must be defeated "at any cost." There were moments when he over-optimistically hoped that the Democratic Party might be persuaded to make anti-imperialism its leading issue and relegate free silver to an inconspicuous place in its platform. If the Democrats, split asunder in 1896 over bimetallism, could only be reconciled, if Cleveland and Bryan could be made to clasp hands in resistance to a common menace, all might be well.

Before the party conventions met, Schurz, although not in good health, did what he could to emphasize the perils of imperialism. To many people, it seemed as if he were singing the same song over and over. He wrote countless letters to Democratic leaders; and he made one long speech, on May 24, 1900, in Cooper Union, in a tone of warning and of prophecy. Events turned out as he had expected. The Republicans, gathering in late June in Philadelphia, nominated not only the obnoxious McKinley for a second term, but also "young Mr. Roosevelt," the militarist and expansionist, the idol of aggressive America, for second place on the ticket. The Democrats, assembling on Independence Day, in Kansas City, did, it is true, declare imperialism to be "the paramount issue of the campaign"; but they also nominated William Jennings Bryan and demanded vociferously again "the immediate restoration of the free and unlimited coinage of silver and gold at the present legal ratio of 16 to 1." Almost in despair, Schurz wrote that the action of the Democratic Convention had "produced the worst possible impression."

Schurz's emotions during this exciting convention period were expressed in two open letters to Senator Joseph B. Foraker, of Ohio, dated June 29 and July 10, and published in the New York *Herald*. Referring to the Philippines, he said, "The trouble is not that we 'cannot let go,' but it is that men of power in politics, moved by a mistaken 'patriotism,' or by ambition, or by greed, will not let go." Schurz challenged Foraker to find in the history of the world a "single act of perfidy committed by any republic more infamous than that which has been committed by President McKinley's administration against our Filipino allies." For our policy of "criminal aggression," he held the President almost solely responsible, for it was he who, in the last analysis, had to stamp it with his approval.

It was a hard summer for Schurz. In late July, he suffered a violent attack of ptomaine poisoning while on one of his regular trips from Lake George to New York. Fortunately he was with his friend, Dr. Abraham Jacobi, who took him to his own city home, where his temperature rose to 105½ degrees. While he was convalescing from this illness, the news arrived of the death of his younger son, Herbert, on July 24, while traveling in England.[1] The body was brought home by Schurz's older son, Carl, who had accompanied his brother. It is not strange that Schurz reported himself on August 7 as hardly "in a condition fit for appearance in public, or to undergo any strain."

There were moments when Schurz felt like striking out boldly in a third-party project. Writing to Edwin B. Smith, on July 8, he said, "There is a very widespread feeling that the people have permitted themselves long enough, and too long, to be forced by two rotten old party carcasses to choose between two evils." When a Liberty Congress was called at Indianapolis in August, Schurz gave the plan his formal approval, and would have been glad to have either Thomas B. Reed or John B. Henderson head an independent movement. Nothing developed from these plans, for no statesman of sufficient ability would accept the dubious honor of a nomination by a third party. Possibly if Schurz had been younger or more robust in health, he might have been able to accomplish something where others failed. But his physical condition forbade any exertion or excitement.

[1] Herbert Schurz, a member of the class of 1897 at Harvard, had later studied law at Columbia. His real ambition was to become an actor, and he was accepted by Henry Irving as a pupil. Later he traveled in South America, Italy, and Germany. It was on his way back to the United States that he died suddenly of heart failure. He was in his twenty-fifth year.

When the third party idea was abandoned, Schurz reached the conclusion that McKinley could be beaten only by a rally of all Independents to Bryan's standard. In early September, his vitality renewed, he sent two open letters to Lyman G. Gage, McKinley's Secretary of the Treasury, refuting the assertion that Bryan, if elected, would force free silver upon the country. Gage took much pains with his reply, reading it to the Cabinet and submitting it to the President for revision; but it was difficult for him to disprove Schurz's evidence that the talk about silver was "a mere rattling of dry bones." Schurz said to Gage, "I am certainly as anxious to maintain the gold standard as you are," but he also added that the battle for sound money was substantially won.

Schurz's most significant utterance during the campaign was made on September 28, at Cooper Union, in a speech which he entitled, "For Truth, Justice, and Liberty." The audience of more than three thousand people was described as "a mixture of Fifth Avenue and the Bowery." Anson Phelps Stokes, as chairman, introduced Schurz as "one of the greatest advocates of the people that ever lived." The latter gave few symptoms of weakness, for his address was eight thousand words long and, when he finished, he seemed as fresh and robust as when he began. He did not mention Bryan's name. He did, however, assail imperialism in burning phrases. It had been commended to the American people by the "systematic use of distortion of history, hypocritical cant, garbling of documents, and false pretense." Of our attitude toward the Filipinos, he said, "No single act in the history of any republic since the world began surpasses this in treacherous villainy." It was a powerful address, but it lacked the judicial tone usually characteristic of Schurz. He was obviously overwrought and nervously "on edge." [1]

[1] "It is really mournful," wrote James Ford Rhodes to Frederic Bancroft apropos of this speech, "to see a champion of sound money and civil service reform like Mr. Schurz using his influence indirectly for Bryan. What twists do get into the brains of good people!" M. A. De Wolfe Howe, *James Ford Rhodes,* 108.

Schurz, who never lost his political sense, was far from optimistic. He wrote on October 7 that, if the election were to take place at once, McKinley would have an easy victory. The only hope for the Democrats, as he saw it, was to extract from Bryan a public declaration that, if elected, he would not interfere with the existing gold standard. This, of course, Bryan would not consent to do. But Schurz still insisted that the important aim was to defeat McKinley. When urged by such a staunch friend as Charles Francis Adams not to persist in his censure of the administration, Schurz replied that "the criminal aggression policy of the present administration was originated and has been carried forward by the Executive" and that he could not conscientiously give even a tacit approval to what he regarded as "deceit, false pretense, unconstitutional assumption of power, downright betrayal of the fundamental principles of our democracy, wanton sacrifice of our soldiers in a wicked war, cruel slaughter of tens of thousands of innocent people." [1]

On the eve of the election, Schurz confessed that he had not for some weeks expected Bryan to win. The situation reminded him of 1872 when, disgusted with Greeley's nomination and knowing that the latter would probably be defeated, he had to make up his own mind whether to support him. He admitted to Adams that he had entered the 1900 campaign "for educational purposes," and he did not cease reiterating that Bryan's election would be "better for the country than McKinley's." He did, however, note regretfully that every one of Bryan's speeches lost him votes. In the last two weeks most of the doubtful voters rushed to McKinley's standard in a vague fear of Bryan's radicalism. It was America's fundamental conservatism

[1] Hay wrote McKinley, November 1, 1900, "Did you ever hear of anything so ridiculous as that Adams and Schurz correspondence? Schurz thinks it will be best to elect a lunatic President, and trust to a sane Congress to keep him in order. Adams thinks that the best way would be to elect a sane man President, and have a lunatic Congress for him to control; and neither of them seems to realize that it makes not the slightest difference what both of them think." Cf. W. R. Thayer, *Life and Letters of John Hay,* II, 257.

which gave McKinley 292 electoral votes against Bryan's 155. If Schurz had expected a revulsion against imperialism, he was sadly disappointed.

Without being altogether conscious of his position, Carl Schurz was out of touch with the times. The United States at the turn of the century was complacent, exultant, confident, and self-assertive, eager to take its proper place in world affairs. Our victory over Spain had made us feel that all Europe was decadent and it was time for our young republic to dictate to dying empires. Schurz did not long remain allied with Bryan. On January 17, 1901, speaking of the "Great Commoner," he said, "To vote for him was the most distasteful thing I ever did." He refused to attend the dinner tendered to Bryan, and expressed the opinion that the Nebraska orator was "the evil genius of the anti-imperialistic cause." In a final defiant gesture, Schurz had once more demonstrated his independence of party ties, but he was obliged to admit ruefully that he had gained nothing by it.

CHAPTER XXVI THE CONCLUDING PHASE

IN NOVEMBER, 1901, Schurz wrote to Edward M. Shepard, "The political life of a public man of character and ability is never ended so long as he is true to his best self and willing to serve the country, and has something to say worth listening to." He was referring, of course, to Shepard, who was at the moment, to Schurz's disgust, running as the Tammany candidate for Mayor of New York against Seth Low: but the words might have been applied without modification to Schurz himself. Although he was chagrined over the reëlection of McKinley and conscious of weakened vitality, he did not withdraw from affairs nor cease to express his opinions. Shepard was one of Schurz's luncheon companions at the club, a man whom he loved and respected; yet Schurz opposed him in the mayoralty campaign. At a great gathering held on October 24, 1901, in Cooper Institute, under the auspices of the German-American Reform League, Schurz, reverting to his native tongue, delivered a stinging indictment of "King" Croker, the Tammany brave, ruler of the "Kingdom" of New York. "No doubt he has extraordinary abilities in his own way," said Schurz. "There never was a successful robber chief who did not have extraordinary abilities for his trade."

This, although he was unaware of it, was to be his valedictory utterance in the vast cheerless auditorium where he had first been introduced forty-one years before during the presidential campaign of 1860. It was a place of thrilling memories. From that platform, on February 27, 1858, Abraham Lincoln, then a badly clothed, awkward, and little known Illinois politician, had delivered his earliest important address before an Eastern audience. On that rostrum had stood Wendell Phillips and Robert G. Ingersoll and William Jennings Bryan and other famous "spellbinders" of that generation. There Schurz himself had spoken during the Civil War and on several occasions afterward, in the fullness of his powers as an orator. Now, after a dramatic career, he stood there again, with head "bloody but unbowed," reiterating the doctrines of liberalism, justice, and honesty in government which, from youth to old age, he had cherished. He was attacking Richard Croker [1] as he had denounced Stephen A. Douglas and Benjamin F. Butler and James G. Blaine. He could have said truthfully in the words of Saint Paul: "I have fought the good fight. I have finished my course. I have kept the faith."

Schurz's withdrawal from his manifold activities was so gradual as to be almost unnoticed. Although he declined, on the ground of ill health, to attend a pro-Boer mass meeting in Chicago in December, 1901, he wrote a letter condemning what he described as "the evil deeds with which the British Government is at present defying the judgment of mankind." During the summer of 1902, he assailed Bryan as being "the evil genius of every cause or party he embraced" and "always preaching discord and internal strife with the whole power of his eloquence." Nevertheless he voted in November for Francis Burton Harrison, the Democratic nominee for Congress in his district. Interviewed in the autumn by the *Staats-Zeitung*, he denounced the protective tariff, declaring it to be the nurse, if not the mother, of many of the iniquitous "trusts" then being condemned by President Roosevelt.

It was a period when Schurz's political ideas, like those of many well-intentioned American citizens, were much confused. The assassination of President McKinley at Buffalo and his subsequent death on September 14, 1901, placed in the White House, at the age of forty-three, a man in whom Schurz felt

[1] In the New York municipal elections of 1901, the Fusion ticket, headed by Low and supported by William Travers Jerome and the Citizens' Union, won an overwhelming victory over Tammany. Most good citizens felt that Shepard had paid the penalty for a fatuous apostasy. When Shepard claimed that Schurz had misrepresented him, the latter replied in an open letter, repeating his charges against Tammany. Despite their sharp divergence at this time on political issues, the friendship between Schurz and Shepard remained unbroken.

little confidence. Theodore Roosevelt was theatrical, unconventional, and boisterous to a degree incomprehensible to a person of Schurz's native dignity. Schurz, peace-loving, cool-headed, and usually logical, was suspicious of Roosevelt's belligerency and volatility, looking upon him much as an adult might regard an impulsive and somewhat destructive child. Schurz would have laughed over John Morley's characterization of Roosevelt as "an interesting combination of St. Vitus and St. Paul." The two were very different. Even when they agreed on aims they could not always concur on policies. But Schurz was prepared to support the President if the latter advocated what seemed to be the right principles and methods.

For some months after Roosevelt took the oath of office as President, he was careful not to commit himself on the question of the Philippines. When rumors of the cruelties and atrocities practiced by our soldiers upon the Filipino natives reached Schurz's ears, he joined Charles Francis Adams Jr., on a committee of investigation. "I am old and sometimes very tired," he wrote on May 8, 1902, "but this is a great and solemn crisis." With Andrew Carnegie and others, he signed an open letter to Roosevelt, urging him to speak out in favor of Philippine autonomy: and later Schurz begged Carnegie to exert all his powerful influence in persuading the President to commit himself on the subject. There were moments in 1903 when Schurz felt optimistic that the obvious distress among the Filipinos might cause a modification of the administration plan. "I have a good deal of evidence that we anti-imperialists are today very much less regarded as 'cranks' than we were three months ago," he wrote Adams on February 8, 1903. When, in December of that year, Roosevelt sent him a gracious note commending an article of his in *McClure's Magazine* entitled, "Can the South Solve the Negro Problem?" Schurz thanked him tactfully and said, toward the close of his letter, "Let me add that, in memory of old times, it does me good to speak with you on things on which we substantially agree, while it makes me feel more keenly the sorrowful regret that there are other things of fundamental importance on which we differ."

As the campaign of 1904 approached, Schurz helped to circulate a petition, eventually signed by President Eliot, Cardinal Gibbons, and scores of other good citizens, asking the two great political parties to pronounce in favor of Philippine independence. It was clear, however, that nothing of this kind could be expected from the Republicans. Certain recent utterances of Roosevelt on this matter had aroused Schurz's anger; indeed he regarded the President's letter to the "Cuba Dinner" in the spring of 1904 as "a symptom of an unbalanced mind." "And to think of this man being in a place of power in which he can bring on war at any time!" Schurz burst out in a note to Rollo Ogden, then the editor of the *Evening Post.* At the Republican Convention in late June, in Chicago, Roosevelt was nominated by acclamation, but without much enthusiasm. The platform, drafted by Lodge and approved by the President, was platitudinous and plausible; but Schurz characterized what he termed its "insolent Philippine paragraph" as meaning "the keeping of the Philippines for military reasons," and made a resolve that this in itself would absolve him from voting the Republican ticket.

At the Democratic Convention held in St. Louis some days later, Judge Alton B. Parker, an uncompromising gold standard man backed by Grover Cleveland, was nominated for President over William Randolph Hearst. Bryan protested, but his party was not willing to go with him for a third time down to inevitable defeat. Schurz, having already ascertained that Parker favored Philippine autonomy and civil service reform, was delighted with the choice and wrote to the Independents asking them to support the Democratic candidate. When John Hay and Elihu Root made speeches in defense of the administration, Parker turned to Schurz as the best available person to produce a refutation.[1] This Schurz did in a long communi-

[1] In his letter, dated August 29, 1904, Parker said to Schurz, "It is of the first importance that the addresses of Secretary Hay and Mr. Root be answered at once by a man of intellectual strength, character, and position. It is a great

cation directed to James W. Pryor, as general secretary of what were over-exuberantly called the "Parker Republican Clubs." In this letter sent out through the press from Bolton Landing in September, Schurz contrasted Roosevelt and Parker, in personality and political philosophy, to the great disadvantage of the former. While admitting that Roosevelt in his young manhood had fought abuses in partisan politics and party management, Schurz declared that since the Spanish War, a new and very dangerous Roosevelt had been evolved. "There are two Roosevelts in the field," he said, "the ideal, the legendary Roosevelt, as he once appeared, and as many people imagine him still to be; and the real Roosevelt, as he has since developed." Roosevelt's temperament, Schurz asserted, had been "altogether too strong for his reason," and he added, "President Roosevelt is an exceedingly interesting, picturesque, and forcible character, who would have found a most congenial and glorious field of action at the time of the Crusades, but sometimes strangely fails to appreciate the higher moral aims of modern civilization." He concluded with something resembling a prophecy, "His is a master nature, but this Republic does not want in the Presidency a master—least of all one who cannot master himself."

But this, apparently, was just what the American people did want. Followers of Bryan and Hearst were reluctant to cast their votes for the dignified but unmagnetic Parker; and, although Cleveland emerged from his retirement long enough to say a few ponderous words for him, this help was inconsequential. The average citizen liked Roosevelt's democracy, his unfailing insistence on a "square deal" for everybody, rich or poor, and his very human qualities. Compared with Roosevelt, statesmen like Parker seemed colorless and uninspiring. Roosevelt, with his insatiable intellectual curiosity and amazing versatility, appealed to all classes and conditions of men. His popularity was demonstrated at the polls, where in November

favor to ask of you, but as no one fills the requirements so well, I make bold to ask you to do it." Schurz, *Writings,* VI, 358.

he secured a popular majority of almost two million and received 336 votes in the Electoral College against 140 for his opponent. Thus Schurz ended his last presidential campaign by seeing his candidate overwhelmingly defeated.

Schurz, though often conscious of the infirmities of age, did not hesitate to take part in the discussion of controversial questions. He criticized pungently Roosevelt's methods in abetting a revolution on the Isthmus of Panama and recognizing the baby Republic of Panama in order to thwart the demands of the Colombian Congress and facilitate the construction of an interoceanic canal. But to Roosevelt's adherents, his prompt and decisive action seemed a just retribution upon Colombia for refusing to comply with our desires, and it undoubtedly pleased more citizens at the time than it offended. For the moment, Schurz was not in touch with the spirit of the younger generation.

Advised by his physicians to refrain from delivering long speeches, he refused most invitations. But he still occasionally deviated from his policy of renunciation. Following the publication of his *Henry Clay*, he had been elected, on December 8, 1887, an honarary member of the Massachusetts Historical Society; but he did not attend a meeting until November 12, 1903, when, at the invitation of Charles Francis Adams Jr., its president, he came to Boston and read before its members a short appreciation of Theodor Mommsen, the historian. A few weeks later, he prepared and read, as a matter of inevitable duty, an address at the unveiling of a bust of George William Curtis, in the Lenox Library, in New York City—an address which, after some alterations, was reprinted in *McClure's Magazine* for October, 1904. In the summer of 1904, he revisited St. Louis, speaking on "German Day," at the Louisiana Purchase Exposition, before an audience a few of whom had known him in his early manhood in that city. He was identified with dozens of philanthropic and educational movements, and never withheld his name when it could be helpful to a worthy cause. His declining vitality was shown chiefly by the admission that his zest for oratory was appeased. "If there is anything I detest, it is making speeches," he wrote to Adams. "It is the bane of my life." And yet, only a few months before his death, he was persuaded by Andrew Carnegie to attend a meeting of leaders of the Negro race, and spoke in Carnegie Hall for nearly an hour with much of his early fervor.

Schurz, believing in the principle of international arbitration, had welcomed the establishment of the Hague Tribunal. In 1905, he and Roosevelt had an interesting interchange of letters on the desirability of national disarmament—a correspondence illustrating beautifully the contrast between their respective temperaments and opinions. It was opened by a note from Schurz commending the President for his interposition between Russia and Japan as "one of the most meritorious and brilliant achievements of our age, not only bold and noble in conception, but most admirable for the exquisite skill and tact with which it was carried through." He then went on to urge Roosevelt to lend his powerful influence to "the gradual diminution of the oppressive burdens imposed upon the nations of the world by armed peace."

Roosevelt evidently felt that this letter offered him an opportunity for explaining his views to a group of reformers whom he regarded as "professional peace advocates." [1] He said in his reply that, while he was substantially in accord with Schurz, he did, however, place peace as "second to righteousness." As far back as 1896, he had written to Schurz, in a vein half-jocular but also half-serious, "I only hope that all of you international arbitration people don't finally bring us literally to the Chinese level." Now, nearly a decade later, he took especial pains to state that, while he did not think it necessary to increase the number of our ships or regiments, he was convinced that the more progressive countries must keep themselves well armed if the peace of the world was to be maintained. "To have the best nations, the free and civilized nations, disarm and leave the despotisms and barbarisms with great

[1] Cf. Theodore Roosevelt, *An Autobiography,* 560–563.

military force, would be a calamity compared to which the calamities caused by all the wars of the nineteenth century would be trivial," he declared with his shadowless dogmatism. He did, however, admit in a postscript that "a general stop in the increase of the war navies of the world *might* be a good thing."

Feeling that some of his ideas might have been misunderstood, Schurz responded, saying that he did not desire the elimination of all armies and navies. He merely wished to "put a limit to the excessive and constantly growing armaments which are becoming so oppressive to the nations of the world." What he hoped for was the gradual ending of the wasteful and cruel rivalry in expenditure among the Great Powers. As a practical suggestion, he pointed out, with tactful flattery, that it would be sufficient for Roosevelt, fresh from his diplomatic success in terminating the conflict between Russia and Japan, to bring the representatives of the Great Powers together and recommend to them a serious consideration of the subject. "You, of all men in the world," he wrote, "can, as you now stand, stir up a public opinion in favor of this course, which the objectors might find it hard to resist." The President answered on September 18, in a letter which he, then or later, would not allow to be published, but which unquestionably assured Schurz that Roosevelt would not refuse his active sympathy to any sane movement for "gradual disarmament." Roosevelt's letters are peculiarly interesting as indicating a struggle in his mind between his natural emotions, which favored a reliance on force, and his reason, which told him that war, even in a good cause, is a great and far-reaching evil.[1] This correspondence was Schurz's last important contribution to national or international affairs.

Importuned by publishers, Schurz had begun in the nineties the preparation of his reminiscences; and in 1901 he devoted himself systematically to their revision for the press. He found

[1] Roosevelt sent to Lodge, September 15, 1905, copies of the entire correspondence, apparently feeling that he had had the better of the discussion. *Letters of Theodore Roosevelt and Henry Cabot Lodge,* II, 194–200.

much pleasure in looking over his letters and manuscripts, and reviving his recollections of his boyhood in the Rhine Valley. Installments appeared serially in *McClure's Magazine*, beginning in 1905, where they attracted much attention because of their interesting material and method of presentation.[1] He had found it easier to write about his early days in German than in English, and this section was translated into English by his friend, Mrs. Eleonora Kinnicutt. Once started, he moved along with some rapidity, stimulated by the cordial reception from the critics. On January 11, 1906, he wrote: "My Memoirs are completed as far as my youth in Europe is concerned. I have also completed the second volume which reaches down to the close of the war, but I am still at work at the third and last, which includes my time in the Senate and Cabinet and what followed." Unfortunately he died before his plan could be fully carried out. His pen stopped forever while he was narrating the events of his senatorial career, and the story was later finished most felicitously by Frederic Bancroft and William A. Dunning. The *Reminiscences* appeared ultimately in three volumes in 1908, with the authority of Schurz's children, Agathe, Marianne, and Carl. Schurz also projected a biography of Charles Sumner, less formidable than that of Edward L. Pierce, but death stole upon him before he could do more than assemble some of his material.

Schurz's income in his declining years was sufficient to provide him with the creature comforts. For some years in the nineties he lived with his children in a house which he called "Solitude," located at Pocantico Hills, in Westchester County, about twenty-five miles north of New York City. One of the residents remembers that once, when it was planned to establish a kindergarten among the children of the workmen on the large estates in that vicinity, Schurz attended the meet-

[1] William Dean Howells wrote Schurz, Mar. 3, 1906, "Your latest chapters are the most moving yet. When I think what your life has been I am ashamed of mine. How well you tell it all, how faithfully, how simply, how greatly!" *Schurz MSS*, Congressional Library.

ing, told the story of how his wife had been the first person to introduce the kindergarten in the United States, and subscribed liberally to put the plan into operation. Schurz had there a large, comfortable library, where he spent most of his waking hours, going two or three times a week to New York to see his friends. Toward the close of the century, feeling somewhat isolated during the long winter months, he moved into the metropolis, living for a time in East Sixty-fourth Street, and, after 1902, in East Ninety-first Street, with Andrew Carnegie as his near neighbor. As he grew older, he depended very much for advice on two younger friends, George McAneny and Oswald G. Villard, to one or both of whom most of his articles and speeches were submitted for comment and criticism.

Schurz's household in these latter days was managed by his two daughters, Agathe and Marianne—known to their friends as "Tante Handi" and "Tante Pussy" respectively—neither of whom ever married. They acted by turns as their father's amanuenses and accompanied him on most of his trips. Carl Lincoln Schurz, the elder son, after graduating from Harvard in 1893, received the degree of LL. B. from New York Law School two years later and built up a fairly extensive law practice in New York City.

Much of Schurz's happiness in his old age was dependent upon his intimate friend of long standing, Dr. Abraham Jacobi, a distinguished New York physician.[1] The two had met first in 1850, at Bonn, where the exiled Schurz, returning to the university town on a secret mission, had been introduced to Jacobi on a dark night in a secluded garden house. They conferred and traveled together for a day or two, but did not see one another again until some years later, in New York, after

[1] Jacobi, born May 6, 1830, at Hartum, in Westphalia, was a little younger than Schurz. He was, in his later life, the author of several noteworthy books on the diseases of children, and was on the medical staff at the University of New York and Columbia University. His only surviving child is Mrs. George McAneny, wife of Schurz's associate on the National Civil Service Reform League.

CARL SCHURZ AND HIS DAUGHTER AGATHE

Jacobi had spent many months in a Prussian prison as a revolutionary. In the United States Jacobi had prospered, had married a remarkable woman, Mary Putnam, like himself a physician, and had become one of the notabilities of New York. When the two refugees were thrown together after Schurz settled in the metropolis, they soon became almost inseparable, and one was rarely seen in public without the other. Strangely enough, they always used the formal German "Sie" to one another until a day or two before Schurz's death, when he, almost unconsciously, addressed his beloved friend as "Du."

Dr. Jacobi had acquired a large tract of woodland on the western shore of Lake George, in the northeastern part of New York State, and had erected there a comfortable summer cottage in the midst of a grove of pines. The nearest settlement was the hamlet of Bolton Landing, and the only railroad station was Lake George, eleven miles to the south. Passengers from New York were obliged to get off here and proceed for the remaining distance either by a small steamboat or by carriage over a somewhat corrugated road.

In 1892, Dr. Jacobi suggested that Schurz bring his family to Bolton Landing for the summer months. Finding the spot and the companionship delightful, the Schurzes built a house for themselves on land provided by Dr. Jacobi. It was a simple two-storied wooden cottage, covered with cedar shingles, not at all unusual from an architectural viewpoint, with a large, irregularly shaped living room opening on to a porch about forty feet long by fifteen feet wide, commanding a glorious outlook up and down Lake George. Facing east, one sees directly in front the long forest-clad ridge on the opposite shore, not sharply serrated, but with smoothly rounded contours. The hills are constantly changing, sometimes clearly outlined in the morning sunshine, sometimes flecked with mist which has lingered in the hollows. A long vista through the trees reveals a widening prospect to the south. At the left, Tongue Mountain rises conspicuously beyond the Northwest Inlet; and, in the foreground, near and far, are a score of low verdurous islands. In certain aspects Bolton Landing reminds one of Montreux, on Lake Geneva. It is less secluded today than when the Schurzes first knew it, but not even automobiles and gasoline stations have effaced its essential charm.

At Bolton Landing, the little group of German Americans led a communal, almost arcadian existence from May to October of each year. What was called the "New House" was built in 1904 for the McAnenys, and the members of the three family groups shared nearly everything together. Schurz's room was at the southern end of his cottage, on the ground floor, lighted by a large three-sided bay window facing toward the east. Between him and the water was an area covered by second-growth timber, including clumps of evergreens of which he was very proud. To nearly every landmark in the forest Schurz gave some characteristic German name. The heavily wooded northwest corner of the estate was christened the "Schwarzwald." Certain rocks were called the "Stones of the Valkyrie," and not far off was the "Bimini Spring." Everywhere he had cut out paths, each one named after one of the Wagnerian operas; and, as he raced along them, his collie, "Friend," and his grotesque dachshunds following close behind him, he would whistle or sing the appropriate motifs from *Lohengrin* or *Tannhäuser* or *Die Meistersinger*. One of his possessions was a quaint one-cylinder "puffboat," the *Hiawatha*, in which he occasionally ventured out upon the lake. He really preferred, however, to ramble through the pines or to sit in quiet meditation on his own broad piazza with Dr. Jacobi, talking over old days and new projects. The two, although Schurz was tall and Jacobi short and stocky, were not unlike in appearance—both with high foreheads, heavy beards and hair, and expressions of dignity and determination. They did not look like men with whom one could take liberties.

Today, when one makes a pilgrimage to Bolton Landing, he soon finds that most of Schurz's trails are overgrown or obscured. Dr. Jacobi's residence burned down in 1918, fortunately without damage to the two adjacent cottages, which are still occupied by the McAneny family. Although there is no living member of the Schurz clan to carry on the tradition, his house is preserved much as it was when he was alive, and a photograph of him looks down from above the fireplace. The landscape itself is very little altered. Tongue Mountain is still there, and Crown Island, and the marvelous panorama from the veranda to the east; and, if one is willing to enter the deep woods and listen, he can even fancy that he hears the baying of the dogs or the ringing voice of Carl Schurz himself as he passes along the slope of "Brunhilde Knoll." Where the driveway enters the main thoroughfare between Glens Falls and Ticonderoga, some of his friends built in 1925 a massive stone seat, with this inscription carved above it:

To the Happy Memory of
CARL SCHURZ
Soldier, Statesman, Scholar, Patriot
For Fourteen Summers, 1892–1905,
He Achieved and Rested in These Precincts
Whose Beauty Was His Never-Ending Joy

In his declining years, Schurz was obliged to guard himself carefully against sudden changes in the weather. He then formed the habit of going to Augusta, Georgia, during the inclement winter months. There he found a climate which suited him perfectly. There, too, he came across old friends and acquired new ones. At the Hotel Bonair in that delightful winter resort he was a welcome guest; and the fact that he had once been a major general in the Northern army added to his prestige among the Southerners by whom he was surrounded.

Although Schurz's health in the spring of 1905 was uncertain, he was able to go with his daughter, Agathe, to Commencement at the University of Wisconsin, where, to his immense satisfaction, he was awarded on June 22 the honorary degree of Doctor of Laws by the institution of which he had, many years before, been a regent, and to which he had been invited, in 1858, as Professor of Modern Languages. President Van Hise, in his citation, described him as "being recognized, by common consent here and abroad, as the foremost German-American"—"a sincere and bold leader of public opinion and an ardent advocate of wise measures of national reform." Schurz was the guest in Madison of Governor Robert M. La-Follette. Those who heard his brief address thought him to be forceful and vigorous.

Early in the following November, as he was descending from a street car in New York on his way to his favorite club, the Century, he was thrown violently to the pavement, suffering a severe head contusion. The shock to a man of his age was severe, and he never recovered from it. As soon as he could be moved, he was sent south, where he spent some weeks at the Hotel Bonair, improving slowly but obviously much exhausted. He had hoped to go to Germany during the ensuing summer for the unveiling of a statue to Gottfried Kinkel, but was obliged to decline the invitation. His last letter, dated April 8, 1906, was written to an unknown correspondent and emphasized the necessity of maintaining peaceful relations between the United States and Germany.

Coming north in the middle of April, he was very cheerful, and wrote to a friend, "I returned from the South last Saturday, having so far escaped the bronchial troubles which used to afflict me about this season, and, save old age, have little to complain of." A few days later, however, he contracted pneumonia—the disease which his physicians had always dreaded for him. His family gathered around him in his home at 24 East Ninety-first Street, aware that, in his weakened condition, he could not long endure the strain. During his illness, Mark Twain sent him a card bearing the message, "Affectionate salutation and good cheer, old friend." On May 14, knowing that the end was near, he bade his son and daughters farewell and, with the words "*Es ist so einfach zu sterben*" on his lips, lapsed into a coma from which he never emerged. He died at 4.35 in the morning from what was technically described as "pulmonary œdema." A death mask was taken at once by the sculptor, Karl Bitter.

Two simple funeral services were held for Carl Schurz. The family and close friends gathered at the house. The pallbearers were Charles Francis Adams Jr., Joseph H. Choate, Dr. Jacobi, Horace White, John B. Henderson, Karl Buenz, Colonel Silas W. Burt, Hubert Cillis, Gustav Lindenthal, Richard Watson Gilder, Oscar S. Straus, Edward M. Shepard, Max Wesendonck, Julius Stahel, Simon Wolf, Andrew Carnegie, Dr. Hans Kudlich, Gustav H. Schwab, Edward L. Preetorius, Isaac N. Seligman, Horace E. Deming, and Udo Brachvogel—a remarkable group of high-minded citizens, many of them, like Schurz, of German parentage or descent. Dr. Felix Adler and Dr. Jacobi made brief eulogistic addresses, the latter speaking in German. Grover Cleveland and Theodore Roosevelt sent notes of condolence, and many other eminent men left cards at the Schurz residence. His death had silenced his enemies and cooled all animosities.

A funeral train bore the body and the mourners to Sleepy Hollow Cemetery, at Tarrytown, New York, not far from his former home at Pocantico Hills. Dr. Frissell, president of Hampton Institute, spoke at the grave. Thus the patriot who was born near the banks of the Rhine was to rest forever on the shores of the Hudson, far from the tomb of his beloved wife in Hamburg, Germany.[1]

On November 21, 1906, Carl Schurz's admirers packed Carnegie Hall at a memorial gathering in his honor. Joseph H. Choate was the Chairman. Grover Cleveland emerged from his retirement at Princeton to pay a tribute to a man with whom he had occasionally disagreed but whom he unreservedly re-

[1] Of the three children who survived him, Agathe died on July 18, 1915, Carl Lincoln Schurz on May 19, 1924, in Nauheim, Germany, and Marianne on May 20, 1929, just after the centennial of her father's birth. Carl Lincoln Schurz was married in 1897 to Harriet Tiedemann, daughter of Carl Schurz's friend, and their only child died at birth. Later he was separated from his wife and married again, but had no children. The line of Carl Schurz is now extinct.

spected. Charles W. Eliot, from Harvard, and Booker T. Washington, from Tuskegee, added their words of eulogy. Two distinguished German scholars—Professor Eugen Kühnemann, of Breslau, and Professor Hermann A. Schumacher, of Bonn—spoke in their native tongue. The Secretary of the Navy, Honorable Charles J. Bonaparte, represented the President of the United States. The music was the kind which Carl Schurz himself loved most: the march from *Götterdämmerung* and the prelude to *Die Meistersinger*, both played by the New York Symphony Orchestra under Frank Damrosch's direction; and certain of his favorite German choruses sung by the Liederkranz and Arion Societies. The great auditorium was very silent when Richard Watson Gilder read his memorial verses. They were not, perhaps, imperishable literature, comparable with *Lycidas* or *In Memoriam.* But they told the truth, as such elegies seldom do. Probably every man and woman in that audience would have agreed with the sentiments of Gilder's noblest stanza:

> The lure of place he well could scorn
> Who knew a mightier joy and fate;—
> The passion of the hope forlorn,
> The luxury of being great.

Nor has Carl Schurz been without his more tangible and enduring memorials. On the afternoon of Saturday, May 10, 1913, the Schurz Memorial Committee dedicated an impressive monument on Morningside Heights at 116th Street, only a few hundred feet from the Columbia University Library. A bronze statue of Schurz nine feet high, the work of Karl Bitter, as sculptor, and Henry Bacon, as architect, stands on a granite pedestal erected on the periphery of a semicircular parapet. The figure of Schurz, attired in the long frock coat which he liked so much to wear, faces west, away from the city. On the pedestal are the words, "Carl Schurz, Defender of Liberty and Friend of Human Right." Two long granite seats extend on either side of the statue, and at each end is a bronze bas-relief, one symbolic of Schurz's work for the Indian, the other of his aid to the Negro. Today, when the weather is good, there is always some one sitting there: it may be two girls, graduate students at the university, discussing a problem in philology; it may be a sight-seer from "up-State," resting after an hour in the cathedral; or it may be a tired German woman, her baby in her arms. Nobody pays very much attention to the stern-looking figure in bronze. Very few of the passers-by are familiar with what he did. But to persons interested in the evolution of the civilized instincts in man, this monument will always have profound significance.

As part of the ceremony of its dedication, a colorful parade marched through the streets, and was reviewed by Mayor Gaynor, General Nelson A. Miles, and a little handful of blue-coated veterans who had been comrades of Carl Schurz in his Civil War campaigns. Joseph H. Choate, chairman of the committee, read a letter from President Wilson. George McAneny, who, since Schurz's death, had been President of the Borough of Manhattan, delivered a biographical address. Count Johann H. von Bernstorff, German Ambassador to the United States, paid a tribute to "the foremost citizen of German descent in this country, whose ideals of German unity in 1848 had been realized by Bismarck twenty years later"—a remark which, in all its implications, was a masterpiece of unconscious irony. A third speaker was Congressman Richard Bartholdt, who represented all German-Americans.

The Carl Schurz Memorial Committee eventually raised somewhat over $93,000. Grover Cleveland headed the list of contributors with a gift of two hundred dollars. Andrew Carnegie and James D. Willis subscribed five thousand dollars each, and the other donors included such men as Anson Phelps Stokes, George Harvey, Richard Watson Gilder, and the Adamses, as well as many German-American admirers. With this sum, the Schurz monument was made possible. A subcommittee on publication, with Oswald Garrison Villard as chairman, arranged for the assembling, under Dr. Frederic Bancroft's editorship, of Schurz's *Speeches, Correspondence, and Political Papers*, which appeared in six volumes in 1913. The amount remaining after these projects were completed was turned over appropriately to Hampton Institute.

Following the World War, at a moment when German-Americans who had been and still were loyal to the United States were realizing the lack in this country of any real appreciation of the literary, artistic, and moral character of the German people, a group of more than a hundred well-known Americans of German ancestry, including Ferdinand Thun, Paul M. Warburg, Felix Warburg, Julius Rosenwald, Henry Janssen, and Gustav Oberlaender, met on May 7, 1930, to establish and organize the Carl Schurz Memorial Foundation. Nearly half a million dollars was raised as an endowment, and the income of this is now being spent in promoting cultural relations between Germany and the United States. An additional and separate gift of one million dollars, contributed by Gustav Oberlaender, is known as the Oberlaender Trust and is constituted to enable American citizens interested in public welfare "to become better acquainted with similar activities in German-speaking countries." Although these two great trusts have been in operation only a few months, they have already demonstrated their value, and they serve to carry on through the years the work which Carl Schurz unconsciously, through his personality and career, so effectively promoted.

At the close of his remarks in dedicating the Schurz Memorial on Morningside Heights, Mr. McAneny said, in eloquent words which may fittingly round out this narrative: "A little way up this river, near Sleepy Hollow, there is a knoll from which every prospect is restful and fair; and from which you can watch the waters coming down from the hills that stand about his beloved lake. There, so near us, Carl Schurz lies. Like the river, the pure stream of his life has reached the eternal sea. But, like the river, it will still flow on, green-banked in the memory of the people and still enriching all the land."

CHAPTER XXVII THE MAN AS HE WAS

No one who ever saw Carl Schurz walking jauntily down Fifth Avenue was likely to forget that slender, erect figure, usually a little cramped in a tight-fitting frock coat; that noble head, crowned with a mass of grizzled hair; that moustache and beard, giving him a foreign appearance in a land of smooth-shaven males; those sharp, twinkling, sometimes whimsical eyes, behind steel-rimmed spectacles; and that bearing of conscious intellectuality and power which befits only those who have matched their abilities successfully against potentates and presidents. "No great man was ever modest," wrote John Hay somewhat impatiently, speaking of Abraham Lincoln. The words smack of heresy, but they hold a strong element of truth. Unquestionably Carl Schurz indicated by his manner that he was a person of some importance in the community. He was not conceited or arrogant, but he did not look meek.

In some respects, he had mellowed with the years. His wit was less mordant, his irony a trifle less disconcerting. The assumption that he was by nature stern and cold had no foundation in fact. The seriousness of his speeches and the unruffled dignity of his deportment sometimes led strangers to think him devoid of humor; but he was, among his family, full of good-natured fun, and he had a quick perception of the ridiculous, even when he himself was involved. While allowing no one to take liberties with him, he was uniformly affable. Even when threatened with disaster, he maintained a stoical equanimity. By nature he was romantic and poetic, animated by cheerfulness and sustained by temperamental optimism. Experience, moreover, had equipped him with a philosophic calm which, combined with his self-confidence, reconciled him to temporary failure. Even defeat could not compel him to admit that he had been wrong.

Schurz's air of assurance was annoying to men of less firmly established principles. In framing his political and moral creed, he was affected very little by personal considerations, seldom considering the effect which a line of conduct would have on his own future. This made him almost unique in an age when "trimming" and duplicity were vices even of the mighty. Having once chosen his policy, he maintained it, without wavering or stooping to compromise, even without troubling himself as to whether others were following him. It is probable that his faith in himself and his genius made him rather indifferent to public opinion. It was said of him justly that "the secret of the conviction which he carried to others was the clearness with which he perceived the moral bearings in the fluctuating policies of the day." Carl Schurz was, from first to last, an idealist. He could, when exigencies arose, play practical politics not unsuccessfully, but he preferred not to rely on such methods. He sincerely believed that, in the long run, honesty, unselfishness, and efficiency would triumph over greed, corruption, and inertia.

Schurz left very little behind him in the form of material possessions. The New York *World*, discussing his career editorially after his death, pointed out "how far his life of devotion to ideals outshone the trumpery success of a regiment of over-prosperous moneygrubbers." Like all sensible men, he desired an income sufficient to support his family and allow him a comfortable old age; but he cared nothing whatever for luxury, and preferred the authority of intellect to that of an inflated bank account. It is not without significance that his bills were always promptly paid. Schurz was very simple in his tastes and habits. He enjoyed music and painting and literature; he loved nature and outdoor life; and he would have been ill at ease in an elaborate household with a large staff of retainers. His aristocracy was of the mind, not of the body. All his days, even when he was a member of the President's Cabinet, he lived unostentatiously, like a man who had reached a full understanding of the importance of spiritual and esthetic values as means of attaining happiness.

Schurz was not, of course, universally beloved. Such placid souls as William McKinley and William Howard Taft managed to emerge from heated political contests without making enemies. But Schurz, like most reformers, had some annoying traits. His air of conscious rectitude was peculiarly irritating to "practical politicians" of the Thomas C. Platt variety. His sharp tongue and dictatorial manner, furthermore, lost him some valuable allies. James G. Blaine, not without reason, hated Schurz and expressed his dislike in his *Twenty Years of Congress.*[1] In 1885, George Hope wrote an article two columns and a half long for a New York newspaper, justifying Blaine, and commenting acidulously on Schurz's "aversion to fixity or constancy," his "passion for novelty and change," "his swiftly serial service in all the camps of opinion," and "his trial of organization after organization, as if he were a political taster instead of a political teacher." An article in the *Cincinnati Enquirer,* for November 18, 1885, signed by "Gath" (George Alfred Townsend), surveys his career, making the most of every opportunity for criticism and ending, "He must be undermining somebody to be entirely virtuous." Accusing Schurz of a succession of disloyalties, this old-school journalist dwelt especially on his relations with the bankrupt Henry Villard, saying, "Schurz never had the courage to stick by a man who had fallen by the wayside." The New York *Tribune,* in a characteristic moment of exasperation, said of Schurz, "He can see no good in an administration which he opposes or a candidate he dislikes."

To the charge of treachery to his friends, Schurz could have challenged his enemies to prove one case of betrayal by him

[1] In Volume II, pp. 438, ff. of his *Twenty Years,* Blaine expressed himself freely regarding Schurz, saying that "as a senator, he did not meet the expectations of his friends"; that his loss of popularity was due "to certain unsteady and erratic tendencies"; that he had boasted himself as "incapable of attachment to party"; and that he was completely independent of "true American feeling." He accused him, furthermore, of having made "his native nationality a political resource."

of any man with whom he had been intimate. In other respects, perhaps, he was more vulnerable. General Howard, the superior officer whom Schurz censured so severely in his *Reminiscences*, declared that the latter "was constitutionally and temperamentally a pessimist, and disposed to settle everybody else's business." Schurz was certainly no pessimist, either personal or philosophical; but he was unable to resist the temptation to administer the affairs of others as well as his own. His fondness for bestowing gratuitous advice without an invitation was vexing to men like Lincoln and Cleveland, who were trying in the face of constant opposition to do their best. In volunteering to be the counselor of Presidents, Schurz was undoubtedly impelled by the best of motives—a desire to promote the public good. It was, however, sometimes difficult for him to realize that he was not the only sincerely high-minded idealist on the continent.

During his tumultuous lifetime, Schurz was drawn into many controversies, notably those with Douglas, Blaine, Foraker, Gallinger, and Roosevelt. On the other hand, he attached to himself scores of admiring and devoted friends. After his death, Mark Twain, in an article in *Harper's Weekly*, declared that, as a political channel-finder, he was "as safe as Ben Thornburgh," a Mississippi River pilot whose instinct for the "best water" was infallible. "I have held him in the sincerest affection, esteem, and admiration for more than a generation," wrote Mr. Clemens, and then proceeded to laud Schurz particularly for his "blemishless honor, his unassailable patriotism, his high intelligence, his penetration." Charles Francis Adams, certainly a good judge of breeding, said that Schurz was "a man of refinement—a gentleman," and added, "Defeat and disaster did not embitter him; and, during one period, he rose supreme when financial pressure, physical injury, political ostracism, and domestic bereavement all seemed to combine to rain affliction on him." With Henry Adams, a true New England aristocrat, Schurz was always on intimate terms, frequently visiting him for several days at his Washington home. Referring to Schurz, Moorfield Storey once said, "Of all the men that I have known, there is not one whom I have admired and respected more utterly, nor one to whom I have turned more constantly for guidance and inspiration."

Looking back from the twentieth century, we can see that Schurz lived through a period of political and moral awakening, not only in the United States but throughout the world. As a youth, he dedicated himself to the cause of national freedom, helping to further the unification of Germany by his efforts to establish a parliamentary and representative government in that jumbled empire. During the next half century or more, he watched the spread of liberal doctrines through such significant movements as the foundation of the French Republic, the extension of the suffrage in Great Britain, and the resistance to monarchical oppression in other sections of Europe.

In the United States, Schurz was consistently on the side of progress, and there were few good causes to which he did not at least lend his name. His career is marked by distinct contributions to at least four great and lasting victories: the liberation of the Negro slave, the preservation of the Federal Union, the establishment of sound money, and the triumph of the merit system in the administration of governmental affairs.[1] In his prolonged effort to eliminate corruption from our municipal, state, and national officialdom, he was, perhaps, less successful, although he did unquestionably raise the standard of party morals. He failed temporarily in his fight against imperialism and against disarmament, but the time may come when his judgment on these matters also will be vindicated. During the period between the Civil War and the Spanish War, Schurz was constantly in the vanguard of reform. It has not

[1] For a carefully considered summary of Schurz's contribution to our history, see Carl Russell Fish's oration at the Carl Schurz Centenary Convocation, March 3, 1929, at Madison, Wisconsin, printed in the *Wisconsin Magazine of History,* Vol. XII, pp. 345, ff. Bliss Perry once said, "For more than fifty years there was hardly a bad cause in our political life which did not have reason to fear this German-born master of English speech."

been possible to touch upon all the philanthropic and humanitarian movements with which he was identified, but it is not improbable that an enlightened posterity will declare him to have been substantially right on every great issue on which he expressed an opinion.

Now that his story has been told, it is worth while asking, "What phases of his career entitle him to a place among the great?" First of all, he was the earliest important practitioner of non-partisanship and independence in American politics. He saw no virtue whatever in blind attachment to party. Blaine declared him to be in the position of a man perched on a fence, with clean boots, watching carefully which way he might leap to keep out of the mud. But Schurz justified his attitude by saying that he set country ahead of party. Other statesmen have, of course, changed their views between campaigns. Caleb Cushing, for reasons which satisfied himself and can be defended by others, was a Whig in 1840, a Democrat in 1844, and a Republican in 1864. The party affiliations of General Grant were somewhat nebulous; and even Mr. Hoover has not been politically consistent throughout his public career. But Schurz was different. He was on principle an Independent, lending his support to that organization which at the moment promised the most in the way of reform.

Consider, for example, how Schurz voted following the Civil War: in 1868 for Grant; in 1872 for Greeley; in 1876 for Hayes; in 1880 for Garfield; in 1884, 1888, and 1892 for Cleveland; in 1896 for McKinley; in 1900 for Bryan; and in 1904 for Parker—four times for a Republican and six for a Democrat. His candidate was elected, it may be added, in six out of the ten contests. Such a record of apparent vacillation would have been impossible in the days of Andrew Jackson, for independence carried to that degree would then have been regarded and treated as party treason.

Those who believe that, in a democracy, party government provides the only feasible method of transacting the nation's business have frequently criticized Carl Schurz. If all voters adopted Schurz's policy, continuity of government would be difficult to maintain. Some form of party organization must be kept up from campaign to campaign if chaos is to be averted. It is probably fortunate for our system that the majority of intelligent voters do not resent the party label and are willing to call themselves broadly Republicans or Democrats. On the other hand, a small body of absolutely independent high-minded citizens may exercise in a two party system a tremendous, often a controlling, influence on nominations and elections. With the balance of power resting in their hands, they can hold both parties to a high standard of honesty and efficiency. This, at any rate, was Carl Schurz's theory. The experiment of "free lance" politics has never been more thoroughly tried than in his case. He and his followers constituted a strong body of reinforcements for which Republicans and Democrats were compelled to make their bids.

In the second place, Carl Schurz, without hypocrisy or ostentation, upheld ideals which can never be presented too often. During an age when corruption in infinite variety was rife even in the highest offices, he presented the pleasing spectacle of a leader with an untarnished record. His enemies spied upon him and set "sleuths" on his trail, only to find that he was invulnerable. They could pick flaws in his temperament and his manners, but never in his integrity. "In his company," said Moorfield Storey, "one felt that he was breathing a purer air." He could wield the scourge all the more effectively because he himself had nothing of which to be ashamed. Thus he assailed the corruption of Blaine and the depravity of Tammany Hall with equal vigor. He dealt blow after blow at the "spoils" system until few self-respecting citizens dared to defend it. Complete honesty is usually offensive to those who do not practice it. Like every reformer, Schurz was regarded by those who belonged to the "machine" as a dissembler, a schemer, and a nuisance. But he did not quail. Courage was a virtue in which he was not lacking.[1]

[1] As an illustration of Schurz's aggressive outspokenness, see the record of

Schurz's most definite contribution to his adopted country was doubtless through his promotion of civil service reform. He had predecessors, like Jenckes, and coadjutors, like Curtis and Roosevelt, from whom credit ought not to be withheld: but the rapid adoption of the "merit" system by successive Presidents was probably due more to him than to any other one man. In achieving his aims, he employed every legitimate device; he threatened, he bargained, he persuaded, he pleaded, he argued. When a friend of his went wrong on the civil service, Carl Schurz reproached him. When one of his political foes helped the cause, Schurz sent him a word of commendation. No matter what else was going on, Schurz had always a watchful eye for government appointments and seldom let a poor one slip by without protesting to the person responsible for it.

Finally, Carl Schurz presented a shining and inspiring example of a foreigner's adaptation to our customs and institutions. In some respects, of course, he always remained a German. To the end of his days it was the *Muttersprache* which was spoken in his house. The quickest way to his heart was through the "Fatherland." One of my uncles, making a social call upon him at Pocantico Hills, found him courteous, but no warmer than an iceberg. "I have often heard of you," observed my uncle. "Yes," answered Mr. Schurz dubiously, apparently not impressed by the compliment. "My father has often talked of you," continued the visitor. "Yes," reiterated his host, in expressionless tones. "My father was a 'forty-eighter,' " added my uncle, in desperation. Then Schurz beamed as if some sun had thawed his frigidity, became all animation, and said eagerly, *"Ach so—und sprechen Sie Deutsch?"* The correct opening had been made, and a long and delightful conversation ensued. It was German music—not the froth of Verdi and Puccini—which he loved to play upon his piano. Some

his heated dinner-table denunciation of Chauncey M. Depew, as a corporation agent who had not only corrupted legislatures and perverted legislation, but had "made corruption respectable in the eyes of the people," in George Cary Eggleston, *Recollections of a Varied Life,* 334, 335.

German-Americans, hailed as "Dutchmen" and ridiculed because of their German accent, grew ashamed of their origin and sometimes tried to conceal it by changing their names. But Carl Schurz was proud of his race, and was happiest in the society of other German-Americans, like Dr. Jacobi, who clung to him as their leader. During the presidential campaign of 1904, several prominent New York German-Americans who inadvertently had allowed their names to be attached to a Roosevelt circular drafted by Jacob Schiff, repudiated the document when they discovered that, in its published form, it included a sentence reflecting on Schurz.

Those interested in the permanence of national characteristics have found in Carl Schurz certain so-called "typical German traits"—his thoroughness, his aggressiveness, his dogmatism, his somewhat didactic manner, and his occasional sentimentality. Doubtless there were qualities in Schurz and his fellow exiles of the fifties which were unlike those marking pure "Yankee" stock. But this does not prove that these immigrants had nothing to teach to members of the Society of Colonial Wars. Even in the decade before Fort Sumter, the United States was neither Yankee nor Puritan nor Cavalier, but a blend of Anglo-Saxon, Teutonic, Latin, and Celtic; and the Germans have no reason to apologize for their own contribution to the "melting pot."

Schurz came to our shores a man full grown, both physically and intellectually; yet he identified himself readily with our civilization, mastered our language, accepted our citizenship, and became a power for good in our affairs. To the assertion that he introduced alien practices and ideals into our country, it may be answered that no man of his generation better understood our peculiar problems; that he was saturated with our history and wrote the best biography of one of our greatest statesmen; and that he qualified himself in the eyes of historians and sociologists as a chronicler and commentator on our institutions. At any time after 1860, if he had been obliged to choose between allegiance to Germany and loyalty to the

United States, he would have stood by his adopted land. If he had lived until the World War, he would unquestionably, though with sorrow, have offered his services to the Wilson administration. His old comrade Dr. Jacobi, who vigorously espoused the Allied cause in 1914 and bitterly assailed the Hohenzollerns, felt sure that Schurz would have stood with him.[1]

Schurz's career has been a convincing refutation of "Know Nothing" doctrines, for he demonstrated that Americanism is more a matter of spirit than of birth. In the eyes of public opinion, he was just as truly one of us as Charles Francis Adams or Josiah Quincy, with generations of New England tradition behind them. What he accomplished should make every immigrant to our shores more ambitious and more hopeful. He stood for all the ideals which we like to think of as most truly American—democracy, liberty, equal opportunity to all and justice to everybody, regardless of financial position, race, or creed. It was Carl Schurz's chief glory that he preserved unblemished his integrity and moral independence, and taught his fellow citizens the primary civic virtues by practicing them himself.

[1] Putnam, *Memoirs of a Publisher,* 86. Mr. Frederic Bancroft shared his conviction.

SELECTED BIBLIOGRAPHY

A complete list of the books and periodicals read in preparation for this biography would include hundreds of items, and would cover many pages of this volume. The following books comprise some of the most important sources for statements in the text. Newspapers in cities like Boston, New York, Cincinnati, St. Louis, Chicago, and Milwaukee are not here mentioned.

Adams, Henry. Letters of Henry Adams. Edited by Worthington Chauncey Ford. Boston, 1930.

Addresses in memory of Carl Schurz, Carnegie Hall, November 21, 1906. New York, 1906.

Alexander, D. S. A political history of the State of New York. 3 vols. New York, 1909.

Andrews, E. Benjamin. The history of the last quarter century in the United States, 1870–1895. 2 vols. New York, 1897.

Bancroft, Frederic. Life of William H. Seward. 2 vols. New York, 1900.

Beveridge, Albert J. Abraham Lincoln, 1809–1858. 2 vols.

Bigelow, John, Jr. The campaign of Chancellorsville. New Haven, 1910.

Blaine, James G. Twenty years of Congress. 2 vols. Norwich, Conn., 1884. Strongly partisan, but interesting because of its comments on Schurz.

Bowers, Claude G. The tragic era. New York, 1929. Reconstruction from a Democratic viewpoint.

Congressional Globe, 1869–1873; *Congressional Record*, 1873–1875. Contains the official report of Schurz's speeches in the Senate.

Cortissoz, Royal. The life of Whitelaw Reid. 2 vols. New York, 1921.

Dannehl, Otto. Carl Schurz, ein deutscher kaempfer. Berlin, 1929.

De Jonge, Alfred R. Gottfried Kinkel as political and social thinker. New York, 1926.

Dewey, Davis R. Financial history of the United States. New York, 1928.

Dictionary of American biography. Exceedingly valuable as a reference source on minor figures. The article on Schurz is by Oswald Villard.

Dodge, Theodore A. The campaign of Chancellorsville. Boston, 1881.

Doubleday, Abner. Chancellorsville and Gettysburg. New York, 1882.

Easum, Chester V. The Americanization of Carl Schurz. Chicago, 1929. A thoroughgoing study of Schurz's career up to 1861.

Eckenrode, H. J. Rutherford B. Hayes. New York, 1930.

Faust, Albert Bernhardt. The German element in the United States. 2 vols. Boston, 1909.

Fish, Carl Russell. Civil service and the patronage. Harvard Historical Studies, Vol. XI. Cambridge, 1924.

Foulke, William D. Fighting the spoilsmen; Reminiscences of the civil service reform movement. New York, 1919.

Foulke, William D. Life of Oliver P. Morton. 2 vols. Indianapolis, 1899.

Garland, Hamlin. Ulysses S. Grant, his life and character. New York, 1920.

Greene, E. B. Lieber and Schurz. "War Information Series," 1918.

Harper's Weekly. Very important for its caricatures of Schurz by Nast, especially in 1872, and for its editorials by Schurz.

Henderson, E. E. A short history of Germany. New York, 1906.

Hibben, Paxton. The peerless leader, William Jennings Bryan. New York, 1929.

Hoar, George F. Autobiography of seventy years. 2 vols. New York, 1903.

Holt, Henry. Garrulities of an octogenarian editor. Boston, 1923.

Howard, Oliver Otis. Autobiography. 2 vols. 1908. Contains sharp criticism of Schurz as a military leader.

Howe, M. A. de W. James Ford Rhodes, American historian. New York, 1929.

Howe, M. A. de W. Moorfield Storey. Boston, 1932.

Husband, J. Americans by adoption. Boston, 1920.

Jackson, Helen Hunt. A century of dishonor. Boston, 1881.

Kühnemann, Eugen. Vom Weltreich des Deutschen Geistes. München. 1914.

Lingley, Charles R. Since the Civil War. New York. 1926.

Lodge Papers, deposited in the Massachusetts Historical Society. A comprehensive and valuable assemblage of material on Henry Cabot Lodge.

Lodge, Henry Cabot. Early memories. Boston, 1913.

McElroy, Robert. Grover Cleveland, the man and the statesman. New York, 1930.

McMasters, John B. History of the people of the United States during Lincoln's administration. New York, 1927.

Millis, Walter. The martial spirit, a study of our war with Spain. Boston, 1930.

Milton, George F. The age of hate. New York, 1930. A valuable book dealing with the critical years of Andrew Johnson's administration.

Mitchell, Edward P. Memoirs of an editor. New York, 1924.

Nathanson, Jerome M. Carl Schurz, idealist in politics (The Senate years). A manuscript dissertation submitted as part of the requirements for a Master's degree at Columbia University.

Nation, The. Contains many references to Schurz, especially from 1869 until 1906.

Nevins, Allan. The emergence of modern America, 1865–1878. New York, 1928.

Nevins, Allan. *The Evening Post*: A century of journalism. New York, 1923. Contains material on Schurz as an editor.

Nicolay and Hay. Abraham Lincoln. 10 vols. New York, 1890.

Oberholtzer, E. P. A history of the United States since the civil war. 3 vols. New York, 1917–1926.

Olcott, Charles S. The life of William McKinley. 2 vols. Boston, 1916.

Paine, Albert Bigelow. Th. Nast, his period and his pictures. New York, 1904. An important and interesting book, now out of print.

Peck, Harry Thurston. Twenty years of the republic, 1885–1905. New York, 1906.

Phillips, W. Alison. Modern Europe, 1815–1899. London, 1903.

Pierce, Edward L. Memoir and letters of Charles Sumner. 4 vols. Boston, 1877.

Platt, Thomas C. The autobiography of Thomas Collier Scott. New York, 1910.

Poore, Ben: Perley. Perley's reminincences. 2 vols. Philadelphia, 1886.

Pringle, Henry F. Theodore Roosevelt, a biography. New York, 1931.

Puck. See especially the issues from March to December, 1884, containing Gillam's famous cartoons.

Putnam, George Haven. Memoirs of a publisher, 1865–1915. New York, 1915.

Report of the board of inquiry to investigate certain charges against S. A. Galpin. Published by the Department of the Interior. Washington, 1878.

Rhodes, James Ford. History of the United States. 8 vols. New York. Vols. III–VIII cover the period when Schurz was active in affairs and are indispensable to any study of his times.

Rhodes, James Ford. History of the civil war, 1861–1865. New York, 1917.

Rhodes, James Ford. The McKinley and Roosevelt administration, 1897–1909. New York, 1922.

Roosevelt, Theodore. Selections from the correspondence of Theodore Roosevelt and Henry Cabot Lodge, 1884–1918. New York, 1925.

Roosevelt, Theodore. Theodore Roosevelt, an autobiography. New York, 1913.

Ropes, John C. The army under Pope. New York, 1881.

Ross, Earle Dudley. The liberal republican movement. New York, 1919.

Russell, Charles E. Blaine of Maine. New York, 1931. The most recent and complete analysis of Blaine's character and career.

Schafer, Joseph. Intimate letters of Carl Schurz. Publications of the State Historical Society of Wisconsin, collections, Vol. XXX, Madison, 1928.

Schafer, Joseph. Schurz's account of the siege of Rastaat, *Wisconsin Magazine of History*, XII, 239–70, March, 1929.

Schafer, Joseph. Carl Schurz, militant liberal. Wisconsin Biography Series, Volume I. Madison, 1930.

Schrader, Frederick F. The Germans in the making of America. Boston, 1924.

Schurz MSS, in the Congressional Library, an important collection, the most valuable items of which, however, were printed in Bancroft's edition of Schurz's *Writings*.

Schurz, Carl. Speeches. Philadelphia, 1865. Twelve of Schurz's earlier speeches, revised and edited by himself, with a short introduction.

Schurz, Carl. Speeches, correspondence, and political papers of Carl Schurz. Selected and edited by Frederic Bancroft. 6 vols. New York, 1913.

Schurz, Carl. Henry Clay. 2 vols. Boston, 1887.

Schurz, Carl. Lebenserinnerungen von Carl Schurz. 3 vols. Berlin, 1912.

Schurz, Carl. Lebenserinnerungen, bis zum jahre 1850. Selections, edited with notes and vocabulary by Edward Manley. Allyn and Bacon, 1913.

Senate executive documents, No. 2, first session, thirty-ninth congress. This is Schurz's much discussed report to President Johnson.

Sherman, John. Recollections of forty years. 2 vols. Chicago, 1895.

Smith, Theodore C. Life and letters of James Abram Garfield. 2 vols. New York, 1926.

Stanwood, Edward. A history of the presidency. Boston, 1898.

Sullivan, Mark. Our times; the United States, 1900–1925. 3 vols. New York, 1926–30. Interesting details about American society and civilization.

Thayer, William R. The life and letters of John Hay. 2 vols. Boston, 1915.

Thompson, Alexander M. A political history of Wisconsin. Wisconsin, 1902.

Villard, Henry. Memoirs. 2 vols. Boston, 1904.

Visit of the Hon. Carl Schurz to Boston, March, 1881. An interesting pamphlet giving the speeches delivered during Schurz's visit.

Watterson, Henry. "Marse Henry," an autobiography. New York, 1919. Diverting Reminiscences.

White, Andrew D. Autobiography of Andrew Dickson White. 2 vols. New York, 1905.

White, Horace. Lyman Trumbull.

Williams, Charles R. The life of Rutherford Birchard Hayes. 2 vols. Boston, 1914.

Wilson, James H. The life of Charles A. Dana. New York, 1907.

Young, Jesse Bowman. The battle of Gettysburg. New York, 1913.

THE END

INDEX